Sport and Exercise Physiology Testing Guidelines

Since its first published edition more than 30 years ago, the BASES (British Association of Sport and Exercise Sciences) Physiological Testing Guidelines have represented the leading knowledge base of current testing methodology for sport and exercise scientists. Sport and exercise physiologists conduct physiological assessments that have proven validity and reliability, both in laboratory and sport-specific contexts. A wide variety of test protocols have been developed, adapted and refined to support athletes of all abilities reach their full potential. This book is a comprehensive guide to these protocols and to the key issues relating to physiological testing.

With contributions from leading specialist sport physiologists and covering a wide range of mainstream sports in terms of ethical, practical and methodological issues, this volume represents an essential resource for sport-specific exercise testing in both research and applied settings. This new edition draws on the authors' experience of supporting athletes from many sports through several Olympic cycles to achieve world leading performances. While drawing on previous editions, it is presented in a revised format matching the sport groupings used in elite sport support within the UK sport institutes. Building on the underpinning general procedures, these specific chapters are supported by appropriate up-to-date case studies in the supporting web resources.

R. C. Richard Davison, PhD, FBASES, CSci, is Professor of Exercise Physiology in the School of Health and Life Sciences at the University of the West of Scotland, UK.

Paul M. Smith, PhD, FBASES, FHEA, is Senior Lecturer in Exercise Physiology in the School of Sport and Health Sciences at Cardiff Metropolitan University, UK.

James Hopker, PhD, is Professor of Sport and Exercise Science and Deputy Director of the Division of Natural Sciences at the University of Kent, UK.

Michael J. Price, PhD, FBASES, is Reader in Exercise Physiology at Coventry University, UK.

Florentina Hettinga, PhD, FACSM, FECSS, SFHEA, is Professor of Sport, Exercise and Rehabilitation and Director of Research and Knowledge Exchange of the Department of Sport, Exercise and Rehabilitation at Northumbria University, UK.

Garry Tew, PhD, FBASES, FHEA, is Professor of Clinical Exercise Science in the Department of Sport, Exercise and Rehabilitation at Northumbria University, UK.

Lindsay Bottoms, PhD, FBASES, is Reader in Exercise and Health Physiology at the University of Hertfordshire, UK, and the Director of the Research Centre for Psychology and Sports Sciences.

Sport and Exercise Physiology Testing Guidelines

Volume II – Exercise and Clinical Testing

Fifth Edition

Edited by R. C. Richard Davison, Paul M. Smith, James Hopker, Michael J. Price, Florentina Hettinga, Garry Tew, and Lindsay Bottoms

Routledge
Taylor & Francis Group
LONDON AND NEW YORK

BASES
The British Association of
Sport and Exercise Sciences

Cover image: © ipopba/Getty Images

Fifth edition published 2022
by Routledge
2 Park Square, Milton Park, Abingdon, Oxon, OX14 4RN

and by Routledge
605 Third Avenue, New York, NY 10158

Routledge is an imprint of the Taylor & Francis Group, an informa business

First edition published by BASES 1988
Fourth edition published by Routledge 2009

British Library Cataloguing-in-Publication Data
A catalogue record for this book is available from the British Library

Library of Congress Cataloging-in-Publication Data
A catalog record for this book has been requested

ISBN: 978-0-367-49239-7 (hbk)
ISBN: 978-0-367-48984-7 (pbk)
ISBN: 978-1-003-04526-7 (ebk)

DOI: 10.4324/9781003045267

Typeset in Baskerville
by Apex CoVantage, LLC

Access the Support Material: www.routledge.com/9780367489847

Contents

List of figures   ix
List of tables   xi
List of contributors   xiii
Foreword   xvi

Introduction   1
R. C. RICHARD DAVISON AND PAUL M. SMITH

PART I   3

1.1 Professional competency and working with others   5
MICHAEL J. PRICE, ANDREW M. MILES AND PAUL M. SMITH

1.2 Physiological exercise testing: ethical considerations   10
STEVE R. BIRD AND ANDREW SMITH

**1.3 Health and safety in duty of care: evaluating
and stratifying risk**   19
S. ANDY SPARKS, KELLY MARRIN AND CRAIG A. BRIDGE

1.4 Safeguarding in physiological testing   26
EMMA KAVANAGH AND DANIEL RHIND

1.5 Influence of medication on typical exercise response   30
THOM PHILLIPS AND PATRICK ORME

PART II   41

2.1 Data intelligence and feedback in a clinical context   43
SARAH GILCHRIST AND MARK HOMER

2.2   Reliability and measurement error   48

SHAUN J. MCLAREN

**2.3   Scaling: adjusting physiological and performance
measures to body size**   53

EDWARD WINTER AND SIMON JOBSON

PART III   59

3.1   Participant pre-test preparation and evaluation   61

RACHEL LORD AND BRIAN BEGG

**3.2   Maintenance and calibration standards: a cornerstone
of laboratory quality assurance**   66

DAVID GREEN AND GLYN HOWATSON

3.3   Lung and respiratory muscle function   72

JOHN DICKINSON AND KARL SYLVESTER

3.4   Surface anthropometry   79

SUSAN C. LENNIE

3.5   Functional screening   86

MIKE DUNCAN, STUART ELWELL AND MARK LYONS

3.6   Assessment of free-living energy expenditure   91

ENHAD A. CHOWDHURY, OLIVER J. PEACOCK
AND DYLAN THOMPSON

3.7   Respiratory gas analysis   97

SIMON MARWOOD AND RICHIE P. GOULDING

**3.8   Metabolic threshold testing: interpretation
and prognostic prescriptive value**   102

MARK BURNLEY AND MATTHEW I. BLACK

3.9   Ratings of perceived exertion   111

JOHN P. BUCKLEY AND ROGER ESTON

3.10 Clinical strength testing   121

DALE CANNAVAN AND KATIE THRALLS-BUTTE

3.11 Blood sampling   126
RONALD J. MAUGHAN AND SUSAN M. SHIRREFFS

3.12 Field-based assessments for determining aerobic fitness and exercise prescription   132
JOHN P. BUCKLEY, JENNIFER REED AND TIM GROVE

3.13 Quantifying free-living physical activity and sedentary behaviours in adults   143
OLIVER J. PEACOCK, ENHAD A. CHOWDHURY
AND DYLAN THOMPSON

3.14 Musculoskeletal assessment   148
NIGEL GLEESON AND ANDREA BAILEY

PART IV   153

4.1 Assessment of peripheral blood flow and vascular function   155
BENJAMIN J. R. BUCKLEY, MAXIME BOIDIN AND
DICK H. J. THIJSSEN

4.2 Application of dual energy X-ray absorptiometry   167
KAREN HIND

4.3 Assessment of cardiac structure and function   182
CHRISTOPHER JOHNSON, KEITH GEORGE AND
DAVID L. OXBOROUGH

4.4 Methods in exercise immunology   197
NICOLETTE C. BISHOP AND NEIL P. WALSH

4.5 Skeletal muscle biopsy: techniques and applications   205
RICHARD A. FERGUSON AND NATALIE F. SHUR

PART V   213

5.1 Exercise testing in obesity   215
DAVID BROOM, MATTHEW CAPEHORN AND ANNA MYERS

5.2 Exercise testing in cardiovascular disease   222
VICTORIA S. SPRUNG, JOHN P. BUCKLEY AND
DAVID L. OXBOROUGH

5.3 Exercise testing in diabetes   231
ROB C. ANDREWS, PARTH NARENDRAN AND
EMMA COCKCROFT

5.4 Exercise testing in chronic kidney disease   241
PELAGIA KOUFAKI, SHARLENE GREENWOOD AND
JAMIE H. MACDONALD

5.5 Exercise testing in chronic lung disease   250
OLIVER J. PRICE, KARL SYLVESTER, JOANNA SHAKESPEARE
AND MARK A. FAGHY

5.6 Exercise testing in breast and prostate cancer   258
JOHN M. SAXTON AND RUTH ASHTON

5.7 Exercise testing in peripheral arterial disease   267
AMY HARWOOD, EDWARD CALDOW AND GABRIEL CUCATO

5.8 Exercise testing in children   277
CRAIG WILLIAMS, MELITTA MCNARRY AND KEITH TOLFREY

5.9 Exercise testing in older adults   284
MATT W. HILL AND MICHAEL J. PRICE

5.10 Exercise testing in females   291
KIRSTY M. HICKS, ANTHONY C. HACKNEY, MICHAEL DOOLEY
AND GEORGIE BRUINVELS

5.11 Exercise testing in pregnancy   296
VICTORIA L. MEAH, AMAL HASSAN, LIN FOO, CHRISTOPH LEES
AND MARLIZE DE VIVO

5.12 Exercise testing in heart failure   307
ERIC J. STÖHR, LAUREN K. TRUBY, VELI TOPKARA,
GORDON MCGREGOR AND MARK J. HAYKOWSKY

Index   317

Figures

1.5.1   Reduction in substrate concentration following first-order
        half-life reaction.   32
1.5.2   Enterohepatic circulation.   34
2.2.1   Test and re-test 10 m linear sprint times in soccer players.   51
3.2.1   Schematic depicting the recommended calibration and control
        processes prior to using equipment for testing purposes.   70
3.6.1   Illustration of the possible relative contribution and variability
        of physical activity energy Expenditure.   93
3.8.1   Illustration of the pulmonary response to a cardiopulmonary
        exercise test (CPET).   104
3.8.2   Schematic representation of methods used to determine the
        heavy-severe boundary during non-incremental exercise tests.   107
3.9.1   Eston-Parfitt (E-P) Scale.   116
3.13.1 Impact of data processing decisions on quantification of
        physical activity outcomes.   146
4.1.1   Illustration of ultrasound measurement of resting blood flow
        and vessel structure (left) and vascular function (FMD and
        CAR; right) in healthy participants.   156
4.1.2   Illustration of the venous occlusion plethysmography technique
        to determine resistance artery structure and function via
        evaluation of blood flow changes in response to vasoactive
        drugs and/or handgrip exercise.   161
4.2.1   Lumbar spine vertebral deformities indicating requirement
        for vertebral exclusion.   173
4.2.2   DXA total-body scan image and region of interest placements.   174
4.2.3   Mid-prone (A – recommended) and prone hand positioning
        (B) for DXA scans.   175
4.3.1   12-lead ECG trace.   183
4.3.2   International consensus standards for electrocardiographic
        interpretation in athletes.   186
4.3.3   Echocardiographic modalities. A) Two-dimensional; B) colour
        Doppler; C) Doppler; and D) tissue Doppler.   187

4.3.4   PLAX view and measurements including 1) LV interventricular
        septum thickness; 2) LV end-diastolic dimension; 3) LV posterior
        wall thickness; 4) LA dimension; 5) Sinus of Valsalva;
        6) RVOT PLAX dimension.   188
4.3.5   LV geometry determined by LV mass index and relative wall
        thickness.   189
4.3.6   PSAX views A) AV; B) MV; C) PM; and D) apical level. RVOT
        dimensions 1) proximal and 2) distal.   190
4.3.7   Apical views at end-diastole A) A4CH; B) A2CH; C) A3CH
        and end-systole; D) A4CH; E) A2CH; F) A3CH.   190
4.3.8   TDI at the A) LV septum; B) LV lateral wall; and C) RV wall.   191
4.3.9   A) LV inflow Doppler; B) A5CH two-dimensional; and
        C) LVOT Doppler.   191
4.3.10 A4CH$_{RV}$ view with measurements 1) RVD1 (basal); 2) RVD2
        (mid-cavity); and 3) RVD3 (length).   192
4.3.11 A) Subcostal four-chamber view; B) subcostal short axis view;
        C) suprasternal notch view.   192
4.4.1   Cell morphology can be used to identify the three main immune
        cell populations in whole blood. Forward scatter (FSC) gives
        an indication of size and side scatter (SSC) gives an indication
        of a cell's internal complexity. The cytometer plots FSC against
        SSC to provide a visual image of the three distinctive white
        blood cell populations   202
4.5.1   Professor Eric Hultman performing a muscle biopsy of the
        vastus lateralis using a Bergström needle.   206
5.3.1   Flowsheet for preparing and carrying out an exercise test
        in patients with diabetes.   234
5.5.1   Schematic detailing test interpretation.   256
5.10.1 Framework for working with female athletes.   292
5.11.1 Physiological adaptation to healthy pregnancy at rest
        and altered responses or considerations for acute, submaximal
        physical activity in pregnant individuals.   297
5.12.1 The contributions to exercise limitations in heart failure.   310

Tables

1.3.1	Classification and explanation of hazard types relevant to physiological testing	21
1.3.2	Example risk quantification guidance assessment tool based on the probability and severity of the outcome impact	23
1.4.1	International Safeguards for Children in Sport	27
1.5.1	Commonly prescribed medications and their half-lives	32
1.5.2	CYP450 Substrates, inducers and inhibitors	35
2.1.1	Key considerations in data management and analysis	45
2.2.1	Reliability of 10 m linear sprint time in soccer players	51
3.2.1	Calibration and control checklist	68
3.2.2	Example – checking the speed of a treadmill	68
3.3.1	Abnormal respiratory function	73
3.4.1	Skinfold measurements	82
3.4.2	Girth measurements	83
3.7.1	Effect of measurement precision on the determined $\dot{V}O_2$ for typical heavy-intensity exercise with 45 s expirate collection	99
3.8.1	The validity, reliability and sensitivity of the metabolic thresholds used to demarcate the exercise intensity domains (EID) and the abbreviations commonly used to describe these in the scientific literature	105
3.9.1	Summary of the relationship between the percentages of maximal aerobic power (%$\dot{V}O_2$max), maximal heart rate reserve (%HRRmax), maximal heart rate (%HRmax) and Borg's RPE (6–20) and CR-10 scales	112
3.10.1	Estimated 1-RM formulas from multiple repetition tests	123
3.12.1	Matching exercise intensities relative to the proportion of aerobic power (%$\dot{V}O_2$max), with %heart rate reserve (%HRR), %$\dot{V}O_2$ Reserve (R) and Borg's ratings of perceived exertion (RPE: 6–20 and CR10 scales)	133
3.12.2	Summary of protocol features of commonly used field-based functional capacity assessments	135

3.14.1   Special tests for anatomical regions (with an appendicular
         skeletal emphasis): Overview of the scope, focus and relevant
         indicative pooled likelihood ratios reflecting positive and
         negative test outcomes and residing within the peer-reviewed
         literature   151
4.2.1   Indications for DXA scans in sport and exercise sciences   169
4.2.2   Standardising DXA body composition scans   171
4.2.3   Interpretation of DXA scans – bone density   172
4.3.1   Training-related ECG changes   185
4.3.2   Left and right heart echocardiographic parameters   193
4.4.1   Case study example of a completed Jackson Common
         Cold Questionnaire   199
5.1.1   Age-related maximum and minimum heart rates for the
         Astrand-Ryhming Test   218
5.2.1   Absolute and relative contraindications for CPET   225
5.2.2   Stepwise increments of the modified Bruce Protocol   226
5.3.1   Exercise and diabetes   231
5.4.1   Classification of CKD stage based on severity of kidney
         function impairment   241
5.4.2   Recommended 'menu' of physical function assessment tools
         based on current available research and practice-based evidence
         on safety, feasibility, validity, research and clinical utility
         characteristics for use in people in all stages of CKD   243
5.5.1   Absolute and relative contraindications   252
5.5.2   Pre-test instructions, test phases and in-test measurements   253
5.6.1   Recommended health-related fitness dimensions to be assessed
         in cancer patients, with specific reference to breast and prostate
         cancer-specific physiological impairments and functional
         limitations   261
5.7.1   Fontaine and Rutherford classifications for peripheral arterial
         disease   268
5.7.2   Interpretation of the ankle brachial pressure index   269
5.8.1   Sex, maturity and ethnic specific equations for estimation
         of percent body fat (%BF) from skinfolds   279
5.9.1   Typical values for key outcome variables in older adults   286
5.9.2   Common tests of balance in older adults   289
5.11.1   Physical reasons to stop antenatal activity and consult a
         healthcare provider   298
5.11.2   Heart rate ranges and corresponding intensities of physical
         activity in individuals with uncomplicated pregnancies   301
5.12.1   New York Heart Association (NYHA) classification
         of heart failure   308

Contributors

Rob C. Andrews
University of Exeter Medical School, UK

Ruth Ashton
University of Derby, UK

Andrea Bailey
Robert Jones and Agnes Hunt Orthapaedic Hospital, UK

Brian Begg
Cardiff Metropolitan University, UK

Steve R. Bird
Royal Melbourne Institute of Technology, Australia

Nicolette C. Bishop
Loughborough University, UK

Matthew I. Black
University of Exeter, UK

Maxime Boidin
Liverpool John Moores University, UK

Craig A. Bridge
Edge Hill University, UK

David Broom
Sheffield Hallam University, UK

Georgie Bruinvels
St Mary's University, UK

Benjamin J. R. Buckley
University of Liverpool, UK

John P. Buckley
University of Chester, UK

Mark Burnley
University of Kent, UK

Edward Caldow
University of Salford, UK

Dale Cannavan
Seattle Pacific University, USA

Matthew Capehorn
Rotherham Institute of Obesity, UK

Enhad A. Chowdhury
University of Bath, UK

Emma Cockcroft
University of Exeter, UK

Gabriel Cucato
Northumbria University, UK

Marlize de Vivo
Canterbury Christ Church University, UK

John Dickinson
University of Kent, UK

Michael Dooley
The Poundbury Clinic Dorset & King Edward VII Hospital London, UK

Mike Duncan
Coventry University, UK

Stuart Elwell
Dudley Physiotherapy Clinic, UK

Roger Eston
University of South Australia, Australia

Mark A. Faghy
University of Derby, UK

Richard A. Ferguson
Loughborough University, UK

Lin Foo
Imperial College London, UK

Keith George
Liverpool John Moores University, UK

Sarah Gilchrist
Gilchrist Performance Ltd, UK

Nigel Gleeson
Queen Margaret University, UK

Richie P. Goulding
Kobe Design University, Japan

David Green
English Institute of Sport, UK

Sharlene Greenwood
King's College Hospital, UK

Tim Grove
Brunel University, UK

Anthony C. Hackney
University of North Carolina, USA

Amy Harwood
Coventry University, UK

Amal Hassan
University College Healthcare NHS Trust and University College London, UK

Mark J. Haykowsky
University of Alberta, Canada

Kirsty M. Hicks
Northumbria University, UK

Matt W. Hill
Coventry University, UK

Karen Hind
Loughborough University, UK

Mark Homer
Buckinghamshire New University, UK

Glyn Howatson
Northumbria University, UK

Simon Jobson
University of Winchester, UK

Christopher Johnson
Liverpool John Moores University, UK

Emma Kavanagh
Bournemouth University, UK

Pelagia Koufaki
Queen Margaret University, UK

Christoph Lees
Imperial College London, UK

Susan C. Lennie
Newcastle University, UK

Rachel Lord
Cardiff Metropolitan University, UK

Mark Lyons
University of Limerick, Ireland

Jamie H. Macdonald
Bangor University, UK

Kelly Marrin
Edge Hill University, UK

Simon Marwood
Liverpool Hope University, UK

Ronald J. Maughan
St Andrews University, UK

Victoria L. Meah
University of Alberta, Canada

Gordon McGregor
Coventry University, UK

Shaun J. McLaren
Durham University, UK

Melitta McNarry
Swansea University, UK

Andrew M. Miles
Cardiff Metropolitan University, UK

Anna Myers
Sheffield Hallam University, UK

Parth Narendran
University of Birmingham, UK

Patrick Orme
Bristol City Football Club, UK

David L. Oxborough
*Liverpool John Moores
University, UK*

Oliver J. Peacock
University of Bath, UK

Thom Phillips
Cwmbran Village Surgery, UK

Michael J. Price
Coventry University, UK

Oliver J. Price
Leeds Beckett University, UK

Jennifer Reed
University of Ottawa Heart Institute, Canada

Daniel Rhind
Loughborough University, UK

John M. Saxton
Northumbria University, UK

Joanna Shakespeare
*University Hospitals Coventry and
Warwickshire NHS Trust, UK*

Susan M. Shirreffs
St Andrews University, UK

Natalie F. Shur
University of Nottingham, UK

Victoria S. Sprung
Liverpool John Moores University, UK

Andrew Smith
Former BASES Chair, UK (retired)

Paul M. Smith
Cardiff Metropolitan University, UK

S. Andy Sparks
Edge Hill University, UK

Eric J. Stöhr
Leibniz University, Germany

Karl Sylvester
*Cambridge University Hospitals NHS
Foundation Trust, UK*

Dick H. J. Thijssen
*Radboud University Medical Center, the
Netherlands*

Dylan Thompson
University of Bath, UK

Katie Thralls-Butte
Seattle Pacific University, USA

Keith Tolfrey
Loughborough University, UK

Veli Topkara
*Columbia University Irving Medical Center,
USA*

Lauren K. Truby
Duke University School of Medicine, USA

Neil P. Walsh
University of Birmingham, UK

Craig Williams
University of Exeter, UK

Edward Winter
Sheffield Hallam University, UK

Foreword

I write this foreword as the current and first female Chair of the British Association of Sport and Exercise Sciences and am delighted to offer support for these Exercise Testing Guidelines. These separate textbooks epitomise the work of the association, through professional collaboration, keeping BASES at the forefront of world-leading science and achieving considerable reach and impact.

The clear expansion of the textbooks, evidenced by overall scale, variety and quality of content as well as the number and diversity of contributors, is commendable. The contributors are highly respected academics and/or practitioners (many of whom are BASES Fellows) and many have collaborated with emerging, early-career colleagues. The quality of these textbooks, combined with the process employed by contributors and the editorial team, reflects a commitment to ensure that the standards for sport and clinical physiological testing remains exemplary. This timely project has produced a model of excellent practice, which other disciplines may consider emulating in future.

Professor Zoe Knowles
FBASES, FHEA, HCPC Practitioner Psychologist
BASES Chair
Liverpool John Moores University, UK

I write as a two-time and first Chair of BASES and commend the editors and authors on the completion of the latest edition of the Exercise Testing Guidelines. This new edition is a true reflection on the development of BASES and the profession since the very first Physiological Testing Guidelines were produced in 1986. In the first edition, the authors produced recommendations that provided the foundations for 'best practice' for physiological testing of athletes. Before its publication, there was no consensus on testing methodologies and often scant regard for the principles of scientific rigour.

Over the ensuing 35 years, each subsequent edition has extended the range of topics and addressed new challenges without compromising the principles of scientific rigour and relevance. In this new edition, the coverage and depth of information is again a significant step forward, providing an exceptional resource for sport and exercise physiologists, particularly for those progressing towards BASES

Accreditation. This series of Guidelines has helped establish and consolidate the Association's reputation as a world leader for physiological testing in health and disease. Therefore, it is with great pride and gratitude that I commend the new Exercise Testing Guidelines to all who study, teach and research in sport and exercise sciences.

Professor Clyde Williams
OBE, DSc, PhD, FBASES, FFSEM
Professor of Sports Science (emeritus)
Loughborough University, UK

Introduction

R. C. Richard Davison and Paul M. Smith

The origins of the BASES Physiological Testing Guidelines date back to 1986, when the Sports Physiology Section of the British Association of Sports Sciences (BASS) created a working group of Neil Armstrong, Adrianne Hardman, Philip Jakeman, Craig Sharp and Edward Winter. Together, they produced a BASS Position Statement on the Physiological Assessment of the Elite Competitor (Hale et al., 1988). As the study of sport science began to grow, BASS established accreditation schemes for individual practitioners and exercise testing laboratories. In 1998, a second edition of the exercise testing guidelines made reference to both accreditation schemes.

Some nine years later, BASS had evolved into the British Association of Sport and Exercise Sciences (BASES) to acknowledge that not all exercise scientists were exclusively interested in sport. In 1997, Steve R. Bird and R. C. Richard Davison took over the responsibility of editing the third edition of the BASES 'Physiological Testing Guidelines'. This consisted of 19 chapters organised in four sections: general issues and procedures; generic testing procedures; sport-specific testing guidelines; and specific considerations for the assessment of the young athlete (Bird and Davison, 1997).

A further gap of ten years elapsed before the fourth edition was published in 2006 (Winter et al., 2006a, 2006b) and this represented a significant expansion of the coverage of the guidelines resulting in two volumes: one with an emphasis on sport, while the other focussed on clinical practices. While both volumes shared chapters linked to common principles of physiological exercise testing, remaining chapters related to either sport or clinical topics. The expansion and creation of distinct textbook volumes reflected the growing number of BASES members and accredited practitioners in respective areas.

Since the last edition, the number of students studying sport and exercise science in the UK has continued to grow, with more than 17,500 students accepted into a sport and exercise science course in 2018/19. At that time, the total number of students studying a higher education course in the UK related to sport and exercise science was just under 49,000 and continues to grow. Mirroring this growth has been the increase in vocational applications of sport and exercise science and many enjoy careers in diverse settings. These settings include sport and exercise support work with national governing bodies, professional clubs, the

DOI: 10.4324/9781003045267-1

Home Countries' Sport Institutes and public and private healthcare providers. Employment opportunities also exist in private enterprises and governmental, voluntary and local authority organisations engaged in the provision of exercise and physical activity for people with, or at high risk of developing, a myriad of diseases and associated disabilities.

In line with this significant increase of student numbers and applied professions has been the expansion of research in the sport and exercise sciences which now provides a significantly expanded evidence base that underpins the physiological assessments in the current two volumes.

This edition provides a reference guide for sport and exercise scientists in training (BASES supervised experience), practitioners, researchers and teachers in sport and exercise science. During very challenging times, members of the editorial team have worked with a wide range of contributors, including many of the United Kingdom's leading sport and exercise scientists and/or practitioners. The two volumes of the BASES Exercise Testing Guidelines provide a comprehensive resource, which is underpinned by the latest research and practice in elite sports and the clinical sciences.

Sadly, since 2006, we have lost several giants of our discipline, who were authors/editors of previous editions: Craig Sharp, Tom Reilly and Edward Winter. Each of these individuals was passionate about BASES and the development of the subject area to whom we owe a great debt.

We would like to pay a particular tribute to Edward Winter who led the editorial team for the last edition and has contributed to every edition of the guidelines, including a chapter in this edition that was completed before his death.

References

Bird, S. and Davison, R. (1997). *Physiological Testing Guidelines* (3rd ed.). Leeds: The British Association of Sport and Exercise Sciences.

Hale, T., Armstrong, N., Hardman, A., Jakeman, P., Sharp, C. and Winter, E. (1988). *Position Statement on the Physiological Assessment of the Elite Competitor* (2nd ed.). Leeds: White Line Press.

Winter, E. M., Jones, A. M., Davison, R. C. R., Bromley, P. D. and Mercer, T. (2006a). *Sport and Exercise Physiology Testing Guidelines: Volume I: Sport Testing: The British Association of Sport and Exercise Sciences Guide*. Abingdon, UK: Routledge.

Winter, E. M., Jones, A. M., Davison, R. C. R., Bromley, P. D. and Mercer, T. (2006b). *Sport and Exercise Physiology Testing Guidelines: Volume 2: Clinical Testing: The British Association of Sport and Exercise Sciences Guide*. Abingdon, UK: Routledge.

Part I

1.1 Professional competency and working with others

Michael J. Price, Andrew M. Miles and Paul M. Smith

Introduction

Achieving and maintaining a *minimum standard of professional competency* is an important aspect of many careers and sport and exercise science is no exception. Careers such as medicine, nursing and physiotherapy require practitioners to record and evidence their ongoing professional development and the relevant professional bodies conduct regular audits in order for practitioners to retain their registration. Whilst BASES does not currently require ongoing evidence of continued development, it does have a strong ethos of achieving and maintaining high standards and professional development as evidenced in its accreditation and re-accreditation pathways. These require practitioners to meet minimum standards to achieve initial accreditation and to evidence continued professional development and sustained growth to secure re-accreditation.

Within the UK, whether as part of a research role, clinical (or sport) service provision or learning and teaching, sport and exercise science practitioners must abide by the BASES Code of Conduct. This code encompasses specific elements of research ethics, personal and professional conduct and competence. Indeed, there are many linked chapters within this textbook, which relate to these specific issues to help you ensure your practice is consistent with good practice.

Members, at all times, must have regard to the following principles:

a) All Clients have the right to expect the highest standards of professionalism, consideration and respect.
b) The pursuit of scientific knowledge requires that research and testing is carried out with utmost integrity.
(c) The law requires that working practices are safe, that the welfare of the Client is paramount, and that data is used and stored in accordance with the law.

BASES Code of Conduct (Paragraph 4.3) March 2017

NB: In anticipation of the publication date of this textbook, note that the BASES code of conduct is currently under review and with a new version available by early 2022.

DOI: 10.4324/9781003045267-3

Maintaining and extending professional competency

The premise underpinning professional competency suggests that an individual achieves some initial baseline, or minimum threshold standard in the form of a measure of his/her *'fitness to practice'* or a *'licence to practice'*. In some professions, this criterion requirement is associated with formal, professional-body-endorsed academic training at either the undergraduate or postgraduate level (e.g., British Association of Sport Rehabilitators and Trainers – BASRaT). In other professions, demonstration of professional competency may be attached to evidencing competence through professional practice or training after graduation to achieve professional-body recognition through an *accreditation scheme* or similar process (e.g., BASES or British Psychological Society). Having achieved this initial baseline, there is an expectation that practitioners maintain and extend their competency and knowledge base through ongoing training and continuous professional development. An employer, a professional organisation and/or private providers can provide ongoing training. Responsibility for maintaining and extending competence lies with the practitioner, but is typically regulated or mandated by the profession.

Employers require minimum knowledge and standards, often identified as 'essential' or 'desirable' skills and knowledge within person specifications and job descriptions. Many identify that a candidate/applicant must have professional-body endorsement/accreditation or similar credentials. This is imperative and ensures an employee can 'hit the ground running' with the minimum acceptable professional knowledge and skills. By ensuring recruits have the required professional skillsets at the outset, employers can focus any initial induction on job- and employer-specific training such as health and safety, data handling and internal policies and practices, some of which are included in chapters of this textbook immediately following this introduction.

Safeguarding and welfare is relevant in all contexts of a client-based industry, but special consideration is required when working with young and/or vulnerable populations. In the UK, anyone working with minors (i.e., participants under 18 years of age) or vulnerable groups (e.g., clinical patients or some individuals with physical and/or learning disabilities) must gain formal clearance through the Disclosure and Barring Service (DBS). Sport and exercise practitioners should thus be aware and informed of such areas, referring to policies of their own organisation, BASES's governance documents or policy documents (e.g., *Safeguarding and Welfare Policy*). In the context of applied sport and exercise science practices, we also refer readers to a wealth of sport- and exercise-science-specific information and applied recommendations within a repository of *BASES Expert Statements* and the *Useful Resources* at the end of this chapter.

Once a practitioner is 'skilled' in both a professional and internal organisational capacity, s/he then needs to *remain up to date of emerging developments* in both contexts. There is a shared responsibility between the employer, the profession and an individual to ensure that practitioners are able to access continued professional development (CPD) opportunities. As alluded to previously, employers and practitioners should be proactive in seeking training opportunities which extend beyond compulsory in-house requirements. Practitioners should be able to clearly demonstrate the retention of their 'fitness to practice' through accessing CPD opportunities such as external (professional) training events, conferences, peer-reviewed publications, opportunities to shadow/observe other practitioners/supervisors, engaging in professional networks and remaining aware of evolving professional regulatory standards. Engagement with a suitable (academic or clinical) mentor (or supervisor) can prove beneficial, helping to ensure a practitioner remains abreast of area-specific requirements, identifying and capitalising upon gainful CPD opportunities.

A fundamental activity to help practitioners recognise those areas of their professional practice in need of improvement is *reflective practice* (Huntley et al., 2019). Reflective practice is a cognitive process that allows practitioners to examine their own professional practice by asking themselves questions about how and why they do things and considering the impact of their actions and decisions on their practice and on the experiences of their clients. Although many reflective practice articles within sport and exercise science appear biased towards sport and exercise psychology (Huntley et al., 2014), reflective practice is key to all applied practice disciplines. However, a study of coach education noted a lack of confidence in understanding reflective practice and thus limited engagement with it (Cropley et al., 2012). Although it is beyond the scope of this chapter to discuss models of reflective practice and the process *per se*, it is important to note the range of reflective practice models available – each with associated pros and cons (Knowles et al., 2014).

Working in multi- and interdisciplinary teams

An important requirement in the context of BASES-supervised experience is the consideration and appreciation of working as a component of an integrated, multidisciplinary (or interdisciplinary) team, a factor that is key for sporting, exercise and health arenas. As a specialist within a particular field of study, you will typically find yourself working alongside others to achieve a common goal: whether evaluating a patient's pre-operative fitness, or the impact of a specific intervention on an elite athlete's performance.

Within the sport and exercise sciences, a subtle difference exists between the terms 'multidisciplinary' and 'interdisciplinarity'. With a client at the centre of a wheel (the hub), a multidisciplinary approach would have professions within their individual silos on the rim, all heading towards the centre with no interaction – a parallel provision of support. However, interdisciplinary work implies that there is some interaction between professional areas. For example, a change in sporting equipment and/or technique (i.e., biomechanics) or improvements in strength (i.e., strength and conditioning) might improve exercise efficiency/economy (i.e., exercise physiology), thus leading to an improvement in situation-specific confidence (i.e., training and/or competition) and an improvement in performance. Likewise, in a clinical setting, an improvement in physiological/metabolic fitness and function (i.e., physiology), resulting from behaviour change (i.e., health psychology; see West et al., 2019), will lead to improved self-efficacy (i.e., psychology), leading to greater independence and improvement in overall quality of life.

Within the clinical sciences, many good examples of the workings of multi- and interdisciplinary teams exist, but the extent of literature pertaining to such an approach in the sport and exercise sciences remains somewhat scant. This situation continues despite Burwitz et al. (1994) raising the importance of this approach more than a quarter of a century ago. In the context of the sport and exercise community, some good examples exist of multidisciplinary approaches to the support and preparation of individual elite athletes and/or squads.

There will always be limitations to research endeavours and/or programmes of clinical provision/sport science support. A frequent shortfall is the poor translation of existing knowledge to applied practice. While the concept of 'evidence-based practice' is broadly accepted, a paradox exists wherein a practitioner may turn to 'practice-based evidence'. To contextualise this point, an example relates to the broad topic of coaching or sport science support of elite athletes. While a vast amount of scientific literature exists for well-trained groups of athletes, little exists for truly elite, international competitors. In this example, Ross et al. (2018) describe a need to adopt a blended approach to the collection and assimilation of knowledge to create often novel and unique solutions and practical applications. Here, one might draw on all available knowledge, gaining insight from a scientific, professional experience and anecdotal perspectives.

This chapter provides the reader with a general overview of professional practice, competency and the concept of multi- and interdisciplinary teams; your challenge is to seek subject-specialist information to help you become more informed and the most competent and effective practitioner possible. Consulting the considerable array of information contained within the BASES policy documents, guidelines and expert statements is highly recommended.

References

Burwitz, L., Moore, P. M. and Wilkinson, D. M. (1994). Future directions for performance-related sports science research: An interdisciplinary approach. *Journal of Sport Sciences*, 12, 93–109.

Cropley, B., Miles, A. and Peel, J. (2012). Reflective practice: Value of, issues, and developments within sports coaching. Sports Coach UK Original Research.

Huntley, E., Cropley, B., Gilbourne, D., Sparkes, A. and Knowles, Z. (2014). Reflecting back and forwards: An evaluation of peer-reviewed reflective practice research in sport. *Reflective Practice*, 15, 863–876.

Huntley, E., Cropley, B., Knowles, Z. and Miles, A. (2019). BASES expert statement: Reflective practice: The key to experimental learning. *The Sport & Exercise Scientist*, 60(Summer), 6–7.

Knowles, Z., Gilbourne, D., Cropley, B. and Dugdill, L. (2014). *Reflective Practice in the Sport and Exercise Sciences: Contemporary Issues*. Edited By Zoe (1st ed.). Abingdon, UK: Routledge.

Ross, E., Gupta, L. and Sanders, L. (2018). When research leads to learning, but not action in high performance sport. *Progress in Brain Research*, 240, 201–217. (Textbook series Chapter 12). https://doi.org/10.1016/bs.pbr.2018.08.001

West, R., Michie, S., Chadwick, P., Atkins, L. and Lorencatto, F. (2019). Achieving behaviour change: A guide for local government and partners. *Public Health England: Protecting and*

Improving the Nation's Health. www.gov.uk/government/publications/behaviour-change-guide-for-local-government-and-partners (accessed 12 May 2021).

Useful resources

BASES Code of Conduct. www.bases.org.uk/imgs/bases_code_of_conduct872.pdf

BASES Safeguarding and Welfare Policy. https://bases.org.uk/imgs/bases_safeguarding__welfare_policy215.pdf (accessed 21 April 2021).

BASES Safeguarding Statement. www.bases.org.uk/imgs/expert_statement_1__pages_380.pdf (accessed 21 April 2021).

The BASES Expert Statement on Ethics and Participation in Research of Young People. (2011). www.bases.org.uk/imgs/ethics_and_participation_in_research_of_young_people625.pdf

General Data Protection Regulations. www.gov.uk/government/publications/guide-to-the-general-data-protection-regulation (accessed 21 April 2021).

1.2 Physiological exercise testing

Ethical considerations

Steve R. Bird and Andrew Smith

The ethics of physiological testing is an important consideration, whether one is conducting tests for research, sport science support, clinical health assessments or teaching. It is an expectation that BASES members will undertake their work in an ethical manner and adhere to the principles of professional practice. This chapter will consider what this means in the context of physiological testing and provide some guidelines on what considerations one must take to ensure that one conducts physiological testing in an ethical manner.

Because regulations and legislation change over time and vary across nations, it is important that readers cross-reference this chapter with the frameworks in the place when and where they are testing. It is the responsibility of the sport and exercise scientist to identify what approvals they need, and which regulations they must adhere to before commencing any test battery.

The application of ethical principles to physiological testing

In relatively recent times, there has been a cultural shift away from the view-point that all-knowing experts perform tests on passive subjects, and instead the activity is now recognised as a partnership between assessors and participants, as well as other potential stakeholders. This is reflected in a change in the terminology from the previous vocabulary of referring to those being tested as 'subjects' and instead to now referring to them as 'participants', which is how they will be referred to throughout this chapter. Likewise, for clarity, those responsible for running tests and collecting data will be referred to as 'assessors' from this point onwards.

This partnership of rights, roles and respect is one of many considerations when determining whether the activity is 'ethical'. Within professional practice, the conduct of physiological testing in an ethical manner is an expectation, whether it be in research, sport science support, clinical health or teaching, so the conduct of physiological tests in an ethical manner is a principal concern for everyone undertaking this work, regardless of the setting.

Today, research that involves either human participants – human organs, tissues, cells, fluids or other biological material – or human data requires

DOI: 10.4324/9781003045267-4

approval by a constituted and recognised human research ethics committee. With human samples, there are also strict codes of conduct and practices set out by the Human Tissue Authority (www.hta.gov.uk). In this context, for example, UK Higher Education Institutions apply for an HTA licence and are subject to ongoing scrutiny to ensure all registered workers abide by the ethical framework set out.

The purpose of human research ethics committees is to ensure that colleagues conduct research ethically and adhere to key principles. The exact wording may differ between codes, but the following directives encapsulate core principles:

1   *Respect* the participants and others involved in the activity;
2   Be fully *transparent* to ensure that all involved are aware of the objectives of the activity, what the activity entails, how data will be managed and any conflicts of interest, and be clear about any risks – large or small;
3   Be scientifically *rigorous* in terms of the methods and protocols used (including the calibration of equipment) to ensure the collection of valid, reliable and accurate data;
4   Only be conducted by people who conform to the highest *professional* standards and who are demonstrably competent assessors holding the appropriate qualifications, certification and insurance;
5   Uphold the highest standards of *honesty* and *integrity*;
6   Put the health and safety of all those involved as the top priority and to always act to *minimise any risks;*
7   Ensure proposed research outcomes are *meaningful and purposeful* for participants involved; and
8   *Comply* with legal and other regulatory frameworks including those of the insurer.

The physiological testing of human participants for other purposes, such as fitness testing for sport or health-related assessments or teaching, should also adhere to these principles, regardless of whether the assessment is physiological, biomechanical, psychological, clinical health or medical. The ethical conduct of these activities not only ensures the protection and minimisation of risk to participants and assessors, but also to any organisations linked to the work, as well as determining that the activity is of benefit to the individual and/or wider community.

In a research context, a consideration of the numerous ethics principles of working with human participants is formalised, itemised and clearly communicated through the completion of an ethics application form. A relevant ethics committee will then review the application and an assessment will be made in accordance with the values and guidelines of the code and culture in which the research is taking place.

These same principles should apply to physiological testing in other contexts, with a constituted panel reviewing the submission and providing feedback to the assessors, and without such approval the physiological testing must not proceed. These formalised procedures and the input from a group with diverse experiences will ensure that the proposed physiological testing activity is undertaken in compliance with recognised ethics requirements and, in doing so, will help to safeguard all involved – participants, assessors, professional organisations and institutions. Forms for physiological testing in 'non-research' contexts can be developed and used to help prevent unethical practice, avoid adverse events and reduce the frequency of complaints, all of which may have detrimental consequences to the participant, assessors, employers of assessors and others.

Where physiological, or other testing activity is approved, assessors are then beholden to comply with the approved procedures and to not deviate from the approved procedures or undertake testing that differs from the approved details. Should there be a need to make subsequent changes, either the chief investigator (CI) or other relevant person must apply to the relevant ethics committee for an amendment to the approved physiological testing activity.

This chapter will deal with the broad principles of ethics for physiological testing, regardless of its context, and highlight any specific issues relating to sport and or clinical exercise testing as they arise.

Ethical issues relating to physiological testing

The following paragraphs consider some of the ethical issues that the assessor needs to address when planning to undertake physiological testing.

Why are you testing: do foreseen benefits outweigh the risks?

Before undertaking any physiological testing, it is important to weigh the risks against likely benefits. To do this, the person responsible for the testing, such as the CI in a research study, the head of sport and sciences services or clinical expert in the health field, needs to make explicit the purpose of the testing and, from this, the benefit that would be derived from the findings. In some cases, these benefits will directly affect the participant, such as identifying a health concern or generating a fitness profile to inform his or her training programme. In other circumstances, indeed in the case of most research, the findings when published may be of little or no immediate benefit to the research participant, but will contribute to knowledge that, when published, may benefit others.

An assessor must consider likely benefits against potential risks for any participant and, in some cases, the assessor(s) and/or their institution or employing organisation. Assessors can view certain risks as being 'negligible' or 'carrying low risk', such as inconvenience and the investment of time by participants, through to discomfort. Other risk may be categorised as 'more than low risk', such as the risk of distress, physical injury or psychological harm. In research, it is the responsibility of the CI to weigh the merits of the potential benefits against the potential risks. At this stage, if intending to proceed, a relevant ethics committee should consider a formal application. At this point, the ethics committee may ask the CI to provide further clarification, or to consider alternative approaches in order to reduce risk. In non-research assessments, other suitable experts within the organisation may fulfil this role if there is no formalised procedure or advisory committee.

Minimisation of risk

Assessors can minimise risk through careful consideration of the intended procedures. These include aspects relating to the participant, the assessors, the exercise protocol, the equipment, the environment and the inclusion of specific safety measures.

• To minimise risks, participants should be screened for contraindications to the exercise or other assessment that they will be asked to undertake, typically using a validated screening tool.
• Those conducting the assessment must be appropriately qualified and have the relevant expertise in the techniques they are using, as well as possessing suitable qualifications in first aid and cardiopulmonary resuscitation (CPR). Furthermore, the assessors should know the appropriate way to respond in the case of any 'adverse event'. It is highly recommended that all assessors complete some form of basic ethics awareness training.
• The protocols used in the testing need to be justified and ideally supported by evidence from previously published work that they are safe, valid and reliable, since collecting data that is not valid or reliable may be deemed unethical since it wastes the participants' time. Many testing protocols will have elements of safety built in, such as the inclusion of electrocardiographic (ECG) monitoring for some forms of exercise and participant groups, or use of a harness if exercising maximally on a treadmill.
• Additionally, assessors must adhere to safety procedures for cleaning and sterilising equipment. Electrical equipment used must have undergone relevant safety checks, including electrical tests, which will generate safety certificates as required by the work environment.
• For the safety of participants and assessors, appropriate personal protective equipment (PPE) should be worn, which, depending on the nature of the testing, may include protective gloves, laboratory coats, safety glasses, masks and others.

Any potential risks associated with testing procedures need to be articulated clearly to the participant, usually as part of a clear and detailed 'Participant Information Sheet' (PIS) and associated 'Informed Consent Form' (ICF). This ensures participants are appropriately informed and can thereby provide genuine informed consent for their participation.

Recruitment and power relationships

When undertaking physiological testing as part of a research study, there is usually a clear process of recruitment. This may range from a broad advertisement to the general population to a specific targeting of individuals with specific characteristics, such as a particular sporting expertise or health condition. In such circumstances, those volunteering to participate are clearly volunteers who have responded to an advertisement without any inherent obligation to do so. However, when undertaking fitness testing for a team or squad, the extent of 'volunteerism' may be compromised if it is the coach or manager who deems that all members of a squad should undergo fitness testing. In such cases, the assessor needs to consider very carefully his or her involvement and whether participation is truly voluntary. A scenario within many professional teams is that the requirement to participate in such activities is part of the participants' contracts, and the assessor needs to consider these issues carefully. In a clinical exercise testing context, the assessor has to be aware of the potential power balance that may exist if the potential participant's doctor, physiotherapist, allied health therapist or pharmacist is involved in the recruitment process. Their involvement in recruitment does not make this process unethical, *per se*, but some scrutiny and careful consideration of how they are involved is required.

Other unbalanced power relationships may exist between university staff and their students; therefore it is important that there should be no perceived obligation for a student to participate in a research study conducted by one of their lecturers. It should be clear that a student's professional relationship with the lecturer and the institution remain unaffected, whether they volunteered or declined to participate. In the context of teaching, those responsible for the physiological testing within academic courses need to carefully consider the ethics of proposed testing which is likely to be included, justifying the inclusion of physiological testing as part of the educational experience. This should always be for the students' benefit of developing their knowledge, understanding, relevant practical skills and awareness through personal experience, but tutors need to consider this matter in light of the students' rights and possible risks.

Power relationships can also influence safeguarding aspects of physiological testing, covered in Chapter 1.4.

Information, consent and the capacity to provide consent or assent (children)

Before participating in any data collection, an assessor must inform all participants of testing procedures and objectives. Participants should know what they will be required to do, how much time may be involved and what, if any, risks they will encounter. Assessors should declare any sources of funding since a prospective participant may have concerns about potential conflicts of interest. The information given to the participant should also include how the data will be stored securely and who will have access to stored data. This may include the participant, assessor, coach or health/medical practitioner, as well as the intention to publish (usually anonymised group data or de-identified data) in research publications or reports. Regardless of the final intentions of the use of the data, the participant needs to be made aware of this. Additionally, the assessors should state for how long the data will be stored. Research ethics codes and guidelines specify minimum durations, as do some publications. These may be of the order of 5 years, but typically 7–10 years for health-related data, and often there is no stated maximum. Thus, provided data is stored securely, it can be maintained far longer, which may be useful if longitudinal comparisons are sought in the future.

This information would normally be in the form of written participant information that is given to them, using language that can be clearly understood and without confusing technical and/or scientific jargon. It should also be in a language that they understand, so translated copies may be required in some circumstances. Without this information, participants cannot provide informed consent. The provision of consent would normally be in writing using an approved 'Participant Information and Consent Form' (PICF), which would include statements saying that the participant understands what the testing entails, any risks, what will happen to the data and that they've had the opportunity to have any questions or concerns addressed. The PIS and ICF would normally be signed by the participant, assessor and a witness. In some cases, there may be a clause that states that if the results indicate a health concern for the participant, test results may be forwarded to a relevant health/medical practitioner, or a medical referral will be made; however, this must be clearly stated to participants and agreed upon by all at the outset.

It should be noted that if the participant is a child, then consent would be provided by his or her parent or guardian, but that this should then be affirmed by the child giving his or her 'assent' to participation.

Confidentiality, privacy, security, data access and usage of data

Data would typically be on secure institution/organisation property in locked cabinets in the case of hardcopies, and/or secure password-protected computers/servers. Increasingly, data is stored on cloud-based servers which also must follow good security practice in password protection and encryption (where possible). In research contexts, data may be collected and stored using coded identifiers, for which only the assessors are able to match the codes to individuals, since this adds further privacy and confidentiality. With research studies, data normally remains confidential, with any identifying data excluded from publications. However, in some cases this may be difficult, if for example the research involves elite sports people, such as Olympic medallists, whereof the population of individuals is so small that it enables accurate deductions about the identity of participants simply from the nature of the research. In such cases, this would need to be made clear to the participants within their PIS and ICF.

In sports physiological testing or clinical health exercise testing, data should be made available to the participant, coach or other relevant staff, health or medical practitioner, and the participant would need to agree to this in the PIS and ICF. In a sporting context, this may cause some concern for the participants, if they perceived that their data may be used in the context of 'team selection' or other means of discrimination. This needs to be clearly established with all concerned and the assessor must comply with the signed agreements. So, for example, if a coach or selection manager asked for the data at a later date, but the participant had not agreed to those individuals having access to the data, then the assessor is not permitted to give it to other persons. Hence, clarity on such matters needs to be established in writing prior to any physiological testing activity and participants may have this access to data included in their contracts.

In some circumstances, photographic images may be taken to illustrate the physiological testing procedures. If this is part of the procedure, then the participant must be made aware of what images will be taken and what they would be used for and agree to this. Furthermore, if any images are to be used in subsequent publications, specific permission must be attained from the participant, and this may or may not involve de-identifying those in the images, for example using pixilation of the face or obscuring the face with a 'black box'. Most institutions will have specific forms that address the publication of images and these would need to be signed by the participant in addition to the standard PICF or equivalent 'non-research' form.

It should be stated that acquired data can only be used for the purposes to which the participant has agreed within the PIS and ICF. If the assessors perceive that they may wish to use the data for secondary purposes at a later date, such as writing a research paper on previously collected fitness or health data, then this must be specified and stated in the PIS and ICF, and the participant must knowingly agree to this possibility.

In some clinical areas, particularly in rare diseases, new models of consent have been developed to enable the collation of data where individual data is scarce. While this wider sharing of data would seem to compromise some aspects of privacy, modified consent clauses have been developed and researched with participants understanding the need for large-scale data sharing and expecting their data to be distributed and reused, but requiring, nonetheless, that they be informed of such activities to maintain a level of protection and control. However, despite this wider sharing, the underlying principle must be that the possible benefit for participants and others like them must surpass the potential consequences for their privacy (Nguyen et al., 2019).

Withdrawal of participant and his or her data

Within a research ethics submission, there would normally be a clause stating that participants are free to withdraw from the study at any stage without it affecting their relationship with the assessors or their organisation. If the participant has already completed the physiological assessments, a further clause may say that s/he can withdraw his/her data, provided it is identifiable as his/her data, prior to it being included in any data analyses or publication, again, without this affecting the participant's relationship with the assessors or their institution. This option should be clearly stated on the PIS and ICF that participants sign, along with whom they should contact in these circumstances.

Monitoring and reporting of activities – annual reports, adverse events, complaints

Ethics committees require regular, typically annual, reporting of the research projects for which they have given ethics approval. This regular monitoring provides those responsible with information on how an approved research project is progressing, and eventually a final report would be required that outlines the outcomes of research undertaken and, where applicable, intended publications. In sports testing or health/clinical testing, there will be similar requirements for regular reporting, and these will be audited at intervals.

In addition to this, even with the best-planned physiological testing procedures, there remains a risk, and this should be included in the PIS and ICF so that the participant is aware of the risk before agreeing to participate. As part of the establishment of the physiological testing activity, there must be a clear procedure for reporting adverse events. This may be both internal and external in the case of clinical trials. Where the physiological testing is for sport science support or health/ medical assessments there must be a clear procedure for reporting these events promptly; this means immediate reporting, rather than waiting to include the information in an annual report. When reported, such occurrences will be investigated by the relevant authorities and the activity may be suspended during the investigation. The findings of the investigation will then determine whether the physiological testing may be resumed or terminated.

Clear procedures must also exist to deal with formal complaints. In the case of research, there will be an established committee, often composed of experts from an institution's research ethics and research governance bodies. The risk of complaints is minimised if the assessors adhere to stated and approved procedures. Complaints often stem from ambiguities, which an assessor can avoid if participants receive comprehensive and clear information within the PIS and signed ICF. Other complaints may relate to the nature of recruitment strategies used, if for example an assessor has randomly displayed unapproved recruitment posters and signs in public areas. Similar organisations and procedures for dealing with complaints must be established within organisations that undertake sports-, health- and medical-related exercise testing.

Other considerations

If the participants are members of particular cultural groups or vulnerable populations, the assessors will need to consider the implications and undertake recruitment, attainment of consent and testing in a way that complies with the expectations of the ethical collection of data with these participants. For example, where children and minors under the age of 18 years are concerned, both participant informed consent and parent/guardian assent must be obtained. Within the UK, it is obligatory for assessors working with minors to have undergone, and be able to present evidence of, a formal, context-specific and up-to-date Disclosure and Barring Service check (see: https://dbscheckonline.org.uk/).

Assessors should not seek ethics approval retrospectively. Situations in which research may be undertaken on existing data sets are a specific scenario, with specific issues that are considered by the research ethics committee, including whether the participants had agreed to their data being used for research or teaching purposes when it was collected.

An assessor cannot recruit participants and collect research until an ethics committee has granted approval; this has to fall within the approval period. If the assessors wish to continue collecting data beyond this point, an assessor must request an extension to ethics approval.

Policies and regulations

American College of Sports Medicine Pre-Participation Screening. www.acsm.org/docs/default-source/default-document-library/read-research/acsm-risk-stratification-chart.pdf?sfvrsn=7b8b1dcd_6

Australian Code for the Responsible Conduct of Research. (2018). *National Health and Medical Research Council, Australian Research Council and Universities Australia.* Commonwealth of Australia, Canberra. www.nhmrc.gov.au/about-us/publications/australian-code-responsible-conduct-research-2018

British Association of Sport and Exercise Sciences (BASES) Code of Conduct. www.bases.org.uk/imgs/bases_code_of_conduct872.pdf

Exercise and Sport Science Australia. *Adult Pre-Exercise Screening System (APSS).* www.essa.org.au/Public/ABOUT_ESSA/Adult_Pre-Screening_Tool.aspx?WebsiteKey=b4460de9-2eb5-46f1-aeaa-3795ae70c687

National Health Service. *Health Research Authority.* www.hra.nhs.uk/about-us/committees-and-services/res-and-recs/research-ethics-service/

Nguyen, M. T., et al. (2019). Model consent clauses for rare disease research. *BMC Medical Ethics*, 20(1), 55.

NHS Health Research Authority. www.hra.nhs.uk/

NHS Research Ethics Service. www.hra.nhs.uk/about-us/committees-and-services/res-and-recs/

UK Government, General Data Protection Regulations. www.gov.uk/government/publications/guide-to-the-general-data-protection-regulation

UK Research and Innovation. www.ukri.org/about-us/policies-and-standards/research-integrity/

1.3   Health and safety in duty of care

Evaluating and stratifying risk

S. Andy Sparks, Kelly Marrin and Craig A. Bridge

The processes involved in data collection and participant, patient or client assessment in exercise physiology present unique challenges for researchers, clinicians and practitioners – collectively referred to as assessors from this point onwards. The need to collect data in diverse environments that are often less controlled than a traditional laboratory setting, but relevant to the assessment and/or research question can further complicate matters. During any physiological testing, an assessor has a duty of care to the individual(s) under his/her supervision. In this context, duty of care represents a formalisation of the social responsibilities that individuals, laboratories and organisations have to research participants, patients or clients in their care. It requires assessors to adhere to standards of reasonable care whilst supervising or conducting any laboratory or field-based procedure that may foreseeably cause harm. Consequently, a key priority is the duty of care for the participant or patient, along with the health and safety of the individuals involved in the data collection itself. Therefore, in order to act reasonably and foresee the possible causes of harm, assessors need to formally identify hazards or risks and implement risk mitigation strategies before any data collection procedures take place. This chapter is intended to provide clear guidelines and suggestions for the processes of hazard identification, risk assessment and mitigation. Assessors and organisations responsible for the physiological assessment of human participants should consider the contents and associated recommendations within this chapter.

Professional obligations

Safe practices and procedures should underpin all laboratory and field-based activities for several vital reasons. Firstly, many assessors will be working either for an organisation or an employer, or as self-employed individuals; in these contexts, assessors and places of work must adhere to the requirements set out in the Health and Safety at Work Act (1974). This outlines the legal requirement for safe practices and environments, along with the paramount importance of client welfare. These principles form the foundation of the BASES Code of Conduct; this framework insists that members use the utmost integrity and concern for their participants, patients or clients and act without jeopardising any individual's safety. Under appropriate assessor supervision, the BASES Code of

DOI: 10.4324/9781003045267-5

Conduct ensures that undue risk is avoided (BASES, 2017) – these issues are also covered in some detail the chapter relating to ethics. It is essential that all aspects of data collection and client sport and exercise science support are assessed for appropriateness and safety before anyone is exposed to unnecessary harm. It is also imperative that there is an appropriate procedure to gain a client's informed consent and that data management occurs in accordance with relevant data protection legislation. Furthermore, the practitioner must recognise his or her limitations in qualifications, experience, expertise and competence and operate safely within these limits. The following sections detail the chronological order in which processes should occur to ensure assessors meet these key considerations.

Hazard identification

The first key step in duty of care-based risk mitigation is the identification of hazards. This should not only focus on research participants or client(s), but also individuals working with these individuals or indeed in isolation. This is especially relevant in cases in which anyone may be exposed to potential risks as part of normal working activities and should be addressed within an organisation's lone working policy. In this context, a hazard represents anything that has the potential to harm the health and safety of any person involved in the process of assessing a client/participant or preparing and/or using equipment, or anyone in proximity to the testing area. Such hazards can typically be categorised into five types (Table 1.3.1). Unless and until an assessor identifies potential hazards, the rest of the risk management process cannot begin. Hazards should also be recorded and reviewed at least annually, following an accident or 'near miss', if something in the environment has changed or if modifications occur to a standard operating procedure.

Risk assessment

The assessment of risk is the key component of health and safety practice and management. It is about taking reasonable and logical steps to prevent ill health (HSE, 2012). Furthermore, there is also a legal requirement that all activities are risk-assessed and documented in order to ensure that what is reasonably practicable has been done to mitigate risks (Health and Safety at Work Act, 1974). This essentially means that there needs to be a balance of the level of risk with the cost, time and practicality of the measures needed to control the risk (HSE, 2016); there is no expectation for an assessor to anticipate unforeseeable risks, nor where mitigation measures are grossly disproportionate to the level of risk (HSE, 2014).

Five steps to risk assessment (HSE, 2014)

1   Identify potential hazards.

   • List the activity in steps and consider the equipment or materials within the specific environment in which it is to be used.
   • List the hazards for each of the steps and/or pieces of equipment.

Table 1.3.1 Classification and explanation of hazard types relevant to physiological testing

Hazard Type	Explanation / Example
Physical	This is the most common hazard and may include trips, slips, falls, noise or extremes of ambient temperature, and changes in physiological state in response to exertion;
Ergonomic / Mechanical	These factors might result in damage to the musculoskeletal system or skin. Such hazards are common with the use of ergometry or sports equipment, but may also be caused by manual handing or repetitive movements;
Chemical	These hazards include exposure to hazardous substances, most likely in wet laboratories or when using cleaning products for hygiene. They may also include the ingestion of substances/supplements used in nutrition-based experimental trials;
Biological	These hazards are common when there is either close contact between individuals or the exposure to human biological samples such as blood, urine or saliva;
Psychological	This form of hazard is possible when either severe exercise is needed and participants are exposed to mental fatigue, or during exposure to confined spaces, such as during some forms of body composition assessment. Risks may also be present when potentially sensitive information is collected (body composition, nutritional analysis, assessments of disordered eating, fitness assessments).

2   Identify who might be harmed and how.

- This is likely to be those in immediate contact or presence of the procedure/equipment but not always.
- Think carefully about the five types of hazards. This is particularly important for those exposed to potentially harmful substances that are chemical, nutritional or biological in nature.
- When exposure is to biological hazards, such as viruses and microorganisms, careful consideration regarding the method of transmission is vital and may require specialised considerations (Tipton et al., 2020). Consultation of the Health and Safety Executive's resources on bloodborne viruses (HSE, 2001), prevention of infection in laboratories (HSE, 2010) and control of substances hazardous to health (COSHH) (HSE, 2012) is recommended.

3   Evaluate the risks – consider the existing controls and assess the extent of the risks which remain.

- List the existing risk controls.

- Use the example (or similar) risk matrix (Table 1.3.2) to calculate the level of risk (the product of the outcome impact and its probability) and then again to calculate the risk with the controls in place.
- List the residual hazards.
- List the additional risk controls required to reduce the residual risk.
- Evaluation should also be done in conjunction with evidence from the literature. This is particularly important for scenarios that involve the ingestion of a substance, because safe consumption thresholds may be subject to change with emerging evidence.

4   Record the findings of the assessment – including the controls necessary and any further action needed to reduce risk sufficiently.

- Use a standardised proforma for the recording of this process. These are often stipulated by institutions or can be adapted from the HSE (2014) examples.
- Document that those affected have been consulted.
- Participant pre-exercise screening is a good example of a risk evaluation process that enables assessment and mitigation of potential risks specific to populations – Warburton et al. (2011) provide a comprehensive set of recommendations for this.

5   Review, revise and modify the assessment – this is especially important if the nature of the procedures or equipment changes, or if developments suggest existing risk assessment may no longer be valid.

Ensure a risk assessment has a suitable title, details the name of the person completing it and is dated. Further, the person with overall responsibility, for example the laboratory manager or head of department, should review all risk assessments and counter-sign them.

Key resources for risk assessment

How to control risks (HSE, 2016).
A brief guide to COSHH (HSE, 2012).
Examples of risk assessment documents (HSE, 2014).

Other key considerations

Hygiene

One underpinning risk mitigation strategy that is essential to exercise physiology is to ensure measures are in place to optimise hygiene via effective handwashing and/or use of alcohol gel, cleaning surfaces regularly, sterilisation of equipment, disposable equipment where appropriate and after-use decontamination (Tipton et al., 2020).

Table 1.3.2 Example risk quantification guidance assessment tool based on the probability and severity of the outcome impact*. Cells denote likely risk with example interpretations in parentheses.

Outcome impact	Rare	Unlikely	Possible	Likely	Probable
Severe	Medium (Moderate)	Medium (Moderate)	High (Substantial)	Extreme (Intolerable)	Extreme (Intolerable)
Major	Low (Acceptable)	Medium (Moderate)	Medium (Substantial)	High (Substantial)	Extreme (Intolerable)
Moderate	Low (Acceptable)	Low (Acceptable)	Medium (Moderate)	Medium (Substantial)	High (Substantial)
Minor	Low (Trivial)	Low (Acceptable)	Low (Acceptable)	Medium (Moderate)	Medium (Moderate)
Minimal	Low (Trivial)	Low (Trivial)	Low (Acceptable)	Low (Moderate)	Low (Moderate)

Probability

Risk Rating	Risk Interpretation
Trivial	No action required.
Acceptable	No preventative action, but consider cost-effective measures. Continued monitoring required.
Moderate	Implement measures to reduce risk. The speed of implementation should be proportional to the number of people exposed.
Substantial	Do not commence procedures until extent of risk is reduced. If this outcome occurs during a review of existing processes, seek to mitigate risk as soon as possible.
Intolerable	The level of risk must be reduced before work can either start or progress. If this is not possible, procedures are prohibited.

* One should use a risk classification matrix as a guide and interpret outcomes with caution.

Use of such a matrix should only form part of the risk assessment process (Peace, 2017).

Incidents and accidents

Appropriate provision for first aid equipment and a suitably qualified first aid-trained individual are minimum requirements. Given the nature of much of the work in sport and exercise physiology, it may also be a reasonable expectation that there is access to an automated external defibrillator (AED). A full assessment of the first aid needs of specific locations and procedures should be part of a risk assessment. Any event or 'near miss' should be formally documented under the regulations of the Reporting of Injuries, Diseases and Dangerous Occurrences Regulations (RIDDOR: – www.hse.gov.uk/riddor), and the current risk assessments should then be reviewed to ensure they are effective.

Emergency procedures

In data collection or client support situations, which may be in the field or laboratory setting, an assessor should consider what to do in an emergency and create a clear emergency plan. A plan should consider what to do in the case of an emergency, how to communicate with others, including the emergency services and how to evacuate, for example. A more detailed list of such considerations is available in the Health and Safety Toolbox (HSE, 2016).

Insurance and personal indemnity

The BASES Code of Conduct (BASES, 2017) requires members working with clients to ensure that suitable insurance indemnity coverage is in place. This needs to be with an authorised insurer (a list of these is available from the Financial Conduct Authority: www.fca.org.uk). In many cases, if activities form part of the work of an organisation, there may be public liability insurance coverage in place, but it is worth checking that this coverage includes all proposed activities, location(s) and individuals involved.

Standard operating procedures

Many institutions that have physiology laboratories will also have a set of standard operating procedures, such as for the procurement of capillary and venous blood samples. Where such documents exist, they should also be used in the development and review of risk assessments.

References

The British Association of Sport and Exercise Sciences. (2017). *Code of Conduct*. www.bases.org.uk/imgs/bases_code_of_conduct872.pdf (accessed 16 April 2020).

Health and Safety at Work Act. (1974). www.legislation.gov.uk/ukpga/1974/37/contents (accessed 15 May 2020).

Health and Safety Executive. (2001). *Blood-Borne Viruses in the Workplace: Guidance for Employers and Employees*. HSE Books. ISBN 978 0 7176 20623.

Health and Safety Executive. (2010). *Safe Working and the Prevention of Infection in Clinical Laboratories and Similar Facilities.* HSE Books. ISBN 978 0 7176 25130. www.hse.gov.uk/pubns/clinical-laboratories.pdf (accessed 4 May 2020).

Health and Safety Executive. (2012). *Working with Substances Hazardous to Health: A Brief Guide to COSHH.* www.hse.gov.uk/pubns/indg136.htm (accessed 4 May 2020).

Health and Safety Executive. (2014). *Risk Assessment: A Brief Guide to Controlling Risks in the Workplace.* www.hse.gov.uk/pubns/indg163.htm (accessed 4 May 2020).

Health and Safety Executive. (2016). *The Health and Safety Toolbox: How to Control Risks at Work.* HSE Books. ISBN 978 0 7176 65877.

Peace, C. (2017). The risk matrix: Uncertain results? *Policy and Practice in Health and Safety*, 15(2), 131–144. doi: 10.1080/14773996.2017.1348571

Tipton, M., Wilkes, M., Long, G., Morgan, P., Roiz de Sa, D., Corbett, J., Montgomery, H., Mekjavic, I. and Friedl, K. (2020). Returning to the laboratory for human testing. *The Physiological Society.* www.physoc.org/covid19/returning-to-the-lab/ (accessed 14 May 2020).

Warburton, D. E., Gledhill, N., Jamnik, V. K., Bredin, S. S. D., McKenzie, D. C., Stone, J., Charlesworth, S. and Shephard, R. J. (2011). Evidence-based risk assessment and recommendations for physical activity clearance: Consensus document. *Applied Physiology, Nutrition and Metabolism*, 36(Suppl 1), S266–S298. doi: 10.1139/h11-062

1.4   Safeguarding in physiological testing

Emma Kavanagh and Daniel Rhind

Introduction

The British Association of Sport and Exercise Sciences (BASES) aims to promote a culture wherein the importance of safeguarding and welfare within the sport and exercise sciences is a priority (Kavanagh et al., 2016). Physiologists working in a variety of settings must be cognisant of their duty of care towards clients, participants and co-workers. Traditionally, a legal duty of care amounts to risk – whether reasonable steps to prevent foreseeable risk have been identified and action(s) are taken to reduce such risks. A duty of care further relies upon the moral obligation placed upon an individual to understand his or her role in the prevention of foreseeable harm to others in order to ensure their safety or well-being (Kavanagh et al., 2020). As a physiologist, you have an obligation both to maintain legal standards of care and to act in accordance with professional standards set out by your regulatory body. The duty of care thus assumes your responsibility for the care of another individual and necessitates the actions you take in order to mitigate foreseeable risk(s).

Safeguarding serves to promote the welfare and well-being of *everyone* in sport and is central in fostering a duty of care (Kavanagh et al., 2020). Safeguarding is of primacy in physiological practice whether it be during research, applied practice, clinical practice or in teaching and learning. Safeguarding concerns a professional obligation to protect all parties (for example the client, athlete and/or self) from maltreatment or harm (Mountjoy et al., 2016). Everyone is potentially involved in the management of safeguarding concerns as a perpetrator, victim or bystander. This includes all stakeholders from athletes, peers and coaches through to parents, sport scientists or other members of the athlete entourage.

The range of potential threats that an individual can be exposed to are recognised to occur across three levels: the individual level, at which there is a potential risk to self (e.g., depression, self-harm, substance abuse and disordered eating); the relational level, a risk that occurs between individuals (e.g., sexual, physical and emotional abuse, discrimination or harassment); and at an organisational level, between an individual and a performance system or organisation (e.g., systems which promote overtraining or competing with an injury, institutional doping or an unhealthy organisational culture). Physiologists should be aware of these levels

DOI: 10.4324/9781003045267-6

Table 1.4.1 International Safeguards for Children in Sport (adapted with permission from Rhind and Owusu-Sekyere, 2018).

Safeguard	Description	Action
1: Developing your policy	Any organisation providing or with responsibility for sports activities should have a safeguarding policy. This is a statement of intent that demonstrates a commitment to safeguard everyone involved in sport from harm, and provides the framework within which procedures are developed. A safeguarding policy makes clear to all what is required. It also helps to create a safe and positive environment and to show that the organisation is taking its duty of care seriously.	You should be familiar with the related policies for the organisations and contexts in which you work. As well as these safeguarding policies, you should also be familiar with any other relevant policies concerning equity, working with vulnerable groups and health and safety. It is good practice to save links to these policies such that they are easily accessible. Be mindful that there may be a number of policies at any given time including those regulations that govern being a BASES accredited practitioner (e.g, BASES Safeguarding and Welfare Policy) and/or those in place for the organisation(s) in which you are working.
2: Procedures for responding to safeguarding concerns	Procedures describe the operational processes required to implement organisational policy and provide clear step-by-step guidance on what to do in different circumstances. They clarify roles and responsibilities, and lines of communication. Procedures help to ensure a prompt response to concerns about a person's safety or well-being	You should be familiar with the procedures required to report and manage any safeguarding concerns. There may also be relevant complaints and disciplinary procedures. It is good practice to make contact with the person to whom you should report concerns after reading this guidance. This should mean that you are more comfortable making a disclosure should a concern arise.
3: Advice and support	Arrangements made to provide essential information and support to those responsible for safeguarding. People should be advised on where to access help and support. An organisation has a duty to ensure advice and support is in place to help people to play their part in safeguarding such that they know who they can turn to for help.	You should identify the people and resources which can support you to effectively fulfil the safeguarding aspects of your role (e.g., Welfare Officer or Safeguarding Manager). The Child Protection in Sport Unit provides a range of helpful resources on their website (www.thecpsu.org.uk).
4: Minimising risks (to children)	The measures which are taken to assess and minimise the risks to people in the organisation. Minimising risks by putting safeguards in place.	Safeguarding should be a part of the planning in physiological testing; make a safeguarding plan. Aim to mitigate risk and work in a matter which prioritises the safety of participants. Key factors to assess may include ages of participants, additional needs or potential vulnerabilities, the nature of the activity being conducted and how the place or space of the activity may increase vulnerability of participants.

(Continued)

Table 1.4.1 (Continued)

Safeguard	Description	Action
5: Guidelines for behaviour	An organisation should have codes of conduct to describe what an acceptable standard of behaviour is and promote current best practice. Standards of behaviour set a benchmark of what is acceptable for all, and codes of conduct can help to remove ambiguity and clarify the grey areas around what is viewed as acceptable behaviour.	You should be familiar with the BASES Code of Conduct and ensure that this is embedded in your practice, for example, the BASES Safeguarding and Welfare Policy (2017a) and the BASES Code of Conduct (2017b). You should also check for any other codes of conduct within the various contexts in which you work.
6: Recruiting, training and communicating	Everyone within an organisation has a role to play in safeguarding. Ensure that you are up to date with safeguarding knowledge and continue to re-educate yourself in this area to identify any changes in legislation or guidance.	You should attend the BASES Safeguarding Welfare in Sport and Exercise Sciences workshop to ensure you are familiar with current legislative, organisational and professional requirements and are aware of relevant reporting and/or referral requirements.
7: Working with partners	Where organisational partnership, membership, funding or commissioning relationships exist or develop with other organisations, the individual and/or organisation should use its influence to promote the implementation of safeguarding measures.	You should be a champion for safeguarding and demonstrate this through your practice. You should work with other physiologists, stakeholders and organisations to identify, share and embed good practice with respect to safeguarding.
8: Monitoring and evaluating	It is essential that there is ongoing monitoring of compliance and effectiveness, involving all key stakeholders. This is necessary because organisations need to know whether safeguarding is effective and where improvements and adaptations are needed, or recognise patterns of risk.	You should conduct an audit of your current knowledge, confidence and behaviours in relation to each of these safeguards. This can help you to identify gaps and set goals to work towards. This can be repeated on an annual basis to ensure that you keep up to date.

in order to prioritise the safety and well-being of participants and to identify or mitigate risks which may arise at each of these levels (Mountjoy et al., 2016).

Safeguarding responsibilities

As a physiologist, you occupy a position of power and authority, particularly when working with children or young people. In this role it is essential to demonstrate moral and ethical standards throughout your practice towards safeguarding yourself and others. Physiologists should be able to recognise and mitigate risks posed to others while understanding how to report or manage safeguarding concerns that they may observe or have disclosed to them during their practice. The International Safeguards (Rhind and Owusu-Sekyere, 2018) outline a number of measures that should be put in place by any organisation providing sports activities. The eight safeguards are outlined in the following table (Table 1.4.1) along with their application to physiological testing.

Following the recommendations of the international safeguards will help to safeguard you as a physiologist, the people with whom you work and your organisation and profession as a whole.

References

British Association of Sport and Exercise Science (BASES). (2017a). *Safeguarding and Welfare Policy.* www.bases.org.uk/imgs/bases_safeguarding___welfare_policy215.pdf (accessed 23 June 2020).

British Association of Sport and Exercise Science (BASES). (2017b). *Code of Conduct.* www.bases.org.uk/imgs/bases_code_of_conduct872.pdf (accessed 23 June 2020).

Kavanagh, E. J., Knowles, Z. R., Rhind, D., Brady, A., Miles, A., Gervis, M. and Davison, R. (2016). The BASES expert statement in safeguarding in the sport sciences. *The Sport and Exercise Scientist*, 49, 20–21.

Kavanagh, E. J., Rhind, D. J. A. and Gordon-Thompson, G. (2020). Duties of care and welfare practices in sport. In R. Arnold and D. Fletcher (eds.), *Stress, Wellbeing and Performance in Sport.* London: Routledge. Chapter 14.

Mountjoy, M., Brackenridge, C., Arrington, M., Blauwet, C., Carska-Sheppard, A., Fasting, K., Kirby, S., Leahy, T., Marks, S., Martin, K., Starr, K., Tiivas, A. and Budgett, R. (2016). The IOC consensus statement: Harassment and abuse (non-accidental violence) in sport. *British Journal of Sports Medicine*, 50, 1019–1029. http://dx.doi.org/10.1136/bjsports-2016-096121

Rhind, D. J. A. and Owusu-Sekyere, F. (2018). *International Safeguards for Children in Sport: Developing and Embedding a Safeguarding Culture.* London, UK: Routledge.

1.5 Influence of medication on typical exercise response

Thom Phillips and Patrick Orme

Introduction

As life expectancy in the UK continues to increase (Statistics, 2021), medical advances allow us to keep people active much later into life. With more complex health conditions, it is inevitable that exercise scientists are likely to encounter people using a variety of medicines to manage their conditions. The effects of the medications on the exercise response will have implications for how you approach any intervention with them. Whether you are working in inpatient cardiopulmonary exercise testing (CPET), outpatient rehabilitation, in the field prescribing exercise or doing research, understanding that medications can have a profound effect on exercise response will be key in executing your chosen processes.

Having read this short chapter, we are not expecting you to become a pharmacist, nor to have developed comprehensive knowledge of all the medications available on the market. As you can imagine, the effects of medication on exercise response are as widespread and varied as the medications themselves. This chapter introduces some of the commonly prescribed medications and considers how they may affect exercise response. From this, you will gain insight and confidence in gathering information about medications, and ways in which to access more information.

With respect to principles of safety and ethical practices, it is important to understand and work within your knowledge and competencies. If you have concerns or questions about a medication and/or its effect on chronic function and/ or acute exercise responses, seek guidance and further advice from a pharmacist or qualified and experienced physician.

Prescription medication

A medication is either a drug or another form of medicine that is used to treat or prevent disease. In the UK, there are two distinct types of medication: those available freely to the public (over the counter, OTC), and those prescribed by a medical doctor (prescription only medicines, POM) (Britain, 2020).

The *British National Formulary* (BNF) provides a comprehensive list of all medicines that are licensed and available within the UK (Britain, 2020). The BNF is

DOI: 10.4324/9781003045267-7

a joint publication between the British Medical Association and the Royal Pharmaceutical Society. It is published quarterly, in print, and is also available online: www.bnf.org. This repository of information provides a quick reference guide to information about a medication. It is important to remember that medications exist in many forms, not always tablets or pills. In this respect, remember to consider inhalers, patches and injections when thinking about possible agents.

Prescriptions are essentially instructions about how to take a medication effectively. They should include the name, formulation, strength and recommended dosing of the medicine. This is important information because many drugs will have a dose-response relationship and drugs within the same class can have vastly different strengths. For example, Bisoprolol and Metoprolol are both beta blockers; one is given in doses of 1.25 mg increments, the other in 50 mg increments. Thus, a patient prescribed 10 mg of Bisoprolol will display a very different cardiac response to someone on 50 mg of Metoprolol.

Pharmacodynamics and pharmacokinetics

These are two principles of pharmacology that are fundamental to the way we understand how a drug works. Essentially one is what the drug does (pharmacodynamics) and the other introduces a temporal aspect since it explains how our bodies metabolise the drug, so giving us a way to predict how long the effects will last (pharmacokinetics). An easy way to think about it is that pharmacokinetics is what the body does to the drug, and pharmacodynamics is what the drug does to the body. As highlighted with the previous example, drugs within the same class can have the same pharmacodynamics (both slow the heart rate) but be metabolised in a different way, meaning the temporal aspect of the effect can be different: Bisoprolol has slow kinetics, Metoprolol has fast kinetics (Rigby et al., 1985).

The rate at which a drug is metabolised and excreted from the body is termed its half-life. The half-life of a drug is the time taken for the plasma concentration of a drug to reduce to half its original value. Conventionally, in pharmacology, half-lives follow the principle of first-order kinetics in which the rate of elimination is constant, irrespective of the concentration of the substance (Ritter et al., 2019), as illustrated in Figure 1.5.1. Following a lapse of time equivalent to five half-lives, less than 97% of the starting concentration remains: at this time, in biological terms, we deem a substance to be eliminated. For example, if a medication has a half-life of 5 hours, one would consider someone drug-free after a 25-hour washout period.

Because biological processes are rarely linear (Berezhkovskiy, 2011), the half-life of a medication is often expressed as a range and should always be accompanied by the mode of delivery (i.e., inhaled, intravenous, oral etc.). With an increase in metabolic rate during exercise, the half-life of a medication can be influenced. In this respect, a drug's half-life may exceed the shortest recorded half-life and exercise scientists should keep this in mind when working with individuals taking various medications. Table 1.5.1 provides examples of commonly prescribed medications and their half-lives.

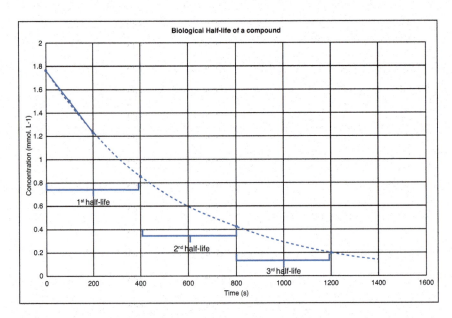

Figure 1.5.1 Reduction in substrate concentration following first-order half-life reaction.

Table 1.5.1 Commonly prescribed medications and their half-lives

Medication (Area of Use)	Biological Half-Life (Mode of Delivery)
Salbutamol (Asthma)	2.7 to 5.5 hours (Inhaled)
Testosterone (Androgen insufficiency)	1.3 to 2 hours (Topical)
Sertraline (Depression)	22 to 36 hours (Oral)
Semaglutide (Type 2 diabetes)	5 to 7 days (Subcutaneous injection)
Adrenaline (Cardiac arrest)	2 to 3 minutes (Intravenous injection)
Caffeine	1.5 to 9 hours (Oral)

The starting concentration of any medication is reliant on the mode of delivery. Obviously, medications administered directly into the blood stream (intravenous) reach higher concentrations compared to an equivalent dose of the same medication administered orally, and exercise can influence some important aspects of this process.

Topical treatments are better absorbed both during and after exercise due to increased sweat rate; however, the adherence to the skin of any patches can be an issue (Lenz and Gillespie, 2011). This is an important consideration for medications such as hormonal preparations and pain relief that one may deliver via a patch (e.g., Lidocaine) or gel (e.g., Ibuprofen).

Gastric motility, gastric emptying and ionisation

Oral absorption is a complex area and there are several influencing factors implicated with exercise. Three intrinsically linked factors are gastric motility, gastric emptying and ionisation. Relative exercise intensity typically displays a u-shaped relationship with the rate of gastric emptying. Low-intensity activity slightly increases the rate at which the stomach contents empty into the small intestine from rest, but as exercise intensity increases, gastric emptying rate decreases. Therefore, if one ingests a dose of medication just before exercise, it will take much longer before it is absorbed. The time taken for an ingested medication to reach permeable membranes is lengthened, potentially resulting in a reduced absorption rate. This is because there is a slowing of gastric emptying time. Paradoxically the transit time through small and large intestines is faster.

For a drug to remain in the stomach longer has other implications, especially for medications that are pH sensitive. Gastric pH is around a value of 3.0, so any medication designed with a gastro-protective coating maybe affected by a longer resident time in the stomach, given that the rate of gastric secretions is reduced during exercise (Ritter et al., 2019). This describes the phenomenon of ionisation.

Splanchnic blood flow

Once absorbed through the bowel wall, substances enter the blood stream. The collective term for the blood supply of the gastrointestinal (GI) tract, liver, spleen and pancreas is referred to as splanchnic circulation. Essentially, the system is composed of two large capillary beds in series (the GI tract and the liver). During submaximal exercise, splanchnic resistance increases to aid with circulatory shunting, meaning the blood flow through this system reduces by 50% (Kolkman and Ter Steege, 2012). This has many potential downstream implications for first-pass metabolism and tissue distribution.

Enterohepatic circulation

Enterohepatic circulation refers to a process whereby medications absorbed in the small intestine become bound to bile salts in the liver and are stored in the gall bladder, before they are excreted back into the small intestine when they can be absorbed again (Figure 1.5.2). At first, this concept may seem strange, but many lipophilic molecules undergo this process. It also means that we can prescribe smaller doses of a drug since this pathway can recycle it. Important for us in this respect is that steroid hormones, derived from cholesterol and other lipophilic medications (e.g., Paracetamol, Aspirin) use this pathway. Exercise speeds up the excretion of bile salts, due to the increased gastric motility (Molina-Molina et al., 2018), but the concurrent reduction in splanchnic blood flow and increase in gastric motility means that less of these types of molecules are reabsorbed.

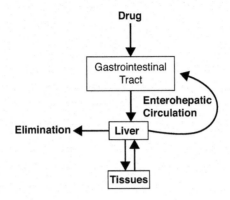

Figure 1.5.2 Enterohepatic circulation.

Source: adapted from Ritter et al. (2019)

First-pass (pre-systematic) metabolism

Phase I reactions – Phase I reactions of drug metabolism involve oxidation, reduction or hydrolysis of the parent drug, resulting in its conversion to a more polar molecule and these simple reactions are often catalysed by enzymes collectively known as the Cytochrome-P450 group. Cytochromes P450 (CYPs) are a superfamily of enzymes, containing haem as a cofactor, that function as mono-oxygenases. They play a vital role in metabolising and clearing multiple compounds, both endo- and exogenous as well as being cofactors in the synthesis of complex fatty acids and hormones. This is important because exercise increases the activity of CYP450 molecules (Gollasch et al., 2019); hence, its effect on any medication also relies on this pathway.

CYP450 is a group of monooxygenase enzymes whose function is to add a hydroxyl group (OH−) onto a substrate. The Iron III cation ($Fe3+$) forms the basis of all CYP enzymes, the poly-valency of this molecule (the complex has five 'valence' electrons) is exploited by drug manufacturers as it is able to accept a large variety of ligands (Ritter et al., 2019). Its ubiquity is also its downfall in respect to drug metabolism, as a considerable number of other substrates can inhibit or induce this cycle: several examples are included in Table 1.5.2.

Phase II reactions – Phase II reactions involve conjugation by coupling a drug or its metabolites to another molecule, such as glucuronidation, acylation, sulfate or glycine. These metabolic pathways are dependent on the availability of a number of cofactors. Chief amongst these cofactors is acetyl coenzyme A (CoA). The effects of exercise on CoA are innumerate, but it is worth considering that they may have implications for any medications prescribed (Sarmiento et al., 2016). This is especially the case in people new to physical activity.

Elimination

Elimination (or excretion) from the body is the final stage in a medication's journey (Wrighton and Stevens, 1992) and is achieved in a variety of ways, including through

Table 1.5.2 CYP450 Substrates, inducers and inhibitors

Substrate	Inducers	Inhibitors
Codeine	Grapefruit juice	Smoking
Beta-blockers	Pomegranate	Broccoli
Caffeine	Black tea	Brussels sprouts
Non-steroidal anti-inflammatory drugs (e.g. Ibuprofen)	Selective serotonin reuptake inhibitors (e.g. Citalopram)	Omeprazole

urine, tears, perspiration, saliva, breast milk and faeces. Exercise can affect any number of these and samples of most excretions can be analysed for traces of medications or their metabolites. This is the premise of antidoping testing in elite sport, and understanding how a medication is eliminated helps scientists at the World Antidoping Association (WADA) design better methodologies for detecting illegal substances in an athlete's urine, hair or blood (Engebretsen, 2021).

Common examples of practical application

When thinking about the typical exercise response, adopt a systems approach and ask, 'How does each system individually react?' Once you understand this, you will be able to amalgamate knowledge of the systems and understand how each interacts with others to determine a whole-body response to a medication.

Similarly, one of the best ways to consider how exercise may affect a medication is to think about the system pharmacology and its associated exercise physiology. For example, when considering cardiovascular medications, consider the effect of exercise on that specific system and establish the purpose of the drug to anticipate its likely effect. One of the more accessible examples is to look at the cardiovascular system and some of the commonly prescribed medications that influence this (Pollock et al., 2000).

Cardiovascular medications are a very commonly prescribed drug: approximately 1 in 6 adults over 18 in the UK is on some form of blood-pressure-lowering medication (Heart Statistics, 2021). Prescriptions for blood pressure medication tend to implicate one of three drug families, considered in the next section.

Angiotensin-converting-enzyme inhibitors

Most angiotensin-converting-enzyme (ACE) inhibitors attenuate the activity of angiotensin-converting enzyme, an important component of the renin-angiotensin system, which can exist as both a membrane-bound and a circulating enzyme. High levels of membrane-bound ACE exist in skeletal muscle. Inhibition of this enzyme prevents the formation of Angiotensin II, which is a potent vasoconstrictor, and it hydrolyses Bradykinin, which is a vasodilator. This synergistic combination of actions drops the blood pressure through reduced peripheral resistance (Byrd et al., 2019). Interestingly, ACE-1 also decreases centrally driven thirst mechanisms

(Dundas et al., 2007) and prevents erythropoiesis (Cruzado et al., 2008). Acute bouts of exercise increase the production of ACE (Magalhães, 2020). Depending on the dosage of the medication, this could lead to profound blood-pressure-lowering effects of ACE, leaving an individual with feelings of light-headedness, nausea or even fainting. Ways to counter this are to check resting blood pressure before exercise and increase the load gradually in order to mitigate this risk. Conversely, chronic exercise exposure leads to lower circulating levels of ACE, which may mean that, in poorly controlled hypertensives, the effect of the medication is diminished (Klöting, 2020).

Beta-blockers

Although use of beta-blockers for high blood pressure is becoming rarer, their use in other conditions such as atrial fibrillation, post cardiac arrest and chronic anxiety remains widespread. They are an old drug, and as such, their impact on multiple systems is well documented (Podbregar and Voga, 2002). As their name implies, the medications are competitive antagonists at the site of β-adrenergic receptors. There are three broad categories of β-adrenergic receptors (Barranger et al., 2006):

β1 – Located in the heart and kidneys
β2 – Located in the lungs, GI tract, liver, uterus, vascular smooth muscle and skeletal muscle
β3 – Located in adipocytes

All three types are receptors for adrenaline and noradrenaline and related to the sympathetic nervous system, especially for mediating the fight-or-flight response. Blocking these sites has the opposite effect of the fight-or-flight response, with slower heart rates, vasodilation and interference with the action of some stress hormones. Many beta-blocking drugs are 'non-selective' meaning that they act on all three types of β-adrenergic receptors, in all tissue types.

During exercise, people on beta-blockers are not able to raise a normal heart rate or blood pressure response, meaning that they may find it more difficult to reach higher intensities. Due to the multitude of tissue types that contain β-adrenergic receptors, there are also other risks to consider including increased shortness of breath, exercise-induced hyperthermia and changes in substrate utilisation (Gordon and Duncan, 1991). Due to the calming effects of beta-blockers, they do feature on the World Antidoping Prohibited List (WADA, 2021).

Thyroxine

Up to 1 in 6 women over 50 have an underactive thyroid and approximately 2% of the entire population take medication to replace their thyroid levels. Levothyroxine is the most commonly prescribed medication for this purpose. Levothyroxine is a synthetic pre-hormone, usually taken in tablet form and mostly absorbed in the jejunum. Levothyroxine absorption is extremely sensitive to a number of factors including dietary fibre, fasting, age and exercise. Once absorbed, it is converted by the body into T4 (the main thyroid hormone) in the liver and undergoes enterohepatic circulation (KGaA, 2013).

Irvine (1968) reported that the rate of levothyroxine degradation in individuals who exercise regularly is as much as 75% faster than non-exercising controls. An excess of thyroxine increases cardiac contractility and resting heart rate, increasing resting metabolic rate by approximately 4% (Johannsen et al., 2012). It is unclear what impact this has on muscle efficiency during aerobic exercise, but regular levothyroxine dosing does stimulate cardiac muscle hypertrophy (KGaA, 2013). At rest for individuals on this medication, expect to see an increased cardiac output caused by a combination of increased resting heart rate, increased contractility and a concomitant decrease in systemic vascular resistance.

This resting hyperdynamic circulation impairs the normal changes in cardiac output observed during exercise and can result in exertional dyspnoea and reduced exercise capacity. In individuals with underlying cardiac conditions, including coronary artery disease, exercise combined with increased doses of levothyroxine can cause angina and in some rare cases precipitate an arrhythmia.

Chapter summary

The ways in which medication can influence the typical exercise response are as wide-ranging and varied as the medications themselves. We have introduced aspects of the fundaments of pharmacology, including how some of the more commonly prescribed drugs act and affect the typical exercise response. Using the systematic approach to understanding how a medication works will allow you to map out the likely impact on exercise. We confirm there is a paucity of good-quality evidence in this area of exercise physiology and medicine. Therefore, we recommend that exercise-testing practitioners proceed with caution in deciding upon the most appropriate course of action, consulting with clients, general practitioners and qualified, experienced physicians.

References

Barranger, K., Peterson, A. M. and Eva, V. (2006). Hypertension. In V. P. Arcangelo, A. M. Peterson and V. A. Arcangelo (eds.), *Pharmacotherapeutics for Advanced Practice: A Practical Approach*. Philadelphia, PA: Lippincott Williams & Wilkins.

Berezhkovskiy, L. M. (2011). The influence of hepatic transport on the distribution volumes and mean residence time of drug in the body and the accuracy of estimating these parameters by the traditional pharmacokinetic calculations. *Journal of Pharmaceutical Sciences*, 100(11), 5031–5047.

Britain, R. P. (2020). *British National Formulary (BNF)*. London: British Medical Association.

Byrd, J. B., Ram, C. V. S. and Lerma, E. V. (2019). Pharmacologic treatment of hypertension. In: E. V. Lerma, M. A. Sparks, and J. M. Topf (eds.), *Nephrology Secrets* (4th ed.), pp. 477–482. New York: Elsevier. https://doi.org/10.1016/B978-0-323-47871-7.00078-2

Cruzado, J. M., Rico, J. and Griñyó, J. M. (2008). The renin angiotensin system blockade in kidney transplantation: Pros and cons. *Transplant International*, 21(4), 304–313.

Dundas, B., Harris, M. and Narasimhan, M. (2007). Psychogenic polydipsia review: Etiology, differential, and treatment. *Current Psychiatry Reports*, 9(3), 236–241.

Engebretsen, L. (2021). Be aware: New rules for corticosteroids! *British Journal of Sports Medicine*, 575–576.

Gollasch, B., Dogan, I., Rothe, M., Gollasch, M. and Luft, F. (2019). Maximal exercise and plasma cytochrome P450 and lipoxygenase mediators: A lipidomics study. *Physiological Reports*, 7(13), e14165.

Gordon, N. and Duncan, J. (1991). Effect of beta-blockers on exercise physiology: Implications for exercise training. *Medicine and Science in Sports and Exercise*, 23(6), 668–676.

Heart Statistics. (2021). British Heart Foundation. www.bhf.org.uk/what-we-do/our-research/heart-statistics?gclid=CjwKCAjw3pWDBhB3EiwAV1c5rGzkKQX0ZZKkcmy-zPsQXUK7lEESeqdGfsCYxsRenIYU3_J460vsohoCuxYQAvD_BwE&gclsrc=aw.ds

Irvine, C. (1968). Effect of exercise on thyroxine degradation in athletes and non-athletes. *The Journal of Clinical Endocrinology & Metabolism*, 28(7), 942–948.

Johannsen, D. L., Galgani, J. E., Johannsen, N. M., Zhang, Z., Covington, J. D. and Ravussin, E. (2012). Effect of short-term thyroxine administration on energy metabolism and mitochondrial efficiency in humans. *PLoS One*, 7(7), e40837.

KGaA, M. (2013, January 1). *Novothyrox (levothyroxine sodium tablets, USP)*. NOVOTHYROX® (levothyroxine sodium tablets, USP. www.accessdata.fda.gov/drugsatfda_docs/label/2009/021292s002lbl.pdf (accessed May 2021).

Klöting, N. R. (2020). Effects of exercise on ACE2. *Obesity*, 28, 2266–2267.

Kolkman, J. J. and Ter Steege, R. W. (2012). The pathophysiology and management of gastrointestinal symptoms during physical exercise, and the role of splanchnic blood flow. *Alimentary Pharmacology & Therapeutics*, 35(5), 516–528.

Lenz, T. L. and Gillespie, N. (2011). Transdermal patch drug delivery interactions with exercise. *Sports Medicine*, 41(3), 177–183.

Magalhães, D. N.-S. (2020). Two protocols of aerobic exercise modulate the counter-regulatory axis of the renin-angiotensin system. *Heliyon*, 6(1), 3.

Molina-Molina, E., Lunardi Baccetto, R., Wang, D. Q., de Bari, O., Krawczyk, M. and Portincasa, P. (2018). Exercising the hepatobiliary-gut axis: The impact of physical activity performance. *European Journal of Clinical Investigation*, 48(8), e12958.

Podbregar, M. and Voga, G. (2002). Effect of selective and nonselective β-blockers on resting energy production rate and total body substrate utilization in chronic heart failure. *Journal of Cardiac Failure*, 8(6), 369–378.

Pollock, M. L., Franklin, B. A., Balady, B. G., Chaitman, B. L., Fleg, J. L., Fletcher, B., Limacher, M., Pina, I. L., Stein, R. A., Williams, M. and Bazzarre, T. (2000). Resistance exercise in individuals with and without cardiovascular disease: Benefits, rationale, safety, and prescription an advisory from the committee on exercise, rehabilitation, and prevention, council on clinical cardiology, American Heart Association. *Circulation*, 101(7), 828–833.

Rigby, J. W., Scott, J., Hawksworth, G. M. and Petrie, J. C. (1985). A comparison of the pharmacokinetics of atenolol, metoprolol, oxprenolol and propranolol in elderly hypertensive and young healthy subjects. *British Journal of Clinical Pharmacology*, 20(4).

Ritter, J., Flower, R. J., Henderson, G., Loke, Y. K., MacEwan, D. J. and Rang, H. P. (2019). *Rang and Dale's Pharmacology*. Edinburgh: Elsevier.

Sarmiento, A., Diaz-Castro, J., Pulido-Moran, M., Kajarabille, N., Guisado, R. and Ochoa, J. (2016). Coenzyme Q10 supplementation and exercise in healthy humans: A systematic review. *Current Drug Metabolism*, 17(4), 345–358.

Statistics, O. O. (2021, May). *Population Estimates*. Office of National Statistics. www.ons.gov.uk/peoplepopulationandcommunity/populationandmigration/populationestimates

WADA. (2021). *World Anti-Doping Code International Standard Prohibited List*. World Anti-Doping. www.wada-ama.org

Wrighton, S. A. and Stevens, J. C. (1992). The human hepatic cytochromes P450 involved in drug metabolism. *Critical Reviews in Toxicology*, 22(1), 1–21.

Part II

2.1 Data intelligence and feedback in a clinical context

Sarah Gilchrist and Mark Homer

The information now available to individuals, exercise physiologists, health clinicians and other health professionals that can inform exercise prescription has increased exponentially during the recent 'data revolution' that has impacted all aspects of our lives. Images of sports science practitioners leaning from car windows with Douglas bags have been replaced with wrist-based super-computers that provide about 1,000 data points per second that can potentially explain and predict multiple components of performance.

This chapter will focus on the processes involved in impactful data intelligence, including collection and management. Finally, the chapter will discuss how to present or visualise information and provide suggestions for feeding back to the client or health professional.

Data intelligence

Data intelligence is the ability to collect, understand and use information for effective performance impact. It is easy to become fixated on the quantity of information when discussing 'data', and exercise physiologists should be wary of 'overload' (see later in chapter). However, in many cases, data intelligence involves better connecting previously unrelated smaller pieces of information. The accessibility of such information is also crucial; if collection, processing and analysis are slow, their impact can be diminished.

In clinical exercise physiology, data intelligence can impact all areas of well-being, exercise prescription and health outcomes. Topics in which an increase in data quantity, quality and variety have had an impact on clinical exercise physiology include, but are not limited to, assessing physiological demands, exercise intensity/volume monitoring and continuous or real-time monitoring of physiological health-related variables. As with other industries in which multiple factors explain the relationship between intervention and outcome, the effective use of data intelligence in exercise and health is dependent on asking the right questions, robust collection, accurate interpretation and impactful feedback.

DOI: 10.4324/9781003045267-9

Data collection, management and feedback

Health questions

When seeking strategies to improve health outcomes, practitioners should consider the precise challenge being raised and how it can be addressed effectively. Planning should involve all relevant parties, with clear understanding and agreement on what is needed to answer the question and how success will be defined. This stage should identify how to ensure how any data collected is valid, reliable and accurate. The impact of any intervention and subsequent data collection on the outcome should not be ignored. A defined timeframe should be arranged with appropriate analysis, monitoring and evaluation considered throughout the process.

Data collection

Quality assurance of the information you are providing to clients is paramount. Processes to ensure data is reliable, valid and repeatable should be the cornerstone of an exercise physiologist's practice. Table 2.1.1 highlights some important considerations for data collection in a health context. Take the time to ensure the equipment calibrations are current, regularly performed and producing correct data. A large part of the relationship between the exercise physiologist and individual/patient is based on trust. If there is confidence that the data provided is consistent, accurate and reproducible, this will help to build strong relationships and enhance confidence during the feedback process.

Finally, ensure you adhere to data protection regulations. Breaches of the government laws designed to safeguard individuals from which any kind of information is collected and stored are severely punishable. Refer to the Data Protection Act (2018) for further information (Data protection – GOV.UK (www.gov.uk)

Data interpretation and visualisation

Data visualisation is an important consideration when dealing with large volumes of information, particularly when balanced with the need to provide feedback succinctly and efficiently. Effective data visualisation techniques are varied, but their shared aim is to communicate data (large or small) in a constructive manner, increase the ease of understanding and highlight key messages. It can also encourage interaction with the data from clients and other members of the multidisciplinary support team. Consider the methods that best explain the data set in question and ensure appropriate scientific rigour in the presentation of information (e.g., report descriptive statistics and typical error of measurements where appropriate). Further, recent advances in data visualisation tools that provide interactive dashboard style reports allow for accessible interrogation of large volumes of information in a wide variety of flexible tables and charts.

In line with quality-assured valid and reliable data, it is important to remain objective in analysing and presenting information. Consciously presenting data

Table 2.1.1 Key considerations in data management and analysis

Considerations	Definition	Practical Example
Accuracy	The degree to which the result of a measurement or calculation relates to the actual value.	A 12-lead ECG used for measurement and interpretation of cardiac function rather than a 2-lead equivalent
Reliability	Synonymous with accuracy, the consistency of a result or measurement. Data can be reliably accurate, or reliably inaccurate.	Collecting 2 blood samples at the same time and achieving the same result. Results repeatedly higher than the true value are reliable but not accurate
Validity	The appropriateness of a measurement. Is the information being collected applicable to the question being asked?	Using an exercise bike to assess improvements in walking after an exercise programme
Analysis	Examination and interpretation of information in order to provide a balanced representation of findings.	Descriptive statistics Traditional statistical analysis Meaningful change
Visualisation	The use of tables, charts, diagrams and the written word to interpret information that is suitable for the audience in question.	Tables and charts used in research papers and presentations, infographics, written reports etc.
Bias	Consciously or unconsciously collecting, interpreting and presenting information in an unbalanced way that prevents a fair evaluation and decision-making process.	Having a pre-existing belief about the effectiveness of an intervention and unfairly presenting results in a way that favours or overexaggerates its success

to highlight particular patterns or holding an unconscious bias towards particular results and opinions is important to recognise and avoid. This can be achieved by remaining neutral and being evidence-based when presenting data and the inferences that can be drawn from it.

Feedback

A vital component of an exercise physiologist's work is his or her relationship with client(s). Providing information that can be used to potentially inform healthier lifestyles is a common scenario, and one that can play a key role in the future influence that an exercise physiologist can have.

The process by which exercise physiologists and clients use information to make decisions is unique to the situation and individuals involved. It is the exercise physiologist's role to ensure scientific rigour throughout the whole (previously described) process, while making allowances for the art and intuition that is a crucial part of exercise prescription and that should not be ignored. How accurate this can be is determined largely by the exercise physiologist's experience and the length of time supporting the individual in question (Guazzi et al., 2016). Therefore, the health professional's relationship with the exercise physiologist should be collaborative when considering adjustments to the exercise prescription. The skill of the exercise physiologist and health professionals involved is to combine quantitative and qualitative information when making decisions.

In line with this is the understanding and interpretation of error. Technical error exists in all measurements and it is the role of exercise physiologists to be acutely aware of the typical error of measurement (TEM) for all their resources, including themselves. An understanding of this is critical in all communication, particularly to the coach and athlete.

Regardless of the dynamic between exercise physiologist and client, data and information should be used to augment the decision-making process rather than lead it. Exercise physiologists should recognise that their clients need data to either tell them something they can't see or provide evidence to support what they can. An exercise physiologist's role is to manage this process and provide the *right* information to help ascertain the right decision in providing health benefits.

Common pitfalls

Data fatigue

In using data to supplement the process of improving physical activity, it is vital that exercise physiologists are conscious not to fall into the pattern of collecting data 'for the sake of it' because it is 'what has always been done'.

A scenario in which data is collected but not used can waste time and resources, potentially leading to inaccurate measurements in the case of subjective data. It can also damage a client's commitment to the process.

Similarly, be cautious when there is a mass of data from various support disciplines and technical data. It can be easy to succumb to 'death by data' in the sense that exercise physiologists are just 'seeing' numbers, so be wary of large data sets and don't observe the data in isolation. Remember that there is a human being, the client, producing the data. Always consider the performance question and the impact of the data intelligence on it. This highlights the importance of setting timeframes for data collection and review to ensure interventions remain impactful over time.

Client engagement

Clients may choose not to engage with new data and analysis. This can often be hard to accept, but originates in the relationship, trust and respect fostered with them during the early stages of a relationship. Consider this before providing them with masses of information they may or may not feel or recognise they would benefit from. Of course, an awareness of the stumbling block is derived from the exercise physiologist's previous experience. Consider a staged approach to using new information, introduce new metrics or feedback one at a time to avoid over-whelming those that are less comfortable with technology, change or both.

Summary

The accuracy and interpretation of 'data' has become an unavoidable influence on modern life. We have access to almost limitless information, but few are trained to properly understand it. With more technology available than ever before, using data and information to scrutinise training and performance is now common practice within sport and health. Crucial to this is establishing an effective plat-form for data management. Ensuring exercise physiologists and clients manage the whole process in the right way, with insight and purpose; employ good data visualisation for understanding; and have excellent insight, experience and com-munication around the data's meaning, will all benefit the collective pursuit of health programme success.

Reference

Guazzi, M., Arena, R., Halle, M., Piepoli, M. F., Myers, J. and Lavie, C. J. (2016). 2016 focused update: Clinical recommendations for cardiopulmonary exercise testing data assessment in specific patient populations. *Circulation*, 133, e694–e711.

2.2   Reliability and measurement error

Shaun J. McLaren

Overview

Reliability refers to the degree of repeatability, reproducibility or consistency in a measure. In sport and exercise science, data obtained from individuals is influenced by both measurement error (associated with equipment and protocols) and the normal, biological variation within systems of the body (or associated functional/performance outputs).

Quantification of reliability has several uses, such as precision of measures and monitoring change within in an individual, setting the target sample size for an experimental trial, determining the variability of performance and guiding decisions where measurement error is an important factor (e.g., purchasing equipment).

The purpose of this chapter is to provide a practical guide to reliability analysis and use within sport and exercise science. It is particularly focussed on the error of interval and ratio level quantitative data measured from individuals in sport and exercise. Some of these concepts are also applicable to method agreement but will not be discussed or elaborated in this regard.

Reliability designs

Reliability can be assessed by taking repeated measures of an outcome when, in theory, it should not change or vary substantially. The purpose of subsequent analysis is to determine the extent of change and variation in the measure. Depending on the goal and use of data, repeated observations can be taken over both short- and long-term periods, such as between repetitions, sets, times within a day, days within a week, between weeks or between months and longer (Hurst et al., 2018). Usually, any factors that may reasonably influence the outcome measure will be controlled for, or concurrently measured when control is not possible.

Test-retest designs are commonly used for reliability assessment and can be analysed using a consecutive pairwise analysis. The following section shall discuss key statistics from such designs – that is, a two-trial (test-retest) study. When two or more re-tests are present (i.e., ≥ 3 trials), or the outcome measure is observed over a longitudinal period, general and mixed-effects linear models (and subsequent use of the sum of squares, or variance parameter estimates) can be used as alternatives.

DOI: 10.4324/9781003045267-10

Key statistics

Statistics from reliability analyses can be used to describe both systematic and random error. For the latter, both absolute reliability (the degree to which repeated measurements vary for individuals) and relative reliability (the degree to which individuals maintain their position in a group during repeated measures) may be quantified (Atkinson and Nevill, 1998).

Mean change

The change in mean between consecutive trials can be used to determine if any systematic (group-level) bias may have influenced change in the outcome measure. This could include, for example, familiarisation effects or changes in the external environment, such as test instructions and subsequent communication with participants during the test (verbal encouragement etc.). In a two-trial test-retest design, the mean change is identical to that derived from a comparison of paired (dependent) means, and can be analysed as such. The most appropriate way to determine this is with the mean of individual change scores (test 2 − test 1).

Standard error of measurement (SEM)

Sometimes referred to as the typical error (TE), the SEM is an estimate of within-subject random variability (absolute reliability). It provides an intuitive and important approximation of how participants may be expected to vary within their own test performance over repeated trials, regardless of any systematic bias. The SEM can be used to calculate additional statistics, such as the minimum detectable change (MDC) and confidence/compatibility limits (CL) for an observed value or an individual change. When expressed in percentage units (see the *Reliability Estimate Uncertainty and Magnitude Interpretation* section), the SEM is referred to as the coefficient of variation (CV).

In a two-trial test-retest design, the SEM can be calculated by dividing the standard deviation (SD) of paired changes scores (SD_Δ) by the square root of 2:

$$SEM = \frac{SD_\Delta}{\sqrt{2}}$$

This is because the variance of the difference scores is equal to the sum of the variances representing the SEM in each trial (Hopkins, 2000). Alternatively, if the interclass correlation coefficient is known, then the SEM can be calculated as:

$$SEM = SD \cdot \sqrt{1 - ICC}$$

in which SD is the observed, pooled (averaged), between-subject standard deviation from trial 1 and trial 2.

Interclass correlation coefficient (ICC)

The ICC is another measure of random error and represents reproducibility in the rank order of participants over two or more trials (relative reliability). It should be used over Pearson's retest correlation coefficient, which can only determine how paired measures vary together, not the extent of agreement between them.

There are several variations of the ICC that depend on the model (one-way random effects, two-way random effects, two-way mixed effects), type (single or multiple measurements) and definition (absolute agreement or consistency). These factors are all determined by the reliability goals and design. For a detailed overview of these ICCs and their calculation, the reader is referred to Koo and Li (2016).

In a pairwise analysis of consecutive trials (test-retest), the most relevant ICC measure is that from a two-way mixed-effects model for consistency in a single measure ($ICC_{3,1}$). That is, the testing equipment or protocols are fixed and participants are random (Hopkins, 2000). In this design, the usual $ICC_{3,1}$ (Koo and Li, 2016) can be simplified (Hopkins, 2015), such that:

$$ICC_{3,1} = \left(\frac{SEM^2}{SD^2} \right)$$

Reliability estimate uncertainty and magnitude interpretation

Confidence (compatibility) limits should accompany all reliability estimates as measures of uncertainty. For the mean change, CL can be derived using a t or z distribution. Confidence (compatibility) limits for the SEM and ICC should be derived from a chi-squared and F-distribution, respectively.

Sometimes it may be appropriate to express the mean change and SEM in percentage or standardised units, as well as raw units. This can be achieved post-hoc, by dividing reliability estimates and their CL by the appropriate denominator (the overall mean for a percentage and the CV, and the between-subject SD for standardised units), or by making appropriate transformation of the data prior to analysis followed by post-hoc back-transformation (the natural, Napierian logarithm for percentage change and the CV, and the between-subject SD for standardised units).

The magnitude of systematic bias (mean change) can be evaluated by scaling its estimate and CL against so-called thresholds of importance. Reference terms include the smallest worthwhile change (SWC), the region of practical equivalence (ROPE), the smallest effect size of interest (SEOI) and the minimum practically or clinically important difference (MPID/ MCID), among others. A brief overview of these distribution- and anchor-based concepts is provided in the online supplementary material to this chapter. The SEM can also be interpreted in this manner, but the estimate (and its CL) must be doubled before being evaluated (Smith and Hopkins, 2011). The magnitude of any ICC can be interpreted as follows: >0.99, extremely high; 0.99–0.90, very high; 0.75–0.90, high; 0.50–0.75, moderate; 0.20–0.50, low; <0.20, very low (Malcata et al., 2014).

Practical applications

An example reliability analysis from on 10 m linear speed in professional soccer players is presented in Table 2.2.1. Supporting descriptive plots are shown in Figure 2.2.1. This sample of 22 players was tested twice, 7 days apart, at the same time of day and on the same indoor artificial turf pitch. Each testing day was preceded by 48 hours of complete rest, and 4 days of light technical-tactical training were performed between sessions. In each testing session, following a standardised warm-up players performed 5 maximal 10 m linear sprint efforts. Sprint time was measured via dual-beam photocell timing gates, with the average time from the final 3 trials retained for analysis.

Table 2.2.1 Reliability of 10 m linear sprint time in soccer players

Statistic	Raw Units		%*		Standardised (d)	
	Est.	90% CL	Est.	90% CL	Est.	90% CL
Mean change	0.01	−0.01; 0.03	0.4	−0.6; 1.4	0.08	−0.12; 0.28
SEM	0.03#	0.03; 0.04	1.9	1.5; 2.5	0.38	0.31; 0.52
ICC$_{3,1}$	0.88	0.77; 0.94	–	–		

Consecutive pairwise analysis was performed on test-retest data measured 7 days apart.
*SEM as a % is the CV.
#to 3 dp = 0.032 (0.026; 0.043)
CL: confidence limits, SEM: standard error of measurement, ICC: interclass correlation coefficient.

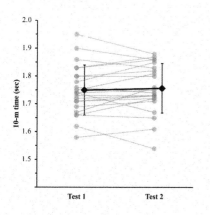 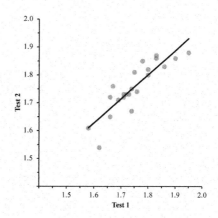

Figure 2.2.1 Test and re-test 10 m linear sprint times in soccer players. Black points and error bars in the left plot are the mean ± standard deviation.

The $ICC_{3,1}$ of 0.88 suggests a high reproducibility (Table 2.2.1). The change in speed required for a soccer player to reach the ball with his or her shoulders in front of the opposition during a one-on-one duel over 10 m is approximately −2% (Haugen and Buchheit, 2016). Therefore, the mean bias of 0.4% is trivial, whereas the SEM of 1.9% is compatible with practically significant values (Table 2.2.1). Despite this, the within-player change required to be clearly meaningful is approximately −5.5% or −0.10 s in this sample. Collectively, these findings support 10-m linear speed as a reliable profiling and monitoring tool in soccer players.

The online supplementary information to this chapter provides more examples of how this reliability analysis can be used in practice, such as monitoring changes in individuals and setting the target sample size for group-based changes or an experimental trial. The raw test-retest data are also provided, along with a step-by-step walkthrough of the reliability analysis.

Summary

Sport scientists and exercise physiologists need to make an informed choice of the most appropriate measurement tool before they start collecting data from athletes or research participants. The degree of test-retest measurement error is one factor that should guide these decisions. Statistics such as the mean change, SEM and ICC can be used to quantify systematic and random variation from re-test designs. Practitioners and researchers can use these data to monitor changes in individuals and set the appropriate sample size target for research investigations.

References

Atkinson, G. and Nevill, A. M. (1998). Statistical methods for assessing measurement error (reliability) in variables relevant to sports medicine. *Sports Medicine*, 26(4), 217–238.

Haugen, T. and Buchheit, M. (2016). Sprint running performance monitoring: Methodological and practical considerations. *Sports Medicine*, 46(5), 641–656.

Hopkins, W. G. (2000). Measures of reliability in sports medicine and science. *Sports Medicine*, 30(1), 1–15.

Hopkins, W. G. (2015). Spreadsheets for analysis of validity and reliability. *Sportscience*, 19, 36–42.

Hurst, C., Batterham, A. M., Weston, K. L. and Weston, M. (2018). Short-and long-term reliability of leg extensor power measurement in middle-aged and older adults. *Journal of Sports Sciences*, 36(9), 970–977.

Koo, T. K. and Li, M. Y. (2016). A guideline of selecting and reporting intraclass correlation coefficients for reliability research. *Journal of Chiropractic Medicine*, 15(2), 155–163.

Malcata, R. M., Vandenbogaerde, T. J. and Hopkins, W. G. (2014). Using athletes' world rankings to assess countries' performance. *International Journal of Sports Physiology and Performance*, 9(1), 133–138.

Smith, T. B. and Hopkins, W. G. (2011). Variability and predictability of finals times of elite rowers. *Medicine and Science in Sports and Exercise*, 43(11), 2155–2160.

2.3 Scaling

Adjusting physiological and performance measures to body size

Edward Winter and Simon Jobson

Introduction

It is well established that measures of performance and physiological character-istics are influenced by the size of the body as a whole or of its principal exercis-ing segments in particular (Åstrand and Rodahl, 1986; Schmidt-Nielsen, 1984). Consequently, if the qualitative properties of tissues are to be explored meaning-fully, differences in size have to be partitioned out by adjusting scores. Scaling is the technique that is used to make these adjustments. However, unverified use of ratio standards whereby for example, a measure is divided simply by body mass, continues to predominate.

It has been suggested that in sport and the physiology of exercise, there are four main uses of scaling techniques (Winter, 1992):

1   To compare an individual against standards for the purpose of assessment.
2   To compare groups.
3   In longitudinal studies that investigate the effects of growth or training.
4   To explore possible relationships between physiological characteristics and performance.

There is enthusiastic debate about when scaling might be appropriate and in par-ticular, how it should be done. In heavyweight rowing for instance, in which the body is supported, absolute measures either of performance or physiological char-acteristic are key and hence do not require adjustment. Conversely, in activities such as running in which body mass is unsupported and has to be carried, some form of scaling might be informative.

However, there is an intuitive attraction to adjust measures so as to develop insight into underlying metabolism and other physiological mechanisms. It is at this point that consideration can be given to possible methods.

Ratio standards

Traditionally, physiological characteristics such as oxygen uptake ($\dot{V}O_2$) have been scaled simply by dividing them by an anthropometric variable, for instance

DOI: 10.4324/9781003045267-11

body mass (BM). This produces a ratio standard and the particular standard $\dot{V}O_2/BM$ expressed as $ml\cdot kg^{-1}\cdot min^{-1}$ is probably the most widely used value in the physiology of exercise. However, it was suggested just over 70 years ago by Tanner (1949) and confirmed by Winter et al. (1991) that these standards can be misleading. Tanner (1949) stated that the ratio standard should be applied only when a 'special circumstance' has been satisfied.

For an outcome physiological or performance measure y, and a predictor body size variable x, the special circumstance that allows the legitimate use of a ratio standard is given by:

$$\frac{\upsilon_x}{\upsilon_y} = r$$

in which υ_x = coefficient of variation of x, i.e., $(SDx/\bar{x}) \times 100$
υ_y = coefficient of variation of y, i.e., $(SDy/\bar{y}) \times 100$
r = Pearson's product-moment correlation coefficient

Rarely is this special circumstance tested and arguably it is even rarer for it to be satisfied. As the disparity between each side of the equation increases, the ratio standard becomes increasingly unstable and distorts measures under consideration.

An effect of the unchallenged use of ratio standards is an apparent favourable economy in submaximal exercise in large individuals compared with those who are diminutive, whereas for maximal responses the opposite occurs. This latter observation has bedevilled researchers in the field of growth and development who see children's endurance performance capabilities increase during adolescence while simultaneously, their aerobic capabilities seemingly deteriorate. The bedevilment is most likely the result of inappropriate scaling (Welsman and Armstrong, 2018).

Allometry

The preferred form of scaling is non-linear allometric modelling (Schmidt-Nielsen, 1984; Nevill et al., 1992). This modelling is based on the relationship:

$$y = ax^b$$

In which y = a performance or physiological outcome measure
x = an anthropometric predictor variable
a = the constant multiplier
b = the exponent

The terms a and b can be identified by taking natural logarithms (ln) of both the predictor variable and outcome measure and then regressing ln y on ln x (Schmidt-Nielsen, 1984; Winter and Nevill, 2001). Groups can be compared either by analysis of covariance on the log-log regression lines (Amara et al., 2000; Amara et al., 2003; Johnson et al., 2000) or via power function ratios, i.e., y/x^b (Nevill et al., 2003). These types of ratios are created firstly by raising x to the power b to create a power function, and then secondly by dividing y by this power function. The power function ratio presents y independent of x. As a note of caution, it should be acknowledged that this simple type of regression is not without its problems and Ricker (1973) provides a useful introduction to some of the vagaries of linear modelling.

The surface law

The surface area of a body is related to its volume raised to the power 0.67. The relationship between these two measures illustrates what is called the *surface law* (Schmidt-Nielsen, 1984). This means that as a body increases in mass and hence volume, there is a disproportionate reduction in the body's surface area. Conversely, as a body reduces in mass, its surface area becomes relatively greater. This is a fundamental principle which underpins, for instance, the action of enzymes during digestion and partly explains differences in thermoregulation in children and adults. Heat exchange with the environment occurs at the surface of a body, so thermogenesis and hence energy expenditure must occur to replace heat lost. The precise rate of thermogenesis is dependent on the temperature differences involved. For bodies that are isometric, i.e., they increase proportionally, surface area increases as volume raised to the power two thirds.

It has been suggested (Åstrand and Rodahl, 1986) and demonstrated (Nevill, 1995; Welsman et al., 1996; Nevill et al., 2003) that maximal oxygen uptake ($\dot{V}O_2$max) and related measures of energy expenditure can be scaled for differences in body mass by means of the surface law; body mass can be raised to the two-thirds power and then divided into absolute values of $\dot{V}O_2$. This produces a power-function ratio that describes the aerobic capabilities of a performer with units of $ml\cdot kg^{-0.67}\cdot min^{-1}$. Typical values for elite athletes are presented by Nevill et al. (2003). They range from (mean ± SD) 192 ± 19 $ml\cdot kg^{-0.67}\cdot min^{-1}$ for women badminton players to 310 ± 31 $ml\cdot kg^{-0.67}\cdot min^{-1}$ for elite standard heavyweight men rowers. When their aerobic capabilities are expressed as ratio standards, the characteristics of the heavyweight men rowers appear to be less than those of other groups, yet their event demands high aerobic capability.

Elastic similarity

An alternative approach has been to use the power three quarters. This is based on McMahon's (1973) model of elastic similarity which acknowledges that growth in most living things is not isometric; body segments and limbs grow at different rates and hence, relative proportions change. In addition, buckling loads and other elastic properties, for instance of tendons, are not accounted for in a simple surface-law approach. Moreover, in inter-species studies, animals that differ markedly in size seem to be described by a body mass exponent that approximates 0.75.

Non-isometric growth

McMahon (1973) identified a key complication to simple surface-law considerations and elasticity: the change in relative size of segments that occurs during growth and development (Medawar, 1944). As humans grow and increase absolutely in body mass and other anthropometric dimensions, the relative sizes of each of the body's segments change. For example, the head of an infant is proportionally larger than that of an adult. Conversely, the length of adult legs is a greater proportion of stature than a child's. This change in relative proportions is allometric, but unlike for regular objects such as cubes and spheres, it is termed non-isometric.

Non-isometric change has implications both for locomotion on land and in water, and physiological characteristics. This adds to the complexity of effects on exercise capability that aggregate during adolescence. Nevill et al. (2004) attempted to model limb circumference for different-sized adults and concluded that fixed scaling exponents can mislead. While ratio standards also mislead and allometric modelling is a distinct improvement, non-isometric growth is probably a key reason why there is still no universally accepted way in which allometry can be applied to investigate human exercise capabilities (Welsman and Armstrong, 2018).

Allometric cascade

However, yet another approach has been advanced: the allometric cascade model for metabolic rate (Darveau et al., 2002). This model acknowledges two important considerations: firstly, the non-isometric changes in the body's segments that accompany growth and development, and training-induced hypertrophy; and secondly, the tripartite nature of $\dot{V}O_2$ and in particular, $\dot{V}O_2max$. The $\dot{V}O_2max$ is the global outcome of the rate at which the body can extract oxygen from the atmosphere via the cardiopulmonary system, transport it via the cardiovascular system and use it in skeletal muscle. The ability to release energy is as strong as the weakest part of this three-link chain.

Darveau et al. (2002) ascribed a weighting to each of these three facets and predicted an exponent for maximal and submaximal metabolic rate. For the former, the exponent was between 0.82 and 0.92. For the latter, equivalent values were 0.76–0.79. Seemingly successful attempts have been made to validate these exponents in exercising humans (Batterham and Jackson, 2003), but without accounting for non-isometric change in the size of body segments.

Recommendations

In the light of these considerations and the possible confusion they create, how should the results of exercise tests be expressed? To report the results of laboratory and field-based tests that meaningfully reflect the performance and physiological status of athletes and exercisers, investigators should:

• Report absolute values of performance measures and physiological characteristics.
• Report ratio standards only when Tanner's special circumstance has been satisfied.

- For expediency, use the surface law exponent of 0.67 to scale $\dot{V}O_2$ or other related assessments of energy expenditure for differences in body mass or the size of exercising segments.
- As appropriate, consider and adjust measures for non-isometric growth.
- Verify the choice of a particular exponent but acknowledge that because of sampling errors, comparisons between groups might be compromised.
- For $\dot{V}O_2$ and $\dot{V}O_2$max consider applying the allometric cascade model.

References

Amara, C. E., Koval, J. J., Johnson, P. J., Paterson, D. H., Winter, E. M. and Cunningham, D. A. (2000). Modelling the influence of fat-free mass and physical activity on the decline in maximum oxygen uptake with age in older humans. *Experimental Physiology*, 85, 877–885.

Amara, C. E., Rice, C. L., Koval, J. J., Paterson, D. H., Winter, E. M. and Cunningham, D. A. (2003). Allometric scaling of strength in an independently living population aged 55–86 years. *American Journal of Human Biology*, 15, 48–60.

Åstrand, P.-O. and Rodahl, K. (1986). *Textbook of Work Physiology* (3rd ed.). New York: McGraw-Hill.

Batterham, A. M. and Jackson, A. S. (2003). Validity of the allometric cascade model at submaximal and maximal metabolic rates in men. *Respiratory Physiology and Neurobiology*, 135, 103–106.

Darveau, C.-A., Suarez, R. K., Andrews, R. D. and Hochachka, P. W. (2002). Allometric cascade as a unifying principle of body mass effects on metabolism. *Nature*, 417, 166–170.

Johnson, P. J., Winter, E. M., Paterson, D. H., Koval, J. J., Nevill, A. M. and Cunningham, D. A. (2000). Modelling the influence of age, body size and sex on maximum oxygen uptake in older humans. *Experimental Physiology*, 85, 219–225.

McMahon, T. (1973). Size and shape in biology. *Science*, 179, 1201–1204.

Medawar, P. B. (1944). The shape of a human being as a function of time. *Journal of the Royal Statistical Society*, 132B, 133–144.

Nevill, A. M. (1995). The need to scale for differences in body size and mass: An explanation of Kleiber's 0.75 mass exponent. *Journal of Applied Physiology*, 77, 2870–2873.

Nevill, A. M., Brown, D., Godfrey, R., Johnson, P. J., Romer, L., Stewart, A. D. and Winter, E. M. (2003). Modelling maximum oxygen uptake of elite endurance athletes. *Medicine and Science in Sports and Exercise*, 35, 488–494.

Nevill, A. M., Ramsbottom, R. and Williams, C. (1992). Scaling physiological measurements for individuals of different body size. *European Journal of Applied Physiology*, 65, 110–117.

Nevill, A. M., Stewart, A. D., Olds, T. and Holder, R. (2004). Are adult physiques geometrically similar? The danger of allometric scaling using body mass power laws. *American Journal of Anthropology*, 124, 177–182.

Ricker, W. E. (1973). Linear regressions in fishery research. *Journal of Fisheries Research Board, Canada*, 30, 409–434.

Schmidt-Nielsen, K. (1984). *Scaling: Why Is Animal Size So Important?* Cambridge: Cambridge University Press.

Tanner, J. M. (1949). Fallacy of per-weight and per-surface area standards and their relation to spurious correlation. *Journal of Applied Physiology*, 2, 1–15.

Welsman, J. and Armstrong, N. (2018). Interpreting aerobic fitness in youth: The fallacy of ratio scaling. *Pediatric Exercise Science*, 31, 184–190.

Welsman, J., Armstrong, N., Nevill, A., Winter, E. and Kirby, B. (1996). Scaling peak O_2 for differences in body size. *Medicine and Science in Sports and Exercise*, 28, 259–265.

Winter, E. M. (1992). Scaling: Partitioning out differences in size. *Pediatric Exercise Science*, 4, 296–301.

Winter, E. M., Brookes, F. B. C. and Hamley, E. J. (1991). Maximal exercise performance and lean leg volume in men and women. *Journal of Sports Sciences*, 9, 3–13.

Winter, E. M. and Nevill, A. M. (2001). Scaling: Adjusting for differences in body size. In R. Eston and T. Reilly (eds.), *Kinanthropometry and Exercise Physiology Laboratory Manual: Tests, Procedures and Data* (2nd ed.). *Volume 1: Anthropometry*), pp. 321–335. London: Routledge.

Part III

3.1   Participant pre-test preparation and evaluation

Rachel Lord and Brian Begg

Regular physical activity is associated with numerous health benefits including lower all-cause mortality and lower risk of cardiovascular and metabolic disease (Kohl et al., 2012). Despite the well-established long-term beneficial effects of exercise, the risk of an acute cardiovascular event including sudden cardiac death (SCD) and/or acute myocardial infarction (AMI) is transiently elevated during and just after vigorous physical exertion (Mittleman et al., 1993). Although there is a small transiently elevated risk during vigorous-intensity exercise, the long-term benefits of exercise far outweigh the acute risks. The exercise pre-participation health-screening process should therefore provide practical assessment while minimising barriers to becoming physically active. The purpose of pre-participation screening is therefore to (i) identify the risk of an adverse event during exercise for the individual concerned, and (ii) inform appropriate risk mitigation strategies.

There are three risk modulators of exercise-related cardiovascular events: 1) the individual's current level of physical activity, 2) presence of signs or symptoms of known cardiovascular, metabolic or renal disease and 3) the desired exercise intensity (Riebe et al., 2015; Franklin, 2014). Cardiovascular disease (CVD) risk factors were traditionally included in the screening process, but these have recently been removed. The ability to predict acute cardiovascular events during exercise by assessing CVD risk factors is poor (Whitfield et al., 2014), and evidence suggests that conventional CVD risk factor-based screening was too conservative and created barriers to exercise testing and prescription (Riebe et al., 2015). The actual incidence of a CV event during very light- to moderate-intensity activities is extremely low and similar to that expected at rest. During vigorous-intensity exercise in healthy, asymptomatic adults, data indicates a risk of cardiac arrest in every 1 per 565,000 patient/hours (Fletcher et al., 2001). In those diagnosed with cardiovascular disease, this incidence increases to 1 in 80,000 patient/hours; however, this can be improved to 1 in 117,000 patient/hours with appropriate monitoring and risk mitigation (Fletcher et al., 2001). In addition, increasing evidence suggests that exercise is safe for most people, exercise-related cardiovascular events are often preceded by warning signs/symptoms and the cardiovascular risks associated with exercise lessen as people become more physically active/fit (Franklin, 2014). Therefore, pre-exercise screening should focus on trying to

DOI: 10.4324/9781003045267-13

identify signs and symptoms of underlying undiagnosed or unstable disease, and those who are least active.

The screening process

Individuals should undergo thorough screening and assessment prior to commencing physical activity, which can reduce/mitigate risk to participants. Screening can be split into subjective and objective assessments.

Subjective assessment

A subjective assessment involves the gathering of relevant information related to the participant. Information gained during a subjective assessment includes:

*   Relevant medical history, both past and current
*   Comorbidities, including mobility issues
*   General appearance
*   Medications
*   Current physical activity status/levels
*   Relevant symptoms including shortness of breath, chest pain, dizziness, fatigue and claudication

Objective assessment

An objective assessment includes observed and/or quantifiable parameters, including:

*   Height
*   Body mass
*   Blood pressure (BP)
*   Heart rate (HR)
*   Body temperature
*   Oxygen saturation
*   Cardiac structure and function, including an evaluation of electrical activity
*   Relevant signs (e.g., angina, palpitations, arrhythmias, oedema, paroxysmal nocturnal dyspnoea, orthopnoea, ascites)
*   Functional capacity, both submaximal and/or maximal evaluations

Absolute and relative contraindications to exercise should be identified (Fletcher et al., 2013). An additional risk assessment is advised for those with known CVD (AACVPR, 2012) and can be used to categorise risk of an adverse event (low, moderate or high risk) during exercise based on the key predictors outlined earlier. For the general population who are symptom-free but sedentary, the 2020 PAR-Q+ (Bredin et al., 2013) should be completed to identify contraindications to exercise that may require medical clearance.

Absolute contraindications

- Acute myocardial infarction (MI), within two days
- Ongoing unstable angina
- Uncontrolled cardiac arrhythmia with haemodynamic compromise
- Active endocarditis
- Symptomatic severe aortic stenosis
- Decompensated heart failure
- Acute pulmonary embolism, pulmonary infarction or deep vein thrombosis
- Acute myocarditis or pericarditis
- Acute aortic dissection
- Physical disability that precludes safe and adequate testing

Relative contraindications

- Known obstructive left main coronary artery stenosis
- Moderate to severe aortic stenosis with uncertain relation to symptoms
- Tachyarrhythmias with uncontrolled ventricular rates
- Acquired advanced or complete heart block
- Hypertrophic obstructive cardiomyopathy with severe resting gradient
- Recent stroke or transient ischaemic attack
- Mental impairment with limited ability to cooperate
- Resting hypertension with systolic or diastolic blood pressures >200/110 mmHg
- Uncorrected medical conditions, such as significant anaemia, important electrolyte imbalance and hyperthyroidism

Information gained can help guide the decision as to whether a participant needs medical clearance before commencing a physical activity/exercise programme. Pre-exercise medical clearance is generally unnecessary for individuals without contraindications prior to beginning light- or moderate-intensity physical activity (Bull et al., 2020). Performing an exercise test on these participants will inform more accurate exercise prescription, but careful consideration about the type of test is required. However, if a participant has unstable disease (showing signs and symptoms suggestive of CV, metabolic or renal disease) irrespective of current activity level, then medical clearance would be necessary and exercise testing and prescription may need to be delayed until these conditions are better controlled (ACSM, 2018). An exercise test in this context is important for the individual participant risk assessment, i.e., functional capacity <5 METS is a moderate risk criterion (AACVPR, 2012).

Which functional capacity measure is best to establish cardiorespiratory fitness?

It is important to analyse the information gained during the subjective and objective assessments and give careful consideration to the risks and benefits of performing a functional capacity test. The choice of maximal or submaximal test depends on the reason for the test, risk level of the client, availability of equipment, skill level of personnel (ACSM, 2018) and comorbidities of the participant.

Maximal cardiopulmonary testing is the 'gold standard' assessment of the cardiovascular, ventilatory and metabolic responses to exercise and is a powerful diagnostic and prognostic tool. This method affords direct measurement of aerobic capacity (Taylor et al., 2015). However, maximal testing requires participants to perform vigorous-intensity exercise, which may be inappropriate or unnecessary for some individuals, or require additional monitoring during exercise testing to mitigate risk.

The aim of submaximal tests is to evaluate parameters such as HR, BP, rating of perceived exertion (RPE) and workload, and then predict $\dot{V}O_2$ max from the HR response. Submaximal tests increase the workload until participants reach 70–75% of HRR or RPE of 14–15, ensuring that participants are only exercising at a moderate exercise intensity.

Both maximal and submaximal exercise tests provide important information about an individual's physiological responses to exercise; however, accuracy is limited in submaximal assessment, and relative risk may be greater during maximal exercise testing. It is important to consider the relative benefits to be gained from maximal testing over and above submaximal methods, and the risk assessment of the individual participant, in making the decision about testing mode.

In summary, the screening process should be used to determine the risk of an adverse event occurring during exercise testing and any subsequent exercise prescription. This screening assessment should allow for the identification of the individual's current level of physical activity, presence of signs or symptoms of known cardiovascular, metabolic or renal disease and the desired exercise intensity. Any participants with absolute contraindications to exercise should receive medical clearance, and potentially further treatment, prior to engaging in an exercise test or programme. Participants with a number of relative contraindications may also require medical clearance, especially for maximal exercise testing.

Overall, there is a low risk of SCD and AMI associated with exercise. Adopting a progressive exercise prescription strategy for each participant reduces this risk even further. For instance, for a sedentary participant, it is recommended to commence exercise at a low to moderate intensity and progress over time as cardiorespiratory fitness increases (ACSM, 2018). Thorough screening and risk assessment, and exercise testing, allow for safer and more effective exercise prescription with informed individualised prescription of the frequency, intensity, time and type of exercise.

References

Aacvpr, A. A. O. C. A. P. R. (2012). *AACVPR Stratification Algorithm for Risk of Event* [Online]. www.aacvpr.org/Portals/0/2014_AACVPR-Risk-Stratification-Algorithm.pdf (accessed 25 February 2021).

ACSM. (2018). In D. Riebe, J. K. Ehrman, G. Liguori, and M. Magal (eds.), *ACSM's Guidelines for Exercise Testing and Prescription* (10th ed.). Philadelphia, PA: Wolters Kluwer.

Bredin, S. S. D., Gledhill, N., Jamnik, V. K. and Warburton, D. E. R. (2013). PAR-Q+ and ePARmed-X+: New risk stratification and physical activity clearance strategy for physicians and patients alike. *Canadian family physician Medecin de famille canadien*, 59, 273–277.

Bull, F. C., Al-Ansari, S. S., Biddle, S., Borodulin, K., Buman, M. P., Cardon, G., Carty, C., Chaput, J.-P., Chastin, S., Chou, R., Dempsey, P. C., Dipietro, L., Ekelund, U., Firth, J., Friedenreich, C. M., Garcia, L., Gichu, M., Jago, R., Katzmarzyk, P. T., Lambert, E., Leitzmann, M., Milton, K., Ortega, F. B., Ranasinghe, C., Stamatakis, E., Tiedemann, A., Troiano, R. P., van der Ploeg, H. P., Wari, V. and Willumsen, J. F. (2020). World Health Organization 2020 guidelines on physical activity and sedentary behaviour. *British Journal of Sports Medicine*, 54, 1451–1462.

Fletcher, G. F., Ades, P. A., Kligfield, P., Arena, R., Balady, G. J., Bittner, V. A., Coke, L. A., Fleg, J. L., Forman, D. E., Gerber, T. C., Gulati, M., Madan, K., Rhodes, J., Thompson, P. D. and Williams, M. A. (2013). Exercise standards for testing and training. *Circulation*, 128, 873–934.

Fletcher, G. F., Balady, G. J., Amsterdam, E. A., Chaitman, B., Eckel, R., Fleg, J., Froelicher, V. F., Leon, A. S., Piña, I. L., Rodney, R., Simons-Morton, D. A., Williams, M. A. and Bazzarre, T. (2001). Exercise standards for testing and training: A statement for healthcare professionals from the American Heart Association. *Circulation*, 104, 1694–740.

Franklin, B. A. (2014). Preventing exercise-related cardiovascular events: Is a medical examination more urgent for physical activity or inactivity? *Circulation*, 129, 1081–1084.

Kohl, H. W., 3rd, Craig, C. L., Lambert, E. V., Inoue, S., Alkandari, J. R., Leetongin, G. and Kahlmeier, S. (2012). The pandemic of physical inactivity: Global action for public health. *Lancet*, 380, 294–305.

Mittleman, M. A., Maclure, M., Tofler, G. H., Sherwood, J. B., Goldberg, R. J. and Muller, J. E. (1993). Triggering of acute myocardial infarction by heavy physical exertion: Protection against triggering by regular exertion: Determinants of myocardial infarction onset study investigators. *New England Journal of Medicine*, 329, 1677–1683.

Riebe, D., Franklin, B. A., Thompson, P. D., Garber, C. E., Whitfield, G. P., Magal, M. and Pescatello, L. S. (2015). Updating ACSM's recommendations for exercise preparticipation health screening. *Medicine & Science in Sports & Exercise*, 47, 2473–2479.

Taylor, C., Nichols, S. and Ingle, L. (2015). A clinician's guide to cardiopulmonary exercise testing 1: An introduction. *British Journal of Hospital Medicine (Lond)*, 76, 192–195.

Whitfield, G. P., Pettee Gabriel, K. K., Rahbar, M. H. and Kohl, H. W., 3rd. (2014). Application of the American Heart Association/American College of Sports Medicine Adult Preparticipation Screening Checklist to a nationally representative sample of US adults aged >=40 years from the National Health and Nutrition Examination Survey 2001 to 2004. *Circulation*, 129, 1113–1120.

3.2 Maintenance and calibration standards

A cornerstone of laboratory quality assurance

David Green and Glyn Howatson

Introduction

Effective maintenance and calibration of laboratory and field equipment is fundamental for ensuring the reliability and validity of testing procedures. By understanding these processes, it is possible to ascertain the error associated with the instrument and hence detect meaningful physiological (biological) changes. Poor practice and user errors during these processes can be detrimental to the quality of data produced and hence have serious implications for research, consultancy and other applied practice. Laboratory accreditation schemes exist, such as that provided by the British Association of Sport and Exercise Sciences (BASES: www.bases.org.uk/spage-organisations-laboratory_accreditation.html).

Such schemes provide external quality assurance of laboratory practices. This external validation is critical in upholding good practice, creating a culture of quality assurance and ensuring acceptable standards are adhered to not just within, but also between laboratories. The aim of this chapter is to provide some guiding principles, central to the BASES Laboratory Accreditation process, that can be employed as good practice for the calibration and maintenance of laboratory or field-testing equipment in the domain of sport and exercise science.

It is important to note that commercial availability does not guarantee the validity, reliability or suitability of a piece of equipment for any given purpose. In this chapter it is assumed due diligence has been performed in the acquisition of any equipment and that, if fully functional, it is fit for purpose. Furthermore, validity and reliability of a testing procedure is influenced by factors other than equipment functionality, such as user competence and biological variation. Therefore, users of all laboratories should make every effort to understand the factors that influence testing validity and reliability, and, where appropriate, be able to report these variables to support data.

Calibration

The function of diagnostic equipment within the sport and exercise community is to measure the value of a specific sample or parameter based upon a pre-determined method of measurement. During production, manufacturers

DOI: 10.4324/9781003045267-14

assess methods of measurement against pre-existing criterion values for reliability and validity; during this process, fine adjustments occur until the manufacturer achieves appropriately equivalent results. This process of adjusting the method of measurement to attain a more accurate result is calibration. The requirement for re-calibration arises when a method of measurement is unstable over time. In this instance, any 'drift' in previous calibration procedures may result in inaccurate measures. Re-calibrating the equipment ensures alignment with the manufacturer's original and acceptable tolerances.

Control

A control test differs from a calibration; a control test uses either known criterion values, or a measuring device, to establish accuracy of an instrument. When running a control test, no adjustment is made to the method of measurement; it is simply a test of accuracy based on the equipment's current calibration. Manufacturers often dictate calibration and control values to ensure optimal performance of a piece of equipment. However, when modifiable, users should prioritise calibration and control values that correspond to an expected testing range. For example, when using controls for blood lactate analysers, the use of a 12 mmol L^{-1} control (standard) would not be suitable for testing athletes that are expected to range between 0.5 mmol L^{-1} and 6 mmol L^{-1}. Appropriate ranges should be determined on a laboratory-by-laboratory basis by the technical staff in consultation with the laboratory director or other appropriately qualified laboratory users. If a piece of equipment calculates results using a non-linear method, multiple calibration values should be considered to determine an appropriate calibration curve that fits within the expected range of values. Using a range of control tests can be useful in assessing the efficacy of different calibration values and thus help to identify the most appropriate calibration protocol.

Quality of calibration and control samples

A calibration sample that does not accurately reflect its designated value will have a detrimental effect on the method of measurement, leading to inaccurate results. A control sample or criterion measure that no longer reflects or measures its designated value will prevent an accurate assessment of equipment functionality and could lead to unnecessary or detrimental follow-up adjustments. The degree of certainty about the value of any individual calibration or control sample can never be 100%. Ultimately, an individual's judgement on the quality and acceptability of a calibrator/control for any given situation must be based on several criteria (see Tables 3.2.1 and 3.2.2 for examples).

How often should I calibrate?

Manufacturers usually advise on the frequency of calibration; however, laboratory-specific knowledge should always complement this fundamental information to

Table 3.2.1 Calibration and control checklist

- Can we trust the supplier?
- Does it have official certification?
- Mechanical degradation (e.g., wear and tear)
- Chemical degradation (e.g., check 'use by' dates and storage conditions)
- Effect of environmental conditions (e.g., cold, hot, humid, hypoxic)
- Does user competence affect its quality?
- Manufacturer's error limits
- Is this error acceptable for the equipment's intended use?

Table 3.2.2 Example – checking the speed of a treadmill

Method 1 – Contact tachometer:
The wheel of the contact tachometer is applied on the treadmill and speed is determined via on-board software.

Considerations:
A tachometer requires specialist calibration, and assessing its functionality 'in house' is not possible; thus, guaranteeing there has been no degradation in the tachometer since the previous calibration is not possible. An instant-read tachometer would be very sensitive to slight perturbations in treadmill belt speed.

Method 2 – Counting belt revolutions:
Using a stopwatch, belt velocity can be calculated from the total distance (belt revolutions x belt length) covered in a given time.

Considerations:
If measured appropriately, you could have high confidence in the length of the belt and, provided the belt length is accurate, error in the calculated speed would decrease as the number of counted revolutions increases. Therefore, it is advisable to use no less than 100 revolutions at a range of velocities. Errors in the calculation of speed can be determined based on possible inaccuracies of belt length and revolution count. Using this method, it is easy to determine treadmill speed within an error of <1%.

Verdict:
A tachometer is more responsive to changes in treadmill speed and therefore maybe the more appropriate tool for assessing instantaneous changes in speed when a load is added to the treadmill (e.g., a foot strike). However, counting revolutions is a more transparent method and has a likely error well within an acceptable level for most treadmill uses.

N.B.: Aside from the method of checking belt speed, consideration should be given to the validity of checking the belt when unloaded when the requirement for confidence in its speed is highest when being loaded (i.e., run on). Importantly, a variety of body masses should be considered across a range of treadmill velocities that are most likely to align with the people exercising on the device. This provides excellent task-specific validity to your instrument.

arrive at a best practice protocol for each piece of equipment, its current use and environment. Some considerations (Figure 3.2.1) for determining the frequency of calibration include:

- When the equipment does not return a satisfactory result from a control test;

- If a change in the environment or equipment has occurred that might affect the method of measurement; and
- When using after a period of non-use.

Maintenance of equipment

Good preventative maintenance will reduce malfunctions, promote early problem identification and maintain the validity and reliability of equipment and results. Users should tailor equipment maintenance plans according to the environment and consideration of how a piece of equipment is used. An effective maintenance plan should include a list of preventative maintenance tasks, the required frequency and documentation/training to promote competent equipment use. The initial creation of a maintenance plan should start with the manufacturer's recommendations, after which users can add components according to the specific, local laboratory environment.

Documentation and user training

Comprehensive operating procedures, risk assessments and user training are essential in preventing avoidable damage to equipment. One should not assume that a user is sufficiently competent to operate equipment because of their experience with 'similar systems'; confidence does not equal competence. Indeed, user training is the first step in ensuring correct usage and should be supplemented with a detailed, step-by-step operating procedure for ongoing reference. Although establishing protocols and procedures takes time to develop, they tend not to change a great deal over time. Importantly, documents of this nature allow for good knowledge transfer and creating them is excellent practice in mitigating risk (loss of knowledge, for example), disaster recovery and business continuity.

Maintenance tasks

Many factors determine the appropriate type and frequency of maintenance tasks for any given piece of equipment. The following list is not exhaustive, but it highlights some common considerations when constructing a maintenance plan:

- What spare parts are required and what is the delivery time on them?
- Do certain parts/consumables have a finite life span?
- Historically, what problems have occurred?
- Can users test constituent parts, individually?
- How often should a user evaluate functionality?
- Document typical calibration and control values to help early identification of problems.
- Track usage to guide maintenance frequency.

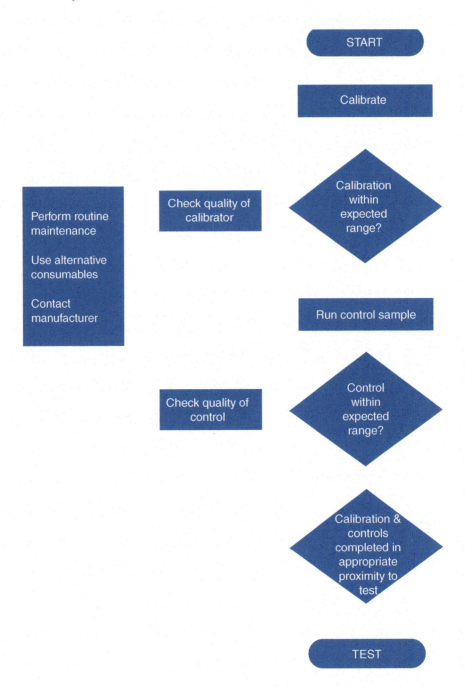

Figure 3.2.1 Schematic depicting the recommended calibration and control processes prior to using equipment for testing purposes.

Summary

Many professionals in the sport and exercise industry make assumptions that all laboratory environments are the same, but this is not true; vast differences will be present between a well-run laboratory and a poorly run laboratory. Accuracy of equipment, safety of the environment, efficacy of exercise testing protocols, quality of analysis and interpretation and competence of staff are critical to ensure good operations. BASES laboratory accreditation provides a schema and level of quality assurance that a laboratory can follow to adhere to industry-based, good practice. As technology improves, new, more affordable equipment becomes available and so it is critically important that laboratories can support their activities with good practice and provide an evidence base for the data produced, both in research and applied practice.

3.3 Lung and respiratory muscle function

John Dickinson and Karl Sylvester

This chapter will consider why the assessment of lung and respiratory muscle function is relevant to sport and exercise science. We will describe the theory behind assessments of lung function, upper airway flow, airway inflammation and respiratory muscle assessments, and will signpost to further reading should more detail on standardisation of performance be required. The online version of this chapter also provides an introduction to breathing.

Individuals will rarely reach their maximal voluntary ventilation limits during most forms of physical activity and exercise; therefore, in many cases it has been assumed that the respiratory system is not a limiting factor to performance. Thus, routine testing and monitoring of respiratory health has taken a back seat to cardiovascular and musculoskeletal issues related to physical activity and exercise. However, times are changing and there is more acceptance from medical, sports science and clinical physiologist teams of the importance of assessing an individual's respiratory health. There is more understanding of the best ways to manage and care for respiratory health and full texts are now available on the subject (Dickinson and Hull, 2020). Even in moderate physical activity the respiratory system may not perform appropriately and can impact health and performance, either directly during exercise or following exercise (e.g., bronchospasm post race). We are therefore able to use assessments of upper and lower airway function at rest and following exercise to assess and monitor the individual's airway performance and health.

Assessments of upper and lower airway function are necessary since exercise respiratory symptoms are non-specific. For example, 50% of athletes who report respiratory symptoms are inappropriately diagnosed with an asthma-related condition when symptoms are used in isolation without an objective assessment of airway function (Rundell et al., 2001). Other issues such as unexplained underperformance, regular early termination of exercise and chronic fatigue can all be linked to underlying respiratory conditions. Many individuals may experience abnormal functioning of the respiratory system that can impact their ability to exercise optimally (see Table 3.3.1).

If practitioners have appropriate resources, it may also be beneficial to screen for respiratory conditions. Several reports (Dickinson et al., 2011) have identified large numbers of elite athletes that are detected with respiratory issues, such as

DOI: 10.4324/9781003045267-15

Table 3.3.1 Abnormal respiratory function

Condition	Pathology	Physiological Impact
Asthma-related conditions	Airway inflammation Airway smooth muscle constriction	Reduction in ability to expire air Compromised gas exchange (usually in moderate to severe forms) Reduction in aerobic exercise capacity (usually in moderate to severe forms) Difficulty in breathing Prolonged time to recover from exercise Post-exercise cough
COPD	Chronic airway inflammation (bronchitis) Chronic damage to the air sacs in the lungs (emphysema) Airway smooth muscle constriction	Reduction in ability to expire air Compromised gas exchange Reduction in aerobic exercise capacity (usually in moderate to severe forms) Difficulty in breathing Prolonged time to recover from exercise Post-exercise cough
Restrictive airway disease (e.g., pulmonary fibrosis)	Lung tissue is damaged and scarred Airway walls become thickened, stiff	Reduction in airway ventilation Compromised gas exchange Limited ability to exercise at moderate and high intensities
Respiratory muscle fatigue/increased respiratory load	Prolonged endurance exercise leads to fatigue of respiratory muscles Poor coordination of respiratory muscle activation Poor conditioning of respiratory muscles	Respiratory muscle fatigue leading to early onset of respiratory metaboreflex
Dysfunctional breathing	Poor coordination of respiratory muscles and overactivation of accessory breathing muscles	Inappropriate ventilation Increased perception of breathing effort Compromised alveolar gas exchange Early termination of exercise
Rhinitis	Inflammation and swelling of the mucous membrane of the nose	Blocked nasal passage prompts mouth breathing Greater exposure to particles entering lower airways which can promote bronchoconstriction in susceptible individuals Can lead some individuals to develop a dysfunctional breathing pattern Can lead to increased perception of breathing effort during exercise

(*Continued*)

Table 3.3.1 (Continued)

Condition	Pathology	Physiological Impact
Exercise-induced laryngeal obstruction	Transient, reversible narrowing of the larynx that occurs during high-intensity exercise	Development of inspiratory wheeze during moderate- to high-intensity exercise Increased perception of breathing effort during exercise Can lead to early termination of high-intensity exercise Can develop persistent dry cough post exercise May promote a dysfunctional breathing pattern or can be present because of a dysfunctional breathing pattern

asthma-related conditions, in the absence of a previous history. When screening for respiratory conditions, it is important to complete a thorough systematic assessment of the individual's airways. This includes assessing the airflow and volumes through the upper and lower airways at rest and following exercise (or surrogate challenge).

Spirometry (dynamic lung function)

Spirometry is probably the most commonly utilised respiratory physiological assessment. It is used to assist with a diagnosis of many respiratory diseases, such as chronic obstructive pulmonary disease (COPD) or asthma. Spirometry is also performed at regular intervals to determine the appropriateness of initiating therapies, such as anti-fibrotic medication in interstitial lung diseases (ILD), should there be a significant decline in spirometry results.

Spirometry is also utilised in other assessments such as bronchial challenge tests. These tests assess the responsiveness of the airways to known bronchoconstricting stimulants, such as methacholine which acts directly on the airways. Indirect airway challenges trigger bronchoconstriction via an indirect pathway. An example of an indirect airway challenge is an exercise challenge, which is useful in confirming the presence of exercise-induced bronchospasm (EIB). Although exercise is a specific indirect airway challenge for EIB, some surrogate challenge assessments (e.g., eucapnic voluntary hyperpnoea or mannitol) have a greater sensitivity when compared to exercise (Dickinson et al., 2006; Holzer et al., 2003). There is an exaggerated response in those who are hyperresponsive or have a diagnosis of asthma that is not detected through more basic assessments. For more detail about specific challenges for asthma-related conditions we refer you to the following American Thoracic Society (ATS) and European Respiratory Society (ERS) guidelines (Hallstrand et al., 2018).

Spirometry must be performed to quality-assured standards to ensure accuracy of the results. Quality assurance includes using calibrated and verified equipment, sufficient training for the professional who will be coaching the participant to perform the manoeuvre and ensuring the results obtained meet acceptability and reproducibility criteria (Sylvester et al., 2020).

Measurement of static lung volumes

In many respiratory diseases, it is important to understand the extent of disease impact on overall lung volumes. Spirometry can measure some constituents of lung volume, but it is unable to measure parameters such as residual volume (RV), the volume of air left in the lungs when the participant completely exhales, or the functional residual capacity (FRC), the volume of air left in the lungs at the end of a normal tidal breath. Both of these parameters are particularly important in obstructive lung diseases because they allow the measurement of gas trapping and hyperinflation respectively.

Being able to measure RV and FRC also allows the calculation of total lung capacity (TLC) to be made. Measuring TLC allows accurate determination of the presence of restrictive lung diseases such as ILD. Analysing all of these measurements also allows more in-depth analysis of the impact of diseases and the potential origin of the disease–for example, whether it is a lung or chest wall problem or how much of an impact obesity is having on the physiology of the lungs.

Static lung volumes can be measured using several techniques that either utilise inhalation of a gas mixture, such as in the helium dilution or nitrogen washout techniques, or pressure-related measurements such as whole-body plethysmography. Each test has its own positives and drawbacks. Gas dilutional techniques may underestimate lung volume, since the gas used may not distribute to airways that aren't being ventilated, particularly in relatively severe obstructive lung diseases. In contrast, the plethysmographic method may overestimate due to measurement of volumes of gas not utilised in the lungs, for example in the buccal cavity or stomach.

Single breath gas transfer

The ability to inspire and expire the desired lung volume, as measured by the preceding techniques, is important but only one aspect of the physiology of respiration. In order for the oxygen required for cellular respiration to reach the cells, it must first cross the alveolar-capillary membrane and enter the pulmonary circulation. The ability of the lungs to exchange gases can be altered by conditions in which there is insufficient ventilation and surface area available, e.g., emphysema, or in conditions in which there is thickening of the alveolar-capillary membrane, e.g., ILD. Measurement of gas exchange is possible through the single breath gas transfer technique. The participant inspires a mix of gas in known concentrations. The gases include an inert gas, such as helium or methane. These gases do not cross the alveolar-capillary membrane and are used to estimate the volume of the lungs available for gas exchange but also the dilutional effect of other gases. The other important gas used in this technique is carbon monoxide. Carbon monoxide is used due to its similar characteristics to oxygen in terms of its molecular weight; however, it has a 250-times greater affinity for haemoglobin than oxygen. When calculating the gas exchange ability of the lungs, the important factors to consider are the thickness of the membrane across which gas diffuses, the surface area available for gas exchange, the diffusivity of the gas, the pulmonary capillary blood volume and the time factor for the gas to combine with haemoglobin. This lattermost can be negated when using carbon monoxide due to its rapid combination with haemoglobin. Therefore, any abnormalities detected can be attributed to either a problem with the lungs or an insufficient pulmonary capillary blood volume.

Fraction of expired nitric oxide (FeNO; airway inflammation)

Fractional exhaled nitric oxide (FeNO) is recognised by the National Institute for Health and Care Excellence (NICE) as an important tool in the detection of airway inflammation, particularly in asthma. Detection of high levels of FeNO predominantly suggests the presence of eosinophilic inflammation, but FeNO levels can be high in other types of airway inflammation. NO itself is derived from the amino acid L-arginine in a process catalysed by three forms of the enzyme NO synthase (NOS). NO production can be in response to airway inflammation, but it is also released to regulate airway function. The inducible form of the enzyme (iNOS) can be induced by proinflammatory cytokines, such as tumour necrosis factor α, interferon γ and IL-1β. It has also been suggested that IL-13 upregulates the iNOS gene and protein expression in epithelial cells, leading to increased levels of FeNO.

FeNO measurements can be used to assess the presence of airway inflammation but can also be utilised in assessing the effectiveness of any treatment intervention provided, such as a course of oral corticosteroids. The manoeuvre required to assess levels of FeNO is relatively simple. It requires a maximal inspiration, sometimes through an NO scrubber which captures any ambient NO, followed by a controlled expiration at a set expiration rate for approximately ten seconds. A result is usually available between 30 and 90 seconds after the manoeuvre is completed.

Mouth pressure

The measurement of respiratory muscles can be conducted in a variety of ways during rest and exercise, as indicated by a recent European Respiratory Society report (Laveneziana et al., 2019). In most cases, the direct measurement of respiratory muscle strength is not feasible since it requires invasive protocols, expensive equipment and skilled respiratory physiologists. Static mouth pressure is a recognised simple assessment of global respiratory muscle strength (Laveneziana et al., 2019). Mouth pressure can be measured during either the inspiratory (PI_{max}) or expiratory (PE_{max}). Most investigations for respiratory muscle strength are focussed on the inspiratory respiratory muscles. Practitioners may choose to ask clients to carry out maximal inspiratory pressure (MIP) assessments to investigate for weak inspiratory muscle function, inform respiratory muscle training programmes or investigate the fatigue of respiratory muscles from various forms of exercise.

The measurement of mouth pressure requires the participant to be fully motivated to perform a maximal effort. The measurement is taken using a respiratory pressure meter. PI_{max} is usually measured at residual volume and PE_{max} at total lung capacity (TLC). At these volumes, participants maximally inspire or expire accordingly against an occluded opening. Efforts should be separated by at least 60 s and continue until the participant has reached a plateau in peak values. Participants should be coached between efforts to ensure their technique is good and they are attempting to provide their best effort. From experience, it usually requires the participant to perform between 5 and 10 efforts. The maximum value of the manoeuvres should be recorded if they vary by less than 10% from second and third best efforts.

Feedback of results to practitioners, patients, coaches and athletes

The results of the assessments are in most cases available as soon as the assessment is complete. Therefore, it is possible if required to inform the client of the test result at the time of the assessment. In some cases in which a direct referral has been made by the client, this is appropriate. However, in many cases the practitioner may report the findings to the clinical practitioner who made the referral. The advantages of reporting results to the referring clinical practitioner include:

* Consistency for the client in the messages they receive about their respiratory care.
* The results may be part of a larger clinical assessment of the client.

Regardless of whether the results are relayed immediately or via the referring practitioner, it is good practice to report the following from the aforementioned assessments:

* Report results from assessments that were conducted in accordance with appropriate guidelines.
* Include predicted values as well as actual values for each variable reported.
* When undertaking diagnostic assessments, report whether diagnostic thresholds have been met (e.g., has FEV_1 fallen greater than 10% from baseline following exercise challenge?).

Although as physiological practitioners we can run and interpret the respiratory assessments, we must be aware of the limits of our scope of practice and not draw conclusions on diagnosis of respiratory disease. Physiological assessments are an excellent aid to determining a differential diagnosis, but other information is pieced together, such as a clinical history or imaging results if available, by an appropriately trained and experienced professional before a definitive diagnosis can be made. We can interpret the results of the test, but the diagnosis of any potential condition must be made by the medical practitioner who is overseeing the care of the client/patient. Building a good relationship between the physiological and medical practitioner team is therefore crucial to ensure that interpretation of assessments is communicated effectively.

References

Dickinson, J. W. and Hull, J. H. (2020). *Complete Guide to Respiratory Care in Athletes*. Abingdon: Routledge.

Dickinson, J. W., McConnell, A. and Whyte, G. (2011). Diagnosis of exercise-induced bronchoconstriction: Eucapnic voluntary hyperpnoea challenges identify previously undiagnosed elite athletes with exercise-induced bronchoconstriction. *British Journal of Sports Medicine*, 45, 1126–1131.

Dickinson, J. W., Whyte, G. P., McConnell, A. K. and Harries, M. (2006). Screening elite winter athletes for exercise induced asthma: A comparison of three challenge methods. *British Journal of Sports Medicine*, 40, 179–182.

Hallstrand, T. S., Leuppi, J. D., Joos, G., Hall, G. L., Carlsen, K. H., Kaminsky, D. A., Coates, A. L., Cockcroft, D. W., Culver, B. H., Diamant, Z., Gauvreau, G. M., Horvath, I., de Jongh, F. H. C., Laube, B. L., Sterk, P. J. and Wanger, J. (2018). American Thoracic Society (ATS)/European Respiratory Society (ERS) bronchoprovocation testing task force: ERS technical standard on bronchial challenge testing: Pathophysiology and methodology of indirect airway challenge testing. *European Respiratory Journal*, 52(5), 1801033.

Holzer, K., Anderson, S. D., Chan, H. K. and Douglass, J. (2003). Mannitol as a challenge test to identify exercise-induced bronchoconstriction in elite athletes. *American Journal of Respiratory Critical Care Medicine*, 167, 534–537.

Laveneziana, P., Albuquerque, A., Aliverti, A., Babb, T., Barreiro, E., Dres, M., Dubé, B. P., Fauroux, B., Gea, J., Guenette, J. A., Hudson, A. L., Kabitz, H. J., Laghi, F., Langer, D., Luo, Y. M., Neder, J. A., O'Donnell, D., Polkey, M. I., Rabinovich, R. A., Rossi, A., Series, F., Similowski, T., Spengler, C. M., Vogiatzis, I. and Verges, S. (2019). ERS statement on respiratory muscle testing at rest and during exercise. *European Respiratory Journal*, 53(6), 1801214.

Rundell, K. W., Im, J., Mayers, L. B., Wilber, R. L., Szmedra, L. and Schmitz, H. R. (2001). Self-reported symptoms and exercise-induced asthma in the elite athlete. *Medicine and Science in Sports and Exercise*, 33, 208–213.

Sylvester, K. P., Clayton, N., Cliff, I., Hepple, M., Kendrick, A., Kirkby, J., Miller, M., Moore, A., Rafferty, G. F., O'Reilly, L., Shakespeare, J., Smith, L., Watts, T., Bucknall, M. and Butterfield, K. (2020). ARTP statement on pulmonary function testing 2020. *BMJ Open Respiratory Research*, 7(1), e000575.

3.4   Surface anthropometry

Susan C. Lennie

Anthropometry is defined as 'measurement of the human body'. Surface anthropometry may therefore be defined as the science of acquiring and utilising surface dimensional measurements which describe the human phenotype. Measurements of mass, stature, skeletal breadths, segment lengths, girths and skinfolds are used, either as raw data or derived ratios or predicted values to describe human size, proportions, shape, composition and symmetry, or to infer aspects of nutritional status or physical performance. Historically, anthropometry draws from diverse disciplines including anatomy, physiology, nutrition and medicine, and the multiplicity of methodologies which prevail may cause some confusion for the exercise scientist in practice today, and impact the comparability of data. The current definitive guide for all anthropometric procedures is the International Society for the Advancement of Kinanthropometry (ISAK) standards manual (Esparza-Ros et al., 2019). The purpose of this chapter is to summarise key principles and methods for measuring stature, mass and the most commonly used skinfolds and girths.

Measurement pre-requisites

For all measurements, participants require appropriate information in advance, and informed written consent should be obtained. Anthropometry requires a spacious (minimum 3 m x 3 m) well-illuminated area, affording privacy. Room temperature should ensure participant comfort. Participants should present for measurement in suitable apparel, recovered from previous exercise, fully hydrated and voided. Clothing should conform to the natural contours of the skin and allow easy access for landmarking and measurement. For males, running shorts or swimwear is ideal, and for females, either a two-piece swimming costume, or running shorts and a sports top which exposes the shoulders and abdominal area, are suitable. One-piece swimwear, rowing suits or leotards are *not* suitable. Some participants may prefer a loose-fitting shirt which can be lifted to access measurement sites. All measurements (except hip girth, which is measured over close fitting clothing for reasons of modesty) are performed on clean, dry, unbroken skin. Cultural differences may preclude the acquisition of some or all measurements in some participants. Measurement of females or children by male anthropometrists requires particular sensitivity and the individual's entitlement to a chaperone. It is

DOI: 10.4324/9781003045267-16

always advisable to have another adult (preferably female) present in such circumstances. (Refer to Chapter 1.4.)

Recommended equipment

Stadiometer – (e.g., Holtain, Crosswell, Crymych, UK, or SECA, Birmingham, UK) mounted on wall or stand with sliding headboard and accurate to 0.1 cm.

Weighing scales – calibrated and graduated to 100 g, suggested range to be up to 150 kg (e.g., SECA, Birmingham, UK).

Skinfold calipers – Harpenden (British Indicators, c/o Assist Creative Resources, Wrexham, UK) calibrated annually to 10 g·mm^2, scale to 80 mm in new models, 40 mm in old ones, which can be read to 0.1 mm by interpolation. Holtain (Crosswell, Crymych, UK) calipers are of similar quality and can be used with equal precision.

Anthropometric tape – flexible metal tape, no wider that 7 mm, with automatic retraction to an enclosed case. A blank 'stub' extending several centimetres beyond the zero line is required. The Rosscraft anthropometric tape (Rosscraft Innovations Inc, Vancouver, Canada) is a modified version of the Lufkin W606PM (Cooper Industries, USA). Both can be read to 0.1 cm and are recommended.

Segmometer – A flexible metal tape with rigid sliding branches for identifying lengths and landmark locations, e.g., Cescorf Segmometer (Cescorf, Porto Alegre, Brazil), or UWA Segmometer (University of Western Australia, Crawley, Australia), read to 0.1 cm.

Anthropometric box – made from plywood or a strong fibre-board equivalent capable of supporting an individual who may weigh 150 kg. The box should be 30 cm x 40 cm x 50 m, to facilitate ease of measuring participants of differing size, with a cut-out at the base for the participant's feet to be positioned during some measures. Commercial anthropometric boxes are available: Anthropometric Box (Scullion Bruce, Aberdeen, UK) or Anthropobox (CartonLab, Murcia, Spain).

Procedures

Descriptions of anthropometric techniques may appear simple but require a high level of technical skill to ensure accuracy and repeatability. Care should be taken at the preparatory stage to confirm calibration of equipment, participant positioning and measurement site location. During measurement, anthropometrists should read values within their line of sight to avoid data error arising from parallax.

Stretch stature is measured to 0.1 cm without footwear and with the head in the Frankfort plane (orbitale and tragion are horizontally aligned). The heels are together, and the back should be in contact with the scale of the stadiometer. The participant inspires for measurement, and the recorder brings down the headboard to compress the hair whilst the anthropometrist applies upward traction to the head to compensate for diurnal variation.

Arm span is measured to 0.1 cm, with the heels, buttocks, upper back and dorsal aspect of the arms against a wall. The arms are stretched maximally and horizontally at 90 degrees, and the measurement is taken at maximal inspiration.

Body mass is measured to 0.1 kg. The participant wears exercise apparel or light clothing but no footwear. If nude mass is required, clothing can be weighed separately. Measurements should be taken after voiding, and 12 hours after food, or record the time of day to consider the impact of diurnal variation.

Skinfolds

Skeletal landmarks (bony locations defining skinfold measurement sites) are located via palpation of overlying soft tissue, or measurement from a palpable site. Since some measurements vary considerably over a short distance, landmarking the correct site is essential for reproducible measurements (Hume and Marfell-Jones, 2008). Landmarks should be located generally and then released. They should then be re-located specifically before marking, since the skin can move several centimetres in relation to underlying bone. Skinfold locations are marked with a cross, with two lines intersecting at right angles, or other similar symbol when there may be cultural concerns. A longer line should represent the orientation of the skinfold, and the shorter line should define the finger and thumb placement. Bony edges are commonly marked with a short (0.5 cm) line, while points (e.g., the inferior tip of the scapula) are marked with a dot, from which linear measurements are made. Measurements should be made on the *right* side of the body, unless prevented by injury; variations in protocol should be recorded. Left-handed participants may have greater muscle mass on the left limb, in which case measurements on both sides can be recorded. Skinfold locations are described in Table 3.4.1.

Participants are encouraged to relax their muscles before measurement to reduce discomfort and improve reproducibility. Ensure the skin is dry and unbroken, and the landmark is clearly visible. The anthropometrist's left hand approaches the participant's skin surface at 90 degrees. The skinfold is raised at the marked site, with the shorter line visible at the edge of the anthropometrist's forefinger and thumb. The fold is grasped firmly in the required orientation, following natural cleavage lines of the skin and raised far enough (but no further) so the fold has parallel sides. Palpation helps avoid incorporating underlying muscle into the grasp. The near edges of the caliper blades are applied to the raised fold 1 cm away from the thumb and forefinger, at a depth of mid-fingernail.

The calipers are held at 90 degrees to the skinfold and, with the skinfold held at all times, the spring pressure is released allowing compression with the full force of the jaws and the measurement value is recorded at 2 s. In the case of large skinfolds, the needle is likely to be moving at this time, but the value is recorded nonetheless. The calipers are removed before the skinfold is released. Measurements should be made in series – moving from one site to the next until the entire protocol is complete – and repeated thereafter according to the measurement proforma.

Table 3.4.1 Skinfold measurements

Skinfold	Location and Landmarking	Orientation	Body Position for Measurement
Triceps[a]	Mid-point of a straight line between the acromiale and the radiale on the posterior aspect of the arm	Vertical	Standing; Shoulder slightly externally rotated
Subscapular	2 cm lateral and 2 cm inferior to the inferior angle of the scapula	Oblique – ~45-degree angle laterally	Standing
Biceps[a]	Mid-point level of a straight line between the acromiale and the radiale on the anterior aspect of the arm	Vertical	Standing; Shoulder slightly externally rotated
Iliac crest	Immediately superior to the crest of the ilium, on the ilio-axilla line	Near horizontal	Standing; Right arm placed across torso
Supraspinale	The intersection of a horizontal line drawn from the crest of the ilium, with a line joining the anterior superior iliac spine and the anterior axillary fold	Oblique	Standing
Abdominal	5 cm lateral of the midpoint of the umbilicus	Vertical	Standing
Thigh[a]	Mid-point of the perpendicular distance between the inguinal crease at the mid-line of the thigh and the mid-point of the posterior border of the patella when seated with the knee flexed to 90 degrees	Longitudinal	Sitting with leg extended and foot supported, the participant extends the knee and clasps hands under hamstrings and lifts gently for measurement
Medial calf	The most medial aspect of the calf, at the level of maximum girth, with participant standing and weight evenly distributed	Vertical	Standing, foot on box, with knee at 90 degrees

Note: [a] These sites ideally require a wide-spreading caliper or segmometer to locate, since curvature of the skin surface affects site location if a tape is used.

Girths

A cross-handed technique is used with the stub held in the left hand, and the case in the right hand. Approaching from the side of the particpant, the stub is passed around the body segment, grasped by the right hand, and then passed back to the left hand which pulls it to the appropriate tension. The middle fingers of both hands can then be used for 'pinning' the tape and moving it a short distance up or down, maintaining its orientation 90 degrees to the long axis of the segment. There should be no visible indentation of the skin at the measurement. In the case of maximal measurements, it is necessary to measure lesser measurements superior and inferior to the final measurement site. If the skin surface is concave, the tape spans the concavity in a straight line. For torso girths, limb position may influence the result so care should be taken to follow standardised protocols (Lennie et al., 2013), and measurements should be made at the end of a normal expiration (Table 3.4.2).

Measurement error

The *mean* of duplicate or the *median* of triplicate measures (when the first two measures differ by more than 5% for skinfolds and 1% for other measures) is recommended to minimise errors as a result of technical variation. Error magnitude varies with the recorder, the measurement type and site, and should be reported as the technical error of measurement (TEM) and expressed as a percentage of the measurement value (Perini et al., 2005).

$$\text{TEM } [(x_2 x_1)^2] \cdot 2n^1$$
$$\% \text{ TEM } 100 \cdot \text{TEM} \cdot m^1$$

In which x_1 and x_2 are replicate pairs of measures, n is the number of pairs and m is the mean value for that measure across the sample.

Table 3.4.2 Girth measurements

Girth	Location	Body Position	Notes
Chest	At level of mid-sternum	Arms abducted slightly	Measure at the end of a normal expiration
Waist	Narrowest circumference between thorax and pelvis	Arms folded, fingertips lightly touching shoulders	Mid-point between iliac crest and tenth rib, if no obvious narrowing
Hip	At the level of maximum posterior protuberance of buttocks	Relaxed, feet together	Measure from the side, over clothing
Upper arm	Mid-acromiale-radiale	Arm abducted slightly, elbow extended	
Arm flexed and tensed	Peak of contracted biceps brachii	Arm forward at 90 degrees horizontally, elbow flexed at 90 degrees and forearm supinated	Measure at maximal contraction
Forearm	Maximum	Shoulder slightly flexed, elbow extended	
Mid-thigh	Mid-trochanterion – tibiale laterale level	Weight equally distributed	
Calf	Maximum	Weight equally distributed	

The TEM is generally used to determine intra-observer error but can also be used to express inter-observer error when two anthropometrists are independently measuring the same participants.

For serial measurements, a statistical basis for detecting real change should be included. Since the TEM equates to the standard error of a single measurement, then overlapping standard errors indicate no significant change in serial measures – either at the 68% (for 1SE) or 95% (for 2SE) level. Clearly, experienced anthropometrists with low TEMs are several times more likely to detect real change than others.

Interpretation of anthropometric data

The conversion of raw data into indices may be justified in terms of fat patterning (Stewart, 2003) (skinfold ratios), corrected girths (Martin et al., 1990), proportions (the ratio of segment lengths) or anthropometric somatotype (Heath and Carter, 1967). Corrected girths involve subtracting the skinfold multiplied by pi from the limb girth and are a useful surrogate for muscularity. Predicting tissue masses of fat (López-Taylor et al., 2018) or muscle (González-Mendoza et al., 2019) has obvious appeal but is problematic (Stewart and Ackland, 2018). Numerous methodological assumptions, such as tissue density, govern the conversion of linear surface measurements into tissue mass, and sample specificity restricts the utility of many equations. If used, the same prediction formulas should be used on all occasions and should be accompanied by the standard error of the estimate or confidence limits, as well as total error of prediction equations (Stewart and Hannan, 2000). The use of raw anthropometric data, such as the sum of skinfolds, is becoming more accepted as a surrogate to quantifying tissue mass (Ackland et al., 2012) and is to be encouraged. For example, Vaquero-Cristóbal et al. (2020) reported positive moderate to high correlations ($r = 0.613$ to 0.849) between fat mass prediction equations and the sums of six and eight skinfolds. Sex- and sport-specific anthropometric reference data are limited (Santos et al., 2014); however, smaller research studies may provide adequate comparisons in specific situations for the exercise scientist in practice.

Conclusion

Surface anthropometry plays an important role in the estimation of body composition and identifying the effect of training regimens. Its portability, together with improvements in defining procedures and control of error, maintain its relevance despite the emergence of newer imaging technologies. Selection of appropriate measures, equipment and attention to measurement procedures are essential to maximising accuracy, reliability and repeatability of results.

References

Ackland, T. R., Lohman, T. G., Sundgot-Borgen, J., Maughan, R. J., Meyer, N. L., Stewart, A. D. and Muller, W. (2012). Current status of body composition assessment in sport. *Sports Medicine*, 42, 227–240.

Esparza-Ros, R., Vaquero-Cristóbal, R. and Marfell-Jones, M. (2019). *International Standards for Anthropometric Assessment*. Spain: Catholic University San Antonio of Murcia.

González-Mendoza, R. G., Gaytán-González, A., Jiménez-Alvarado, J. A., Villegas-Balcázar, M., Jáuregui-Ulloa, E. E., Torres-Naranjo, F. and López-Taylor, J. R. (2019). Accuracy of anthropometric equations to estimate DXA-derived skeletal muscle mass in professional male soccer players. *Journal of Sports Medicine*. 2019. https://doi.org/10.1155/2019/4387636

Heath, B. H. and Carter, J. E. L. (1967). A modified somatotype method. *American Journal of Physical Anthropology*, 27, 57–74.

Hume, P. and Marfell-Jones, M. (2008). The importance of accurate site location for skinfold measurement. *Journal of Sport Sciences*, 26, 1333–1340.

Lennie, S. C., Amofa-Diatuo, T., Nevill, A. and Stewart, A. D. (2013). Protocol variations in arm position influence the magnitude of waist girth. *Journal of Sport Sciences*, 31, 1353–1358.

López-Taylor, J. R., González-Mendoza, R. G., Gaytán-González, A., Jiménez-Alvarado, J. A., Villegas-Balcázar, M., Jáuregui-Ulloa, E. E. and Torres-Naranjo, F. (2018). Accuracy of anthropometric equations for estimating body fat in professional male soccer players compared with DXA. *Journal of Sports Medicine*. 2018. https://doi.org/10.1155/2018/6843792

Martin, A. D., Spenst, L. F., Drinkwater, D. T. and Clarys, J. P. (1990). Anthropometric estimation of muscle mass in men. *Medicine and Science in Sports and Exercise*, 22, 729–733.

Perini, R. A., de Oliveira, G. L., dos Santos Ornellas, J. and de Oliveira, F. P. (2005). Technical error of measurement in anthropometry. *Revista Brasileira de Medicina do Esporte*, 11, 86–90.

Santos, D. A., Dawson, J. A., Matias, C. N., Rocha, P. M., Minderico, C. S., Allison, D. B., Sardinha, L. B. and Silva. A. M. (2014). Reference values for body composition and anthropometric measurements in athletes. *PLoS One*, 9(5), e97846.

Stewart, A. D. (2003). Anthropometric fat patterning in male and female subjects. In T. Reilly and M. Marfell-Jones (eds.), *Kinanthropometry VIII*, pp. 195–202. London: Routledge.

Stewart, A. D. and Ackland, T. (2018). Anthropometry in physical performance and health. In H. C. Lukaski (ed.), *Body Composition: Health and Performance in Exercise and Sport*, pp. 89–108. Boca Raton: CRC Press.

Stewart, A. D. and Hannan, W. J. (2000). Prediction of fat and fat free mass in male athletes using dual X-ray absorptiometry as the reference method. *Journal of Sports Sciences*, 18, 263–274.

Vaquero-Cristóbal, R., Albaladejo-Saura, M., Luna-Badachi, A. E. and Esparza-Ros, R. (2020). Differences in fat mass estimation formulas in physically active adult population and relationship with sums of skinfolds. *International Journal of Environmental Research and Public Health*, 17, 7777.

3.5 Functional screening

Mike Duncan, Stuart Elwell and Mark Lyons

Functional movement screening is a process that is highly debated and has become widely used within the sport and exercise sciences with both general and athletic populations (Cook et al., 2010). This chapter will provide an overview of functional screening to guide sport and exercise scientists in their selection and use of screening tools in practice. Functional movement screening is defined by the International Movement Screening and Interventions Group (IMSIG, 2016) as the quantitative or qualitative observation of a single movement and/or a composite battery of movements. Such a broad focus has resulted in numerous movement screens being developed that assess different aspects of movement, often with varying degrees of validity and reliability. It is therefore important for sport and exercise scientists to understand the main forms of functional screening tests and the key challenges when employing them with both general and athletic populations. Functional screening tests can broadly be distinguished into two types of testing: Quantitative Movement Tests (QMTs) and Movement Quality Tests (MQTs).

Quantitative Movement Tests: QMTs are more commonly considered akin to physical fitness tests and include the quantitative measurement of strength and power, often through multi-joint movements. Tests such as the Triple Hop Test, Y-Balance Test or the Six-Foot Timed Up and Go Test constitute QMTs in which outcomes tend to be continuous, such as distance covered or repetitions completed. QMTs are sometimes referred to as physical performance or functional fitness tests.

Movement Quality Tests: MQTs are more commonly considered 'functional screens' and include identification and rating of movement patterns. This includes compensations, asymmetries, efficiency of movement through transitional (e.g., sit-to-stand) or dynamic (e.g., hopping, landing) movement tasks. Outcomes from MQTs tend to provide a classification of movement quality using some form of scoring system. These typically categorise movement as dichotomous (e.g., movement present vs. not present or pass/fail) or trichotomous (e.g., poor/fair/good) classifications. Some MQTs have more than three categories and others such as the Functional Movement Screen use a numerical tetrachotomous classification applied to a series of different movements which can then be summed to represent overall functional movement quality. For the majority of MQTs, specific training in administration and scoring of the different functional screens available is required.

DOI: 10.4324/9781003045267-17

Why employ functional screening?

Functional screens have been employed for a variety of reasons and while marker-based motion capture and electromyography have become the gold standard for evaluating movement patterns and biomechanical musculoskeletal deficits in sport and exercise science (Kraus et al., 2014), functional screens tend to be used in real-world settings to provide an appraisal of movement quality. Numerous functional screens have been developed for use in athletic and general populations with the most widely used being the Functional Movement Screen (FMS) (Cook et al., 2010) and the Landing Error Scoring System (LESS) (Padua et al., 2009). These two screens will be outlined in greater depth in the next section.

Irrespective of which functional screen is selected, they are most commonly employed for one or more reasons including, but not limited to:

* Determining movement quality
* Identifying risk (of injury)
* Guiding management and prevention strategies

Commonly used functional screening tools

Functional movement screen

The FMS, developed by Cook et al. (1998), was developed under the assumption that strength, movement, flexibility and stability are pre-requisites for optimal athletic performance; it is one of the most widely used functional screens world-wide. The FMS comprises seven movements that, combined, provide a screening tool to assess functional mobility and postural stability in different settings without locomotion. The FMS involves seven tests that examine three different levels of movement difficulty. The squat, lunge and hurdle step tests are described as higher-level patterns which are proposed to examine the three essential foot positions taken up in sport. The rotary stability and press-up tests are known as transitionary patterns and predominantly assess tri-planar and sagittal stability. Finally, the primitive mobility patterns of the body are assessed by the active straight leg raise and the shoulder mobility tests (Cook et al., 2010). The tests within the FMS can be scored individually or summed to reflect a composite functional movement score (Cook et al., 2006). Performance of each test is rated on a scale of 0–3 by an assessor. A score of 0 is given if pain occurs during the test, 1 if the participant cannot perform the movement, 2 if the participant can perform the movement but with some form of compensation and 3 if the movement is performed correctly by the participant (Cook et al., 2006). The maximum score attainable in the FMS is 21, although more recently, a 100-point scoring scale has been developed (Butler et al., 2012), which is suggested to be more sensitive and useful in research contexts, whereas the 21 point scale may be more practical in applied situations. Within the FMS, a score of 3 is taken as 'correct' movement and anything less than this, per individual test, indicates a 'compensatory movement pattern' which leads to individuals 'sacrificing efficient movements for inefficient ones' (Cook et al., 2006).

Current research suggests that performance on the FMS is related to physical activity and obesity in children (Duncan and Stanley, 2012), injury prevalence in professional athletes (Bushman et al., 2016), fitness test performance in military recruits (Lisman et al., 2013) and performance improvement in track and field athletes (Chapman et al., 2014). An arbitrary cut-off value of 14 in the FMS has been associated with greater/lower injury risk but is controversial in the literature (Monaco and Schoenfeld, 2019) and the sensitivity and specificity of the FMS in predicting injury has been questioned (Monaco and Schoenfeld, 2019). The FMS demonstrates good inter-and intra-rater reliability (Bonazza et al., 2017, inter-rater ICC = 0.84; intra-rater ICC = 0.81), but its validity in relation to injury prediction is questionable (Monaco and Schoenfeld, 2019). This has led to recommendations that the FMS is useful and valid as a screen to assess the quality of human movement (not injury) and should be employed by practitioners as such (Monaco and Schoenfeld, 2019).

The landing error scoring system

The LESS was developed to provide a standardised instrument to identify potentially high-risk movement patterns ('errors') during a jump-landing manoeuvre (Padua et al., 2009). The jump-landing task includes both vertical and horizontal movements as participants jump forward off a 30 cm-high box to a distance equal to 50% of their height away from the box. On landing, they immediately rebound for a maximal vertical jump with instruction to jump as high as they can once they land from the box. Trials are video recorded from the frontal and sagittal planes for subsequent scoring.

The LESS score is simply a count of landing technique 'errors' on a range of readily observable items of human movement. A higher LESS score indicates poor technique in landing from a jump; a lower LESS score indicates better jump-landing technique. There are 17 scored items in the LESS (see Padua et al., 2009 for operational definitions and scoring details of each item) derived from previous research that identified specific movements that may contribute to increased risk of injury; particularly anterior cruciate ligament (ACL) injury (Padua et al., 2009). Items 1–15 are scored dichotomously as either 1 or 0. Items 16 and 17 score values 0, 1 or 2 depending on joint displacement and overall impression of technique, respectively. Scores of <5 are regarded as 'good' and assume low risk for ACL injury. A maximal score of 19 can be reached for exceptionally poor performance.

Studies to date (Padua et al., 2009; Onate et al., 2010) report good to excellent inter- and intra-rater reliability for the screen (inter-rater kappa = 0.459–0.875 [Onate et al., 2010], ICC = 0.84 [Padua et al., 2009]; intra-rater ICC = 0.84–0.91 [Padua et al., 2009; Onate et al., 2010]). There is conflicting and limited evidence, however, related to the ability of the LESS to predict injury with some studies finding no relationship between LESS scores and ACL injury risk (Smith et al., 2013) and others reporting significantly poorer LESS scores in athletes sustaining ACL injuries over a season compared to uninjured athletes (Padua et al., 2015).

Finally, Everard et al. (2017), while examining the relationship between the FMS and LESS, found a significant moderate correlation between FMS and LESS scores but poor shared variance. Performing well in one of the screens, therefore, does not necessarily equate to performing well in the other and both screens should not be used interchangeably.

Conclusion

Functional screening, as a process, provides effective means to assess movement quality and outcomes in general and athletic populations. There are validated and reliable tools such as the FMS and the LESS that can be used to determine movement quality and guide management of training programmes and pre/rehabilitation. However, the evidence relating to the ability of functional screens to be a sole means of determining injury risk is less robust, and functional screens should instead be used as a collective of filters to qualify relative risk of injury with physical activity.

References

Bonazza, N. A., Smuin, D., Onks, C. A., Silvis, M. L. and Dhawan, A. (2017). Reliability, validity, and injury predictive value of the functional movement screen: A systematic review and meta-analysis. *American Journal of Sports Medicine*, 45, 725–732.

Bushman, T. T., Grier, T. L. and Canham-Chervak, M. (2016). The functional movement screen and injury risk: Association and predictive value in active men. *American Journal of Sports Medicine*, 44(2), 297–304.

Butler, R. J., Plisky, P. J. and Kiesel, K. B. (2012). Interrater reliability of videotaped performance on the functional movement screen using the 100-point scoring scale. *Athletic Training & Sports Health Care*, 4(3), 103–109.

Chapman, R. F., Laymon, A. S. and Arnold, T. (2014). Functional movement scores and longitudinal performance outcomes in elite track and field athletes. *International Journal of Sports Physiology and Performance*, 9(2), 203–211. https://doi.org/10.1123/ijspp.2012-0329

Cook, G., Burton, L., Fields, K. and Kiesel, K. (1998). *The Functional Movement Screen*. Danville, VA: Athletic Testing Services Inc.

Cook, G., Burton, L. and Hoogenboom, B. (2006). Pre-participation screening: The use of fundamental movements as an assessment of function – Part 1. *North American Journal of Sports Physical Therapy*, 1, 62.

Cook, G., Hoogenboom, B., Burton, L., Plisky, P. and Rose, G. (2010). *Movement*. Santa Cruz, CA, USA: On Target Publications.

Duncan, M. J. and Stanley, M. (2012). Functional movement is negatively associated with weight status and positively associated with physical activity in British primary school children. *Journal of Obesity*, (7244), 697563.

Everard, E. M., Harrison, A. J. and Lyons, M. (2017). Examining the relationship between the functional movement screen and the landing error scoring system in an active, male collegiate population. *Journal of Strength and Conditioning Research*, 31(5), 1265–1272.

IMSIG. (2016). *Working definitions of movement screening* [WWW document]. https://www. sportsarthritisresearchuk.org/international-movement-screening-and-interventions-group-imsig/working-definitions-of-movement-screening.aspx (accessed 25 October 2021).

Kraus, K., Schutz, E., Taylor, W. R. and Doyscher, R. (2014). Efficacy of the functional movement screen: A review. *Journal of Strength and Conditioning Research*, 28(12), 3571–3584.

Lisman, P., O'Connor, F. G., Deuster, P. A. and Knapik, J. J. (2013). Functional movement screen and aerobic fitness predict injuries in military training. *Medicine and Science in Sports and Exercise*, 45(4), 636–643.

Monaco, J.-T. and Schoenfeld, B. J. (2019). A review of the current literature on the utility of the functional movement screen as a screening tool to identify athletes' risk for injury. *Strength & Conditioning Journal*, 41, 17–23. https://doi.org/10.1519/SSC. 0000000000000481

Onate, J., Cortes, N. and Welch, C. (2010). Expert versus novice inter-rater reliability and criterion validity of the landing error scoring system. *Journal of Sport Rehabilitation*, 19(1), 41–48.

Padua, D. A., DiStefano, L. J., Beutler, A. I., de la Motte, S. J., DiStefano, M. J. and Marshall, S. W. (2015). The landing error scoring system as a screening tool for an anterior cruciate ligament injury-prevention program in elite-youth soccer athletes. *Journal of Athletic Training*, 50, 589–595. https://doi.org/10.4085/1062-6050-50.1.10

Padua, D. A., Marshall, S. W., Boling, M. C., Thigpen, C. A., Garrett, W. E. and Beutler, A. I. (2009). The Landing Error Scoring System (LESS) is a valid and reliable clinical assessment tool of jump-landing Biomechanics the JUMP-ACL study. *American Journal of Sports Medicine*, 37(10), 1996–2002.

Smith, C. A., Chimera, N. J., Wright, N. J. and Warren, M. (2013). Interrater and intrarater reliability of the functional movement screen. *Journal of Strength and Conditoning Research*, 27, 982–987. https://doi.org/10.1519/JSC.0b013e3182606df2

3.6 Assessment of free-living energy expenditure

Enhad A. Chowdhury, Oliver J. Peacock and Dylan Thompson

Measurement and understanding of energy expenditure (EE) are important for many applications, such as researchers trying to characterise an intervention, or practitioners/clinicians attempting to establish the energy demands of an athlete or patient. As one half of the energy balance equation, energy expenditure plays a critical part in both the short-term regulation of physiology and the longer-term regulation of energy balance, ultimately determining body mass and composition.

The three main components of energy expenditure are:

Resting Metabolic Rate (RMR), which is the largest single component of EE in most individuals, is the energy required by the body at rest. RMR can be assessed using laboratory methods for the determination of EE (see Compher et al., 2006 for considerations). However, in most cases, RMR is estimated using prediction equations commonly based on sex, age, stature and mass. Specific equations may be required, since accuracy can be population-dependent (Bedogni et al., 2019).

Diet-Induced Thermogenesis (DIT), which represents increased expenditure above RMR due to food intake, is the smallest component of EE. In free-living contexts, DIT is commonly assumed to be 10% of energy intake (or expenditure, if an individual is in energy balance) (Westerterp, 2004).

Physical Activity Energy Expenditure (PAEE), which is expenditure above rest associated with bodily movement, is the most malleable component of EE. Inter-individual differences can be considerable due to variation in physical activity behaviour (see Chapter 3.13 for details) and, thus, this chapter will specifically focus on categories of methods for assessing PAEE as the most variable sub-component of EE.

Methods for assessing PAEE

Due to the rapid evolution of technologies and large volume of measurement devices, this section will consider general principles and guidance relating to broad approaches for determining PAEE in ambulatory adults. Historically,

DOI: 10.4324/9781003045267-18

measurement of PAEE was often based upon various self-report measures, but these instruments are constrained to ranking of individuals at best. Individuals tend to over-report PAEE, with the degree also varying dependent upon participant characteristics, resulting in systematic and random errors. As such, these instruments have extremely limited use for determining absolute EE or PAEE (see Dhurandhar et al., 2015 for critique). Therefore, subsequent focus will predominantly be on device-based measures of EE/PAEE.

Doubly labelled water (DLW): DLW is widely considered the 'gold standard' measure of free-living EE and often used for method validation. DLW relies upon measurement of labelled isotope elimination as a way of determining carbon dioxide production (and, indirectly, metabolic rate). Access to DLW is limited because specialised centres are needed to analyse samples, and cost is prohibitive for many applications. If the objective is the most accurate assessment of total EE during a free-living period (e.g., 7–14 days), and budget is not a consideration, DLW is the best choice. However, DLW is not perfect, a key limitation being despite providing accurate *total* EE estimation (PAEE is derived by subtracting RMR and DIT), DLW provides no information on the intensities or distributions of physical activity (see Westerterp, 2017 for DLW overview).

Heart rate monitors: The use of heart rate (HR) is based upon the relatively linear relationship between HR and EE in most individuals and is relatively accessible. Accuracy of EE estimation from HR is best during moderate- to high-intensity activity, and on an individual level is improved with calibration of the HR-EE relationship around the Flex-HR concept that uses a threshold HR to differentiate between separate 'resting' and 'active' HR-EE relationships (Leonard, 2003).

Accelerometers: Accelerometers can be used to convert movement 'counts' to PAEE estimates using various (potentially proprietary) models specific to devices/populations. Some devices have been validated against DLW in adults (White et al., 2016, 2019). Accelerometers were historically hip/waist-mounted but are increasingly worn at other locations (e.g., wrist). Accelerometers are inexpensive, generally easy to use, and often the device of choice for small- to medium-size research studies.

Combined devices: Due to theoretically independent limitations associated with accelerometry (e.g., specific activities not generating acceleration) and HR (e.g., values changing due to confounding factors such as stress), the combination of these measurements has been suggested. This technique requires mathematical modelling to balance estimation between accelerometry or HR based on pre-determined criteria (Brage et al., 2004). Such combined instruments are commercially available but practitioners could, in principle, develop their own approach using a carefully synchronised HR monitor and accelerometer. This is an area of innovation, particularly within the commercial sector, and new devices are drawing on other (combined) physiological measures to try to improve estimation of PAEE.

Consumer devices: In applied settings, practitioners are likely to encounter many different consumer devices, often marketed with an array of sensors. These devices are also increasingly utilised in research settings, with some blurring of the lines between 'research' and 'consumer' devices. As a note of caution, the precise methodology is usually proprietary and, due to the pace of product development, independent validation is often unavailable. While these commercial devices to date do not seem to match estimates of EE from research devices (O'Driscoll et al., 2020), they are often affordable for practitioners. Some devices provide reasonable estimates that may be useful for observing behaviour changes, but users should be aware of potentially large variation between devices (Chowdhury et al., 2017).

Expression of energy expenditure data

Depending on the application, the most straightforward expression of EE is total kilojoules or kilocalories expended ('calories' to lay individuals). However, users should consider that body size substantially influences total EE estimates, so benchmarking between individuals is often advisable using normalised data. A common method of normalisation is to use physical activity level (PAL), which represents total EE (DIT+RMR+PAEE) divided by RMR, giving comparability across individuals (Figure 3.6.1). PAL could theoretically be as low as 1.10 in a

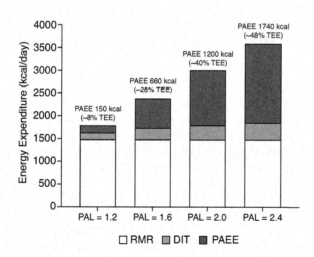

Figure 3.6.1 Illustration of the possible relative contribution and variability of physical activity energy Expenditure.

bed-bound individual, with most individuals falling between 1.40 and 2.00 (see FAO/WHO/UNU, 2004 for population benchmarks). In extremely active individuals (e.g., athletes) the greatest *sustainable* EE is represented by a PAL of ~2.5, due to the corresponding limit on energy intake (Thurber et al., 2019), but PAL may be much higher for short periods.

An example could be an individual with a resting metabolic rate (RMR) of 1,500 kcal/d and a wide range of theoretical physical activity energy expenditures (PAEE). The physical activity level (PAL) values represent an extremely sedentary lifestyle that may be related to a movement-limiting pathology (1.2), a low-activity lifestyle (1.6), the lower boundary of a highly active lifestyle (2.0) and reaching the upper limit of a sustainable lifestyle (2.4). It should be noted that the majority of the population falls within a PAL range of 1.4–2.0. Diet-induced thermogenesis (DIT) has been assumed at 10% of total energy expenditure.

Considerations for application

From a pragmatic perspective, the choice of EE measure is likely to be determined by logistical restrictions. Researchers are likely to have more options than practitioners, but some underlying principles apply across all settings. Potential users should consider the necessary monitoring duration to achieve desired objectives for daily wear time (illustration in Chapter 3.13), and number and nature (weekday/weekend) of representative measurement days (Scheers et al., 2012). Practitioners should bear in mind that, while many approaches produce reasonable group-level EE estimates often sufficient for research interventions (see Dowd et al., 2018 for a comprehensive performance overview of validity and reliability of techniques), and are deemed 'validated' on that basis, caution is advised in attempting to provide individual-level information (e.g., exact dietary prescription). All methods struggle to provide highly accurate and precise individual-level estimates of EE, even the 'gold standard' measure of DLW, in which discrepancy to indirect calorimetry can be up to ~20% for an individual (Melanson et al., 2018). Practitioners working in specific populations (e.g., clinical, paediatric) should establish methods as valid and appropriate for their context. Users may decide that, whilst accurate EE estimates might be desired, the reproducibility of measures is more important to monitor or track changes over time. In this scenario, devices with poorer accuracy could be used if measurements are reproducible, but users should bear in mind that absolute estimates of PAEE are unlikely to be 'true' and some behaviours will have been (systematically) over- or under-recorded due to variability in measurement accuracy for different activities (Chowdhury et al., 2017).

As technology develops, the volume and sophistication of options is likely to increase, and researchers and practitioners alike will have opportunities (and challenges) to make the most appropriate choices to capitalise on the many benefits from the measurement of energy expenditure.

References

Bedogni, G., Bertoli, S., Leone, A., De Amicis, R., Lucchetti, E., Agosti, F., Marazzi, N., Battezzati, A. and Sartorio, A. (2019). External validation of equations to estimate resting energy expenditure in 14952 adults with overweight and obesity and 1948 adults with normal weight from Italy. *Clinical Nutrition*, 38(1), 457–464.

Brage, S., Brage, N., Franks, P. W., Ekelund, U., Wong, M. Y., Andersen, L. B., Froberg, K. and Wareham, N. J. (2004). Branched equation modeling of simultaneous accelerometry and heart rate monitoring improves estimate of directly measured physical activity energy expenditure. *Journal of Applied Physiology*, 96(1), 343–351.

Chowdhury, E. A., Western, M. J., Nightingale, T. E., Peacock, O. J. and Thompson, D. (2017). Assessment of laboratory and daily energy expenditure estimates from consumer multi-sensor physical activity monitors. *PLoS One*, 24, 12(2), e0171720.

Compher, C., Frankenfield, D., Keim, N., Roth-Yousey, L. and Evidence Analysis Working Group. (2006). Best practice methods to apply to measurement of resting metabolic rate in adults: A systematic review. *Journal of American Dietetic Association*, 106(6), 881–903.

Dhurandhar, N. V., Schoeller, D., Brown, A. W., Heymsfield, S. B., Thomas, D., Sørensen, T. I., Speakman, J. R., Jeansonne, M., Allison, D. B. and Energy Balance Measurement Working Group. (2015). Energy balance measurement: When something is not better than nothing. *International Journal of Obesity*, 39(7), 1109–1113.

Dowd, K. P., Szeklicki, R., Minetto, M. A., Murphy, M. H., Polito, A., Ghigo, E., van der Ploeg, H., Ekelund, U., Maciaszek, J., Stemplewski, R., Tomczak, M. and Donnelly, A. E. (2018). A systematic literature review of reviews on techniques for physical activity measurement in adults: A DEDIPAC study. *International Journal of Behavioral Nutrition and Physical Activity*, 8, 15(1), 15.

FAO/WHO/UNU. (2004). *Human Energy Requirements*. Rome: FAO Food and Nutrition Report Series 1.

Leonard, W. R. (2003). Measuring human energy expenditure: What have we learned from the flex-heart rate method? *American Journal of Human Biology*, 15(4), 479–489.

Melanson, E. L., Swibas, T., Kohrt, W. M., Catenacci, V. A., Creasy, S. A., Plasqui, G., Wouters, L., Speakman, J. R. and Berman, E. S. F. (2018). Validation of the doubly labeled water method using off-axis integrated cavity output spectroscopy and isotope ratio mass spectrometry. *American Journal of Physiology and Endocrinology and Metabolism*, 314, E124–E130.

O'Driscoll, R., Turicchi, J., Beaulieu, K., Scott, S., Matu, J., Deighton, K., Finlayson, G. and Stubbs, J. (2020). How well do activity monitors estimate energy expenditure? A systematic review and meta-analysis of the validity of current technologies. *British Journal of Sports Medicine*, 54(6), 332–340.

Scheers, T., Philippaerts, R. and Lefevre, J. (2012). Variability in physical activity patterns as measured by the SenseWear Armband: How many days are needed? *European Journal of Applied Physiology*, 112(5), 1653–1662.

Thurber, C., Dugas, L. R., Ocobock, C., Carlson, B., Speakman, J. R. and Pontzer, H. (2019). Extreme events reveal an alimentary limit on sustained maximal human energy expenditure. *Scientific Advances*, 5, 5(6), eaaw0341.

Westerterp, K. R. (2004). Diet induced thermogenesis. *Nutrition and Metabolism*, 18, 1(1), 5.

Westerterp, K. R. (2017). Doubly labelled water assessment of energy expenditure: Principle, practice, and promise. *European Journal of Applied Physiology*, 117(7), 1277–1285.

White, T., Westgate, K., Hollidge, S., Venables, M., Olivier, P., Wareham, N. and Brage, S. (2019). Estimating energy expenditure from wrist and thigh accelerometry in free-living adults: A doubly labelled water study. *International Journal of Obesity*, 43(11), 2333–2342.

White, T., Westgate, K., Wareham, N. J. and Brage, S. (2016). Estimation of physical activity energy expenditure during free-living from wrist accelerometry in UK adults. *PLoS One*, 9, 11(12), e0167472.

3.7   Respiratory gas analysis

Simon Marwood and Richie P. Goulding

Respiratory gas analysis is a cornerstone of physiological testing procedures, perhaps most commonly for the determination of pulmonary gas exchange (PGE) variables, particularly oxygen uptake ($\dot{V}O_2$) and carbon dioxide production ($\dot{V}CO_2$). However, end-tidal gas tensions (PETO$_2$, PETCO$_2$), expired minute ventilation ($\dot{V}_E$) and derived variables such as the respiratory exchange ratio (RER) and ventilatory equivalents ($\dot{V}_E/\dot{V}O_2$, $\dot{V}_E/\dot{V}CO_2$) are widely applied.

Collectively, these measurements provide parameters of human function that can be used to determine metabolic rate, substrate oxidation, exercise economy/efficiency, gas exchange thresholds, gas exchange kinetics and maximal $\dot{V}O_2$. In turn, these parameters of human function can be utilised to evaluate performance, health and causes of exercise intolerance. The purpose of this chapter is to outline key aspects for ensuring the accuracy of respiratory gas data collection and describe methods of data analysis for the subsequent derivation of parameters of physiological function (see supplementary material).

Douglas bag technique

The Douglas bag technique incorporates a mouth-piece (requiring a nose-clip) or face-mask attached via a sample tube to a 100–200 litre polyvinyl chloride sealed 'bag' which captures the expirate via a one-way valve operated by the practitioner. Two one-way valves at the mouth ensure flow of air from the environment to the mouth, and from the mouth to the bag. The discrete and relatively prolonged duration of expired gas collections required for the Douglas bag method indicates that this method is best utilised for steady state gas exchange measurements. Practitioners should be aware of the significant delay (exercise intensities above the gas exchange threshold [GET]), or lack of (exercise intensities above critical power [CP]) achievement of a steady state during high-intensity exercise (Whipp and Ward, 1992). However, this approach may be reasonably utilised during incremental exercise assuming the underlying speed or power output does not continue to change during the period of expired gas collection.

The supplementary material (Section 1) details the calculations for $\dot{V}_E$, $\dot{V}O_2$ and $\dot{V}CO_2$ which provides a basis for understanding error in respiratory gas analysis using the Douglas bag technique. Accordingly, sources of error for the

DOI: 10.4324/9781003045267-19

Douglas bag method include determination of the expired gas fractions, volume and duration of gas collection. The entire apparatus should thus be checked for leaks before commencing measurements with the expirate from a whole number of breaths collected. Timing of gas collection may be improved by the installation of time switches on the Douglas bag valves. The expirate should be analysed immediately upon collection to avoid volume losses and contamination.

Error in the determination of gas fractions (FeO_2 and $FeCO_2$) is highly influential in the calculation of $\dot{V}O_2$ and $\dot{V}CO_2$. A 1% overestimation of FeO_2 leads to a ~3–8% underestimation of $\dot{V}O_2$ for typical moderate- to severe-intensity exercise (respectively), whereas a 1% overestimation in $FeCO_2$ leads to a ~0.2–0.3% underestimation for $\dot{V}O_2$ and a ~1% overestimation for $\dot{V}CO_2$ (Sandals, 2003). The extent of the error for $\dot{V}O_2$ is a function of using FeO_2 twice in its calculation.

Consequently, prior to undertaking measurements, the Douglas bag should be evacuated of any residual air to avoid contamination of the sample. However, air remains within the non-compressible components (i.e., neck, valve). Minimising the volume of these components is desirable. Moreover, by knowing the volume of the non-compressible components and flushing them with a gas of known content (e.g., inspired air) prior to gas evacuation and subsequent collection, it is possible to correct the measured FeO_2 for this residual volume:

$$cFeO_2 = \{mFeO_2(\dot{V}_E + V_{NC}) - V_{NC}*FiO_2\} / \dot{V}_E$$

[$cFeO_2$ and $mFeO_2$: corrected and measured FeO_2, respectively; V_{NC}: volume of non-compressible components; FiO_2 could be replaced by another gas of known concentration such as the O_2 span calibration (see next section)]

Alternatively, the collection of a few seconds of expired gas, followed by rapid flushing of the bag and valve through the collection ports immediately prior to collection of the sample, can similarly eliminate the error due to residual air in the Douglas bag.

Errors may also be made if it is assumed that inspired gas fractions in a laboratory are equivalent to atmospheric, especially if these are standardised to 0.2093 and 0.0003 for O_2 and CO_2 respectively when values of 0.2095 and 0.0004 better represent precise measurement of atmospheric gases (Machta and Hughes, 1970; Keeling et al., 1995). Even in a well-ventilated laboratory with one participant and two practitioners, Sandals (2003) found the mean (95% confidence limits) for FiO_2 and $FiCO_2$ to be 0.20915 ($\pm$0.00035) and 0.0007 ($\pm$0.0003), respectively. These values translated into a systematic error of 0.18% and 0.99% for $\dot{V}O_2$ and $\dot{V}CO_2$, respectively, for typical heavy-intensity exercise when atmospheric conditions were otherwise assumed in the laboratory. The only way to correct for such systematic errors is either to determine average inspired gas fractions over a series of exercise tests in normal laboratory conditions, or preferably to determine inspired gas fractions for every test.

Calibration of the gas analyser is usually through a two-point (zero and span) approach for both O_2 and CO_2, with N_2 being used as the zero setting in both cases. For the O_2 span, either a gravimetrically prepared gas of known O_2 fraction should be used (recommended to be ~0.2 O_2) or the sampling of outside air set at 0.2095 O_2 on the gas analyser. In the latter case, sampling of laboratory air is not an adequate substitute (see previous discussion). For CO_2, a span calibration of 0.04–0.08 is typical, though the higher end of the range is recommended to place typical $FeCO_2$ values approximately at the midpoint of the span.

Accurate determination of the expirate volume is subject to error at the volume-measuring device, the volume of gas removed for fractional composition analysis and the determination of ambient pressure and expirate temperature. Volume is typically determined 'offline' by evacuating the expirate through a dry gas meter. The dry gas meter should be calibrated across a range of known volumes reflective of the test conditions (i.e., exercise intensity range, mode, participant characteristics), delivered to the gas meter from the Douglas bag which itself is filled with a known volume via a gas syringe. The flow rate on the gas meter during this process should match that used during normal testing and analysis. A regression equation can then be derived to correct future meter readings to actual volume. Similarly, the sample flow rate of the fractional gas analyser can be determined by filling a Douglas bag of known volume (using a gas syringe) and timing the emptying of the bag. A barometer with a resolution of 0.05 mmHg should be utilised, with regular accuracy checks performed (WMO, 1996). Temperature probes should have a resolution of 0.1°C; errors here have a cumulative effect since temperature is used twice in the conversion of ambient temperature pressure saturated (ATPS) to standard temperature pressure dry (STPD) (see supplementary material, Section 1). Table 3.7.1 shows potential sources of error, their degree of measurement precision with best-practice approaches as indicated in this chapter and the resultant outcome on the precision in $\dot{V}O_2$ for a 45 s collection of expirate during typical heavy-intensity exercise (Sandals, 2003).

The overall effect of precision of measurement on final $\dot{V}CO_2$ values is similar to that of $\dot{V}O_2$, with precision improving for higher exercise intensities and/or longer expirate sample durations (Sandals, 2003). During typical moderate intensity exercise, precision is ~3% for a 30 s sample duration, improving to <1% during typical severe-intensity exercise with a sample duration of 45 s and above (Sandals, 2003). The duration of gas collection should therefore be considered in the context of the exercise intensity.

Table 3.7.1 Effect of measurement precision on the determined $\dot{V}O_2$ for typical heavy-intensity exercise with 45 s expirate collection

Measurement	Precision in Measurement	Precision in $\dot{V}O_2$ (%)
Expired gas fractions	± 0.0001*	0.34
Residual volume in Douglas bag	± 0.031 l	0.05
Volume for gas fraction analysis	± 0.007 l.min[1]	0.11
Volume (with dry gas meter)	± 0.057 l	0.86
Ambient pressure (via barometer)	± 0.2 mmHg	0.03
Expired gas temperature (via thermistor probe)	± 0.2°C	0.10

*BOC Gases, New Jersey, USA

Breath-by-breath method

Commercial metabolic carts for respiratory gas analysis on a breath-by-breath basis typically incorporate a measurement of ventilatory flow (either via turbine, pitot tube or ultrasonic or variable orifice flowmeter) with simultaneous, continuous sampling of gas fractions by directing samples of expirate to gas analysers. The equipment for flow measurement, with attached sample tubes for gas fractions, is normally held in place using a full-face mask or other apparatus that prevents the mass being held by force applied by the participant at the mouth. Breath-by-breath respiratory gas analysis enables the determination of physiological parameters requiring a more rapid sampling rate than can be accurately achieved using the Douglas bag technique (e.g., $\dot{V}O_2$ kinetics, gas exchange and ventilatory thresholds; see supplementary material). However, the principles outlined earlier to ensure precision for the Douglas bag technique also hold for breath-by-breath measures.

Most metabolic carts utilise chemical and non-dispersive infrared cells for the determination of fractional O_2 and CO_2, respectively. The CO_2 cell is generally very stable unless it accumulates dust; the pump on the metabolic carts should therefore only be on when a suitable particle filter is connected to the sample port. Chemical O_2 cells degrade with time such that 'drift' following calibration is increasingly rapid. Given the small amount of gas required for calibration, it is therefore advised to calibrate for gas fractions prior to every test. Moreover, in light of the issue of FiO2 in laboratory conditions (see previous), careful attention should be paid to the manner in which the metabolic cart determines this variable. Measurement of gas fractions must be time-aligned with flow, since gas fraction analysis will be delayed relative to the measurement of flow. Depending on the system, time alignment may be undertaken during the calibration procedures (which are normally semi-automated) or in a period pre-test with the participant breathing through the system, possibly with additional delay optimisation in-test. In the former case, if following calibration, the sample tubes need to be changed, then the calibration process should be restarted. When utilising hypoxic or hyperoxic gas as the inspirate, the linearity of the O_2 cell should be checked with the manufacturer to see if an alternate span is required for the O_2 calibration. In such cases, the viscosity of inspirate is altered, thus impacting time alignment. Ideally, the gas utilised during the time alignment procedure will therefore match the inspirate.

Calibration of flow should be undertaken across a wide range of flow rates and ideally the calibration should be linear across this range to avoid the use of correction factors in-test. It is advised to check the linearity of the flow calibration with the manufacturer. Common errors arise during this process due to incomplete use of the gas syringe volume, which the user should be careful to avoid.

The validity of PGE measurements with metabolic carts is ideally checked every few weeks by simultaneous measurement of PGE using the Douglas bag technique (assuming that error in the latter is both known and minimised; see earlier). These measurements should be undertaken over a wide range of exercise intensities (moderate, heavy and severe) in a range of participants. A difference of <5% in measurements of PGE and $\dot{V}_E$ is generally considered acceptable in such comparisons (Lamarra et al., 1987). There is considerable breath-to-breath variability in measures of PGE even in the steady state. An effective solution in many situations is to average the PGE values over 10–15 s periods, though this may be inappropriate when determining parameters of PGE kinetics (see supplementary material, Section 5). The user should also discuss with the metabolic cart manufacturer the manner in which lung gas stores are corrected for since changes here will dissociate measured respiratory variables from those at the alveoli (Whipp et al., 2005).

References

Keeling, C. D., Whorf, T. P., Wahlen, M. and van der Plichtt, J. (1995). Interannual extremes in the rate of rise of atmospheric carbon dioxide since 1980. *Nature*, 375(6533), 666–670. https://doi.org/10.1038/375666a0

Lamarra, N., Whipp, B. J., Ward, S. A. and Wasserman, K. (1987). Effect of interbreath fluctuations on characterizing exercise gas exchange kinetics. *Journal of. Applied Physiology*, 62(5), 2003–2012.

Machta, L. and Hughes, E. (1970). Atmospheric oxygen in 1967 to 1970. *Science (New York, N.Y.)*, 168(3939), 1582–1584. https://doi.org/10.1126/science.168.3939.1582

Sandals, L. E. (2003). *Oxygen Uptake during Middle Distance Running.* http://eprints.glos.ac.uk/3085/

Whipp, B. J. and Ward, S. A. (1992). Pulmonary gas exchange dynamics and the tolerance to muscular exercise: Effects of fitness and training. *The Annals of Physiological Anthropology*, 11(3), 207–214. https://doi.org/10.2114/ahs1983.11.207

Whipp, B. J., Ward, S. A. and Rossiter, H. B. (2005). Pulmonary O2 uptake during exercise: Conflating muscular and cardiovascular responses. *Medicine and Science in Sports and Exercise*, 37(9), 1574–1585. https://doi.org/10.1249/01.mss.0000177476.63356.22

WMO: World Meteorological Organization. (1996). Guide to meteorological instruments. *WMO Publication*, 8, 1–21.

3.8   Metabolic threshold testing

Interpretation and prognostic prescriptive value

Mark Burnley and Matthew I. Black

The exercise intensity spectrum is composed of identifiable 'exercise intensity domains', within which predictable physiological and perceptual responses can be observed. These domains, in turn, are separated by specific metabolic thresholds, namely the lactate threshold (LT) and the maximal steady state (MSS) or critical power (CP). Appreciation of these domains, and the metabolic thresholds that separate them, is of great importance for the assessment of functional capacity and provides valuable insights into the severity of the disease. These domains can inform and evaluate surgical, pharmacological and exercise rehabilitation interventions in a variety of patient groups. Accordingly, the determination of metabolic thresholds is a key part of clinical exercise testing. The aim of this chapter is to outline the physiological basis of these thresholds, and to broadly describe how exercise testing should be constructed to identify them in patients. Specific disease states will only be mentioned where and when they may be relevant. Subsequent chapters will address the specific needs of individuals with different conditions.

Exercise intensity domains

Four domains of exercise intensity have been identified: moderate (below the LT), heavy (above LT but below the MSS/CP), severe (above the MSS/CP) and extreme (wherein exercise duration is too short to achieve maximal oxygen uptake [$\dot{V}O_2$max] before task failure; for review see Burnley and Jones, 2018). The metabolic thresholds of interest, therefore, are the LT and its ventilatory and gas exchange equivalents (separating the moderate and heavy domains), and the MSS or CP (separating the heavy and severe domains). It is important to note that numerous methods, and associated nomenclature, have been proposed to determine the boundaries between moderate-, heavy- and severe-intensity exercise, and the appropriate methodology remains a topic of heated debate (Jones et al., 2019; Table 3.8.1). Whichever method of threshold determination is selected, its validity should be based on whether it can, to a reasonable and quantifiable degree of confidence, establish the intended exercise intensity domain boundary.

DOI: 10.4324/9781003045267-20

The moderate/heavy boundary: lactate threshold

The moderate-intensity domain is characterised by a steady state physiological response profile after an initial transient response (the 'on-transient' kinetics of oxygen uptake [$\dot{V}O_2$]). Thus, in this domain, steady states in gas exchange, ventilation and heart rate can be achieved within 2–3 minutes in healthy participants, although it may require considerably longer to achieve in diseases that severely impact heart, lung or muscle function. In this domain, blood [lactate] (brackets denote concentration) may rise transiently, if at all, before returning to resting concentrations. In contrast, in the heavy-intensity domain, a steady state is achieved following a delay of 10–15 minutes, in which $\dot{V}O_2$ rises to a greater value than expected based on the relationship of $\dot{V}O_2$ and work rate below LT, and blood [lactate] is elevated above resting concentrations. This rise in blood [lactate] results in bicarbonate buffering of its associated proton, and thus CO_2 production increases. This increases respiratory drive and therefore minute ventilation ($\dot{V}_E$). The contrasting responses between moderate- and heavy-intensity exercise are the basis for the determination of the LT and its gas exchange and ventilatory equivalents.

To identify the moderate-heavy domain boundary, practitioners have two options (see Table 3.8.1): first, to detect the LT by direct measurement of the blood lactate response to incremental exercise (using an incremental test with stage durations ≥ 3 minutes); or second, to detect the gas exchange and ventilatory consequences of exceeding the LT, which does not require blood sampling (using a ramp or incremental test with stage durations of not more than 1 minute, see Figure 3.8.1 and after). In the context of clinical testing, the standard incremental lactate threshold protocol is usually too long in duration to apply to patients who are unaccustomed to, anxious of or experiencing pain during exercise. Nevertheless, there may be utility in lactate sampling following standardised exercise testing in the clinical setting. The six-minute walk test, for example, could be concluded with a fingertip blood sample, and the blood [lactate] can be interpreted in the context of the patient's performance (Casas et al., 2005).

The most appropriate and undoubtedly the most commonly used method of determining the LT in the clinical setting is indirectly by gas exchange or minute ventilation (see Figure 3.8.1, for example). To determine the LT indirectly using gas exchange variables (the gas exchange threshold [GET]), a ramp or rapid incremental test is preferred, since the evolution of CO_2 from the bicarbonate buffering of lactate is most clearly identified with relatively rapid incrementation and breath-by-breath gas exchange measurement. The advantages of this test are that there are normative data for healthy participants as well as typical responses for patient groups (Wasserman and McIlroy, 1964; Wasserman et al., 2011). Further, it is relatively short (~10 minutes, of which only 2–3 minutes are strenuous), and it can be used to identify a range of parameters beyond the LT/GET which are relevant to integrated cardiorespiratory function (such as efficiency/economy and the maximal oxygen uptake, $\dot{V}O_2$max). In patient groups, the achievement of ~10 min test duration requires a relatively modest incrementation rate (of 5–15 W·min^{-1}).

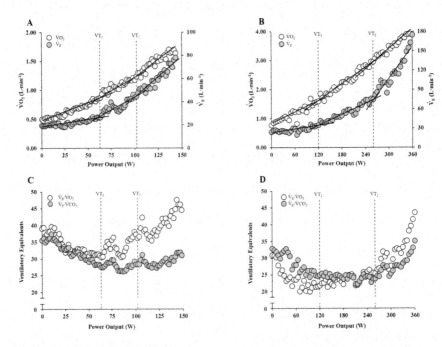

Figure 3.8.1 Illustration of the pulmonary response to a cardiopulmonary exercise test (CPET). The data presented in panels A and C were obtained from a 53-year-old male with idiopathic pulmonary fibrosis, and a forced vital capacity (FVC) of 77%. Panels C and D were obtained from a recreationally active, healthy, 21-year-old male. Panels A and B plot the relationship between pulmonary oxygen uptake ($\dot{V}O_2$; white circles), and pulmonary minute ventilation ($\dot{V}_E$; grey circles) with power output, and panels C and D plot the relationship between the ventilatory equivalents ($\dot{V}_E/\dot{V}O_2$, white circles; $\dot{V}_E/\dot{V}CO_2$, grey circles) with power output. The first ventilatory threshold (VT_1; dashed vertical line) is indicated in panels A and B by the first disproportionate increase in 1) $\dot{V}O_2$ versus power output, and 2) $\dot{V}_E$ versus power output. VT_1 is also identified by an increase in $\dot{V}_E/\dot{V}O_2$ with power output with no change in $\dot{V}_E/\dot{V}CO_2$ (panels C and D). The second ventilatory threshold (VT_2) is indicated by the second disproportionate increase in 1) $\dot{V}O_2$ versus power output, and 2) $\dot{V}_E$ versus power output (panels A and B). VT_2 is also determined by an increase in $\dot{V}_E/\dot{V}CO_2$ with power output (panels C and D).

To detect the GET, a cluster of variables is usually used, including an increase in $\dot{V}_E/\dot{V}O_2$ without a corresponding increase in $\dot{V}_E/\dot{V}CO_2$, a breakpoint in the $\dot{V}O_2/\dot{V}CO_2$ x-y plot identified using the V-slope method (Beaver et al., 1986; Figure 3.8.1 C-D), and the corresponding increase in $PETO_2$ without a change in $PETCO_2$. All of these are easily identified from data acquired using standard on-line gas analysis systems, and require only linear regression to establish the V-slope. Minute ventilation can also be interrogated to detect the LT (that is, the ventilatory threshold, VT; Figure 3.8.1 A-B), but practitioners should be wary of

Table 3.8.1 The validity, reliability and sensitivity of the metabolic thresholds used to demarcate the exercise intensity domains (EID) and the abbreviations commonly used to describe these in the scientific literature

	Common Abbreviation(s)	Strong Evidence for Validity, Reliability and Sensitivity?	Determined from an Incremental Exercise Test?	Easily Assessed in the Field?
Moderate-heavy EID				
Lactate Threshold	LT; LT1; Tlac	✓	✓	✓
Ventilatory Threshold or Gas Exchange Threshold	VT; VT1; Tvent; GET	✓	✓	✗
Heavy-severe EID				
Lactate Threshold or Lactate Turnpoint	LT; LT2; LTP	✗	✓	✓
Ventilatory Threshold or Respiratory Compensation Point	VT; VT2; RCP	✗	✓	✗
Onset of blood lactate accumulation	OBLA	✗	✗	✓
Maximal lactate steady state	MLSS	✓	✗	✓
Individual anaerobic threshold	IAT	✗	✗	✗
Lactate minimum speed	LMS	✗	✗	✓
Critical power/speed	CP; CS; P_{crit}	✓	✗	✓
Functional threshold power	FTP	✗	✗	✓

using $\dot{V}E$ exclusively due to low signal-to-noise ratio and idiosyncratic breathing patterns that can distort the identification of the VT.

Given that the GET (or VT) is detected under non-steady state conditions, and is the consequence of lactate efflux and buffering, the relationship between the metabolic rate at which GET (or VT) occurs and its corresponding walking/running speed or power output is dissociated by an amount related to the 'mean response time' of the $\dot{V}O_2$ response. This lag can vary considerably depending on the type and severity of disease, but can be estimated by back-extrapolation from the current $\dot{V}O_2$ value to the speed or power output associated with it. This can be performed by plotting both variables against time on the same graph and drawing a horizontal line from the $\dot{V}O_2$ back to the power or speed and noting the time difference.

Heavy-severe boundary: maximal steady state/critical power

The defining feature of severe-intensity exercise is that it is non-steady state. In this domain, blood [lactate] cannot be stabilised and $\dot{V}O_2$ will usually rise until $\dot{V}O_2$max is attained (Gaesser and Poole, 1996). However, the termination of exercise may occur before $\dot{V}O_2$max is attained in clinical populations, due to either symptom limitation (e.g., maximal voluntary ventilation being attained in chronic obstructive pulmonary disease [COPD] patients, angina or predefined ST segment depression in cardiac patients), limb pain or anxiety. Nevertheless, in this domain, exercise at any fixed speed or power output will result in task failure within minutes, and the precise duration is a predictable function of the speed or power output above the heavy-severe boundary.

There are two methods of determining this boundary. The first is a 'bottom-up' approach, in which the MSS is determined, usually from serial measurements of blood [lactate] (the maximal lactate steady state, MLSS) during a series of 30-min constant speed (or power) exercise bouts. When a non-steady state profile is identified, the previous bout is defined as the MLSS (see Figure 3.8.2). The second method is a 'top-down' approach, in which a series of constant speed or power tests in the severe-intensity domain are performed, and a mathematical function is applied to the resulting power vs. time to task failure data, with the asymptote being the estimated heavy-severe domain boundary (CP; Figure 3.8.2) (Morton, 2006). Both methods have their advantages and disadvantages, but the requirement for repeated and strenuous testing is a disadvantage common to both. Efforts have been made, therefore, to associate parameters derived from incremental or ramp testing with the MLSS or CP, including the lactate turn-point, the D_{max} and modified D_{max} method, the 4 mM 'Onset of Blood Lactate Accumulation' (OBLA) and the respiratory compensation point (RCP). Unfortunately, these parameters do not appear to provide valid and reliable estimates of the heavy-severe domain boundary (e.g., Dekerle et al., 2003; Broxterman et al., 2015) and the duration of these tests also precludes their use in routine clinical testing.

The heavy-severe domain boundary typically occurs halfway between the LT and $\dot{V}O_2$max. Thus, to conduct an MLSS determination, several 30-minute efforts bracketing this intensity should be performed. Blood sampling should be performed at rest and at every fifth minute of exercise. Typically, a difference in blood [lactate] of <1 mM between minutes 10 and 30 is considered representative of a steady state (but see Jones et al. [2019]). The choice of intensities used, and the difference between them (e.g., 1 km·h^{-1} or 25 W), requires judgement, with the goal to establish MLSS with the highest possible precision in the fewest number of tests. Usually, no more than 4–5 tests should be required to identify the MLSS. Starting at, or just above, the GET would be prudent in patients if this technique is chosen, with 0.5 km·h^{-1} or 5–10 W separating each trial.

Two advantages of using CP in establishing the heavy-severe domain boundary are that the number of trials required can be decided before the testing begins, and the testing itself also characterises exercise tolerance in the severe-intensity

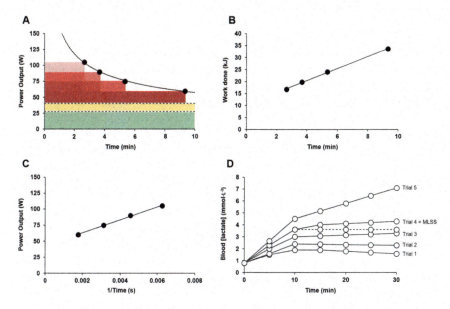

Figure 3.8.2 Schematic representation of methods used to determine the heavy-severe boundary during non-incremental exercise tests. Panels A-C illustrate the determination of CP and W′ via a series of severe-intensity exercise trials performed to task failure (black markers). In panel A, the work performed above CP (red) indicative of W′ and the severe-intensity domain, and the moderate (green) and heavy (orange) intensity domains, are provided. Panel D shows the blood [lactate] response, measured every 5 min (white markers) to a series of constant speed (or power) trials, in which each trial (1–5) is indicative of an increment in speed (or power). Blood [lactate] did not increase by more than 1 mM between minutes 10 and 30 during trial 4 (Δ 0.7 mM) and is therefore defined as MLSS. The dashed line is indicative of the blood [lactate] attained at the 10 min mark during trial 4, and is projected to the end of the exercise trial.

domain. The only reason to increase the number of tests is if the CP estimate is associated with a high standard error, and usually only one extra test is then required. The tests themselves have the disadvantage of needing to be performed to the limit of tolerance, but the duration of each test is relatively short (between 2 and 15 min; Hill, 1993). Curve fitting of the resulting speed- or power-duration relationship can then provide the CP and curvature constant (distance, D′, or work, W′) parameters. The simplest way of representing this relationship is to plot the linear distance or external work vs. time to task failure, wherein the slope of the relationship is the critical speed or power, and the intercept is the D′ or W′ (Figure 3.8.2; panel B). Alternatively, non-linear regression of the speed/power and time to task failure can be performed, fitting a rectangular hyperbola to the data (for cycle ergometry):

$$T_{lim} = W'/(P - CP) \quad [1]$$

in which Tlim is the time to task failure and P is power output. CP will then be represented by the asymptote (i.e., the flattened portion) of the power-duration relationship (Figure 3.8.2; panel A). Finally, the inverse time model can be used to provide a linear fit to the data, with the intercept being CP and the slope being W′ (Figure 3.8.2; panel C). It is common to establish all three relationships, and then rely on the fitting with the smallest standard error. This procedure also guards against inadvertent errors in data entry that would result in the models producing wildly different parameter estimates. It should also be noted that the estimates are only estimates; the confidence limits associated with them are also important. In this respect, practitioners should seek to maximise the degrees of freedom in the model used. For a two-parameter model, we suggest at least four predicting trials be performed, since 95% confidence limits of ± 60 W are not uncommon using only three predicting trials.

The MLSS and CP do not typically agree in the literature, and this highlights a major source of controversy in the field. MLSS is, by definition, a measure of the upper limit of the heavy domain, whereas the CP is a parameter estimate of the lower limit of the severe domain (Jones et al., 2019). Both are subject to experimental error and biological variation, but the CP tends to return a higher estimate for the boundary than does the MLSS. Space does not permit us to explore these issues, but we refer readers to Jones et al. (2019). Whichever method is chosen, practitioners should seek to minimise the associated measurement errors. As a rule of thumb, however, exercise above CP is almost certainly in the severe domain, and exercise at or below MLSS is, by definition, in the heavy domain.

Prognostic prescriptive value of metabolic threshold testing

Due to the routine use of cardio-pulmonary exercise testing (CPET) in healthcare settings, determination of LT/GET occurs frequently. Ramp or rapid incremental tests are straightforward for experienced technicians to perform and relatively straightforward for clinicians to interpret. This is, in part, because there are a number of clinical resources and CPET courses that provide practitioners with guidance on the use of gas exchange responses in clinical decision-making. It has been shown, for example, that the $\dot{V}O_2$ at GET predicted mortality following abdominal surgery in 187 cardiac patients: 18% of those with a GET below 11 ml.kg^{-1}.min^{-1} died following surgery, compared to only 0.8% of those with a GET above this cut-off (Older et al., 1993). In those with pre-operative ischaemia during exercise testing, a low GET was associated with 42% mortality compared to 4% in those ischaemic patients with a GET >11 ml.kg^{-1}.min^{-1}. Clearly, increasing the GET should be a major goal in the context of patient rehabilitation given the 'metabolic extravagance' that exceeding this threshold causes (Whipp, 1987). But the CPET can provide a host of variables and parameters beyond threshold measures that can indicate the normalcy, or otherwise, of a patient's physiological response to exercise.

The clinical use of MLSS or critical power is rare. The strenuous nature of the tests used to determine the heavy-severe domain boundary, coupled with the requirement for multiple tests, limits the utility of this landmark in patients. Those protocols intended for a single-visit determination of CP either lack evidence of validity and reliability, or are simply too strenuous to apply to patient populations (e.g., Vanhatalo et al., 2007). That said, there are notable studies investigating CP in chronic heart failure and COPD, with both confirming that, as in healthy and athletic populations, CP occurs at a higher metabolic rate than GET, and below the $\dot{V}O_2$max (Mezzani et al., 2010; Neder et al., 2000). In these studies, the critical power was in the range of 40–80 W, in contrast to the 200–400 W seen in healthy groups and athletes.

Despite the limited use of MLSS or CP in clinical exercise testing, Casas et al. (2005) reported that the speed attained in the last three minutes of the six-minute walk test (5.4 $km·h^{-1}$) was not different from critical walking speed (5.2 $km·h^{-1}$) in eight moderate to severe COPD patients. This is, of course, far too small a sample to recommend for clinical use. However, that this study showed the six-minute walk test to be performed in the severe-intensity domain means that it is likely to correlate well with critical speed in patient groups, although considerably more validation is required to confirm this.

Summary

The proximity of an exercise task to metabolic thresholds is a key determinant of the resulting physiological responses; in patients, trespassing the LT/GET results in significantly increased demands on the respiratory and cardiovascular systems. Increasing this threshold is therefore a key target in any rehabilitation programme. A low value for this parameter is also associated with poor exercise tolerance in general, and high mortality during surgical interventions. Although seldom measured in healthcare situations, the heavy/severe domain boundary occurs in the same region of the intensity spectrum as found in health (between the GET and the $\dot{V}O_2$max). The critical walking speed has been shown to correlate with the performance of a six-minute walk test, albeit in a very small number of COPD patients, suggesting that CP is a key determinant of performance in both health and disease.

References

Beaver, W. L., Wasserman, K. and Whipp, B. J. (1986). A new method for detecting anaerobic threshold by gas exchange. *Journal of Applied Physiology*, 60, 2020–2027.

Broxterman, R. M., Ade, C. J., Craig, J. C., Wilcox, S. L., Schlup, S. J. and Barstow, T. J. (2015). The relationship between critical speed and the respiratory compensation point: Coincidence or equivalence. *European Journal of Sport Science*, 15, 631–639. doi: 10.1080/17461391.2014.966764

Burnley, M. and Jones, A. M. (2018). Power-duration relationship: Physiology, fatigue, and the limits of human performance. *European Journal of Sport Science*, 18, 1–12.

Casas, A., Vilaro, J., Rabinovich, R., Mayer, A., Albert Barberà, J., Rodriguez-Roisin, R. and Roca, J. (2005). Encouraged 6-min walking test indicates maximum sustainable exercise in COPD patients. *Chest*, 128, 55–61.

Dekerle, J., Baron, B., Dupont, L., Vanvelcenaher, J. and Pelayo, P. (2003). Maximal lactate steady state, respiratory compensation threshold and critical power. *European Journal Applied Physiology*, 89, 281–288.

Gaesser, G. A. and Poole, D. C. (1996). The slow component of oxygen uptake kinetics in humans. *Exercise and Sport Sciences Reviews*, 24, 35–70.

Hill, A. V. (1993). The critical power concept: A review. *Sports Medicine*, 16, 237–254.

Jones, A. M., Burnley, M., Black, M. I., Poole, D. C. and Vanhatalo, A. (2019). The maximal metabolic steady state: Redefining the "gold standard". *Physiological Reports*, 7, e14098.

Mezzani, A., Corrà, U., Giordano, M., Colombo, S., Psaroudaki, M. and Giannuzzi, P. (2010). Upper intensity limit for prolonged aerobic exercise in chronic heart failure. *Medicine and Science in Sports and Exercise*, 42, 633–639.

Morton, R. H. (2006). The critical power and related whole-body bioenergetic models. *European Journal of Applied Physiology*, 96, 339–354.

Neder, J. A., Jones, P. W., Nery, L. E. and Whipp, B. J. (2000). Determinants of the exercise endurance capacity in patients with chronic obstructive pulmonary disease: The power-duration relationship. *American Journal of Respiratory and Critical Care Medicine*, 162, 497–504.

Older, P., Smith, R., Courtney, P. and Hone, R. (1993). Preoperative evaluation of cardiac failure and ischemia in elderly patients by cardiopulmonary exercise testing. *Chest*, 104, 701–704.

Vanhatalo, A., Doust, J. H. and Burnley, M. (2007). Determination of critical power using a 3-min all-out cycling test. *Medicine and Science in Sports and Exercise*, 39, 548–555.

Wasserman, K., Hansen, J. E., Sue, D. Y., Stringer, W. W., Sietsema, K. E., Sun, X.-G. and Whipp, B. J. (2011). *Principles of Exercise Testing and Interpretation* (5th ed.). Philadelphia: Lippincott, Williams and Wilkins.

Wasserman, K. and McIlroy, M. B. (1964). Detecting the threshold of anaerobic metabolism in cardiac patients during exercise. *American Journal of Cardiology*, 14, 844–852.

Whipp, B. J. (1987). Dynamics of pulmonary gas exchange. *Circulation*, 76, VI18–VI28.

3.9 Ratings of perceived exertion

John P. Buckley and Roger Eston

Following two decades of research, Gunnar Borg's original rating of perceived exertion (RPE) 6–20 scale was accepted in 1973 as a valid tool within the field of exercise science and sports medicine (Noble and Robertson, 1996). His seminal research provided the basic tool for numerous studies in which an individual's effort perception was of interest. It also provided the basis and incentive for the development of other scales, particularly those used with children. Borg's initial research validated the scale against heart rate and oxygen uptake. Later research focussed on the curvilinear growth of perceived exertion with lactate, ventilation and muscle pain responses, and led to the development of the category-ratio (CR-10) scale. The RPE 6–20 and CR-10 scales and their accompanying instructions can be found in the British Association for Cardiovascular Prevention and Rehabilitation (BACPR) Reference Tables Booklet via this link: www.bacpr.com/pages/page_box_contents.asp?PageID=787.

The general aim of using RPE is to quantify an individual's perception of exertion as a means of determining or regulating exercise intensity (Borg, 1998). In this way it acts as a surrogate or concurrent marker to key relative physiological responses including percentage of maximal heart rate (%HRmax), percentage of maximal aerobic power (%$\dot{V}O_2$max) and blood lactate. The strongest stimuli influencing an individual's RPE are breathing/ventilatory work and sensations of strain from the muscles (Chen et al., 2002).

Modes of using the RPE

Traditionally, RPE was developed as a dependent response variable to a given exercise intensity known as *estimation mode* (Noble and Robertson, 1996). Smutok et al. (1980) were among the first to evaluate RPE as an independent exercise intensity regulator (i.e., *production mode*), in which participants exercise to a target effort perception and other measures become dependent response variables.

RPE and relative measures of exercise intensity

The RPE is commonly used to complement physiological measures of exercise during graded exercise testing (GXT) and prescribe intensity levels in healthy and clinical populations (ACSM, 2021; Eston and Connolly, 1996; Parfitt et al., 2012;

DOI: 10.4324/9781003045267-21

Kang et al., 2003; Scherer and Cassady, 1999; Williams and Eston, 1989). The strong relationship between RPE and exercise intensity during GXT was demonstrated in a study involving 2,560 men and women (Scherr et al., 2013), 'independent of age, gender, medical history (with respect to coronary artery disease), level of physical activity and exercise modality'. They concluded that RPE can be used to monitor and regulate exercise intensity for primary and secondary disease prevention. They recommended RPE 11–13 for less-trained individuals, and RPE 13–15 when more intense aerobic training is desired. In cardiac rehabilitation patients, the recommended range of RPE 11 (for low-fit low-active patients) to 14 (for higher fit, more active patients) was shown to represent exercise at the anaerobic/ventilatory threshold (Nichols et al., 2020).

Several studies have shown that RPE is a useful tool for guiding exercise intensity in healthy and clinical populations. For example, Parfitt et al. (2012) observed a 17% increase in $\dot{V}O_2$max from a self-paced, 8-week treadmill training program (3 × 30 min/wk) clamped at RPE 13 in previously sedentary participants. During training at RPE 13, the average $\dot{V}O_2$ increased from 61% of the baseline $\dot{V}O_2$max to 64% of the higher $\dot{V}O_2$max in week 8. Since participants were blinded to speed, HR and other intensity feedback, the data provide strong evidence and proof of principle for the efficacy of RPE 13 (particularly because it was also perceived to be *pleasant*) to self-regulate training over a long period. Illarraza et al. (2004) reported similar results in post-operative cardiac patients whose exercise intensity was solely regulated by RPE 13 with similar gains in fitness and ventricular ejection fraction compared to a similar group exercising at a target intensity of 70% heart rate reserve. Table 3.9.1 summarises the relationship between RPE and related physiological markers. For example, once an individual has given an RPE of 13–14 on the RPE scale or 3–4 on the CR-10 scale, it is highly probable that the participant is exercising at or around the ventilatory threshold.

Use of RPE to predict and assess $\dot{V}O_2$max

The RPE elicited from submaximal increments in a GXT can be used to provide estimations of $\dot{V}O_2$max that are as good as, or better than, heart rate. Morgan and Borg (1976) first observed that the linear relationship of RPE and work rate during a GXT in physically active and sedentary men permits extrapolation to a

Table 3.9.1 Summary of the relationship between the percentages of maximal aerobic power (%$\dot{V}O_2$max), maximal heart rate reserve (%HRRmax), maximal heart rate (%HRmax) and Borg's RPE (6–20) and CR-10 scales

%VO$_2$max	<37	37–45	46–63	64–90	>91	100
%HRRmax	<30	30–39	40–59	60–89	>90	100
%HRmax	<57	57–63	64–76	77–95	>96	100
RPE (6–20)	<9	9–11	12–13	14–17	18+	20
CR-10	<1	1–1.5	2.5–3	4–6	7–9	10 +

Source: Adapted from ACSM (2021) and Borg (1998)

theoretical end point, enabling prediction of maximal work capacity with better accuracy than heart rate. Many studies have since confirmed the efficacy of sub-maximal RPE to estimate $\dot{V}O_2max$ or maximal work rate (Coquart et al., 2014; Evans et al., 2015).

On the basis that RPE alone may be used to regulate exercise intensity, percep-tually regulated exercise testing (PRET) was proposed as an alternative method of estimating maximal exercise capacity and training status (Eston et al., 2005). This method has the advantage of allowing individual autonomy to set exercise intensity at a given RPE through changes in pace, work rate or gradient. It is also a closed-loop task in which the number of bouts and time at each RPE-regulated intensity are known, allowing the participant to set a pace accordingly. The proce-dure was first conceived by Eston et al. (1987) and later applied in cardiac patients (Eston and Thompson, 1997). Their research provided initial proof of concept and rationale for a series of studies on the efficacy of PRET, with a known end-point RPE, involving different exercise modalities and population groups as a valid means of predicting $\dot{V}O_2peak$. The validity of submaximal PRET has been confirmed across a broad range of age, ability, fitness levels and chronic health conditions (Eston et al., 2012; Coquart et al., 2014).

There has been considerable interest in extending Eston and colleagues' orig-inal concept of the PRET to include a maximal stage at RPE 20 ($PRET_{max}$), also interchangeably referred to as a self-paced $\dot{V}O_2peak$ test (SPV) to measure $\dot{V}O_2peak$. The initial $PRET_{max}$ (Mauger and Sculthorpe, 2012) consisted of the same two-minute, verbally anchored RPE stages (11, 13, 15, 17) as those applied by Eston et al. (2006) with the addition of RPE 20 to produce a maximal effort and freedom to change power output or speed on a moment-to-moment basis during each of the perceptually regulated bouts. Others have used protocols with seven stages at RPE 8, 10, 12, 14, 16 and 20 (Chidnok et al., 2013) and six 3-minute stages at RPE 9, 11, 13, 15, 17 and 20 (Evans et al., 2014). These closed-loop pro-tocols have the advantages of known duration and autonomy to control exercise intensity within a fixed RPE (see Eston and Parfitt, 2019 for critical review).

Factors influencing RPE

During exercise testing, the inter-trial agreement of either RPE or a concurrent physiological response at a given RPE increases with each use of the RPE scale (Buckley et al., 2000, 2004; Eston et al., 2000, 2005). Typically, the agreement is shown to be acceptable within three trials when the participant is exposed to a variety of exercise intensities.

Psychosocial factors can influence up to 30% of the variability in an RPE score (Dishman and Landy, 1988; Williams and Eston, 1989). Furthermore, the litera-ture has identified numerous modulators of RPE including: the mode of exer-cise, age, audio-visual distractions, circadian rhythms, gender, haematological and nutritional status, medication, muscle mechanics and biochemical status, the phys-ical environment and the psycho-social status or competitive milieu of the testing and training environment. These factors are exemplified in Borg's effort continua proposed in 1973 (Borg, 1998). Beta-blocking medication exerts an influence during extended periods of exercise and at intensities greater than 65% $\dot{V}O_2$max (Eston and Connolly, 1996; Head et al., 1997).

In healthy or clinical populations that may be fearful of the exercise testing environment (e.g., cardiac patients), it is likely that they will inflate RPE (Morgan, 1973, 1994; Rejeski, 1981; Kohl and Shea, 1988; Biddle and Mutrie, 2001; Buckley et al., 2009). Such inflation of RPE relates to individuals who either lack self-efficacy or who are unfamiliar or inhibited by the social situation of the exercise training or testing environment.

Throughout this guidance, most of the focus is on using RPE as an intensity monitor. However, like heart rate, it responds to more than just intensity stimuli. Similar to cardiovascular drift, in which during a fixed submaximal intensity and constant or steady state $\dot{V}O_2$, RPE will grow *linearly* as a function of time as linked to the onset of sensations of 'fatigue' (Utter et al., 2002; Fontes et al., 2010; Buckley and Borg, 2011; Borg, 1998), which may be disrupted by a change in the anticipated duration of the task (Eston et al., 2012). Furthermore, any underlying perception of fatigue could be present as a function of the time of day (Micklewright et al., 2017). From the previous evidence, the slope or rate of RPE growth as a function of time is proportional to the intensity and becomes especially pronounced when exercise is performed above the ventilatory/anaerobic threshold. Faulkner et al. (2008) showed the same pattern for long-distance competitive running in which the rate of increase in RPE was greater for a faster-paced shorter distance (7 cf. 13 mile). During marathon running, the growth of RPE is more gradual in that it takes several hours to see a similar amount of growth in RPE, when compared with strength training (Buckley and Borg, 2011). In health-promoting or rehabilitative exercise, when aerobic activities typically last for 30 minutes, RPE for the same work rate or metabolic equivalent (METs) could increase by 2 points on the RPE scale (Joseph et al., 2008). Similarly for a given RPE (e.g., used in RPE production mode) the work rate ($\dot{V}O_2$ or METs) over this time is likely to decrease (Cochrane et al., 2015).

RPE and strength/power testing and training

Up until the late 1990s, most of the evidence in RPE focussed on application and research with aerobic-type exercise. There is now a growing body of evidence in the use of monitoring somatic responses to local muscle sensations during resistive or strength training exercise (Borg, 1998; Gearhart et al., 2002; Pincivero et al., 2003; Lagally and Costigan, 2004). The important aspect to consider is that during short-term high-intensity exercise for a localised muscle group, in which 8 to 15 repetitions are performed, RPE will typically grow by one point on the RPE or CR-10 for every 3 to 4 repetitions (Buckley and Borg, 2011). For example, if after 12 repetitions, one wishes to end his/her last repetition at an RPE of 15 or a CR-10 scale rating of 5 (hard, heavy), then the first or second repetition should elicit an RPE of 12 or a CR-10 rating of 2 (between light and somewhat hard). Ultimately, during strength training, the rate of growth is rapid; for example, at the beginning of work at 70% of a 1-repetition maximum, the perception of intensity is moderate/somewhat hard, but rapidly grows to extremely hard/maximum in less than 30 seconds.

Which scale should I use?

In both Borg's RPE and CR-10 scale, semantic verbal anchors and their corresponding numbers have been aligned to accommodate for the curvilinear nature (a power function between 1.6 and 2.0) of human physiological responses (Borg, 1998). The CR-10 scale, with its ratio or semi-ratio properties, was specifically designed with this in mind. The RPE 6–20 scale was originally designed for whole-body aerobic-type activity in which perceived responses are pooled to concur with the linear increments in heart rate and oxygen uptake, as exercise intensity is increased. The CR-10 scale is best suited when there is an overriding sensation arising either from a specific area of the body, for example, muscle pain, ache or fatigue in the quadriceps or from pulmonary responses. Examples of this individualised or differentiated response have been applied in patients with McArdle disease (Buckley et al., 2014) and chronic obstructive pulmonary disease (O'Donnell et al., 2004).

Perceived exertion in children

There have been important advances in the study of effort perception in children (Kasai et al., 2020; Eston and Parfitt, 2019; Lamb et al., 2017 for reviews). In summary, a developmentally appropriate 1–10 Children's Effort Rating Table (CERT, Williams et al., 1994; Eston et al., 1994) laid the foundation for several linearly sloped pictorial scales (OMNI, Robertson, 1997; Robertson et al., 2000; PCERT, Yelling et al., 2002; Cart and Load Effort Rating Scale, CALER, Eston et al., 2000). More recently, the E-P scale (Figure 3.9.1; Eston and Parfitt, 2007) depicts a character at various stages of exertion on a concave slope. The scale is intuitive and valid and has been applied in several studies (Eston et al., 2009; Lambrick et al., 2011, 2016). Steeper slopes are harder to ascend and the area under the curve is shaded progressively from light to dark red to further reflect increasing intensity. The horizontal distance between increments (0 to 10) is successively reduced to create equidistant intervals on the vertical axis, which allows for linear analyses and interpretation of RPE and other data.

Key points for the effective use of RPE

The following points for instructing participants are recommended (adapted from Maresh and Noble, 1984; Borg, 1998, 2004):

1   Before using the RPE scale, it is important that the participant understands the concept of sensing the exercise responses (breathing, muscle movement/ strain, joint movement/speed).

2   It is also important to anchor the perceptual range, which includes relaying the fact that no exertion at all is sitting still and maximal exertion is a

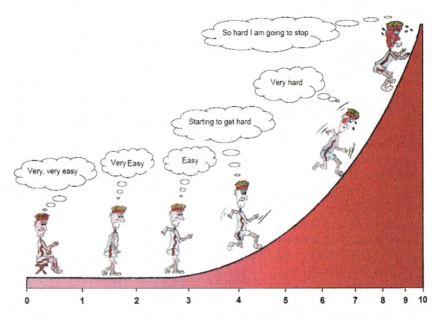

Figure 3.9.1 Eston-Parfitt (E-P) Scale.

theoretical concept of pushing the body to its absolute physical limits. Participants should then be exposed to several levels of exercise intensity to understand what various levels on the scale feel like.

3   The participant should first concentrate on the sensations arising from the activity, look at the scale to see which verbal descriptor relates to the effort he/she is experiencing and then link this to the corresponding numerical value.

4   Unless specifically directed, ensure that the participant focusses on all the different sensations arising from the exercise being performed. For aerobic exercise, the participant should pool all sensations to give one rating. If there is an overriding sensation, then additionally make note of this differentiated rating. Differentiated ratings can be used during muscular strength activity or when exercise is limited more by breathlessness or leg pain, as in the case of pulmonary or peripheral vascular disease, respectively.

5   Confirm that there is no right or wrong answer and it is what the participant perceives. There are three important cases in which the participant may give an incorrect rating:

(a)   When there is a preconceived idea about what exertion level is elicited by a specific activity (Borg, 1998).

(b)   When participants are asked to recall the exercise and give a rating. As with heart rate, RPEs should be taken while the participant is actually engaged in the movements, not after they have finished an activity.

(c) When participants attempt to please the practitioner by stating what should be the appropriate level of RPE. This is typically the case when participants are advised ahead of time of the target RPE (e.g., in education sessions or during the warm-up). In the early stages of using RPE, the participant's exercise intensity should be set by heart rate or work rate (e.g., in METs) and participants need to reliably learn to match their RPE to this level in estimation mode. Once it has been established that the participant's rating concurs with the target heart rate or MET level reliably, then moving them on to production mode can be considered.

6   Keep RPE scales in full view at all times (e.g., on each machine or station or in fixed view in the exercise testing room) and keep reminding participants throughout their exercise session or test to think about what sort of sensations they have while making their judgement rating. Elite endurance athletes are known to be good perceivers since they are well used to associating sensations to regulate an optimal pace. (Morgan, 2000).

References

ACSM. (2021). *ACSM's Guidelines for Exercise Testing and Prescription* (11th ed.) Baltimore: Lippincott, Williams and Wilkins.

Biddle, S. J. H. and Mutrie, N. (2001). *Psychology of Physical Activity: Determinants, Well-Being and Interventions.* London: Routledge.

Borg, G. (1998). *Borg's Perceived Exertion and Pain Scales.* Champaign, IL: Human Kinetics.

Borg, G. (2004). *The Borg CR10 Folder: A Method for Measuring Intensity of Experience.* Stockholm, Sweden: Borg Perception.

Buckley, J. P. and Borg, G. A. (2011). Borg's scales in strength training from theory to practice in young and older adults. *Applied Physiology and Nutrition Metabolism,* 36, 682–692.

Buckley, J. P., Eston, R. G. and Sim, J. (2000). Ratings of perceived exertion in Braille: Validity and reliability in production mode. *British Journal of Sports Medicine,* 34, 297–302.

Buckley, J. P., Quinlivan, R. C. M., Sim, J., Eston, R. G. and Short, D. S. (2014). Heart rate and perceived muscle pain response to a functional walking test in McArdle disease. *Journal of Sports Sciences,* 32, 1561–1569.

Buckley, J., Sim, J. and Eston, R. G. (2009). Reproducibility of ratings of perceived exertion soon after myocardial infarction: Responses in the stress-testing clinic and the rehabilitation gymnasium. *Ergonomics,* 52, 421–442.

Buckley, J. P., Sim, J., Eston, R. G., Hession, R. and Fox, R. (2004). Reliability and validity of measures taken during the Chester step test to predict aerobic power and to prescribe aerobic exercise. *British Journal of Sports Medicine,* 38, 197–205.

Chen, M. J., Fan, X. and Moe, S. T. (2002). Criterion-related validity of the Borg ratings of perceived exertion scale in healthy individuals: A meta-analysis. *Journal of Sports Sciences,* 20, 873–899.

Chidnok, W., DiMenna, F. J., Bailey, S. J., Burnley, M., Wilkerson, D. P., Vanhatalo, A., et al. (2013). VO2max is not altered by self-pacing during incremental exercise. *European Journal of Applied Physiology,* 113, 529–539.

Cochrane, K. C., Housh, T. J., Bergstrom, H. C., et al. (2015). Physiological responses during cycle ergometry at a constant perception of effort. *International Journal of Sports Medicine,* 36, 466–473.

Coquart, J. B., Garcin, M., Parfitt, G., et al. (2014). Prediction of maximal or peak oxygen uptake from ratings of perceived exertion. *Sports Medicine*, 44, 563–578.

Dishman, R. K. and Landy, F. J. (1988). Psychological factors and prolonged exercise. In D. R. Lamb and R. Murray (eds.), *Perspectives in Exercise Science and Sports Medicine*, pp. 281–355. Indianapolis, IN: Benchmark Press.

Eston, R. G. and Connolly, D. (1996). The use of ratings of perceived exertion for exercise prescription in patients receiving /ß-blocker therapy. *Sports Medicine*, 21, 176–190.

Eston, R. G., Davies, B. and Williams, J. G. (1987). Use of perceived effort ratings to control exercise intensity in young, healthy adults. *European Journal of Applied Physiology*, 56, 222.

Eston, R. G., Faulkner, J. A., Parfitt, C. G. and Mason, E. (2006). The validity of predicting maximal oxygen uptake from a perceptually regulated graded exercise tests of different durations. *European Journal of Applied Physiology*, 97, 535–541.

Eston, R. G., Lamb, K. L., Bain, A., Williams, M. and Williams, J. G. (1994). Validity of a perceived exertion scale for children: A pilot study. *Perceptual and Motor Skills*, 78, 691–697.

Eston, R. G., Lamb, K. L., Parfitt, C. G. and King, N. (2005). The validity of predicting maximal oxygen uptake from a perceptually regulated graded exercise test. *European Journal of Applied Physiology*, 94, 221–227.

Eston, R. G., Lambrick, D. and Rowlands, A. V. (2009). The perceptual response to exercise of progressively increasing intensity in children aged 7–8 years: Validation of a pictorial curvilinear ratings of perceived exertion scale. *Psychophysiology*, 46, 843–851.

Eston, R. G. and Parfitt, G. (2007). Perceived exertion. In N. Armstrong (ed.), *Paediatric Exercise Physiology*, pp. 275–298. London: Elsevier.

Eston, R. G. and Parfitt, G. (2019). Perceived exertion, heart rate and other non-invasive methods for exercise testing and intensity control. In K. Norton and R. Eston (eds.), *Kinanthropometry and Exercise Physiology*, pp. 464–499. New York: Routledge.

Eston, R. G., Parfitt, G., Campbell, L. and Lamb, K. L. (2000). Reliability of effort perception for regulating exercise intensity in children using a Cart and Load Effort Rating (CALER) Scale. *Pediatric Exercise Science*, 12, 388–397.

Eston, R. G., Stansfield, R., Westoby, P. and Parfitt, G. (2012). Effect of deception and expected exercise duration on psychological and physiological variables during treadmill running and cycling. *Psychophysiology*, 49, 462–469.

Eston, R. G. and Thompson, M. (1997). Use of ratings of perceived exertion for prediction of maximal exercise levels and exercise prescription in patients receiving atenolol. *British Journal of Sports Medicine*, 31, 114–119.

Evans, H., Ferrar, K., Smith, A., et al. (2015). A systematic review of methods to predict maximal oxygen uptake from submaximal, open circuit spirometry in healthy adults. *Journal of Science and Medicine in Sport*, 18, 183–188.

Evans, H., Parfitt, G. and Eston, R. (2014). Use of a perceptually-regulated test to measure maximal oxygen uptake is valid and feels better. *European Journal of Sport Science*, 14, 452–458.

Faulkner, J. A., Parfitt, C. G. and Eston, R. G. (2008). The rating of perceived exertion during competitive running scales with time. *Psychophysiology*, 45, 977–985.

Fontes, E. B., Smirmaul, B. P., Nakamura, F. Y., et al. (2010). The relationship between rating of perceived exertion and muscle activity during exhaustive constant-load cycling. *International Journal of Sports Medicine*, 31, 683–688.

Gearhart, R. F., Jr., Goss, F. L., Lagally, K. M., Jakicic, J. M., Gallagher, J., Gallagher, K.1. and Robertson, R. (2002). Ratings of perceived exertion in active muscle during high-intensity and low-intensity resistance exercise. *Strength and Conditioning Research*, 16(1), 87–91.

Head, A., Maxwell, S. and Kendall, M. J. (1997). Exercise metabolism in healthy volunteers taking celiprolol, atenolol, and placebo. *British Journal of Sports Medicine*, 31, 120–125.

Illarraza, H., Myers, J., Kottman, W., et al. (2004). An evaluation of training responses using self-regulation in a residential rehabilitation program. *Journal of Cardiopulmonary Rehabilitation*, 24, 27–33.

Joseph, T., Johnson, B., Battista, R. A., et al. (2008). Perception of fatigue during simulated competition. *Medicine & Science in Sports & Exercise*, 40, 381–386.

Kang, J., Hoffman, J. R., Walker, H., et al. (2003). Regulating intensity using perceived exertion during extended exercise periods. *European Journal of Applied Physiology*, 89, 475–482.

Kasai, D., Parfitt, G., Eston, R. and Tsiros, M. (2020). The use of ratings of perceived exertion in children and adolescents a scoping review. *Sports Medicine*, 51, 33–50.

Kohl, R. M. and Shea, C. H. (1988). Perceived exertion: Influences of locus of control and expected work intensity and duration. *Journal of Human Movement Studies*, 15, 225–272.

Lagally, K. M. and Costigan, E. M. (2004). Anchoring procedures in reliability of ratings of perceived exertion during resistance exercise. *Perceptual and Motor Skills*, 98(3 Pt 2), 1285–1295.

Lamb, K. L., Parfitt, G. and Eston, R. G. (2017). Effort perception. In N. Armstrong and W. Van-Mechelen (eds.), *The Oxford Textbook of Children's Sport and Exercise Medicine* (3rd ed.), pp. 213–224. Oxford: Oxford University Press.

Lambrick, D., Bertelsen, H., Eston, R., et al. (2016). Prediction of peak oxygen uptake in children using submaximal ratings of perceived exertion during treadmill exercise. *European Journal of Applied Physiology*, 116, 1189–1195.

Lambrick, D., Rowlands, A. V. and Eston, R. G. (2011). The perceptual response to treadmill exercise using the Eston-Parfitt scale and a marble dropping task, in children aged 7–8 years. *Pediatric Exercise Science*, 23, 36–48.

Maresh, C. and Noble, B. J. (1984). Utilization of perceived exertion ratings during exercise testing and training. In L. K. Hall, G. C. Meyer and H. K. Hellerstein (eds.), *Cardiac Rehabilitation: Exercise Testing and Prescription*, pp. 155–173. Great Neck, NY: Spectrum.

Mauger, A. R. and Sculthorpe, N. (2012). A new VO2max protocol allowing self-pacing in maximal incremental exercise. *British Journal of Sports Medicine*, 46, 59–63.

Micklewright, D., St Clair Gibson, A., Gladwell, V., et al. (2017). Development and validity of the rating of-fatigue scale. *Sports Medicine*, 47, 2375–2393.

Morgan, W. P. (1973). Psychological factors influencing perceived exertion. *Medicine and Science in Sports and Exercise*, 5, 97–103.

Morgan, W. P. (1994). Psychological components of effort sense. *Medicine and Science in Sports and Exercise*, 26, 1071–1077.

Morgan, W. P. (2000). Psychological factors associated with distance running and the marathon. In D. Tunstall-Pedoe (ed.), *Marathon Medicine*. London: Royal Society of Medicine Press.

Morgan, W. P. and Borg, G. A. V. (1976). Perception of effort in the prescription of physical activity. In T. Craig (ed.), *The Humanistic Aspects of Sports, Exercise and Recreation*, pp. 126–129. Chicago, IL: American Medical Association.

Nichols, S., Engin, B., Carroll, S., et al. (2020). Ratings of perceived exertion at the ventilatory anaerobic threshold in people with coronary heart disease: A CARE CR study. *Annals of Physical Rehabilitation and Medicine*, 101462.

Noble, B. and Robertson, R. (1996). *Perceived Exertion*. Champaign, IL: Human Kinetics.

O'Donnell, D. E., Fluge, T., Gerken, F., Hamilton, A., Webb, K., Make, B. and Magnussen, H. (2004). Effects of tiotropium on lung hyperinflation, dyspnoea and exercise tolerance in COPD. *European Respiratory Journal*, 23(Payne), 832–840.

Parfitt, G., Evans, H. and Eston, R. G. (2012). Perceptually-regulated training at RPE 13 is pleasant and improves physical health. *Medicine and Science in Sports and Exercise*, 44, 1613–1618.

Pincivero, D. M., Campy, R. M. and Coelho, A. J. (2003). Knee flexor torque and perceived exertion: A gender and reliability analysis. *Medicine and Science in Sports and Exercise*, 35(NICE), 1720–1726.

Rejeski, W. J. (1981). The perception of exertion: A social psychophysiological integration. *Journal of Sport Psychology*, 4, 305–320.

Robertson, R. J. (1997). Perceived exertion in young people: Future directions of enquiry. In J. Weisman, N. Armstrong and B. Kirby (eds.), *Children and Exercise XIX*, Vol. 2, pp. 33–39. Exeter and Washington: Singer Press.

Robertson, R. J., Goss, F. L., Boer, N. F., Peoples, J. A., Foreman, A. J., Dabayebeh, L. M., Millich, N. B., Balasekaran, G., Riechman, S. E., Gallagher, J. D. and Thompkins, T. (2000). Children's OMNI Scale of perceived exertion: Mixed gender and race validation. *Medicine and Science in Sports and Exercise*, 32, 452–458.

Scherer, S. and Cassady, S. L. (1999). Rating of perceived exertion: Development and clinical applications for physical therapy exercise testing and prescription. *Cardiopulmonary Physical Therapy*, 10, 143–147.

Scherr, J., Wolfarth, B., Christle, J. W., et al. (2013). Associations between Borg's rating of perceived exertion and physiological measures of exercise intensity. *European Journal of Applied Physiology*, 113, 147–155.

Smutok, M. A., Skrinar, G. S. and Pandolf, K. B. (1980). Exercise intensity: Subjective regulation by perceived exertion. *Archives of Physical Medicine and Rehabilitation*, 61, 569–574.

Utter, A. C., Kang, J., Robertson, R. J., et al. (2002). Effect of carbohydrate ingestion on ratings of perceived exertion during a marathon. *Medicine & Science in Sports & Exercise*, 34, 1779–1784.

Williams, J. G. and Eston, R. G. (1989). Determination of the intensity dimension in vigorous exercise programmes with particular reference to the use of the rating of perceived exertion. *Sports Medicine*, 8, 177–189.

Williams, J. G., Eston, R. G. and Furlong, B. (1994). CERT: A perceived exertion scale for young children. *Perceptual and Motor Skills*, 79, 1451–1458.

Yelling, M., Lamb, K. and Swaine, L. L. (2002). Validity of a pictorial perceived exertion scale for effort estimation and effort production during stepping exercise in adolescent children. *European Physical Review*, 8, 157–175.

3.10 Clinical strength testing

Dale Cannavan and Katie Thralls-Butte

Maximum strength is the ability of a muscle or muscle group to generate force against an external resistance at a given velocity. The literature describes three modalities of strength testing; however, given the complex interaction of neuromuscular and tendinous factors, these systems should not be interchanged. *Isokinetic* testing is considered to be the 'gold standard' for measuring strength; however, advanced technology and expertise typically dictate that this approach be limited to laboratory and/or clinical settings. *Isometric* tests are applicable in the field setting, but some techniques are limited to laboratory or clinical settings (i.e., manual muscle assessment). *Isotonic (isoinertial)* tests are easy/feasible to administer/implement in field and laboratory settings. Operationally, clinical strength testing will occur in the clinical or laboratory settings. After injury or surgery, regaining strength and restoring muscle balance is required for successful return to sport (RTS).

Isokinetic testing

During isokinetic dynamometry, torque production can be measured at a wide range of velocities demonstrating different strength expressions (slow to fast movements). Testing is typically used for force-velocity or torque-angle relationships of a muscle group/limb, muscle fatigability and joint excursion. Other measures include isometric, reactive eccentric and passive torques.

Isokinetic dynamometers are useful in the rehabilitative/pre-operative/clinical process in which common injuries (such as to the anterior cruciate ligament [ACL]) are assessed. Bilateral, position-specific muscle weakness/pain can be compared using a number of contractile modes (concentric-concentric, concentric-eccentric and eccentric-eccentric) to present a limb symmetry index (Undhein et al., 2015). Hamstring-to-quadriceps ratio (HQR) can be assessed for RTS protocols when significant alterations exist post ACL injury (Kim et al., 2016). Additionally, the rate of force development (RFD) of HQR has shown high reliability (Zebis et al., 2011) and may be a useful tool in RTS protocols given the importance of RFD in joint stabilisation and athletic success. Furthermore, eccentric strength improvements have been shown to reduce the prevalence of hamstring injuries (Peterson et al., 2011). Isokinetic dynamometers have shown very good to excellent reliability, although joint dependent, and validity up to 300 degrees/s (for a review see

DOI: 10.4324/9781003045267-22

Caruso et al., 2012). However, a strict testing protocol with at least one familiarisation session is needed.

Suggested protocol for isokinetic testing

1   Warm-up with full range of motion (ROM; within injury constraints) and incremental load progression for physical, mental preparation and familiarity of the test without fatigue.
2   Minimal duration of static stretching to prevent stretch-induced strength deficits (Kay and Blazevich, 2012); dynamic stretching/mobility may be preferred.
3   Repeated testing at the same time of day in the same environmental conditions (see the following) and same warm-up procedure. Nutrition, stimulants (caffeine) and sleep should be considered and noted.
4   Ensure a reproducible environment to assure representation of the individual's strength, rather than another factor (e.g., temperature, weight machine/technique used, motivational factors etc.). For females, time of menstruation is an important consideration with strength variation between the late luteal phase the early follicular phase (Blagrove et al., 2020). Practitioners should aim to conduct subsequent tests at the same menstrual phase.
5   Participant secured with joint and dynamometer axes aligned.
6   Gravity corrections performed as per manufacturer's guidelines.
7   Careful selection of ROM and velocities required to prevent joint hyperextension.
8   Three trials performed, although more are necessary as velocity increases (e.g., for knee extension, 4 and 5 trials should be given at 180 degrees and 300 degrees/s^{-1} respectively).
9   Ensure adequate rest intervals (> 30 s); periods up to 4 min are warranted with slower velocities when perceived exertion and contraction time are greater.
10 Test order generally progresses from slower to faster velocities, being identical for subsequent testing sessions.

Isometric testing

Isometric strength testing requires participants to exert a maximal force (at a specified joint angle) against an immovable object, or hold a set level of force for an extended time. Typical systems include dynamometers, force platforms and strain gauges recording maximal force/torque or RFD. The simplicity of these movements requires little familiarisation with moderate to strong correlations ($r = 0.76$ to 0.97) between isoinertial force and isometric force, although this is highly dependent on the joint position (McMaster et al., 2014). For example, test-retest isometric trunk strength shows acceptable measurement error in patients with chronic low back pain (Kienbacher et al., 2016). Short duration (3 s) isometric tests have recently been used, with excellent reliability ($r > 0.86$) to measure fatigue and recovery of football players (McCall et al., 2015).

Isometric strength testing in manual muscle assessment (MMA) has shown good reliability with experienced practitioners, with hand-held dynamometry techniques showing acceptable reliability if strict protocols are followed. Importantly, these techniques correlate significantly with isokinetic dynamometers and sit-to-stand protocols (Bohannon, 2019).

RFD is known as an athletic discriminator with early (<100 ms; intrinsic neuromuscular properties) and late (>200 ms; maximal strength) phases (Andersen and Aagaard, 2006). Contralateral monitoring of isometric RFD during rehabilitation may be a useful identifier in RTS protocols given the need for joint stabilisation.

Suggested protocol for isometric testing

1 As per points 1–4 for isokinetic testing described earlier.
2 Careful consideration should be given to changes in tissue stiffness with excessive stretching and maximal isometric contractions during measures of RFD.
3 MMA should follow specific guidelines depending on the system used.

(for a review, see Bohannon, 2019)

Isotonic (isoinertial) testing

Isotonic (isoinertial) contractions have traditionally been defined as moving a fixed resistance through a ROM. This type of strength testing is commonplace and generally measured using various methods including free weights (see Chapter 3.9 Strength testing, Sports testing volume). Given the strength deficits after injury, a new strength assessment will be required for RTS protocols. Although the 1-RM (the maximum load that a person can lift for one repetition) is the 'gold standard', during rehabilitation, the body will not be ready to withstand heavy loads and a submaximal 1-RM test (using regression equations) will be more appropriate. Most studies support good predictive validity (Table 3.10.1) for multiple repetitions up

Table 3.10.1 Estimated 1-RM formulas from multiple repetition tests

Test	Estimated 1-RM	Adjusted r^2	SEE
Athletic population male[a]	$100 \times$ repetition mass/ $(36.1115 \times \exp[-0.1240 \times \text{reps}] + 67.9776)$	0.96	1.67
Strength trained male[a]	$100 \times$ repetition mass/ $(36.1133 \times \exp[-0.1352 \times \text{reps}] + 68.2982)$	0.96	2.06
Endurance trained male[a]	$100 \times$ repetition mass/ $(37.4720 \times \exp[-0.1056 \times \text{reps}] + 66.2090)$	0.97	1.97
Moderately trained male[b]	$(1.17 \times \text{repWt(kg)} + [2.15 \times \text{reps}] - 12.31)$	0.98	3.7
Female[c]	$100 \times$ repetition mass/ $(41.9 \times \exp[-0.055 \times \text{reps}] + 52.2)$	0.98	Unavailable

Note: reps = repetitions to fatigue, exp = exponent

[a] Formula from Desgorces et al. (2010) experienced male athletes
[b] Formula from Macht et al. (2016) moderately trained men
[c] Formula taken from Mayhew et al. (1992) untrained to moderately trained

to 10-RM, although fewer repetitions are more predictive of a true 1-RM and can be used by either gender (see Mayhew et al., 2008). Furthermore, sit-to-stand protocols show good-to-excellent reliability (0.81 to 0.92) with moderate-strong correlations for knee extensor and leg press strength (Bohannon, 2019).

Suggested protocol for isotonic (isoinertial) testing

1   As per points 1–4 isokinetic testing described previously.
2   Sport/movement-specific tests are preferred to provide appropriate information.

Conclusion

Clinical muscular strength assessment is important to ensure an athlete's RTS competency. Isometric and isokinetic testing are valuable in RTS protocols ensuring correct neuromuscular function before isoinertial strength testing (i.e., 1-RM or submaximal equations) and RTS. It is important to choose an appropriate protocol with attention to validity and reliability in the population/injury of interest. Also, careful analysis and considerations related to the client characteristics as well as their goals must be considered when choosing the most appropriate test(s).

References

Andersen, L. L. and Aagaard, P. (2006). Influence of maximal muscle strength and intrinsic muscle contractile properties on contractile rate of force development. *European Journal of Applied Physiology*, 96, 46–52.

Blagrove, R. C., Bruinvels, G. and Pedlar, C. R. (2020). Variations in strength-related measures during the menstrual cycle in eumenorrheic women: A systematic review and meta-analysis. *Journal of Science and Medicine in Sport*, 1, 1–11.

Bohannon, R. W. (2019). Considerations and practical options for measuring muscle strength: A narrative approach. *Biomed Research International*. doi: 10.1155/2019/8194537

Caruso, J. F., Brown, L. E. and Tufano, J. J. (2012). The reproducibility of isokinetic dynamometry data. *Isokinetics and Exercise Science*, 20, 239–253.

Desgorces, F. D., Berthelot, G., Dietrich, G. and Testa, M. S. A. (2010). Local muscular endurance and prediction of 1 repetition maximum for bench in 4 athletic populations. *Journal of Strength and Conditioning Research*, 24(2), 394–400.

Kay, A. D. and Blazevich, A. J. (2012). Effect of acture static stretch on maximal muscle performance: A systematic review. *Medicine and Science in Sports and Exercise*, 44(1), 154–164.

Kienbacher, T., Kollmitzer, J., Anders, P., Habenicht, R., Starek, C., Wolf, M., Paul, B., Mair, P. and Ebenbichler, G. (2016). Age-related test-retest reliability of isometric trunk torque measurements in patients with chronic low back pain. *Journal of Rehabilitative Medicine*, 48(10), 893–902.

Kim, H., Lee, J., Ahn, S., Park, M. and Lee, D. (2016). Influence of anterior cruciate ligament tear on thigh muscle strength and hamstring-to-quadriceps ratio: A meta analysis. *PLoS One*, 11(1). https://doi.org/10.1371/journal.pone.0146234

Macht, J. W., Abel, M. G., Mullineaux, D. R. and Yates, J. W. (2016). Development of 1RM prediction equations for bench press in moderately trained men. *Journal of Strength and Conditioning Research*, 30(10), 2901–2906.

Mayhew, J. L., Ball, T. E., Arnold, M. D. and Bowen, J. C. (1992). Relative muscular endurance performance as a predictor of bench press strength in college men and women. *Journal of Applied Sport Science Research*, 6(4), 200–206.

Mayhew, J. L., Johnson, B. D., LaMonte, M. J., Lauber, D. and Kemmler, W. (2008). Accuracy of prediction equations for determining one repetition maximum bench press in women before and after resistance training. *Journal of Strength and Conditioning Research*, 22(5), 1570–1577.

McCall, A., Nedelec, M., Carling, C., Le Gall, F., Berthoin, S. and Dupont, G. (2015). Reliability and sensitivity of a simple isometric posterior lower limb muscle test in professional football players. *Journal of Sports Sciences*, 33(12), 1–7.

McMaster, D. T., Gill, N., Cronin, J. and McGuigan, M. (2014). A brief review of strength and ballistic assessment methodologies in sport. *Sports Medicine*, 44, 603–623.

Peterson, J., Thorborg, K., Nielson, M. B., Budtz-Jørgensen, E. and Hölmich, P. (2011). Preventive effect of eccentric training on acute hamsting injuries in men's soccer: A cluster-randomized controlled trial. *American Journal of Sport Medicine*, 39(11), 2296–2303.

Undhein, M. B., Cosgrove, C., King, E., Strike, S., Marshall, B., Falvey, E. and Franklyn-Miller, A. (2015). Isokinetic muscle strength and readiness to return to sport following anterior cruciate ligament reconstruction: Is there and association? A systematic review and a protocol recommendation. *British Journal of Sports Medicine*, 49, 1305–1310.

Zebis, M. K., Anderson, L. L., Ellinggsgaard, H. and Aagaard, P. (2011). Rapid hamstring/quadricep force capacity in male vs. female elite soccer players. *Journal of Strength and Conditioning Research*, 25(7), 1989–1993.

3.11 Blood sampling

Ronald J. Maughan and Susan M. Shirreffs

The collection of blood samples from human participants is required in many physiological, biochemical and nutritional investigations. The purpose of the sample will determine the method of collection, the volume of blood required and the way in which the specimen is handled and stored.

Blood sampling and handling

Many different methods and sites of blood sampling can be used to collect samples for analysis, and the results obtained will be affected by the procedures used in sample collection. A detailed discussion of the sampling procedures and of the consequences for measurement of various haematological parameters is presented by Maughan et al. (2001). Standardisation of sampling conditions is crucial if meaningful results are to be obtained. If or when the study design makes this impossible, it is important to appreciate the extent to which the sample is influenced by the conditions under which it is collected.

The main sampling procedures involve collection of arterial, venous, arterialised venous or capillary blood. In most routine laboratory or field investigations of interest to the sports scientist, arterial blood sampling is impractical and unnecessarily invasive, and will not be considered in detail here. When arterial blood is required, arterial puncture may be used, but in most situations, collection of arterialised venous blood as described later gives an adequate representation of arterial blood.

Pre-sampling standardisation

The composition of blood is influenced by many factors, including recent food and fluid intake and exercise. It is also influenced, however, by many less-obvious factors, including posture and ambient temperature. Failure to control for these will result in an increased variability in the composition of any samples collected, but the controls that should be applied will depend in part on the variables to be measured in the sample.

Blood and plasma volumes are markedly influenced by the physical activity, hydration status and posture of the participant prior to sample collection. In many

DOI: 10.4324/9781003045267-23

cases, samples are collected after an overnight fast of at least 8 hours' duration and without prior exercise. Difficulties may arise in the case of athletes who are training two or three times per day. It is also known that prolonged (1–2 hours) hard exercise typically results in haemoconcentration, but this is followed within a few hours by a marked haemodilution that may persist for several (at least five) days (Robertson et al., 1990).

The sampling site and method can also affect the haemoglobin concentration, since arterial, capillary and venous samples differ in a number of respects due to fluid exchange between the vascular and extravascular spaces and to differences in the distribution of red blood cells (Harrison, 1985). The venous plasma-to-red-cell ratio is higher than that of arterial blood, although the total-body haemoglobin content is clearly not acutely affected by these factors. Haemodynamic changes caused by postural shifts will alter the fluid exchange across the capillary bed, leading to plasma volume changes that will cause changes in the circulating concentration. Moving from a supine position to standing, plasma volume falls by about 10% and whole blood volume by about 5% (Harrison, 1985). This corresponds to a change in the measured haemoglobin concentration of about 7 g L^{-1}. These changes are reversed moving from an upright to a seated or supine position. These changes make it imperative that posture is controlled in studies in which haemoglobin changes are to be used as an index of changes in blood and plasma volume over the time course of an experiment. It is, however, common to see studies reported in the literature in which samples were collected from participants resting in a supine position prior to exercising in a seated (cycling or rowing) or upright (treadmill walking or running) position. The changing blood volume not only invalidates any haematological measures made in the early stages of exercise, it also confounds cardiovascular measures because the stroke volume and heart rate will also be affected by the blood volume. Likewise, studies of running exercise often allow participants to sit or lie down before collecting post-exercise samples.

Flow through the superficial forearm veins is very much influenced by skin blood flow, which in turn depends on ambient temperature and the thermoregulatory strain imposed on the individual. The composition of venous blood is affected by the degree of arterialisation: when sampling occurs over time, therefore, and when the degree of arterialisation of the venous blood will influence the measures to be made, this may cause major problems. In cold conditions, flow to the limbs and to the skin will be low, and venous blood will be highly desaturated. In prolonged exercise in a warm environment, a progressive increase in skin blood flow results in a corresponding increase in the degree of arterialisation of samples collected from superficial veins, the normal sampling site in such experimental conditions. For some substrates and metabolites which are routinely measured, the difference between arterial and venous concentrations is relatively small and in many cases it may be ignored. If a difference does occur and is of importance, the effect of a change in arterialisation of the blood at the sampling site may be critical. Pre-exercise warming of the hand on the limb from which samples are to be collected may reduce the risk of results being influenced by changes in flow.

There is some debate as to which, if any, concentration measurements should be corrected for changes in blood or plasma volume. The modern Coulter counter incorporates an autosampler and spectrophotometer which permits automated measurement of haemoglobin concentration. While this automation has considerable attractions, including a high level of accuracy in the measures of red cell count and haemoglobin concentration, care must be taken in the interpretation of the measures of cell volume. The diluent commonly used in the preparation of samples for analysis is not isotonic with normal human blood plasma: Isoton II has an osmolality of about 340 $mosmol\,kg^{-1}$, compared with an osmolality of human plasma of about 285–290 $mosmol\,kg^{-1}$. Because the red cell membrane is freely permeable to water, a rapid equilibration will take place on mixing of blood with the diluent, leading to a change (in the case of Isoton II there will be a decrease) in the red cell volume. The measured volume is therefore different, by an amount proportional to the difference in osmolality between the plasma and the diluent, from the volume of the cells while in the circulation. In situations in which the plasma osmolality changes substantially, as during intense or prolonged exercise, this will invalidate measures made using automated cell-counting procedures (Watson and Maughan, 2014).

Venous blood

Venous blood sampling is probably the method of choice for most routine purposes: sampling from a superficial hand, forearm or ante-cubital vein is simple, painless and relatively free from risk of complications. During exercise involving the lower limbs, the composition of venous blood collected from a hand or arm vein will be very different from that of veins draining the active muscles. In exercise involving the arms, such as in many Paralympic sports, account needs to be taken of the sampling site and of the consequences of changes in flow rate that occur during exercise. Sampling may be by venous puncture or by an indwelling cannula. When repeated sampling is necessary at short time intervals, introduction of a cannula is obviously preferred to avoid repeated venous punctures. Either a plastic cannula or a butterfly-type cannula can be used. The latter has obvious limitations if introduced into an ante-cubital vein, since movement of the elbow is severely restricted. However, because it is smaller and therefore less painful for the participant, it is often preferable if used in a superficial hand or forearm vein, provided that long-term (more than a few hours) access is not required. A 21 gauge cannula is adequate for most purposes, and only when large volumes of blood are required will a larger size be necessary. In most situations in which vigorous movements are likely, the forearm site is preferred to the elbow. Clotting of blood in the cannula is easily avoided by flushing with sterile isotonic saline. When intermittent sampling is performed, the cannula may be flushed with a bolus of saline to which heparin (10–50 $IU\,ml^{-1}$ of saline) is added, allowing the participant freedom to move around between samples. Alternatively, when the participant is to remain static, as in a cycle or treadmill exercise test, a continuous slow infusion (about 0.3 $ml\,min^{-1}$) of isotonic saline may be used, avoiding the need to add heparin. Collection of samples by repeated venous puncture is not practical in most exercise situations and increases the risk that samples will be affected by venous occlusion applied during puncture.

Arterialised venous blood

When arterial blood is required, there is no alternative to arterial puncture, but for most practical purposes, blood collected from a superficial vein on the dorsal surface of a heated hand is indistinguishable from arterial blood. This reflects both the very high flow rate and the opening of arterio-venous shunts in the hand. Sampling can conveniently be achieved by introduction of a butterfly cannula into a suitable vein. The hand is first heated, either by immersion up to the forearm for at least 10 min in hot (about 42°C) water (Forster et al., 1972) or by insertion into a hot air box (McGuire et al., 1976). If hot water immersion is used prior to exercise, arterialisation – as indicated by oxygen saturation – can be maintained for some considerable time by wearing a glove, allowing this technique to be used during exercise studies. This procedure allows large volumes of blood to be collected without problems.

Capillary blood

When only small samples of blood are required, capillary blood samples can readily be obtained from a fingertip or ear lobe. The use of micromethods for analysis means that the limited sample volume that can be obtained should not necessarily be a problem in metabolic studies. It is possible to make duplicate measurements of the concentrations of glucose, lactate, pyruvate, alanine, glycerol, acetoacetate and 3-hydroxybutyrate as well as several other metabolites on a single 20 μl blood sample using routine laboratory methods (Maughan, 1982).

The sampling site should be arterialised, by immersion of the whole hand in hot (42°C) water in the case of the fingertip, and by the use of a rubefacient in the case of the ear lobe. Samples can be obtained without stimulating vasodilatation, but bleeding is slower, the volumes that can be reliably collected are smaller, and the composition of the sample is more variable. It is essential that a free-flowing sample is obtained. If pressure is applied, an excess of plasma over red cells will be obtained. Samples are most conveniently collected into graduated glass capillaries when only small volumes are required (typically 10–100 μl). The blood must never be expelled from these tubes by mouth, because of the obvious risks involved. Volumes greater than about 0.5 ml are difficult to obtain by this method.

Blood treatment after collection

Analysis of most metabolites can be carried out using whole blood, plasma or serum, but the differential distribution of most metabolites and substrates between the plasma and the intracellular space may affect values. It is convenient to use whole blood for the measurement of most metabolites. Glucose and lactate are commonly measured in either plasma or whole blood, but glycerol and free fatty acid concentrations should be measured using plasma or serum. The differences become significant when there is a concentration difference between the intracellular and extracellular compartments.

If plasma is to be obtained by centrifugation of the sample, a suitable anticoagulant must be added. A variety of agents can be used, depending on the measurements to be made. The potassium salt of EDTA is a convenient anticoagulant, but is clearly inappropriate when plasma potassium is to be measured. Heparin is a suitable alternative in this situation. For serum collection, blood should be added to a plain tube and left for at least one hour before centrifugation: clotting will take place more rapidly if the sample is left in a warm place. If there is a need to stop glycolysis in serum or plasma samples (for example, when the concentration of glucose, lactate or other glycolytic intermediates is to be measured), fluoride should be added: failure to do this will result in measurable decreases in glucose concentration and increases in lactate concentration. When metabolites of glucose are to be measured in whole blood, the most convenient method is immediate deproteinisation of the sample to inactivate the enzymes which would otherwise alter the concentrations of substances of interest after the sample has been withdrawn.

Safety issues

Whatever method is used for the collection of blood samples, the safety of the participant and of the investigator is paramount. Strict safety precautions must always be followed in the sampling and handling of blood. It is wise to assume that all samples are infected and to treat them accordingly. This means wearing gloves and appropriate protective clothing and following guidelines for handling of samples and disposal of waste material. Appropriate antiseptic procedures must always be followed, including ensuring cleanliness of the sampling environment, cleaning of the puncture site and use of clean materials to staunch bleeding after sampling. Blood sampling should be undertaken only by those with appropriate training and insurance coverage, and a qualified first-aider should be available at all times. All contaminated materials must be disposed of using appropriate and clearly identified waste containers. Used needles, cannulae and lancets must be disposed of immediately in a suitable sharps bin: resheathing of used needles must never be attempted. Sharps – whether contaminated or not – must always be disposed of in an approved container and must never be mixed with other waste. Any spillage of blood must be treated immediately.

There is clearly a need for appropriate training of all laboratory personnel involved in any aspect of blood sampling and handling. Most major hospitals run courses for the training of phlebotomists, who are often individuals with no medical background. The taking of blood samples is a simple physical skill, and medical training is not required when expert assistance is at hand. What is essential, though, is the necessary back-up if something goes wrong, and a suitable training in first aid and resuscitation should be seen as a necessary part of the training for the sport scientists who collects blood samples outside a hospital setting.

References

Forster, H. V., Dempsey, J. A., Thomson, J., Vidruk, E. and DoPico, G. A. (1972). Estimation of arterial PO_2, PCO_2, pH and lactate from arterialized venous blood. *Journal of Applied Physiology*, 32, 134–137.

Harrison, M. (1985). Effects of thermal stress and exercise on blood volume in humans. *Physiological Reviews*, 65, 149–209.

Maughan, R. J. (1982). A simple rapid method for the determination of glucose, lactate, pyruvate, alanine, 3-hydroxybutyrate and acetoacetate on a single 20μl blood sample. *Clinical Chimica Acta*, 122, 232–240.

Maughan, R. J., Leiper, J. B. and Greaves, M. (2001). Haematology. In R. G. Eston and T. P. Reilly (eds.), *Kinanthropometry and Exercise Physiology Laboratory Manual*, 2nd ed., Vol. 2, pp. 99–115. London: Spon.

McGuire, E. A. H., Helderman, J. H., Tobin, J. D., Andres, R. and Berman, M. (1976). Effects of arterial versus venous sampling on analysis of glucose kinetics in man. *Journal of Applied Physiology*, 41, 565–573.

Robertson, J. D., Maughan, R. J., Walker, K. A. and Davidson, R. J. L. (1990). Plasma viscosity and the haemodilution following distance running. *Clinical Hemorheology and Microcirculation*, 10, 51–57.

Watson, P. and Maughan, R. J. (2014). Artifacts in plasma volume changes due to hematology analyzer derived hematocrit. *Medicine & Science in Sports & Exercise*, 46, 52–59.

3.12 Field-based assessments for determining aerobic fitness and exercise prescription

John P. Buckley, Jennifer Reed and Tim Grove

This chapter provides the rationale and guidance for using field-based assessments (FBAs) of cycle ergometry, walking/running (treadmill or shuttle/timed walks/runs) and step tests in at-risk or clinical populations. FBAs are used to save expense and as a pragmatic solution to allow a large number of tests to be conducted in clinical, community and home settings (Cowie et al., 2019). The evidence is robust with applications in many clinical populations: cardiovascular, pulmonary, metabolic conditions, cancer, mental health, neuromotor and musculoskeletal conditions (Noonan and Dean, 2000). FBAs can provide data to support three main objectives:

1 Determining clinical or health risk
2 Informing physical activity guidance and exercise prescription
3 Determining functional capacity changes between baseline and follow-up, to provide individual client/patient feedback, service audit or research data

Underpinning assumptions of cardiorespiratory-metabolic estimates of exercise intensity

FBAs are used to estimate maximal aerobic power ($\dot{V}O_2max$) based on the relationship between work-rate (walking/running speed, cycle watts, step height and rate) and the following parameters: age-estimated maximal heart rate (HRmax); ratings of perceived exertion (RPE) (Borg, 1998); and the estimated $\dot{V}O_2$ or METs (Ainsworth et al., 2011; ACSM, 2021). One MET ($\dot{V}O_2$ at rest) is assumed to be ~3.5 ml·kg^{-1}·min^{-1} with multiples used to described physical activity intensity. Older adults and those with disease or on cardiovascular medications can have, however, resting $\dot{V}O_2$ values as low as 2.5 ml·kg^{-1}·min^{-1} (Savage et al., 2007; Franklin et al., 2018; Byrne et al., 2005). During submaximal exercise, slowed $\dot{V}O_2$ and HR kinetics (chronotropic incompetence) are features of older diseased populations, in whom it can take as long as 5–6 minutes for a steady-state $\dot{V}O_2$ (MET) or HR to be achieved (Murias and Paterson, 2015; George et al., 2018; Brubaker and Kitzman, 2011; Keteyian et al., 2012). For most FBAs, in which exercise testing stages are between 1–3 minutes, a lower MET value and lower-than-expected HR can paradoxically represent a prolonged use of anaerobic sources. Therefore,

DOI: 10.4324/9781003045267-24

it is important to make close observations of a client's breathing rate, pallor, motor coordination and RPE.

For HRmax estimates in individuals over 40 years old or with a specific disease, there are several more-appropriate formulae available than the typical HRmax = 220 – age (Robergs and Landwehr, 2002). However, whatever formula is chosen, there remains an error margin of up to $+/-10$ beats·min^{-1} in up to two thirds of a population, and up to $+/-15$ to 20 beats·min^{-1} in the remaining third. HRmax error estimates also increase as a function of age (Robergs and Landwehr, 2002). For individuals taking rate-limiting medications (beta-blockers, ivabradine and some calcium channel blockers), HRmax is likely to be reduced by 20 to 30 beats·min^{-1} and this has to be subtracted from the chosen HRmax estimation (Davies and Sargeant, 1979; Joannides et al., 2006; Liu et al., 1999; Wonisch et al., 2003). For beta-blocked heart failure patients, a specific HRmax estimation equation has been recommend (Keteyian et al., 2012):

119 + 0.5(resting HR) − 0.5(age) − (5 for cycle ergometry)

The heart rate reserve (HRR) method (Karvonen et al., 1957) is well suited to represent relative physiological strain in clinical and older populations, in whom the reserve between rest and maximum capacity decreases with ageing. Compared to the more common use of %HRmax, %HRR accommodates for age-related changes to both resting and HRmax, thus reducing chances of under-estimating exercise intensity (da Cunha et al., 2011).

Table 3.12.1 summarises relationships between %$\dot{V}O_2$max, %$\dot{V}O_2$ reserve, %HRR and RPE. In younger adults (<35 years) %HRR matches best with the same %$\dot{V}O_2$ reserve (not %$\dot{V}O_2$ max), whereas in older or less-active and less-fit individuals %HRR can represent the same percentage values as %$\dot{V}O_2$max (da Cunha et al., 2011; Gaskill, 2004; Skinner et al., 2003; Swain and Leutholtz, 1997; Swain et al., 1998).

Table 3.12.1 Matching exercise intensities relative to the proportion of aerobic power (%$\dot{V}O_2$max), with %heart rate reserve (%HRR), %$\dot{V}O_2$ Reserve (R) and Borg's ratings of perceived exertion (RPE: 6–20 and CR10 scales)

%$\dot{V}O_2$max and %HRR Values Match for Older, or Less-Active, or Less-Fit Adults	%$\dot{V}O_2$R and %HRR Values for Younger (<35 yrs) Adults	RPE 6–20	CR-10
30%	22%	≤10	≤1.5
40%	33%	11	2
50%	44%	12	2.5
60%	55%	13	3
70%	66%	14	4
80%	78%	15	5

Source: (da Cunha et al., 2011; Gaskill, 2004; Skinner et al., 2003; Swain and Leutholtz, 1997; Swain et al., 1998)

General methods of testing protocols

Protocols to estimate $\dot{V}O_2$max (Table 3.12.2) are typically derived and validated against cardiopulmonary exercise testing using one of three methods:

a   An incremental protocol that takes participants to an observed volitional maximal exertion at which point the highest $\dot{V}O_2$ is translated into a known external work rate (cycle watts, treadmill speed and gradient, over-ground walking/running speed) (Singh et al., 1992; Myers et al., 2002; Jolly et al., 2008; Lee et al., 2010).

b   A 'timed' endurance task (distance or total work achieved), which is then correlated with a set of normative population $\dot{V}O_2$max mean scores (e.g., 12 or 6 min walk test or fixed-rate step test) (Johnson et al., 1942; McGavin et al., 1976; Guyatt et al., 1985; ATS, 2002; Troosters et al., 2002).

c   A 'submaximal' incremental protocol that takes participants up to a target intensity (e.g., 65–75% HRR or 14 on Borg's 6–20 RPE scale) (Borg, 1998), and extrapolates this data to an age-estimated HRmax or RPE 19/20 paralleled by the corresponding $\dot{V}O_2$, which becomes the assumed $\dot{V}O_2$max (Astrand and Ryhming, 1954; Buckley et al., 2004; Sykes and Roberts, 2004; Karloh et al., 2013; Reed et al., 2019; Izquierdo et al., 2019; Morris et al., 2019; Coquart et al., 2015; Byrne et al., 2005; Legge and Banister, 1986; Beekley et al., 2004; ACSM, 2021).

Risk stratification

The ACSM (2021), the American Association of Cardiovascular and Pulmonary Rehabilitation (AACVPR, 2020) and the European Society of Cardiology (ESC) (Abreu et al., 2020) all use $\dot{V}O_2$max and/or maximal METs for risk stratification of a clinical event occurring during moderate-to-vigorous exertion and/or risk of developing significant disease or premature mortality. The two categories are defined as follows:

1   *High risk – $\dot{V}O_2$max < 14–17.5 ml·kg^{-1}·min^{-1} (< 4–5 METs)
2   Low risk – $\dot{V}O_2$max > 21–25 ml·kg^{-1}·min^{-1} (> 6–7 METs)

*When assessing suspected higher-risk patients/clients, it may be advisable to use a cycle ergometer that not only starts at a very low work rate (<10 W or 2 METs), but clinically makes it easier and more accurate than all other modes of testing to assess exercising blood pressure, pulse oximetry and, if required, a simple 1- to 3-lead ECG to check for arrhythmias.

For most FBAs cited in this chapter, the validation studies report a minimum mean error of 10–15% between estimated and actual $\dot{V}O_2$max. To mitigate a lack of confidence in the validity of such error, a more pragmatic observational approach to performing the tests can be used to make the results more valuable, as exampled in these two cases:

Case 1: A male client (85 kg) completes a step test (step height of 15 cm at 15 steps per min). The test was stopped here due to not maintaining stepping

Table 3.12.2 Summary of protocol features of commonly used field-based functional capacity assessments

Test	Protocol Design	Lowest Starting Intensity	Non-Clinical Event End Point
Cycle ergometer			
1. Astrand/ ACSM	2–3 min increments, submaximal, predicted $\dot{V}O_2$max from HR/RPE extrapolation to max	0 W electromechanically braked, 25 W mechanically braked, 40 W self-powered fitness cycle	70–75% HRR, RPE 14–15 (CR10 4–5)
Step test			
2. Astrand-Ryhming	5 min, 22.5 steps/min, 33 or 40 cm step height for females and males, respectively	33 cm step, 22.5 steps/min	
3. Chester step test	2 min increments of 5 steps/min, submaximal predicted $\dot{V}O_2$max from HR/RPE extrapolation to max	15 cm step, 15 steps/min = 3 METs	70–75% HRR, RPE 14–15 (CR10 4–5)
4. Canadian aerobic-fitness test	3 min, 1 MET increments, submaximal, predicted $\dot{V}O_2$max from HR correlated to population norm	= 4 METs	85% HRmax (~RPE 15)
Shuttle walking			
5. Six-minute walk test (20–30 m)	Self-paced clinician choice of submaximal or maximal effort. Predicted $\dot{V}O_2$max from population norm for distance achieved in	Clinician-guided, client-agreed	End of 6 min, client can take rest-breaks during test if required but clock continues
6. Incremental 10 m shuttle walk test	1 min increments. Choice of maximal effort with predicted $\dot{V}O_2$max from population norm for distance achieved or submaximal predicted VO$_2$max from HR/RPE extrapolation to max	30 m/min; 1.8 kph; 1.1 mph = 2.1 METs	Maximal exertion or symptom limited or submaximal: 70–75% HRR, RPE 14–15 (CR10 4–5). See profession-specific guidance on condition-specific end points
Treadmill tests	All treadmill protocols have choice of maximal protocol for predicting $\dot{V}O_2$max from final speed/grade or submaximal predicted $\dot{V}O_2$max from HR/RPE extrapolation to max		All treadmill protocols have clinician choice of maximal exertion or submaximal protocols. Submaximal ends at 70–75% HRR, RPE 14–15 (CR-10 4–5)

(Continued)

Table 3.12.2 (Continued)

Test	Protocol Design	Lowest Starting Intensity	Non-Clinical Event End Point
7. Bruce	3 min increments, speed and gradient change	45 m/min, 2.7 kph, 1.7 mph: on 10% grade = 5 METs	
8. Modified Bruce	3 min increments, starts with two prior stages to full Bruce at 0% and 5%, respectively	45 m/min, 2.7 kph, 1.7 mph: on 0% grade = 2 METs on 5% grade = 3 METs	
9. Fox Naughton	2 min increments; at second stage speed remains constant at 2 mph and gradient is only changed thereafter	30 m/min, 1.8 kph, 1 mph, 0% grade = 1.5 METs	
10. Balke	3 min increments, constant speed of 3 mph and only gradient changed	50 m/min, 4.8 kph, 3 mph, 0% = 3 METs	

For specific details on individual stages and METS: 1, 2, 7–10. (Astrand and Ryhming, 1954; ACSM, 2021; Jette et al., 1990); 3. (Sykes and Roberts, 2004; Buckley et al., 2004); 4. (Weller et al., 1995); 5. (ATS, 2002); 6. (Singh et al., 1992; Hanson et al., 2018; Buckley et al., 2016; Buckley and Jones, 2019) in time/coordination with metronome tempo, noticeably breathing harder, Borg RPE of 15 and HR at 75% HRR. This step height and rate equates to a $\dot{V}O_2$ of ~10.5 ml·kg^{-1}·min^{-1} or 3.0 METs. It was obvious he would struggle to sustain 2 minutes at this level, and considering his breathing, RPE and HR, he was likely exercising at >75% $\dot{V}O_2$max and would thus not be able to achieve >17.5 ml·kg^{-1}·min^{-1} or 5 METs; thus, the performance was categorised as high risk.

Case 2: A female client (68 kg) performs a cycle ergometer test. At 6 min, she has attained a work rate of 130 W ($\dot{V}O_2$ = 26.5 ml·kg^{-1}·min^{-1} or ~7.5 METs); breathing more heavily but still steady and controlled and able to keep a steady pedal frequency without any added accessory muscle movements. RPE score was 15 and she is at 75% HRR. At this submaximal level she has already surpassed the low-risk threshold of requiring a maximum of 7.0 METs.

(ACSM, 2021;Astrand et al., 2003;BACPR, 2014;
Buckley and Jones, 2019)

Physical activity guidance and exercise prescription following an FBA

Physical activity guidance using FBA data involves two key steps:

1   Noting the HR, RPE and MET level at the onset of either symptoms or other notable changes in motor coordination, breathing control and posture as obvious upper limits of safe intensity for subsequent exercise.
2   Taking the determined safe-effective METs noted in point 1 and translating this into known activity work rates (walking/running speed, cycle ergometer watts or other activities in daily life), then setting appropriate durations (e.g., >20 min) and weekly frequencies of participation.

For higher-risk, older or low-fitness individuals, the public health definition of moderate-intensity activity of 3–6 METs (WHO, 2021) could actually be vigorous-to high-intensity (>70% max) when functional capacity is <6 METs. Intensities of light moving and slow walking (1.5–3 METs) for younger or healthier individuals may constitute moderate-to-vigorous intensity.

Reporting changes in exercise capacity for individual clients and service outcomes

As noted earlier, FBAs can have a wide margin of error between estimated and actual values of $\dot{V}O_2$max (Reed et al., 2019; Sartor et al., 2013). To add confidence to the reporting or feedback of changes in aerobic fitness, a long-standing classic 'text-book' principle must be remembered: look for a reduced heart rate (e.g., >5 beats·min^{-1}) or RPE for any given submaximal work-rate (Astrand et al., 2003). Two service case-accounts provide examples of such an application. The first case was an 8-week cardiac rehabilitation programme, wherein there was a large 42% improvement in walking test performance (Buckley et al., 2010), but in respecting the notion of improvement from a practice effect being ~10–15% (Nevill and Atkinson, 1997; Jolly et al., 2008), 17% of this improvement was assessed to be a practice effect. The true change was a 25% improvement (not 42%) in aerobic fitness, which corresponded to a 25% lower heart rate at any given walking speed. The second case reported a 25% improved six-minute walk test performance over a 12-week programme but they did not perform a practice test (Grove et al., 2019). In respecting the aforementioned 'practice effect' lead to 10–15% of the improvement, the actual change in HR-to-walking-speed ratio was calculated as a similar 13% lower HR for a given walking speed. It is the presence of the reduced heart rate for any given intensity which gives confidence to an actual change in aerobic fitness (Grove et al., 2017). RPE/pain scores relative to a given work rate (e.g., walking speed or cycle ergometer power) have been used in a similar way to HR (Buckley et al., 2014; Sartor et al., 2013).

Summary

The use of field-based assessments in clinical practice aids in a cost-effective means of increasing access and delivery to wider populations of clients and patients. There are challenges to the validity of such assessments, influenced by the error range of the physiological assumptions of key parameters, including estimates of maximal heart rate, metabolic equivalents, ratings of perceived exertion and psycho-social influences on exercise performance. This chapter has however shown how practitioners can accommodate for these error margins when determining individual client physical activity guidance and outcomes or when using results to report larger population or service evaluation outcomes.

References

AACVPR. (2020). *American Association of Cardiopulmonary Rehabilitation Guidelines for Cardiac Rehabilitation Programs* (6th ed.). Champaign, IL: Human Kinetics.

Abreu, A., Schmid, J. P. and Piepoli, M. F. (2020). *The ESC Handbook of Cardiovascular Rehabilitation*. Oxford: Oxford University Press.

ACSM. (2021). *ACSM's Guidelines for Exercise Testing and Prescription* (11th ed.). Baltimore: Lippincott, Williams and Wilkins.

Ainsworth, B. E., Haskell, W. L., Herrmann, S. D., Meckes, N., Bassett, D. R., Jr., Tudor-Locke, C., Greer, J. L., Vezina, J., Whitt-Glover, M. C. and Leon, A. S. (2011). 2011 Compendium of Physical Activities: A second update of codes and MET values. *Medicine & Science in Sports & Exercise*, 43, 1575–1581.

Astrand, P. O., Rodahl, K., Dahl, H. and Stromme, S. B. (2003). *Textbook of Work Physiology-4th Edition; Physiological Bases of Exercise*. Champaign, IL: Human Kinetics.

Astrand, P. O. and Ryhming, I. (1954). A nomogram for calculation of aerobic capacity (physical fitness) from pulse rate during sub-maximal work. *Journal of Applied Physiology*, 7, 218–221.

ATS. (2002). ATS statement: Guidelines for the six-minute walk test. *American Journal of Respiratory and Critical Care Medicine*, 166, 111–117.

BACPR. (2014). *A Practical Approach to Exercise and Physical Activity in the Prevention and Management of Cardiovascular Disease*. London: British Association for Cardiovascular Prevention and Rehabilitation.

Beekley, M. D., Brechue, W. F., Dehoyos, D. V., Garzarella, L., Werber-Zion, G. and Pollock, M. L. (2004). Cross-validation of the YMCA submaximal cycle ergometer test to predict VO2max. *Research Quarterly for Exercise and Sport*, 75, 337–342.

Borg, G. (1998). *Borg's Perceived Exertion and Pain Scales*. Champaign, IL: Human Kinetics.

Brubaker, P. H. and Kitzman, D. W. (2011). Chronotropic incompetence: Causes, consequences, and management. *Circulation*, 123, 1010–1020.

Buckley, J. P., Cardoso, F. M., Birkett, S. T. and Sandercock, G. R. (2016). Oxygen costs of the incremental shuttle walk test in cardiac rehabilitation participants: An historical and contemporary analysis. *Sports Medicine*, 46(12), 1953–1962.

Buckley, J. P. and Jones, J. (2019). *BACPR Reference Tables for Assessing, Monitoring and Guiding Physical Activity and Exercise Intensity* [Online]. www.bacpr.com/resources/BACPR%20 Reference%20Table%20Booklet%20April%202019.pdf: British Cardiovascular Society and the British Association for Cardiovascular Prevention and Rehabilitation (accessed 26 February 2021).

Buckley, J. P., Quinlivan, R. M., Sim, J., Eston, R. G. and Short, D. S. (2014). Heart rate and perceived muscle pain responses to a functional walking test in McArdle disease. *Journal of Sports Sciences*, 32, 1561–1569.

Buckley, J. P., Reardon, M., Innes, G. and Morris, M. (2010). Using a heart rate walking speed index to report truer physiological changes when using walking performance tests in cardiac rehabilitation. *Journal of Cardiopulmonary Rehabilitation and Prevention*, 30, 346–347.

Buckley, J. P., Sim, J., Eston, R. G., Hession, R. and Fox, R. (2004). Reliability and validity of measures taken during the Chester step test to predict aerobic power and to prescribe aerobic exercise. *British Journal of Sports Medicine*, 38, 197–205.

Byrne, N. M., Hills, A. P., Hunter, G. R., Weinsier, R. L. and Schutz, Y. (2005). Metabolic equivalent: One size does not fit all. *Journal of Applied Physiology (1985)*, 99, 1112–1119.

Coquart, J. B., Eston, R. G., Lemaitre, F., Bart, F., Tourny, C. and Grosbois, J. M. (2015). Prediction of peak oxygen uptake from ratings of perceived exertion during a submaximal cardiopulmonary exercise test in patients with chronic obstructive pulmonary disease. *European Journal of Applied Physiology*, 115, 365–372.

Cowie, A., Buckley, J., Doherty, P., Furze, G., Hayward, J., Hinton, S., Jones, J., Speck, L., Dalal, H., Mills, J., British Association for Cardiovascular, P. and Rehabilitation. (2019). Standards and core components for cardiovascular disease prevention and rehabilitation. *Heart*, 105, 510–515.

Da Cunha, F. A., Farinatti Pde, T. and Midgley, A. W. (2011). Methodological and practical application issues in exercise prescription using the heart rate reserve and oxygen uptake reserve methods. *Journal of Science and Medicine in Sport*, 14, 46–57.

Davies, C. T. and Sargeant, A. J. (1979). The effects of atropine and practolol on the perception of exertion during treadmill exercise. *Ergonomics*, 22, 1141–1146.

Franklin, B. A., Brinks, J., Berra, K., Lavie, C. J., Gordon, N. F. and Sperling, L. S. (2018). Using metabolic equivalents in clinical practice. *American Journal of Cardiology*, 121, 382–387.

Gaskill, S., Bouchard, C., Rankinen, T., Rao, D. C., Wilmore, J., Art, S. and Skinner, J. (2004). Percent heart rate reserve is better related to percent VO2max than to percent VO2 reserve. *Medicine & Science in Sports & Exercise*, 36, S3.

George, M. A., McLay, K. M., Doyle-Baker, P. K., Reimer, R. A. and Murias, J. M. (2018). Fitness level and not aging per se, determines the oxygen uptake kinetics response. *Frontiers in Physiology*, 9, 277.

Grove, T., Jones, J. and Connoly, S. (2017). Cardiorespiratory fitness, oxygen pulse and heart rate response following the MyAction programme. *British Journal of Cardiology*, 24, 25–29.

Grove, T., Jones, J. and Connoly, S. (2019). Changes in 6-minute walk test distance and heart rate walking speed index following a cardiovascular prevention and rehabilitation programme. *British Journal of Cardiac Nursing [Online]*, 14, 1–12.

Guyatt, G. H., Sullivan, M. J., Thompson, P. J., Fallen, E. L., Pugsley, S. O., Taylor, D. W. and Berman, L. B. (1985). The 6-minute walk: A new measure of exercise capacity in patients with chronic heart failure. *Canadian Medical Association Journal*, 132, 919–923.

Hanson, L. C., McBurney, H. and Taylor, N. F. (2018). Is the 10 m incremental shuttle walk test a useful test of exercise capacity for patients referred to cardiac rehabilitation? *European Journal of Cardiovascular Nursing*, 17, 159–169.

Izquierdo, M. C., Lopes, S., Teixeira, M., Polonia, J., Alves, A. J., Mesquita-Bastos, J. and Ribeiro, F. (2019). The Chester step test is a valid tool to assess cardiorespiratory fitness in adults with hypertension: Reducing the gap between clinical practice and fitness assessments. *Hypertension Research*, 42, 2021–2024.

Jette, M., Sidney, K. and Blumchen, G. (1990). Metabolic equivalents (METS) in exercise testing, exercise prescription, and evaluation of functional capacity. *Clinical Cardiology*, 13, 555–565.

Joannides, R., Moore, N., Iacob, M., Compagnon, P., Lerebours, G., Menard, J. F. and Thuillez, C. (2006). Comparative effects of ivabradine, a selective heart rate-lowering agent, and propranolol on systemic and cardiac haemodynamics at rest and during exercise. *British Journal of Clinical Pharmacology*, 61, 127–137.

Johnson, R. E., Brouha, J. and Darling, R. C. (1942). A test of physical fitness for strenuous exertion. *Canadian Journal of Biochemistry and Cell Biology*, 1, 491.

Jolly, K., Taylor, R. S., Lip, G. Y., Singh, S. and Committee, B. S. (2008). Reproducibility and safety of the incremental shuttle walking test for cardiac rehabilitation. *International Journal of Cardiology*, 125, 144–145.

Karloh, M., Correa, K. S., Martins, L. Q., Araujo, C. L., Matte, D. L. and Mayer, A. F. (2013). Chester step test: Assessment of functional capacity and magnitude of cardiorespiratory response in patients with COPD and healthy subjects. *Brazilian Journal of Physical Therapy*, 17, 227–235.

Karvonen, M. J., Kentala, E. and Mustala, O. (1957). The effects of training on heart rate: A longitudinal study. *Annales Medicinae Experimentalis et Biologiae Fenniae*, 35, 307–315.

Keteyian, S. J., Kitzman, D., Zannad, F., Landzberg, J., Arnold, J. M., Brubaker, P., Brawner, C. A., Bensimhon, D., Hellkamp, A. S. and Ewald, G. (2012). Predicting maximal HR in heart failure patients on beta-blockade therapy. *Medicine & Science in Sports & Exercise*, 44, 371–376.

Lee, D. C., Artero, E. G., Sui, X. and Blair, S. N. (2010). Mortality trends in the general population: The importance of cardiorespiratory fitness. *Journal of Psychopharmacology*, 24, 27–35.

Legge, B. J. and Banister, E. W. (1986). The Astrand-Ryhming nomogram revisited. *Journal of Applied Physiology (1985)*, 61, 1203–1209.

Liu, X., Brodie, D. and Bundred, P. (1999). Difference in exercise heart rate, oxygen uptake and ratings of perceived exertion relationships in male post myocardial infarction patients with and without beta blockade therapy. *Coronary Health Care*, 4, 48–53.

McGavin, C. R., Gupta, S. P. and McHardy, G. J. (1976). Twelve-minute walking test for assessing disability in chronic bronchitis. *BMJ*, 1, 822–823.

Morris, M., Deery, E. and Sykes, K. (2019). Chester treadmill police tests as alternatives to 15-m shuttle running. *Occupational Medicine (Lond)*, 69, 133–138.

Murias, J. M. and Paterson, D. H. (2015). Slower VO(2) kinetics in older individuals: Is it inevitable? *Medicine & Science in Sports & Exercise*, 47, 2308–2318.

Myers, J., Prakash, M., Froelicher, V., Do, D., Partington, S. and Atwood, J. E. (2002). Exercise capacity and mortality among men referred for exercise testing. *New England Journal of Medicine*, 346, 793–801.

Nevill, A. M. and Atkinson, G. (1997). Assessing agreement between measurements recorded on a ratio scale in sports medicine and sports science. *British Journal of Sports Medicine*, 31, 314–318.

Noonan, V. and Dean, E. (2000). Submaximal exercise testing: Clinical application and interpretation. *Physical Therapy*, 80, 782–807.

Reed, J. L., Cotie, L. M., Cole, C. A., Harris, J., Moran, B., Scott, K., Terada, T., Buckley, J. P. and Pipe, A. L. (2019). Submaximal exercise testing in cardiovascular rehabilitation settings (BEST study). *Frontiers in Physiology*, 10, 1517.

Robergs, R. A. and Landwehr, R. (2002). The surprising history of the "HRmax=220-age" equation. *Journal of Exercise Physiologyonline*, 5, 1–10.

Sartor, F., Vernillo, G., De Morree, H. M., Bonomi, A. G., La Torre, A., Kubis, H. P. and Veicsteinas, A. (2013). Estimation of maximal oxygen uptake via submaximal exercise testing in sports, clinical, and home settings. *Sports Medicine*, 43, 865–873.

Savage, P. D., Toth, M. J. and Ades, P. A. (2007). A re-examination of the metabolic equivalent concept in individuals with coronary heart disease. *Journal of Cardiopulmonary Rehabilitation and Prevention*, 27, 143–148.

Singh, S. J., Morgan, M. D., Scott, S., Walters, D. and Hardman, A. E. (1992). Development of a shuttle walking test of disability in patients with chronic airways obstruction. *Thorax*, 47, 1019–1024.

Skinner, J. S., Gaskill, S. E., Rankinen, T., Leon, A. S., Rao, D. C., Wilmore, J. H. and Bouchard, C. (2003). Heart rate versus %VO2max: Age, sex, race, initial fitness, and training response: HERITAGE. *Medicine & Science in Sports & Exercise*, 35, 1908–1913.

Swain, D. P. and Leutholtz, B. C. (1997). Heart rate reserve is equivalent to %VO2 reserve, not to %VO2max. *Medicine & Science in Sports & Exercise*, 29, 410–414.

Swain, D. P., Leutholtz, B. C., King, M. E., Haas, L. A. and Branch, J. D. (1998). Relationship between % heart rate reserve and % VO2 reserve in treadmill exercise. *Medicine & Science in Sports & Exercise*, 30, 318–321.

Sykes, K. and Roberts, A. R. (2004). The Chester step test: A simple yet effective tool for the prediction of aerobic capacity. *Physiotherapy*, 90, 183–188.

Troosters, T., Gosselink, R. and Decramer, M. (2002). Six-minute walk test: A valuable test, when properly standardized. *Physical Therapy*, 82, 826–827; author reply 827–828.

Weller, I. M., Thomas, S. G., Gledhill, N., Paterson, D. and Quinney, A. (1995). A study to validate the modified Canadian Aerobic Fitness Test. *Canadian Journal of Applied Physiology*, 20, 211–221.

WHO. (2021). *What Is Moderate-Intensity and Vigorous-Intensity Physical Activity?* [Online]. Geneva: World Health Organisation (accessed 3 May 2021).

Wonisch, M., Hofmann, P., Fruhwald, F. M., Kraxner, W., Hodl, R., Pokan, R. and Klein, W. (2003). Influence of beta-blocker use on percentage of target heart rate exercise prescription. *European Journal of Cardiovascular Prevention and Rehabilitation*, 10, 296–301.

3.13 Quantifying free-living physical activity and sedentary behaviours in adults

Oliver J. Peacock, Enhad A. Chowdhury and Dylan Thompson

Low physical activity is a major public health problem and an important independent risk factor for chronic diseases such as cardiovascular disease (Lee et al., 2012). Healthcare systems worldwide are being called upon to implement effective physical activity assessment and promotion strategies (Lobelo et al., 2018). With the development of device-based measurement tools it is now possible to characterise 24-hour free-living physical activity and sedentary behaviour over days and weeks. Technological progress means feedback from monitor-based devices creates unprecedented opportunities for practitioners to initiate discussions and provide personalised physical activity prescriptions for patients/users. However, the rapid development in monitor-based technologies and techniques makes it challenging for practitioners and exercise professionals to make decisions about how to collect, process and quantify physical activity data. This is important, because different approaches for handling the same data can have a substantial impact on values derived for the same physical activity outcomes and thus alter interpretation of these outcomes.

This chapter will introduce some of the key considerations for healthcare professionals regarding (1) monitor selection and data collection, (2) physical activity patterns and data processing and (3) newer monitoring technologies.

Monitor selection and data collection

The measurement of free-living physical activity has improved dramatically in recent years, and valid, affordable and feasible device-based measures are increasingly available. The majority of devices use internal accelerometers to produce raw indicators of movement often referred to as 'activity counts'. These raw activity data are typically converted into more physiologically meaningful outcomes such as energy expenditure or multiples of Resting Metabolic Rate (RMR) known as Metabolic Equivalents (METs). A detailed technical specification of motion sensors has been described previously (Chen et al., 2012).

Recognising that there is an inherent administrative 'burden' with the use of activity monitors (i.e., wear/care instructions, calibration/setup, distribution/

DOI: 10.4324/9781003045267-25

collection and battery charging), most devices are generally easy to use. However, there are several decisions to be made to inform monitor selection and the data collection strategy. An initial consideration is to define the population of interest in terms of age, sex, body mass, clinical condition (e.g., cardiovascular disease) and other characteristics, since this will impact many other data collection and processing decisions. For example, compared with healthy populations, patients with chronic disease are likely to engage in lower levels/intensities of activity. Physical activities are usually classified according to type, frequency, duration and intensity (i.e., sedentary, light, moderate and vigorous) and outcomes of interest will determine monitor selection, e.g., some monitors have low sensitivity for detecting sedentary time or light intensity activity and multi-sensor devices (that collect data on both physiological and mechanical variables) are typically required for detecting non-ambulatory activities or to account for additional load carriage. Another critical decision is the epoch or sampling timeframe over which physical activity data are collected since this may directly influence outcomes. Most research-grade devices allow the selection of sampling frequency, and a common epoch length is 60 seconds because a minute is a pragmatic unit for evaluation. However, shorter epoch lengths may be required to capture intermittent/sporadic or vigorous-intensity activities. Traditionally, activity monitors have been worn on the waist or hip, but there has been a transition towards the use of wrist-mounted devices for practical reasons such as improved compliance (i.e., less need to remove the monitor). Other protocol decisions that can be made *a priori* include the number of valid days needed to capture habitual activity (e.g., 4 to 7 days and number of week or weekend days) and the length of registration period (e.g., waking-hour versus 24-hour).

Physical activity patterns and data processing

It is important to recognise that, whilst device-based measurements may provide 'objective' measures of physical activity, this is not the same as 'impartial'. Physical activity assessments comprise thousands of data points collected over extended periods of time, and overall interpretation about a given person/group will involve many decisions by practitioners/users. Data processing typically requires 'quality control' checks for identifying spurious or physiologically implausible data and any periods of non-wear time. Figure 3.13.1 (Plot A) illustrates the impact of low or incomplete monitor data compared to a more complete day (i.e., 75% versus 100% of a total day) on time engaged in moderate-intensity activity. In this example, a period of non-wear time failed to account for 90 minutes of moderate-intensity activity. Importantly, procedures to account for missing data (e.g., removing non-wear time and/or interpolating with RMR) should be planned and systematic. Other key decisions include whether to use absolute energy expenditure or energy expenditure normalised to mass or some other factor such as RMR (i.e., METs). The factor (denominator) that is used will influence interpretation, as will the intensity thresholds used to define specific features of free-living physical activity (e.g., moderate-intensity physical activity). Another critical decision is whether judgements are benchmarked against pattern-based physical activity measures (e.g., time engaged in moderate intensity) or average summative scores, e.g., daily physical activity level (PAL; total energy expenditure expressed in multiples of RMR). Figure 3.13.1 (Plot B) shows the influence of using different absolute 'cut-off points' for the estimation of intensity-specific physical activity levels. In this example, moderate-intensity activity above 3 METs was 3-fold greater than moderate intensity activity above 4 METs, and shows how 'where you draw the line' can impact interpretation of the same raw data. This issue is further complicated since processing criteria can be age-specific to account for differences in physical activity patterns (Garber et al., 2011). Even using summative scores such as PAL is not entirely straightforward, since the definition of an 'active' PAL is not universally agreed upon (Brooks et al., 2004). All of these choices will influence physical activity outcomes and judgements about whether a given individual or group is considered 'active' or 'sedentary' (Thompson et al., 2009). Thus, practitioners should carefully consider their approach to free-living physical activity assessment and take this into account when forming judgements. It is quite feasible that a person could score well according to one outcome (e.g., PAL) but poorly according to another (e.g., time engaged in moderate-intensity activity or sedentary time). Given this heterogeneity in performance, practitioners may want to consider the assessment and provision of a profile across multiple outcomes (Thompson and Batterham, 2013). This approach enables feedback and advice on which aspects of behaviour are more or less appropriate and provides a platform for practitioners to initiate discussion with individuals about increasing participation in health-harnessing physical activity (Thompson et al., 2015).

Newer monitoring technologies

There has been an explosion in the number of consumer-based wearable activity monitors, and these are of increasing interest for use by health professionals and clinicians. It is important to highlight that not all monitors have the same utility and many products have been released into the marketplace with no or minimal evidence of validity or reliability. However, the accuracy and precision of these technologies will continue to improve, and some monitors produce similar free-living energy expenditure estimates to research devices (Chowdhury et al., 2017). The pace of change is rapid and it will be up to the practitioner to be aware of the methodological effectiveness and feasibility of any activity monitor selected for use when examining physical activity and sedentary behaviour. There are now millions of people worldwide who are self-monitoring their physical activity in a way that was never possible in the past, and practitioners will have an increasingly important role in helping people to make sense of the output from these devices if they are to be used successfully to help support and/or monitor health-enhancing physical activity behaviour.

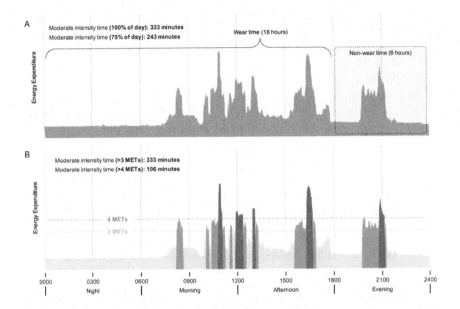

Figure 3.13.1 Impact of data processing decisions on quantification of physical activity
outcomes. This example depicts 24-hour energy expenditure data collected
using an activity monitor. **Plot A** shows the potential influence of incomplete
monitor wear time in the evening versus perfect compliance across an entire
day (i.e., 75% vs. 100% data across a 24-hour period) on time engaged in
moderate intensity physical activity above 3 METs. In this example, non-
wear time failed to capture 90 minutes of moderate activity. This shows
how non-wear time (i.e., whereby the monitor is accidentally or purposefully
removed) can lead to incomplete data and inappropriate conclusions about
a person's physical activity. **Plot B** shows the potential influence of using
different intensity thresholds (i.e., >3 METs or >4 METs) for estimating time
engaged in moderate-intensity physical activity using the same raw energy
expenditure data. In this example, moderate intensity time above 3 METs
was approximately 3-fold greater than moderate intensity time above 4
METs. This shows how the use of different cut-off points and processing
decisions around 'where you draw the line' can impact values derived for the
same physical activity outcomes and the interpretation of data.

References

Brooks, G. A., Butte, N. F., Rand, W. M., Flatt, J.-P. and Caballero, B. (2004). Chronicle
of the Institute of Medicine physical activity recommendation: How a physical activity
recommendation came to be among dietary recommendations. *American Journal of Clinical Nutrition*, 79(5), 921S–930S.
Chen, K. Y., Janz, K. F., Zhu, W. M. and Brychta, R. J. (2012). Redefining the roles of
sensors in objective physical activity monitoring. *Medicine & Science in Sports & Exercise*,
44, S13–S23.

Chowdhury, E. A., Western, M. J., Nightingale, T. E., Peacock, O. J. and Thompson, D. (2017). Assessment of laboratory and daily energy expenditure estimates from consumer multi-sensor physical activity monitors. *PLoS One*, 12(2), e0171720.

Garber, C. E., Blissmer, B., Deschenes, M. R., Franklin, B. A., Lamonte, M. J., Lee, I. M., et al. (2011). American College of Sports Medicine position stand: Quantity and quality of exercise for developing and maintaining cardiorespiratory, musculoskeletal, and neuromotor fitness in apparently healthy adults: Guidance for prescribing exercise. *Medicine & Science in Sports & Exercise*, 43(7), 1334–1359.

Lee, I. M., Shiroma, E. J., Lobelo, F., Puska, P., Blair, S. N., Katzmarzyk, P. T., et al. (2012). Effect of physical inactivity on major non-communicable diseases worldwide: An analysis of burden of disease and life expectancy. *The Lancet*, 380(9838), 219–229.

Lobelo, F., Young, D. R., Sallis, R., Garber, M. D., Billinger, S. A., Duperly, J., et al. (2018). Routine assessment and promotion of physical activity in healthcare settings: A scientific statement from the American Heart Association. *Circulation*, 137(18), E495–E522.

Thompson, D. and Batterham, A. M. (2013). Towards integrated physical activity profiling. *PLoS One*, 8(2).

Thompson, D., Batterham, A. M., Markovitch, D., Dixon, N. C., Lund, A. J. S. and Walhin, J. P. (2009). Confusion and conflict in assessing the physical activity status of middle-aged. *PLoS One*, 4(2).

Thompson, D., Peacock, O., Western, M. and Batterham, A. M. (2015). Multidimensional physical activity: An opportunity, not a problem. *Exercise and Sport Sciences Reviews*, 43(2), 67–74.

3.14 Musculoskeletal assessment

Nigel Gleeson and Andrea Bailey

Musculoskeletal as an adjective describes aspects of, or involving, both the musculature and the skeleton of the body. There are more than 150 musculoskeletal conditions or disorders affecting the locomotor system. These conditions are burdensome, typically associated with pain, exhibit relatively high prevalence (> 21%; World Health Organization [WHO], 2021) and significantly limit mobility, dexterity and overall level of functioning (Cieza et al., 2020). Conditions range from those arising acutely (fractures, sprains, strains) to ones involving life-long persistence affecting joints (osteoarthritis, rheumatoid arthritis, ankylosing spondylitis), bones (osteoporosis, osteopenia, traumatic and fragility fractures), muscles (sarcopenia), spine (back and neck pain) and multiple areas and systems involving regional or widespread pain disorders and inflammatory diseases affecting connective and vascular tissue.

This chapter offers a brief overview of key aspects underpinning musculoskeletal assessments. Readers are directed to definitive reviews of peer-reviewed evidence and respected volumes detailing complementary subjective and physical core and special musculoskeletal tests for the various peripheral and central regions of the body (for example, Clarkson, 2020; National Institute for Health and Care Excellence [NICE] guidelines; Goodman et al., 2017, and other references [see supplementary materials]).

Assessment approaches

Assessment of the musculoskeletal system by means of clinical examination is a central tenet for diagnosing conditions, disorders and injury. Accumulation and interpretation of relevant information facilitates identification of the characteristics and stage of injury or disease, the need for further investigation, cost-effective treatment guidance and outcome assessment. Identifying sources of pain by means of physical testing and reproducible symptoms offers immediate feedback and reassurance of diagnosis to both the sufferer and skilled practitioner.

The plethora of musculoskeletal conditions, disorders and injuries affecting exercisers and sportspeople has been matched by the burgeoning number of core and additional or special tests available to the assessor. In this context, clinical reasoning and focal selection of the most appropriate tests from amongst a vast array, not all of which have confirmed precision and reproducibility, is crucial

DOI: 10.4324/9781003045267-26

to diagnosis. Similarly, diagnostic acuity is dependent on favourable interactions amongst an assessor's technical, clinical and interpretative skills.

Musculoskeletal assessments demand consideration of all factors impacting health (see Framework of Health and Disability, World Health Organization [WHO], 2001), within a wide-ranging subjective examination involving precise communication between clinical assessor and patient and relevant clinical reasoning (Huhn et al., 2018). Assessment involves identification of primary and secondary expectations about the cause of symptoms, and the reasoned planning of safe and effective physical musculoskeletal assessment to challenge the targeted expectations (Rotter et al., 2020). Nevertheless, identifying contraindications to physical examination involving pathologies of a non-musculoskeletal origin such as visceral or systematic conditions, or in conjunction with a patient's history, of symptoms known as 'red flags', signifying the potential for serious pathology associated with tumours, infections or cord/cauda equina compression, must be a priority for an assessor.

Amongst other purposes, a physical musculoskeletal assessment should be targeted to the patient's presentation with aims of determining (i) whether or not specific structures or features might be responsible for provoking or preserving the presenting symptoms, (ii) effects on functionality and (iii) behavioural interactions with a patient's condition and presentation (Health Education England and NHS England, 2018). Musculoskeletal assessments can also act as markers for treatment progression and efficacy.

Influences on test outcomes

Test findings may reflect several influences including that (i) a single test stresses multiple structures (such as anatomical in combination with physiological mechanisms, both proximally and distally linked) rather than any in isolation, (ii) reproduction or easing of symptoms implies a physical test has impacted the faulty structure, (iii) referred pain may be implicated and (iv) objectivity may not be assured since tests are reliant on the assessor's skill in observation, manipulation and palpation. Point (iv) underscores the need to be mindful of a musculoskeletal test's sensitivity and specificity. Sensitivity represents the proportion of individuals testing *positive* and who *do* exhibit the condition. High test sensitivity, often expressed as a percentage, offers testing assurance that a condition is absent if there is a negative test outcome. Specificity represents the proportion of individuals testing *negative* and who *do not* exhibit the condition. High specificity offers testing assurance that a condition is present if there is a positive test outcome, and the avoidance of 'false positives' and 'false negatives' especially, to correctly attribute symptoms and inform decisions of condition management in the process towards optimal outcomes (Simoneau and Allison, 2010). By directly utilising a test's sensitivity and specificity attributes for dichotomous outcomes (i.e., condition present/not present), likelihood ratios can be used to summarise a test's diagnostic precision. Tests offering a large likelihood ratio for a positive test outcome (i.e., >10.0 and pathology present) or a small likelihood ratio for a negative test (i.e., <0.1 and pathology absent), are considered to provide strong evidence to rule in or rule out diagnoses (Deeks and Altman, 2004). While sensitivity, specificity and likelihood ratio constitute popular clinimetric descriptors of a physical musculo-skeletal test, other indicators such as predictive scores (Altman and Bland, 1994), receiver operator characteristic (Hanley and McNeil, 1982) and diagnostic odds ratio (Glas et al., 2003) also have relevance and clinical utility.

Core musculoskeletal tests

The following list offers an overview of core tests constituting a physical musculo-skeletal examination (Atkins et al., 2015), which may be varied in order of delivery depending on symptoms and relevance amongst body regions:

1   *Observation*: Informal and formal observation of posture, muscle bulk and tone, soft tissues, gait, function and patient's response
2   *Active physiological movement*: Active movements, with adjunct targeted adaptations, e.g., repeated, sustained, involving functional and/or combined positions
3   *Passive physiological movement*: Passive movements, including adjunct targeted adaptations, e.g., repeated, sustained, involving functional and/or combined positions, passive physiological accessory movement
4   *Joint integrity tests*: e.g., knee adduction (varus) and abduction (valgus) stress tests
5   *Muscle tests*: Strength, control, length, static action
6   *Nerve tests*: Neurological integrity and neurosensitivity tests, responses to loading and palpation of nerve pathways
7   *Vascular, soft tissue tests*
8   *Palpation*: Soft tissues (superficial and deep), bone, joint, ligament, muscle, tendon and nerve
9   *Joint tests*: Accessory movements testing glide pathways in relevant directions (anterior-posterior, medial-lateral, caudad-cephalad)

Special musculoskeletal tests

As adjuncts to core physical musculoskeletal tests, special tests have flourished and are typically incorporated within the examination framework derived from the wide-ranging subjective examination and relevant clinical reasoning noted earlier. Special musculoskeletal tests are likely to offer the most utility within populations presenting heterogeneous conditions and diminished access to specialist care services, and the least utility amongst environments such as specialist orthopaedic research hospitals, in which rare conditions are routinely experienced and investigated. In this latter scenario, special tests might not necessarily be capable of enhancing diagnostic processes significantly. The evidential basis for a test's diagnostic utility therefore needs to reside amongst that gathered from a range of patients (including condition-mimicking comorbidities), and ideally, from research that has applied a reference or 'gold standard' confirmation with known precision (e.g., magnetic resonance imaging [MRI], or surgery in this context), to all participants, including those who are asymptomatic. Ethical, cost and risk considerations may preclude or relegate the use of reference comparisons to those involving less-invasive approaches, and thus, proffer inferior estimates of specificity. The

Table 3.14.1 Special tests for anatomical regions (with an appendicular skeletal emphasis): Overview of the scope, focus and relevant indicative pooled likelihood ratios reflecting positive and negative test outcomes and residing within the peer-reviewed literature

Anatomical Region	Test Focus	Most Common Disorder	Indicative Positive/Negative Likelihood Ratios
Shoulder	Impingement tests	Spectrum of pathologies associated with subacromial space	~1.82/~0.45
	Tendon tests	Integrity of the 'rotator cuff'	~1.49/~0.96
	Labral tests	Damage to the glenoid labrum	~2.47/~0.78
	Instability tests	Anterior instability of glenohumeral joint	~5.73/~0.32
	Acromioclavicular joint tests	Ligamentous integrity	~1.08/~0.82
Elbow	Tendon tests	Extensor and flexor tendinopathies	Na
	Ligament-instability tests	Valgus (medial) instability and varus instability (including posterolateral rotary instability)	~3.70/~0.05
	Neurological tests	Cubital tunnel syndrome	~1.30/~0.51
Wrist-hand	Ligament-instability tests	Instability of carpal joints; intra-articular wrist pathology	~2.40/~0.51
	Triangular fibrocartilage complex tests	Integrity of structure for soft tissue stabilisation	~1.90/~0.53
	Thumb tests	Osteoarthritis of the trapeziometacarpal joint	~1.4/~0.51
	Carpal tunnel tests	Causal differentiation of hand paraesthesia	~5.40/~0.38
Hip	Articular tests	Detection of pathology or injury within the joint	~1.40/~0.41
	Muscle tests	Pathophysiological changes in muscle extensibility	~5.3/~0.18
	Stability tests	Functional dynamic stabilisation (micro-instability regulating functional capability)	Na
Knee	Ligament-instability tests	Passive movements assessing integrity of ligamentous structures (basic/uniplanar advanced/multiplanar-rotatory)	~9.40/~0.1 ~12.20/~0.43
	Meniscal tests	Detection of meniscal injury	~1.60/~0.79
	Patellofemoral tests	Inter alia, anterior knee pain (chondromalacia patellae), medial plicas, patella tendinopathy, bursitis, neuromas	~1.40/~0.85
Ankle-foot	Ligament stress and instability tests	Ligament lesions and sprains (syndesmosis injuries; Achilles rupture; fractures); inter alia, anterior talofibular, calcaneofibular, calcaneocuboid, medial collateral	~1.80/~0.62

Note: *na* = Not available; robust data lacking.

following listing (Table 3.14.1) of special tests for anatomical regions (with an appendicular skeletal emphasis) offers an overview of the scope, focus and relevant indicative pooled likelihood ratios residing within the peer-reviewed literature and compiled for this chapter from recent database searches (CINAHL, EMBASE, Cochrane, Medline).

References

Altman, D. G. and Bland, J. M. (1994). Statistics Notes: Diagnostic tests 2: predictive values. *BMJ*, 309, 102. doi:10.1136/bmj.309.6947.102.

Atkins, E., Kerr, J., Goodlad, E., Atkins, E. and Kesson, M. (2015). *A Practical Approach to Musculoskeletal Medicine: Assessment, Diagnosis, Treatment* (4th ed.). Edinburgh: Elsevier Health Sciences.

Cieza, A., Causey, K., Kamenov, K., Wulf Hanson, S., Chatterji, S. and Vos, T. (2020). Global estimates of the need for rehabilitation based on the Global Burden of Disease study 2019: A systematic analysis for the Global Burden of Disease Study 2019. *The Lancet*, Published Online 1 December 2020. https://doi.org/10.1016/ S0140–6736(20)32340–0

Clarkson, H. M. (2020). *Musculoskeletal Assessment: Joint Range of Motion, Muscle Testing, and Function* (4th ed.). Philadelphia, PA: Lippincott Williams & Wilkins. ISBN 9781975152406)

Deeks, J. J. and Altman, D. G. (2004). Statistics notes, diagnostic tests 4: Likelihood ratios. *BMJ*, 329, 168–169.

Glas, A. S., Lijmer, J. G., Prins, M. H., Bonsel, G. J. and Bossuyt, P. M. (2003). The diagnostic odds ratio: A single indicator of test performance. *Journal of Clinical Epidemiology*, 56(11), 1129–1135.

Goodman, C. C., Heick, J., Lazaro, R. T. (2017). *Differential Diagnosis for Physical Therapists: Screening for Referral* (6th ed.). Philadelphia: Saunders. ISBN 9780323478496.

Hanley, J. A. and McNeil, B. J. (1982). The meaning and use of the area under a Receiver Operating Characteristic (ROC) curve. *Radiology*, 143, 29–36.

Health Education England and NHS England. (2018). *Musculoskeletal Core Capabilities Framework for First Point of Contact Practitioners*. https://www.hee.nhs.uk/our-work/ musculoskeletal-msk-first-contact-practitioners

Huhn, K., Black, L., Christensen, N., Furze, J., Vendrely, A. and Wainwright, S. (2018). Clinical reasoning: Survey of teaching methods and assessment in entry-level physical therapist clinical education. *Journal of Physical Therapy Education*, 32(3), 241–247.

Rotter, G., Noeres, K., Fernholz, I., Willich, S. N., Schmidt, A. and Berghöfer, A. (2020). Musculoskeletal disorders and complaints in professional musicians: A systematic review of prevalence, risk factors, and clinical treatment effects. *International Archives of Occupational and Environmental Health*, 93(2), 149–187.

Simoneau, G. G. and Allison, S. C. (2010). Physical therapists as evidence-based diagnosticians. *Journal of Orthopaedic and Sports Physical Therapy*, 40(10), 603–605.

World Health Organization. (2001). *International Classification of Functioning, Disability and Health*. Geneva: World Health Organization. www.who.int/classifications/icf/en/.

World Health Organization. (2021). *Musculoskeletal Conditions*. www.who.int/news-room/ fact-sheets/detail/musculoskeletal-conditions (accessed March).

Part IV

4.1 Assessment of peripheral blood flow and vascular function

Benjamin J. R. Buckley, Maxime Boidin
and Dick H. J. Thijssen

Whilst exercise-induced cardioprotection can be partly attributed to improvements in traditional cardiovascular risk factors, the magnitude of effect does not fully explain the risk reduction seen in cardiovascular outcomes and all-cause mortality (Joyner and Green, 2009). Peripheral vascular dysfunction represents a precursor of atherosclerosis (Takase et al., 1998), subsequently leading to the development and progression of cardiovascular disease (Davignon and Ganz, 2004). For this reason, measurement of peripheral vascular dysfunction shows strong predictive capacity for future coronary vascular events (Green et al., 2011). Moreover, the potent cardioprotective effects of regular exercise training is at least partly explained through improvement in vascular function (Green et al., 2017).

The improvements in vascular function that are observed with chronic exercise training appear to be mediated through elevations in haemodynamic stimuli (e.g., blood flow). This makes peripheral vascular function and blood flow central features in the protection against cardiovascular events. The assessment of peripheral blood flow and vascular function is therefore an important area of investigation. These procedures allow insight into the development of cardiovascular disease, but also contribute to better understanding of the detrimental effects of modern lifestyle behaviours, such as reduced physical activity, increased sedentary behaviour and poor diet. These measurements of vascular function and blood flow also provide a promising avenue for early risk identification, but also to evaluate the cardioprotective effects of exercise training. This chapter provides an overview of testing guidelines for common, non-invasive assessments of vascular physiology in humans. This overview is categorised based on techniques evaluating first conduit arteries (large, elastic vessels that maintain high-pressure blood flow) and then resistance arteries (small-diameter vessels in the microcirculation that constitutes major sites of vascular resistance).

Conduit arteries

Ultrasonography

Given the size of peripheral conduit arteries, typically varying between 2 and 10 mm (Thijssen et al., 2008), ultrasound can be used to visualise these arteries and to evaluate blood velocity. This allows for the evaluation of resting blood flow and

DOI: 10.4324/9781003045267-28

vessel structure, but also the assessment of functional characteristics such as flow-mediated dilation (FMD) and carotid artery reactivity (CAR). Ultrasound measures of vascular function typically use high-resolution duplex ultrasound with a 10–12 MHz probe, since most arteries of interest are relatively superficial (~2–5 cm depth). Duplex ultrasound provides a two-dimensional image of the vessel diameter (B-mode), combined with determination of blood flow velocity (Doppler; Figure 4.1.1) (Harris et al., 2010). A sonographer will optimise ultrasound parameters to achieve a satisfactory image of the artery, from which the ultrasound probe's position should be maintained for the remainder of the protocol. Training of the sonographer is important to guarantee high-quality output (Robbin et al., 2011). For research purposes, post-test analysis of the artery diameter and blood flow velocity is recommended to be performed using custom-designed edge-detection and wall-tracking software that is largely independent of investigator bias (Woodman et al., 2001).

Blood flow

Ultrasonography can be used to examine conduit artery diameter and blood velocity, which can be used to calculate blood flow through a conduit artery. These procedures are also used to calculate shear stress or shear rate, the frictional force of blood on the arterial wall. Shear stress represents a highly relevant area in science, which plays an important role in inducing changes to the arterial wall,

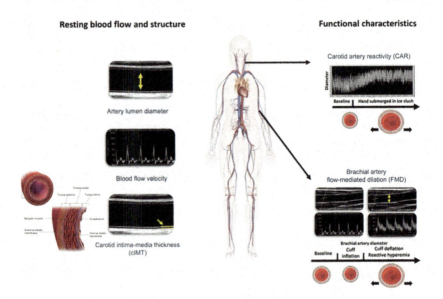

Figure 4.1.1 Illustration of ultrasound measurement of resting blood flow and vessel structure (left) and vascular function (FMD and CAR; right) in healthy participants.

typically via endothelial cell signal transduction (Green et al., 2017). Shear stress is the tangential force of blood flow on the endothelial surface of the artery. The magnitude of shear stress (τ) in straight vessels can be estimated as being directly proportional to the viscosity of blood (μ) and inversely proportional to the third power of the inner radius of the vessel (R), with flow rate represented as Q (Fung, 2013; Malek et al., 1999).

$$\tau = 4\mu Q/R^3$$

In vivo observations indicate that fluctuations in blood flow or shear stress play critical roles in vascular homeostasis and remodelling, and consequently improve vascular health (Cheng et al., 2006; Holder et al., 2019). For example, at the onset of acute exercise, mean blood flow and shear stress drastically increase in the active limbs (Thijssen et al., 2009; Green et al., 2005), whilst decreases are seen in the inactive limbs (Green et al., 2017). The distinct patterns of shear stress have important consequences for acute and chronic adaptations in conduit artery structure (Atkinson et al., 2015). This highlights the importance of assessing conduit artery blood flow and shear stress, both under resting and during various conditions that cause alterations in blood flow and shear stress (e.g., exercise).

Vascular function

Ultrasound can also be used to examine the function of conduit arteries, which is typically performed by examining the change in conduit artery diameter in response to a physiologically relevant stimulus (e.g., shear stress). Here, we discuss two procedures that can be used to evaluate peripheral (flow-mediated dilation; FMD) and central (carotid artery reactivity; CAR) conduit artery vascular function (Figure 4.1.1).

Flow-mediated dilation (FMD)

As introduced by Celermajer (1992), peripheral vascular function can be assessed with the flow-mediated dilation (FMD) technique. Using ultrasound, brachial or femoral FMD relates to the evaluation of the artery diameter in response to a 5-minute period of ischaemia, typically induced by inflating a pneumatic cuff around the forearm or the thigh (distal from the imaged artery) to supra-systolic levels. The artery is typically recorded for a 1-minute baseline period, followed by a 5-minute epoch of cuff occlusion (ischaemia), and then a 3-minute period of post-cuff release (reperfusion). It is important to note that substantial between-laboratory variation is present in the FMD protocol, which impairs reproducibility and comparability between studies. Therefore, it is essential to follow expert-consensus guidelines in the performance of the FMD (Thijssen et al., 2019). Following these guidelines, studies have demonstrated that the brachial artery FMD likely represents an endothelium-dependent, largely nitric oxide-mediated dilation of conduit arteries (Thijssen et al., 2019). Moreover, this non-invasive method has been validated against coronary endothelial function (Takase et al., 1998) and independently predicts cardiac events in participants with cardiovascular disease and even in asymptomatic individuals (Green et al., 2011). Specifically, each 1% increase in FMD has been associated with an 8–15% decreased risk of cardiovascular events and mortality (Xu et al., 2014; Inaba et al., 2010; Matsuzawa et al., 2015; Ras et al., 2013). This demonstrates the clinical relevance of using the FMD technique in (pre)clinical studies.

Carotid artery reactivity (CAR)

More recently, a procedure has been introduced to evaluate central artery vascular function, which adopts activation of the sympathetic nervous system to subsequently evaluate the carotid artery diameter response. Sympathetic nervous system activation is an important and clinically relevant prognostic stimulus, which can be used to evaluate coronary artery function (Schachinger et al., 2000). For example, the cold pressor test (placing one hand in ice slush), is a potent sympathetic stimulus resulting in coronary artery vasodilation in healthy individuals, yet a marked vasoconstriction in people with cardiovascular disease (Nitenberg et al., 2004; Monahan et al., 2013). Although this test of coronary artery vascular function holds independent prognostic value, the invasive and technical nature of coronary angiography prohibits large-scale clinical use. Interestingly, similar to coronary arteries (Zeiher et al., 1991), carotid artery dilation occurs in healthy participants, whereas high-risk participants demonstrate a vasoconstrictive response during cold pressure test-induced sympathetic stimulation (Buckley et al., 2019). Based on this remarkable observation, ultrasound can be used to examine carotid artery reactivity (CAR) in response to sympathetic stimulation using the cold pressor test (Peace et al., 2020; van Mil et al., 2017). Following 10 minutes of supine rest, carotid artery diameter and blood flow velocity are recorded using ultrasound sonography. The participant then immerses his or her left hand (up to the wrist) in ice slush (≤4°C) for 3 minutes. During this, the ultrasound probe position should be maintained, and the participant instructed to remain still, not hyperventilate, or talk unless necessary (Thijssen et al., 2019; van Mil et al., 2017). Finally, because the sympathetic stimulus (ice slush) can cause hyperventilation (Peebles et al., 2007), this should be controlled for by monitoring gaseous exchange when feasible. Previous work has found strong correlation between coronary and carotid artery responses to the cold pressor test (van Mil et al., 2018). Moreover, the CAR test independently predicts adverse clinical events in patients with peripheral arterial disease (van Mil et al., 2019). Finally, it was recently demonstrated that carotid vasoconstriction in response to sympathetic stimulation can be reversed following exercise training (Buckley et al., 2019). This highlights the utility of this novel test of central vascular function in (pre)clinical studies.

Structure

Arterial structure, including vessel diameter and wall thickness, are key variables to measure both independently and in conjunction with vascular function (Figure 4.1.1). For example, resting diameter is inversely associated with shear rate and directly related to peak flow (Pyke et al., 2004). As such, baseline artery diameter is inversely associated with FMD response, with smaller arteries producing a larger functional stimulus (and higher FMD) (Thijssen et al., 2008). It is therefore essential to consider potential differences in artery size when comparing FMD results between participants. It is also important to measure the peak diameter responses in order to exclude the impact of vasodilators and/or constrictors that influence resting vessel diameter (Thijssen et al., 2019).

In addition to the evaluation of the resting and peak diameter, ultrasound can also be used to examine the intima-media thickness (IMT). IMT, measured via ultrasound as the distance between the lumen-intima and media-adventitia interfaces, is a marker of subclinical atherosclerosis and can be measured in multiple arteries, most commonly the common carotid artery. In the evaluation of conduit artery IMT, it is important to use automated wall-tracking software to measure the far wall of the vessel because this improves reproducibility (Naqvi and Lee, 2014; Nambi et al., 2012). Following automated calibration of vessel diameter (a pixel-density algorithm can automatically identify the angle-corrected near and far wall e-lines for every pixel column for diameter assessment), the same algorithm can be used to identify the far wall media-adventitia interface, allowing for IMT interpretation on every frame selected (Green et al., 2010). Regardless of target vessel, IMT is associated with risk of atherosclerosis (Thijssen et al., 2012) and carotid IMT is associated with increased risk of cerebral events (Sun et al., 2020). Carotid IMT may also precede and predict future cardiovascular events (Lorenz et al., 2007, 2012), though does not seem to improve conventional risk prediction models (Den Ruijter et al., 2012; Lorenz et al., 2010). Importantly, exercise training can decrease arterial wall thickness in healthy asymptomatic individuals and those with cardiovascular disease that present with already increased arterial wall thickness (Thijssen et al., 2012). This highlights the utility of measuring vascular structure in (pre)clinical studies.

Arterial stiffness – pulse wave velocity (PWV)

Despite the various possible sites of measurement and devices used, pulse wave velocity (PWV) is typically determined by measuring the velocity of waveforms at two different locations and the time delay (or transit time) measured between the two waveforms. The transit time is therefore the time the waveform takes over a known distance. A variety of different waveforms can be used including pressure, distension and Doppler (Laurent et al., 2006). The distance covered by the waveforms is typically measured by the surface distance between the two recording sites:

$$PWV = Distance\ (metres)\ /\ time\ (seconds)$$

Typically, the higher the PWV, the higher the arterial stiffness and consequent risk of cardiovascular disease. The most common devices for assessing PWV include applanation tonometry (i.e., SphygmoCor or PulsePen devices), piezoelectric mechanotransducer (i.e., Complior or aortic devices), and cuff-based oscillometry (i.e., Arteriograph or Mobil-O-Graph devices).

PWV has been developed as a feasible and clinically important direct marker of arterial stiffness, able to independently predict cardiovascular events and mortality risk (Vlachopoulos et al., 2010). Indeed, aortic PWV (aPWV) improves the prediction of cardiovascular events beyond more traditional risk factors (Laurent et al., 2006; Ben-Shlomo et al., 2014). Although carotid-femoral pulse wave velocity (cfPWV) has been defined as the gold standard for determining arterial stiffness (van Bortel et al., 2012), a number of other sites have been validated as useful surrogates, including brachial-ankle, cardiac-ankle and finger-toe PWV (Milan et al., 2019). Nonetheless, PWV (regardless of measurement site) is an important and independent marker of cardiovascular risk, and useful in (pre) clinical studies.

Resistance arteries

Blood flow (plethysmography)

Introduced in 1909, venous occlusion plethysmography is a non-invasive and low-cost tool that can be used to assess blood flow and reactive hyperaemia in the forearm, calf and thigh (Zwaluwenburg, 1909; Thijssen et al., 2005; Rosenberry and Nelson, 2020). The central principle is that when venous outflow from an extremity is blocked, typically performed by inflating a cuff to sub-diastolic levels, any immediate increase in volume reflects the rate of arterial inflow (i.e., blood flow). Since conception, venous occlusion plethysmography has been used to examine resting blood flow, but also study the acute effects of various physiological stimuli (e.g., sympathetic activation) and/or pharmacological stimuli (e.g., endothelium-dependent and -independent dilators/constrictors) (Arciero et al., 2001; Benjamin et al., 1995; Greyling et al., 2018; Patterson and Ferguson, 2010; Thijssen et al., 2007; Stephen and Richard, 2011). These studies contribute to a better understanding of the (patho)physiology of resistance artery vascular function within and between patient subgroups.

In brief, venous outflow from the target limb is interrupted by a cuff inflated above venous pressure and below arterial diastolic pressure (~40–60 mmHg), proximal to the area of interest (typically lasting ~8 heart beats). The target limb is positioned at the level of the heart to ensure adequate venous emptying during cuff deflation (lasting ~8 heart beats). When examining the forearm, the hands are usually excluded from the circulation during measurements by initial rapid inflation of smaller cuffs, placed around the wrist to supra-systolic pressure (~220 mmHg) (Lenders et al., 1991). The wrist-cuffs must be inflated at least 60 s before starting measurements of flow to allow forearm blood flow to stabilise (Kerslake, 1949). Upon cuff inflation, limb volume immediately changes. These changes in volume can be measured using mercury-in-silastic strain gauges. Peripheral limb blood flow, determined via venous occlusion plethysmography, is then usually expressed as ml of blood per 100 ml of fore-arm volume per minute.

Vascular function and structure (plethysmography + pharmacology)

Venous occlusion plethysmography is most frequently used to assess changes in resistance artery blood flow when combined with physiological or pharmacological stimuli (Figure 4.1.2). For example, maximal blood flow can be examined after a prolonged (5–10 minutes) ischaemic exercise, induced by combining handgrip exercise with inflating a blood pressure cuff to supra-systolic pressure. Peak blood flow values can then be used to examine resistance artery structure. By maximally dilating resistance arteries through this ischaemic stimulus, peak blood flow reflects the structure of the resistance artery vascular bed. Furthermore, vascular function can be examined using venous occlusion plethysmography through evaluation of blood flow changes in response to vasoactive drugs, typically administered intra-arterially via a cannula under local anaesthesia. For example, infusion of power-ful vasoconstrictors (endothelin 1 [Thijssen et al., 2007]), endothelium-dependent dilators (acetylcholine [Walker et al., 2001]), endothelium-independent dilators (glyceryl trinitrate [Ranadive et al., 2017]) or selective blockers (e.g., L-NG-Monomethyl-arginine [McVeigh et al., 1992]), have been used to varying degrees to explore vascular function. An important advantage to this technique is the abil-ity to investigate local effects of selected vasoactive substances, without invoking concomitant systemic effects. To control for potential systemic effects, evaluation

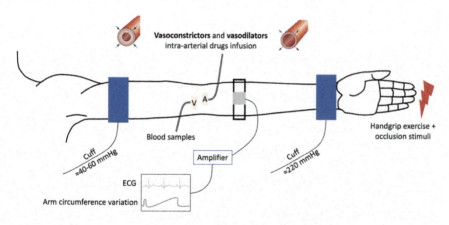

Figure 4.1.2 Illustration of the venous occlusion plethysmography technique to determine resistance artery structure and function via evaluation of blood flow changes in response to vasoactive drugs and/or handgrip exercise.

of venous occlusion plethysmography is typically performed on both forearms; one forearm is used to locally infuse vasoactive substances and the contra-lateral arm is used to evaluate and control for potential systemic effects (including effects affecting blood pressure).

In addition, venous occlusion plethysmography can be used to differentiate endothelium-dependent from endothelium-independent responses (Figure 4.1.2). For example, McVeigh et al. (1992) demonstrated *in vivo* for the first time that patients with type 2 diabetes present with impaired endothelium-dependent and -independent vasoactive responses to acetylcholine and glyceryl trinitrate, respectively. By using L-NG-Monomethyl-arginine to inhibit endothelium-dependent vasodilation via nitric oxide release, the authors were able to investigate endothelium-independent vasodilation in isolation. Impaired endothelial-independent function is associated with structural vascular alterations and alterations in smooth muscle cells (Flammer et al., 2012). It is therefore important to also evaluate endothelial-independent vascular function, though many studies do not, and we therefore know little about non-endothelial vascular adaptations to exercise training. Further investigation will help elucidate the multiple and interconnected pathways underlying upregulated conduit artery function in response to haemodynamic stimuli training in humans (Green et al., 2017).

Summary

Peripheral and central artery blood flow and vascular function are centrally involved in the development of cardiovascular disease. Thus, the investigation of blood flow and vascular function is of great interest for our understanding of the mechanisms, and more clinically, for primary and secondary prevention of cardiovascular disease. The techniques presented in this chapter, therefore, play an integral role in our understanding of the impact of physical activity and exercise on improving vascular function and health.

References

Arciero, P. J., Hannibal, N. S., Nindl, B. C., Gentile, C. L., Hamed, J., and Vukovich, M. D. (2001). Comparison of creatine ingestion and resistance training on energy expenditure and limb blood flow. *Metabolism*, 50(12), 1429–1434.

Atkinson, C. L., Carter, H. H., Naylor, L. H., Dawson, E. A., Marusic, P., Hering, D., Schlaich, M. P., Thijssen, D. H. J. and Green, D. (2015). Opposing effects of shear-mediated dilation and myogenic constriction on artery diameter in response to handgrip exercise in humans. *Journal of Applied Physiology*, 119(8), 858–864.

Benjamin, N., Calver, A., Collier, J., Robinson, B., Vallance, P. and Webb, D. J. H. (1995). Measuring forearm blood flow and interpreting the responses to drugs and mediators. *Hypertension*, 25(5), 918–923.

Ben-Shlomo, Y., Spears, M., Boustred, C., May, M., Anderson, S. G., Benjamin, E. J., et al. (2014). Aortic pulse wave velocity improves cardiovascular event prediction: An individual participant meta-analysis of prospective observational data from 17,635 subjects. *Journal of the American College of Cardiology*, 63(7), 636–646.

Buckley, B. J. R., Watson, P. M., Murphy, R. C., Graves, L. E. F., Whyte, G. and Thijssen, D. H. J. (2019). Carotid artery function is restored in subjects with elevated cardiovascular disease risk after a 12-week physical activity intervention. *The Canadian Journal of Cardiology*, 35(1), 23–26.

Celermajer, D. S., Sorensen, K. E., Gooch, V. M., Spiegelhalter, D. J., Miller, O. I., Sullivan, I. D., et al. (1992). Non-invasive detection of endothelial dysfunction in children and adults at risk of atherosclerosis. *Lancet*, 340(8828), 1111–1115.

Cheng, C., Tempel, D., Van Haperen, R., Van Der Baan, A., Grosveld, F., Daemen, M., et al. (2006). Atherosclerotic lesion size and vulnerability are determined by patterns of fluid shear stress. *Circulation*, 113(23), 2744–2753.

Davignon, J. and Ganz, P. (2004). Role of endothelial dysfunction in atherosclerosis. *Circulation*, 109(23_suppl_1), III-27–III-32.

Den Ruijter, H. M., Peters, S. A., Anderson, T. J., Britton, A. R., Dekker, J. M., Eijkemans, M. J., et al. (2012). Common carotid intima-media thickness measurements in cardiovascular risk prediction: A meta-analysis. *JAMA*, 308(8), 796–803.

Flammer, A. J., Anderson, T., Celermajer, D. S., Creager, M. A., Deanfield, J., Ganz, P., et al. (2012). The assessment of endothelial function: From research into clinical practice. *Circulation*, 126(6), 753–767.

Fung, Y.-C. (2013). *Biomechanics: Circulation*. New York: Springer Science & Business Media.

Green, D. J., Bilsborough, W., Naylor, L. H., Reed, C., Wright, J., O'Driscoll, G., et al. (2005). Comparison of forearm blood flow responses to incremental handgrip and cycle ergometer exercise: Relative contribution of nitric oxide. *The Journal of Physiology*, 562(2), 617–628.

Green, D. J., Jones, H., Thijssen, D. H. J., Cable, N. T. and Atkinson, G. (2011). Flow Mediated Dilation (FMD) and cardiovascular event prediction: Does nitric oxide matter? *Hypertension*, 57, 363–369.

Green, D. J., Hopman, M. T., Padilla, J., Laughlin, M. H. and Thijssen, D. H. (2017). Vascular adaptation to exercise in humans: Role of hemodynamic stimuli. *Physiological Reviews*, 97(2), 495–528.

Green, D. J., Swart, A., Exterkate, A., Naylor, L. H., Black, M. A., Cable, N. T., et al. (2010). Impact of age, sex and exercise on brachial and popliteal artery remodelling in humans. *Atherosclerosis*, 210(2), 525–530.

Greyling, A., Wolters, T. L., de Bresser, D. M., Roerink, S. H., Riksen, N. P., Mulder, T. P., et al. (2018). The acute effect of black tea consumption on resistance artery endothelial function in healthy subjects: A randomized controlled trial. *Clinical Nutrition ESPN*, 23, 41–47.

Harris, R. A., Nishiyama, S. K., Wray, D. W. and Richardson, R. S. (2010). Ultrasound assessment of flow-mediated dilation. *Hypertens Dallas Tex 1979*, 55(5), 1075–1085.

Holder, S. M., Dawson, E. A., Brislane, Á., Hisdal, J., Green, D. J. and Thijssen, D. H. (2019). Fluctuation in shear rate, with unaltered mean shear rate, improves brachial artery flow-mediated dilation in healthy, young men. *Journal of Applied Physiology*, 126(6), 1687–1693.

Inaba, Y., Chen, J. A. and Bergmann, S. R. (2010). Prediction of future cardiovascular outcomes by flow-mediated vasodilatation of brachial artery: A meta-analysis. *The International Journal of Cardiovascular Imaging*, 26(6), 631–640.

Joyner, M. J. and Green, D. J. (2009). Exercise protects the cardiovascular system: Effects beyond traditional risk factors. *The Journal of Physiology*, 587(23), 5551–5558.

Kerslake, D. M. (1949). The effect of the application of an arterial occlusion cuff to the wrist on the blood flow in the human forearm. *Journal of Physiology*, 108(4), 451.

Laurent, S., Cockcroft, J., Van Bortel, L., Boutouyrie, P., Giannattasio, C., Hayoz, D., et al. (2006). Expert consensus document on arterial stiffness: Methodological issues and clinical applications. *European Heart Journal*, 27(21), 2588–2605.

Lenders, J., Janssen, G.-J., Smits, P. and Thien, T. (1991). Role of the wrist cuff in forearm plethysmography. *Clinical Science (London)*, 80(5), 413–417.

Lorenz, M. W., Markus, H. S., Bots, M. L., Rosvall, M. and Sitzer, M. (2007). Prediction of clinical cardiovascular events with carotid intima-media thickness. *Circulation*, 115(4), 459–467.

Lorenz, M. W., Polak, J. F., Kavousi, M., Mathiesen, E. B., Völzke, H., Tuomainen, T.-P., et al. (2012). Carotid intima-media thickness progression to predict cardiovascular events in the general population (the PROG-IMT collaborative project): A meta-analysis of individual participant data. *The Lancet*, 379(9831), 2053–2062.

Lorenz, M. W., Schaefer, C., Steinmetz, H. and Sitzer, M. (2010). Is carotid intima media thickness useful for individual prediction of cardiovascular risk? Ten-year results from the Carotid Atherosclerosis Progression Study (CAPS). *European Heart Journal*, 31(16), 2041–2048.

Malek, A. M., Alper, S. L. and Izumo, S. (1999). Hemodynamic shear stress and its role in atherosclerosis. *JAMA*, 282(21), 2035–2042.

Matsuzawa, Y., Kwon, T. G., Lennon, R. J., Lerman, L. O. and Lerman, A. (2015). Prognostic value of flow-mediated vasodilation in brachial artery and fingertip artery for cardiovascular events: A systematic review and meta-analysis. *Journal of the American Heart Association*, 4(11), e002270.

McVeigh, G. E., Brennan, G. M., Johnston, G. D., McDermott, B. J., McGrath, L. T., Henry, W. R., et al. (1992). Impaired endothelium-dependent and independent vasodilation in patients with type 2 (non-insulin-dependent) diabetes mellitus. *Diabetologia*, 35(8), 771–776.

Milan, A., Zocaro, G., Leone, D., Tosello, F., Buraioli, I., Schiavone, D., et al. (2019). Current assessment of pulse wave velocity: Comprehensive review of validation studies. *Journal of Hypertension*, 37(8), 1547–1557.

Monahan, K. D., Feehan, R. P., Sinoway, L. I. and Gao, Z. (2013). Contribution of sympathetic activation to coronary vasodilatation during the cold pressor test in healthy men: Effect of ageing. *Journal of Physiology*, 591(11), 2937–2947.

Nambi, V., Chambless, L., He, M., Folsom, A. R., Mosley, T., Boerwinkle, E., et al. (2012). Common carotid artery intima-media thickness is as good as carotid intima-media thickness of all carotid artery segments in improving prediction of coronary heart disease risk in the Atherosclerosis Risk in Communities (ARIC) study. *European Heart Journal*, 33(2), 183–190.

Naqvi, T. Z. and Lee, M. S. (2014). Carotid intima-media thickness and plaque in cardiovascular risk assessment. *Journal of the American College of Cardiology Cardiovascular Imaging*, 7(10), 1025–1038.

Nitenberg, A., Chemla, D. and Antony, I. (2004). Epicardial coronary artery constriction to cold pressor test is predictive of cardiovascular events in hypertensive patients with angiographically normal coronary arteries and without other major coronary risk factor. *Atherosclerosis*, 173(1), 115–123.

Patterson, S. D. and Ferguson, R. A. (2010). Increase in calf post-occlusive blood flow and strength following short-term resistance exercise training with blood flow restriction in young women. *European Journal of Applied Physiology*, 108(5), 1025–1033.

Peace, A., Pinna, V., Timmen, F., Speretta, G., Jones, H., Lotto, R., et al. (2020). Role of blood pressure in mediating carotid artery dilation in response to sympathetic stimulation in healthy, middle-aged individuals. *American Journal of Hypertension*, 33(2), 146–153.

Peebles, K., Celi, L., McGrattan, K., Murrell, C., Thomas, K. and Ainslie, P. N. (2007). Human cerebrovascular and ventilatory CO2 reactivity to end-tidal, arterial and internal jugular vein PCO2. *The Journal of Physiology*, 584(Pt 1), 347–357.

Pyke, K. E., Dwyer, E. M. and Tschakovsky, M. E. (2004). Impact of controlling shear rate on flow-mediated dilation responses in the brachial artery of humans. *Journal of Applied Physiology (1985)*, 97(2), 499–508.

Ranadive, S. M., Eugene, A. R., Dillon, G., Nicholson, W. T. and Joyner, M. J. (2017). Comparison of the vasodilatory effects of sodium nitroprusside vs. nitroglycerin. *Journal of Applied Physiology* (Bethesda, Md: 1985), 123(2), 402–406.

Ras, R. T., Streppel, M. T., Draijer, R. and Zock, P. L. (2013). Flow-mediated dilation and cardiovascular risk prediction: A systematic review with meta-analysis. *International Journal of Cardiology*, 168(1), 344–351.

Robbin, M. L., Lockhart, M. E., Weber, T. M., Tessler, F. N., Clements, M. W., Hester, F. A., et al. (2011). Ultrasound quality and efficiency. *Journal of Ultrasound in Medicine*, 30(6), 739–743.

Rosenberry, R. and Nelson, M. D. (2020). Reactive hyperemia: A review of methods, mechanisms, and considerations. *American Journal of Physiology-Regulatory, Integrative and Comparative Physiology*, 318(3), R605–R618.

Schachinger, V., Britten, M. B. and Zeiher, A. M. (2000). Prognostic impact of coronary vasodilator dysfunction on adverse long-term outcome of coronary heart disease. *Circulation*, 101(16), 1899–1906.

Stephen, D. P. and Richard, A. F. (2011). Enhancing strength and postocclusive calf blood flow in older people with training with blood-flow restriction. *Journal of Aging and Physical Activity*, 19(3), 201–213.

Sun, P., Liu, L., Liu, C., Zhang, Y., Yang, Y., Qin, X., et al. (2020). Carotid intima-media thickness and the risk of first stroke in patients with hypertension. *Stroke*, 51(2), 379–386.

Takase, B., Uehata, A., Akima, T., Nagai, T., Nishioka, T., Hamabe, A., et al. (1998). Endothelium-dependent flow-mediated vasodilation in coronary and brachial arteries in suspected coronary artery disease. *American Journal of Cardiology*, 82, 1535–1539.

Thijssen, D. H. J., Bleeker, M. W., Smits, P. and Hopman, M. T. E. (2005). Reproducibility of blood flow and post-occlusive reactive hyperaemia as measured by venous occlusion plethysmography. *Clinical Science (London)*, 108(2), 151–157.

Thijssen, D. H. J., Bruno, R. M., van Mil, A. C., Holder, S. M., Faita, F., Greyling, A., et al. (2019). Expert consensus and evidence-based recommendations for the assessment of flow-mediated dilation in humans. *European Heart Journal*, 40(30), 2534–2547.

Thijssen, D. H. J., Cable, N. T. and Green, D. J. (2012). Impact of exercise training on arterial wall thickness in humans. *Clinical Science* (London, England: 1979), 122(7), 311–322.

Thijssen, D. H. J., Dawson, E. A., Black, M. A., Hopman, M. T. E., Cable, N. T. and Green, D. J. (2008). Heterogeneity in conduit artery function in humans: Impact of arterial size. *American Journal of Physiology – Heart and Circulatory Physiology*, 295(5), H1927–H1934.

Thijssen, D. H. J., Dawson, E. A., Black, M. A., Hopman, M. T. E., Nigel, T. and Green, D. J. (2009). Brachial artery blood flow responses to different modalities of lower limb exercise. *Medicine and Science in Sports and Exercise*, 41(5), 1072–1079.

Thijssen, D. H. J., Rongen, G. A., van Dijk, A., Smits, P. and Hopman, M. T. E. (2007). Enhanced endothelin-1-mediated leg vascular tone in healthy older subjects. *Journal of Applied Physiology*, 103(3), 852–857.

van Bortel, L. M., Laurent, S., Boutouyrie, P., Chowienczyk, P., Cruickshank, J. K., De Backer, T., et al. (2012). Expert consensus document on the measurement of aortic stiffness in daily practice using carotid-femoral pulse wave velocity. *Journal of Hypertension,* 30(3), 445–448.

van Mil, A. C., Hartman, Y., Van Oorschot, F., Heemels, A., Bax, N., Dawson, E. A., et al. (2017). Correlation of carotid artery reactivity with cardiovascular risk factors and coronary artery vasodilator responses in asymptomatic, healthy volunteers. *Journal of Hypertension,* 35(5), 1026–1034.

van Mil, A. C., Pouwels, S., Wilbrink, J., Warlé, M. C. and Thijssen, D. H. J. (2019). Carotid artery reactivity predicts events in peripheral arterial disease patients. *Ann Surg,* 269(4), 767–773.

van Mil, A. C., Tymko, M. M., Kerstens, T. P., Stembridge, M., Green, D. J., Ainslie, P. N., et al. (2018). Similarity between carotid and coronary artery responses to sympathetic stimulation and the role of α(1)-receptors in humans. *Journal of Applied Physiology (1985),* 125(2), 409–418.

Vlachopoulos, C., Aznaouridis, K. and Stefanadis, C. (2010). Prediction of cardiovascular events and all-cause mortality with arterial stiffness: A systematic review and meta-analysis. *Journal of the American College of Cardiology,* 55(13), 1318–1327.

Walker, H. A., Jackson, G., Ritter, J. M. and Chowienczyk, P. J. (2001). Assessment of forearm vasodilator responses to acetylcholine and albuterol by strain gauge plethysmography: Reproducibility and influence of strain gauge placement. *British Journal of Clinical Pharmacology,* 51(3), 225–229.

Woodman, R. J., Playford, D. A., Watts, G. F., Cheetham, C., Reed, C., Taylor, R. R., et al. (2001). Improved analysis of brachial artery ultrasound using a novel edge-detection software system. *Journal of Applied Physiology,* 91(2), 929–937.

Xu, Y., Arora, R. C., Hiebert, B. M., Lerner, B., Szwajcer, A., McDonald, K., et al. (2014). Non-invasive endothelial function testing and the risk of adverse outcomes: A systematic review and meta-analysis. *European Heart Journal: Cardiovascular Imaging,* 15(7), 736–746.

Zeiher, A. M., Drexler, H., Wollschläger, H. and Just, H. (1991). Modulation of coronary vasomotor tone in humans: Progressive endothelial dysfunction with different early stages of coronary atherosclerosis. *Circulation,* 83(2), 391–401.

Zwaluwenburg, J. (1909). The rate of blood flow in the arm. *Heart,* 1, 87.

4.2 Application of dual energy X-ray absorptiometry

Karen Hind

Dual energy X-ray absorptiometry (DXA) is a quantitative imaging procedure for the measurement of bone mineral density (BMD) and the diagnosis of osteopenia and osteoporosis. Given the ability of DXA to concurrently measure whole-body and regional bone, lean and fat mass, DXA has become the method of choice for bone and body composition assessment in athletes. In applied science research and practice, linked to both sporting and clinical groups, DXA is valuable for the evaluation of athlete bone health, recovery from injury and for monitoring the effects of interventions. In a sporting context, DXA is particularly useful for the evaluation of athletes at risk of relative energy deficiency in sports (RED-S), a condition associated with overtraining and/or undernutrition. However, poor-quality DXA acquisition, analysis or reporting may lead to inappropriate scan interpretation, drawing of inaccurate conclusions and uninformed advice to athletes, patients and other colleagues who form part of a multidisciplinary support team. One must also consider the frequency of DXA scanning exposure: although the ionising radiation exposure from DXA is low, scans must always be justified.

This chapter informs on the safe and effective practice of DXA scanning and provides informed guidelines to promote high quality standards in DXA scan acquisition and interpretation in sport and exercise sciences research and practice. These guidelines have been prepared in conjunction with the International Society for Clinical Densitometry (ISCD) position statements, but one must also consider local ionising radiation regulations. Within this chapter, reference is made to 'an athlete', but principles covered apply to any active person presenting for a DXA scan or a participant in sport, exercise and/or health-related research.

DXA technology

DXA uses two X-ray beams of different energies that are diversely attenuated by bone and soft tissue. The X-ray source (which in most models of DXA is usually below the scanner table), generates the X-ray beams containing photons which are transmitted through electromagnetic energy. As the photons pass through the body, there is differential attenuation depending on the density of the tissues. The level of attenuation also depends on the energy of the photons and the tissue thickness. The measurement of bone is based on the assumption that the body is made up of two compartments, bone and soft tissue. Bone has a higher density

DOI: 10.4324/9781003045267-29

than soft tissue and therefore the photon energies are attenuated less. In order to image either tissue, the two energy beams are subtracted from one another, to either subtract the soft tissue and image the bone, or subtract the bone and image the soft tissue. In distinguishing what is lean and what is fat tissue, the bone is subtracted and the ratio of the two photon energies is linearly related to the proportion of fat in the soft tissue (Laskey, 1996). The resulting outcomes are bone mineral, lean tissue mass and fat mass.

Since the introduction of DXA in the 1980s, there have been numerous advancements in the technology including a move from pencil beam to narrow fan beam densitometers and an increased number of detectors, which improve resolution. Such advancements have led to superior image quality and reduced scan times with the average bone density scan taking less than 2 minutes and the total body scan taking around 7–14 minutes (depending on manufacturer, model and scan mode). The most common DXA systems used in the UK are GE Lunar (Madison, Wisconsin) and Hologic Inc. (Waltham, Massachusetts). Both provide bone density and body composition measurements, and additional features such as visceral fat assessment, advanced hip structural analysis and paediatric applications.

Radiation dose

DXA involves a small amount of ionising radiation. The effective dose to an adult from a typical bone density scan is around 7 µSv depending on the manufacturer, model and scan mode used. The total body scan brings a lower effective dose of around 3.0 µSv. It is useful to compare these values to the natural background radiation dose in the UK, which is approximately 7.3 µSv daily (2.7 mSv annually) (Public Health England, 2011). For example, a standard mode total-body scan would give an exposure that is less than one day of natural background radiation. Although the dose of radiation from DXA is small, all laboratories or centres performing DXA scans must follow the regulations set out in the Ionising Radiation Regulations 2017 (IRR17) (Health and Safety Executive, 2018) and the Ionising Radiation for Medical Exposure Regulations (IRMER) (Department of Health and Social Care, 2018), and all operators must have received IRMER-specific training. DXA scans performed for human participant research, with accompanying ethical approval from an NHS Research Ethics Committee where the input from a medical imaging expert and a clinical radiation expert are required.

Indications and contraindications

DXA has an integral place in sport and exercise sciences, given its unique ability to measure bone, lean and fat mass status concurrently, with a high degree of precision. Table 4.2.1 provides information relating to indications for DXA scans. DXA bone density scans have primarily been used for the assessment of BMD and diagnosis of osteoporosis. These scans require a medical referral, unless part of an ethically approved research study. Information is particularly useful for bone

Table 4.2.1 Indications for DXA scans in sport and exercise sciences

Bone Density*	Body Composition
Low body mass index (<18.5 kg.m^{-2})	Chronic LEA/RED-S
Low trauma fracture	Monitor the effect of training and/or nutritional interventions
Bone stress injury, e.g., stress fracture	Monitor the effect of detraining
Chronic LEA/RED-S, eating disorder and/or frequent weight fluctuations	Investigate regional mass to understand injury risk and rehabilitation
Hypogonadism including menstrual disturbances	Inform on body composition for weight-category sports
Glucocorticoid medications	
Malabsorption conditions	

*See also NICE guidelines: www.nice.org.uk/guidance/cg146/chapter/1-guidance

LEA: low energy availability; RED-S: relative energy deficiency in sports

health investigations in athletes with bone injuries such as stress fracture, and in athletes suspected to have chronic low energy availability (LEA) and at risk of relative energy deficiency in sports (RED-S) (Hind et al., 2006; Mountjoy et al., 2014; Barrack et al., 2017; Keay et al., 2019). RED-S is a condition that arises from undernutrition and/or overexercise, increasing risk of low BMD in athletes of both sexes (Mountjoy et al., 2014). In female athletes, amenorrhea (which can develop as a result of chronic low energy availability) is an overt sign there is a risk to bone health. In male athletes, the signs are less clear, but a screening tool can be helpful to identify those at risk and who might benefit from DXA evaluation (Keay et al., 2018, 2019). In clinical practice, bone density scans are not usually repeated more than once annually, but in research studies, scans may need to be repeated more frequently, for example, when investigating the effects of a specific intervention on bone density.

Body composition scans provide invaluable data to inform health and injury management plans for athletes and clinical patients. For example, if an athlete is suspected to be in chronic LEA, DXA has proven useful in the body composition profiling of athletes from different sports (Bartlett et al., 2020); by ethnicity (Zemski et al., 2019); or to monitor maintenance of an optimal body composition status across an intense, competitive season (Harley et al., 2011; Lees et al., 2017). Information is also useful to evaluate risk and recovery from injury by examining any asymmetry between left and right limbs (Jordan et al., 2015). It is reasonable to include a body composition scan alongside bone density investigations, justified on the grounds of providing additional, important information on the health of the athlete, for example, very low body fat or lean mass atrophy. Although the radiation dose is very low, body composition scans must still be justified. With consideration to radiation exposure and the time required to observe a significant change in lean or fat mass, unless a change in body composition over a shorter period is expected, one should not perform repetitive body composition scans more frequently than every six weeks.

One should not perform a DXA scan when:

- an individual is pregnant or suspects that they may be pregnant, or is breastfeeding;
- an individual is unable to provide informed consent;
- it is not possible to provide feedback;
- when a scan will result in an annual ionising radiation exposure that is greater than 1 mSv;
- if there has been an exposure to nuclear medicine examinations or radio-graphic agents in the previous 48 hours;
- if there is a risk that performing a body composition scan may exacerbate body image concerns or an eating disorder; or
- if an individual exceeds a stipulated maximum weight capacity – most DXA models can accommodate a weight capacity range between 160 and 204 kg.

Quality densitometry

Pre-scan standardisation

Prior to any DXA scan, athletes should receive detailed information about the scans and guidance relating to how to prepare. Furthermore, as part of a consistent protocol, athletes complete a pre-DXA screening questionnaire, which covers the contraindications and gathers other important information including the reason for the scan and any internal artefacts such as metal plates and rods, that may jeopardise scan quality. For example, if an athlete reports a metal artefact in the right proximal femur, one should only perform a bone density scan on the left hip and the lumbar spine. Because clothing can impact bone density and body composition outcomes (Siglinsky et al., 2018), it is recommended that athletes wear minimal clothing, avoiding heavy-textile materials, reflective materials, metallic thread and metal artefacts such as zips and clasps.

Diurnal variations in biological factors can also influence information stemming from a DXA body composition scan, namely hydration and stomach and intestinal content. DXA assumes that fat-free tissue is euhydrated with a constant of 73%, to enable the separation of fat tissue mass and lean tissue mass (Laskey, 1996). However, euhydration can vary significantly from 67% to 85% (Pietrobelli et al., 1998; Andreoli et al., 2009) and for athletic groups there are additional considerations for hydration based on fluid losses during exercise training and fluid replenishment post exercise (Nana et al., 2016). Minimising potential errors arising from biological variation is especially relevant in sports science and when working with elite athletes, when the detection of the smallest change is of the highest importance. To ensure that variability is as low as practicably possible, standardised pre-scan conditions should be adopted (Table 4.2.2). To date, research indicates that morning scans following an overnight fast (rested and with normal hydration) provides the ideal condition for detecting small, but true and meaningful changes (Nana et al., 2016).

Table 4.2.2 Standardising DXA body composition scans

Source	Potential Variation	Standardisation
Clothing	Technical error arising from metal artefacts on clothing presenting as bone mass.	One should undertake measurements on participants with them wearing lightweight clothing with no metal artefacts or residues such as chlorine, salt water or sweat. Jewellery and clothing that contains metal (e.g., hair clips, zips, underwire garments) should be removed.
Meal/fluid consumption	Biological variation reflected in changes to total mass and lean mass, arising from the meal consumed (Nana et al., 2012).	Participants should ideally present in an overnight fasted state (no food or fluid for 8 hours). However, it is advised that athletes should be glycogen replete and be euhydrated, with dietary guidance to facilitate this process. If it is not possible to perform a morning scan, advise no food or fluid for 5 hours. If it is not possible to avoid consumption of food or fluids, then it has been suggested that the total content should be no more than 500 g (Kerr et al., 2017).
Hydration	Biological variation reflected in decreases (dehydrated) or increases (overhydrated) in lean mass. Variable hydration of soft tissue can also result in fat estimation error (Pietrobelli et al., 1998).	Participants should be euhydrated and advised to drink one to two glasses of water with each meal/snack the day before the scan. Prior to scanning, participants should empty their bladder. One can obtain confirmation of hydration status by collecting a mid-stream urine sample for the analysis of USG.
Exercise	Biological variation arising from i) the effect of exercise on tissue hydration (loss of fluid through sweat during exercise, and gain through fluid replenishment post exercise), ii) exercise-associated fluid shifts to regional body compartments and iii) shifts in blood volume.	Participants should present in a rested state with no exercise on the morning of the scan and participants should not have undertaken intense exercise since lunchtime the day before.

Scan acquisition and analysis

Calibration

Alterations in the accuracy and precision of DXA information can occur suddenly (calibration shift) or gradually (calibration drift; Lewiecki et al., 2006). To identify such alterations in performance and to ensure stable DXA performance over time, it is important to have a calibration and quality assurance protocol in place. This should involve the daily scanning of the calibration block and the weekly scanning of a phantom (standardised object with a known BMD content), which are provided by the DXA manufacturer. Attention should be given to shifts or drifts in calibration that exceed 1.5% (Lewiecki et al., 2006).

Bone density

One must take care to ensure a consistent approach in the interpretation of bone density assessment (see Table 4.2.3). The ISCD and the National Osteoporosis Guideline Group (NOGG) recommend bone density testing at the lumbar spine (L1-L4) and hip (including femoral neck). If either site is unsuitable for scanning, for example, due to an artefact or injury, the focus should shift to the distal radius for scanning. A manufacturer's instructions linked to scan acquisition should be followed carefully, with particular attention given to the analysis of lumbar spine scans to ensure that the region of interest (ROI) lines must be placed accurately,

Table 4.2.3 Interpretation of DXA scans – bone density

Age <50 years

Z-Score	Interpretation	Action(s)
> −1.0	**Normal** bone density for age	Advise on maintaining a bone-positive lifestyle (weight-bearing and resistance exercise, energy balance, calcium and vitamin D).
≤ −1.0	**Low** bone density for age	Advise GP/sports doctor appointment. Advise on training and nutrition to promote bone health. Supervised plan to include RED-S screen (Mountjoy et al., 2014).

Postmenopausal women and men ≥50 years

T-Score	Interpretation	Recommended Action(s)
> −1.0	**Normal** bone density	Advise on maintaining a bone-positive lifestyle (weight-bearing and resistance exercise, energy balance, calcium and vitamin D).
−1.0 to −2.4	**Osteopenia**	Advise GP appointment. Advise on exercise and nutrition for bone health. Athletes – supervised plan to include RED-S screen (Mountjoy et al., 2014).
≤ −2.5	**Osteoporosis**	Advise GP appointment. Advise on exercise* and nutrition for bone health. Athletes – supervised plan to include RED-S screen (Mountjoy et al., 2014).

*Refer to Royal Osteoporosis Society guidance (ROS, 2022).

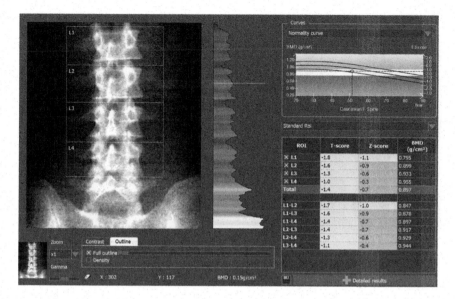

Figure 4.2.1 Lumbar spine vertebral deformities indicating requirement for vertebral exclusion.

according to the manufacturer instructions. These scans should also be carefully scrutinised for abnormalities, such as vertebral fracture and degenerative changes (Figure 4.2.1), which can be prevalent in athletes and former athletes from contact sports (Entwistle et al., 2021). An operator should manually remove any affected vertebrae from the analysis region to ensure bone density is not falsely elevated. When a lumbar spine scan is not readable, for example, two or more vertebrae excluded, results of a hip scan can interpret bone density.

Body composition

Each DXA centre should have standard procedures for body composition positioning that ensures consistency and accuracy. An athlete should be positioned supine with the head in the Frankfort plane position, and with the whole body within the marked boundaries of the scan table. The ROI placements are summarised in Figure 4.2.2.

For tall athletes who exceed the scan boundaries there are two options depending on the system and software. First, the latest Encore software (version 18) from GE offers a new total body-less head scan which starts at the level of the mandible. This can be adopted as a consistent protocol for all athletes given that the composition of the head is unlikely to change, but does not provide absolute body composition. The second option is to combine two partial scans; one for the head and one for the body (Silva et al., 2013). For the head scan, the crown of the head should be ~1–3 cm below the upper scan boundary and the head placed in the

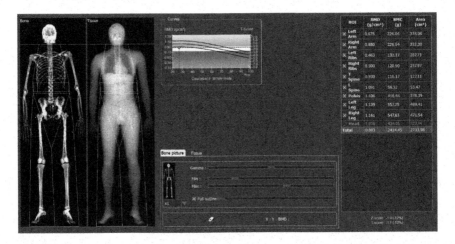

Figure 4.2.2 DXA total-body scan image and region of interest placements.

Frankfort plane. Once one has captured an image of the whole head, the scan should be terminated and saved. For the body scan, the athlete should be repositioned so that the feet are fully captured within the lower scan area to allow a 1 cm gap. The ROIs should be reviewed and the head, arm, trunk and leg compartments combined.

For broad athletes who exceed the width of the scan boundaries, there are also two options. The first is the offset (mirror image) scan procedure in which the DXA software (GE – mirror mode, Hologic – reflection mode) estimates composition on the left side from the right side by assuming symmetry of the body. While this does not allow for the accurate evaluation of regional compartments or asymmetries, it is helpful for total body composition so long as care is taken to ensure the correct ROI placement (Rothney et al., 2009). The second option is to combine two partial scans. This is appropriate when there is a need for accurate evaluation of regional compartments and differences between left and right sides. The whole right side should be included in the scan window, and the scan should be performed without offsetting. Once this scan is complete, the same should be repeated for the left side and the results from the two scans combined, after careful scrutiny of ROI placement.

It is recommended that the hands are placed in the mid-prone position with 1 cm air space between the hand and the upper leg (Figure 4.2.3). This position is particularly useful for broad athletes, although care should be taken to ensure that the hand does not overlap the upper leg. Foam positioning aids may help consistent placement (Nana et al., 2012). The interchanging of hand position, for example hands placed prone at baseline and hands mid-prone at follow-up, is not recommended given the impact on total BMD, arm bone and fat mass and precision (Thurlow et al., 2018).

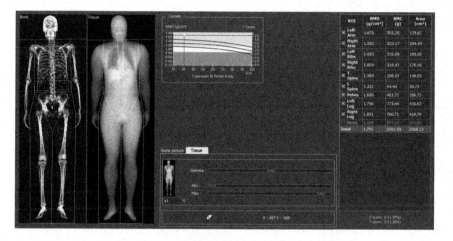

Figure 4.2.3 Mid-prone (A – recommended) and prone hand positioning (B) for DXA scans.
Source: (from Thurlow et al., 2018)

Interpretation and reporting

DXA scans, particularly body composition scans, provide a large amount of useful information, which one must interpret accurately. Those interpreting scans must have received appropriate training and if there are incidental health findings, one must refer an athlete to his or her GP or sports doctor. When preparing bone and body composition scan reports, it is important to include the model, manufacturer and software of the DXA system used. This is because there can be small differences between scans conducted on different systems (Shepherd et al., 2012; Oldroyd et al., 2018). It is also important to report scan mode (thin, standard or thick) (Hind et al., 2018). One should also record reference data used to help interpret scan results. The ISCD recommend the NHANES 1999–2004 reference data as most appropriate for bone density and body composition. However, one should recognise that reference data associated with body composition are likely to be of limited value for comparisons in highly trained athletes given their unique physical traits (Hangartner et al., 2013; Petak et al., 2013).

Bone density

Bone density in athletes under 50 years of age is interpreted using Z-scores (age-matched). In postmenopausal athletes, or male athletes aged 50 years or older, T-scores (young adult reference) should be used (Table 4.2.3). One can use the lowest Z-score or T-score calculated from completed scans for diagnosis.

Body composition

Total-body scan reports include total and regional (arms, trunk, legs) estimates of total mass, fat mass, fat-free mass (which comprises lean mass and bone mass), lean mass, bone mineral content (BMC) and BMD. Further detailed information includes regional and tissue percent fat mass, appendicular lean mass index (appendicular lean mass/height^2) and fat mass index (fat mass/height^2). If measured, values of urine specific gravity can be included in the notes of the body composition report, as can any other relevant information. When two partial scans are used, one must collate data manually using the Excel report.

Longitudinal scans

In sport and exercise sciences, follow-up DXA scans are valuable for examining the effects of a training programme, injury rehabilitation, a competitive season or exercise or nutrition intervention on bone and body composition. To interpret change accurately, it is important to ensure the following:

• Standardised protocols are established and followed at each time point for consistency;
• Height and body mass are measured and updated at each time point;
• Consistent application of reference data;
• Careful inspection of scan images from each time point to ensure correct and consistent placement of ROIs;
• Knowledge and application of *precision* and *least significant change* (see the following); and
• To ensure consistency, one should always use the same densitometer. If this is not possible, one must perform a *cross-calibration* procedure (see the following).

Precision and least significant change

DXA precision is the ability of the same system and the same operator to obtain the same result when measuring an individual at multiple points over a short period of time (Baim et al., 2005). All densitometrists should complete an *in vivo* precision study for bone and body composition outcomes in order to estimate precision error (Hangartner et al., 2013; Hind et al., 2018). In addition to operator precision, precision can vary by athlete size (Barlow et al., 2015) and it is important that the precision study sample is reflective of the usual population scanned (Hangartner et al., 2013; Hind et al., 2018).

Performing a precision study involves repeat scans, with re-positioning on either a minimum sample of $n = 30$ scanned twice or $n = 15$ scanned three times, as described by the ISCD. Published precision studies exist for a range of populations using different DXA systems (Hind et al., 2010, 2011; Hangartner et al., 2013; Bilsborough et al., 2014; Barlow et al., 2015; Farley et al., 2020). Precision error is calculated as the root-mean-square standard deviation (RMS-SD) or % coefficient of variation (www.iscd.org/learn/resources/calculators/). Once precision error is established, one can calculate least significant change (LSC) as follows:

$$RMS\text{-}SD \times 2.77 = LSC$$

The LSC represents the minimum change between two measurements that is required for 95% confidence that an actual change has occurred. For example, the LSC for DXA lean mass in high performance rugby players might be 888 g; therefore, to confirm a meaningful change (i.e., a loss or gain of lean mass) would need to exceed this value (Lees et al., 2017). In sport and exercise science research, it is common to focus on the statistical analysis of change in group mean (±SD) values. However, there is a significant limitation associated with this group-based approach, because it is not easy for one to identify important individual changes. In sport science particularly, an individualised, case-study approach is recommended, whereby an individual athlete's changes in body composition compartments are plotted against LSC using a Bland Altman chart.

Cross calibration

One should conduct follow-up scans on the same DXA system: if this is not possible, one must perform a cross calibration between the original and subsequent DXA systems. Cross calibration is also required for multi-centre studies in which different DXA models are used, and following a DXA system upgrade. Cross calibration can be performed *in vitro* with a phantom (only recommended if the two DXA systems are of the same model), or *in vivo*. Jankowski et al. (2019) describe an *in vivo* method for cross calibration. If differences exist between systems, one should create and apply a suitable regression equation (Shepherd et al., 2006; Hangartner et al., 2013).

Professional practice and communication

DXA bone and body composition assessments provide important information on athlete conditioning, injury rehabilitation and changes in response to nutrition and training interventions. However, it is important to recognise that these assessments have the potential to unfavourably impact athletes who are sensitive about their body shape and composition, and who might be recovering from or at risk for disordered eating. As such, care should be taken when communicating with athletes during scan preparation and positioning and when discussing results. Protocols should be in place to create a safe environment for DXA assessments and to guide on appropriate communication:

- Provide an athlete with an information sheet relating to suitable clothing for DXA scans prior to the appointment. This information should advise on not wearing undergarments that contain underwire or clasps;

- Advise athletes to wear lightweight clothing; for example, shorts and a fitted t-shirt or vest. This will enable quality of data and athlete privacy;
- Provide access to a private room for the athlete to get changed in (if required) prior to and following the scan;
- Where possible, ensure that the scanning room temperature is suitable to accommodate the athlete wearing only lightweight clothing;
- Ensure that only the necessary people are in the DXA imaging room; for example, the densitometrist, the athlete and if required the athlete's chaperone. If an additional member of staff or a student is present for training purposes, the athlete must be consulted and provide assent;
- When measuring body weight before the scan, do not read out the weight;
- At all times, avoid comment on the physical appearance, shape, weight or stature of the athlete;
- If there is a need to physically adjust the athlete to ensure appropriate positioning within the scan boundaries, inform the athlete before doing so. When using positioning aids, inform the athlete of their purpose and location; and
- Ensure DXA results remain confidential: only qualified and experienced staff (for example, densitometrists trained in DXA scan interpretation and sports dieticians) should be responsible for providing feedback on results.

Training requirements

In addition to IRMER-specific training, DXA technicians must also complete practical and theoretical training on the acquisition, analysis and interpretation of DXA scans, and demonstrate competency. When the DXA model is purchased, an equipment manufacturer will provide basic training; however, this is not sufficient to attain competency in DXA. Further (advanced) training can be achieved through completion of educational courses such as those offered by the ISCD (bone and body composition) or the Royal Osteoporosis Society (bone density). In-house, certified densitometrists can also provide training. One must keep records of training and certificates and refresher training is necessary to keep up to date with regulatory and emerging technical developments.

References

Andreoli, A., Scalzo, G., Masala, S., Tarantino, U. and Guglielmi, G. (2009). Body composition assessment by Dual-Energy X-Ray Absorptiometry (DXA). *La radiologia medica*, 114(2), 286–300.

Baim, S., Wilson, C. R., Lewiecki, E. M., Luckey, M. M., Downs, R. W., Jr. and Lentle, B. C. (2005). Precision assessment and radiation safety for dual-energy X-ray absorptiometry: Position paper of the International Society for Clinical Densitometry. *Journal of Clinical Densitometry*, 4, 371–378.

Barlow, M. J., Oldroyd, B., Smith, D., Lees, M. J., Brightmore, A., Till, K., Jones, B. and Hind, K. (2015). Precision error in dual-energy X-ray absorptiometry body composition measurements in elite male rugby league players. *Journal of Clinical Densitometry*, 18(4), 546–550.

Barrack, M. T., Fredericson, M., Tenforde, A. S. and Nattiv, A. (2017). Evidence of a cumulative effect for risk factors predicting low bone mass among male adolescent athletes. *British Journal of Sports Medicine*, 51(3), 200–205.

Bartlett, J. D., Hatfield, M., Parker, B. B., Roberts, L. A., Minahan, C., Morton, J. P. and Thornton, H. R. (2020). DXA-derived estimates of energy balance and its relationship with changes in body composition across a season in team sport athletes. *European Journal of Sport Science*, 20(7), 859–867.

Bilsborough, J. C., Greenway, K., Opar, D., Livingstone, S., Cordy, J. and Coutts, A. J. (2014). The accuracy and precision of DXA for assessing body composition in team sport athletes. *Journal of Sports Sciences*, 32(19), 1821–1828.

Department of Health and Social Care. (2018). *Ionising Radiation (Medical Exposure) Regulations 2017: Guidance*. www.gov.uk/government/publications/ionising-radiation-medical-exposure-regulations-2017-guidance (Accessed 5 April 2021).

Entwistle, I., Hume, P., Francis, P. and Hind, K. (2021). Vertebral anomalies in retired rugby players and the impact on bone density calculation of the lumbar spine. *Journal of Clinical Densitometry*, 24(2), 200–205.

Farley, A., Slater, G. J. and Hind, K. (2020). Short-term precision error of body composition assessment methods in resistance-trained male athletes. *International Journal of Sport Nutrition and Exercise Metabolism*, 31(1), 55–65.

Hangartner, T. N., Warner, S., Braillon, P., Jankowski, L. and Shepherd, J. (2013). The official positions of the international society for clinical densitometry: Acquisition of dual-energy X-ray absorptiometry body composition and considerations regarding analysis and repeatability of measures. *Journal of Clinical Densitometry*, 16(4), 520–536.

Harley, J. A., Hind, K. and O'hara, J. P. (2011). Three-compartment body composition changes in elite rugby league players during a super league season, measured by dual-energy X-ray absorptiometry. *The Journal of Strength & Conditioning Research*, 25(4), 1024–1029.

Health and Safety Executive. (2018). Working with ionising radiation. *Ionising Radiation Regulations 2017*. Approved code of practice and guidance. www.hse.gov.uk/pubns/books/l121.htm (accessed 5 April 2021).

Hind, K., Oldroyd, B. and Truscott, J. G. (2010). In vivo precision of the GE Lunar iDXA densitometer for the measurement of total-body, lumbar spine, and femoral bone mineral density in adults. *Journal of Clinical Densitometry*, 13(4), 413–417.

Hind, K., Oldroyd, B. and Truscott, J. G. (2011). In vivo precision of the GE Lunar iDXA densitometer for the measurement of total body composition and fat distribution in adults. *European Journal of Clinical Nutrition*, 65(1), 140–142.

Hind, K., Slater, G., Oldroyd, B., Lees, M., Thurlow, S., Barlow, M. and Shepherd, J. (2018). Interpretation of dual-energy X-ray Absorptiometry-Derived body composition change in athletes: A review and recommendations for best practice. *Journal of Clinical Densitometry*, July 1;21(3), 429–443.

Hind, K., Truscott, J. G. and Evans, J. A. (2006). Low lumbar spine bone mineral density in both male and female endurance runners. *Bone*, 39(4), 880–885.

Jankowski, L. G., Warner, S., Gaither, K., Lenchik, L., Fan, B., Lu, Y. and Shepherd, J. (2019). Cross-calibration, least significant change and quality assurance in multiple dual-energy x-ray absorptiometry scanner environments: 2019 ISCD official position. *Journal of Clinical Densitometry*, 22(4), 472–483.

Jordan, M. J., Aagaard, P. and Herzog, W. (2015). Lower limb asymmetry in mechanical muscle function: A comparison between ski racers with and without ACL reconstruction. *Scandinavian Journal of Medicine & Science in Sports*, 25(3), e301–e309.

Keay, N., Francis, G., Entwistle, I. and Hind, K. (2019). Clinical evaluation of education relating to nutrition and skeletal loading in competitive male road cyclists at risk of Relative Energy Deficiency in Sports (RED-S): 6-month randomised controlled trial. *BMJ Open Sport & Exercise Medicine*, 5(1), e000523.

Keay, N., Francis, G. and Hind, K. (2018). Low energy availability assessed by a sport-specific questionnaire and clinical interview indicative of bone health, endocrine profile and cycling performance in competitive male cyclists. *BMJ Open Sport & Exercise Medicine*, 4(1).

Kerr, A., Slater, G. J. and Byrne, N. (2017). Impact of food and fluid intake on technical and biological measurement error in body composition assessment methods in athletes. *British Journal of Nutrition*, 117(4), 591–601.

Laskey, M. A. (1996). Dual-energy X-ray absorptiometry and body composition. *Nutrition*, 12(1), 45–51.

Lees, M. J., Oldroyd, B., Jones, B., Brightmore, A., O'Hara, J. P., Barlow, M. J., Till, K. and Hind, K. (2017). Three-compartment body composition changes in professional rugby union players over one competitive season: A team and individualized approach. *Journal of Clinical Densitometry*, 20(1), 50–57.

Lewiecki, E. M., Binkley, N. and Petak, S. M. (2006). DXA quality matters. *Journal of Clinical Densitometry*, 9(4), 388–392.

Mountjoy, M., Sundgot-Borgen, J., Burke, L., Carter, S., Constantini, N., Lebrun, C., Meyer, N., Sherman, R., Steffen, K., Budgett, R. and Ljungqvist, A. (2014). The IOC consensus statement: Beyond the female athlete triad–relative energy deficiency in sport (RED-S). *British Journal of Sports Medicine*, 48(7), 491–497.

Nana, A., Slater, G. J., Hopkins, W. G. and Burke, L. M. (2012). Effects of daily activities on dual-energy X-ray absorptiometry measurements of body composition in active people. *Medicine and Science in Sports and Exercise*, 44(1), 180–189.

Nana, A., Slater, G. J., Hopkins, W. G., Halson, S. L., Martin, D. T., West, N. P. and Burke, L. M. (2016). Importance of standardized DXA protocol for assessing physique changes in athletes. *International Journal of Sport Nutrition and Exercise Metabolism*, 26(3), 259–267.

Oldroyd, B., Treadgold, L. and Hind, K. (2018). Cross calibration of the GE prodigy and iDXA for the measurement of total and regional body composition in adults. *Journal of Clinical Densitometry*, 21(3), 383–393.

Petak, S., Barbu, C. G., Elaine, W. Y., Fielding, R., Mulligan, K., Sabowitz, B., Wu, C. H. and Shepherd, J. A. (2013). The official positions of the international society for clinical densitometry: Body composition analysis reporting. *Journal of Clinical Densitometry*, 16(4), 508–519.

Pietrobelli, A., Gallagher, D., Baumgartner, R., Ross, R. and Heymsfield, S. B. (1998). Lean R value for DXA two-component soft-tissue model: Influence of age and tissue or organ type. *Applied Radiation and Isotopes*, 49(5–6), 743–744.

Public Health England. (2011). *Ionising Radiation Dose Comparisons*. www.gov.uk/government/publications/ionising-radiation-dose-comparisons/ionising-radiation-dose-comparisons (accessed 5 April 2021).

Rothney, M. P., Brychta, R. J., Schaefer, E. V., Chen, K. Y. and Skarulis, M. C. (2009). Body composition measured by dual-energy X-ray absorptiometry half-body scans in obese adults. *Obesity*, 17(6), 1281–1286.

Shepherd, J. A., Fan, B., Lu, Y., Wu, X. P., Wacker, W. K., Ergun, D. L. and Levine, M. A. (2012). A multinational study to develop universal standardization of whole-body bone density and composition using GE Healthcare Lunar and Hologic DXA systems. *Journal of Bone and Mineral Research*, 27(10), 2208–2216.

Shepherd, J. A., Lu, Y., Wilson, K., Fuerst, T., Genant, H., Hangartner, T. N., Wilson, C., Hans, D. and Leib, E. S. (2006). Cross-calibration and minimum precision standards for dual-energy X-ray absorptiometry: The 2005 ISCD Official Positions. *Journal of Clinical Densitometry*, 9(1), 31–36.

Siglinsky, E., Binkley, N. and Krueger, D. (2018). Do textiles impact DXA bone density or body composition results?. *Journal of Clinical Densitometry*, 21(2), 303–307.

Silva, A. M., Heymsfield, S. B. and Sardinha, L. B. (2013). Assessing body composition in taller or broader individuals using dual-energy X-ray absorptiometry: A systematic review. *European Journal of Clinical Nutrition*, 67(10), 1012–1021.

Thurlow, S., Oldroyd, B. and Hind, K. (2018). Effect of hand positioning on DXA total and regional bone and body composition parameters, precision error, and least significant change. *Journal of Clinical Densitometry*, 21(3), 375–382.

Zemski, A. J., Keating, S. E., Broad, E. M., Marsh, D. J., Hind, K. and Slater, G. J. (2019). Preseason body composition adaptations in elite white and polynesian rugby union athletes. *International Journal of Sport Nutrition and Exercise Metabolism*, 29(1), 9–17.

4.3 Assessment of cardiac structure and function

Christopher Johnson, Keith George and David L. Oxborough

This chapter details the importance of cardiac structure and function assessment in sport and exercise science and describes investigative techniques including the resting 12-lead electrocardiogram (ECG), resting transthoracic echocardiogram (ECHO) and stress ECHO. The equipment and procedures for data collection and interpretation will be described with direction for further reading. For the purposes of this topic, the reader is directed to British Society of Echocardiography (BSE) guidance documents which provide a comprehensive protocol for resting and stress ECHO and its interpretation (Harkness et al., 2020; Steeds et al., 2019; Wharton et al., 2015; Zaidi et al., 2020).

12-lead electrocardiogram

The 12-lead ECG is an inexpensive, efficient and widely available cardiac assessment technique. Interpretation of the ECG provides information on cardiac rate, rhythm, electrical conduction and, indirectly, structure. This technique has various applications in sports and exercise science and clinical practice including monitoring cardiac rate and rhythm during interventional studies; identifying training-related ECG changes in physically active individuals and athletes; and defining training-unrelated or potentially pathological ECG alterations. Due to its high sensitivity, the ECG is able to identify, or suggest, the majority of abnormalities associated with sudden cardiac death (SCD) and is therefore used in cardiac pre-screening programs with the aim to identify athletes at risk.

The standard 12-lead ECG involves 10 electrodes placed at strategic points on the chest and limbs to generate traces which represent multiple 'views' of the heart commonly referred to as 'leads' (Figure 4.3.1). The six chest electrodes are placed at the fourth intercostal space on the right and left sternal edge (V1 and V2, respectively), at the fifth intercostal space on the midclavicular line (V4), halfway between V2 and V4 (V3), at the left axillary line on the same horizontal plane as V4 (V5), and at the left midaxillary line on the same horizontal plane as V4 and V5 (V6). The four limb electrodes are placed at the site of the right and left wrists (R and L, respectively) and right and left ankles (N and F, respectively). The traces provide a series of deflections (or waveforms) representative of depolarisation or repolarisation of regions of the heart throughout the cardiac cycle. By convention,

DOI: 10.4324/9781003045267-30

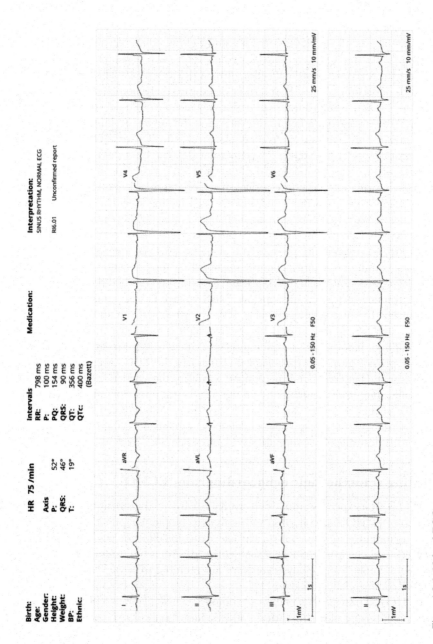

Figure 4.3.1 12-lead ECG trace.

the waveforms are labelled PQRST. Cardiac conduction spreads from the sino-atrial node through the atria causing atrial depolarisation (P wave) to reach the atrioventricular node. Specialised fibres called the bundle of His slow the rate of conduction to the ventricles (the P-R interval is a measure from the start of atrial depolarisation to the start of ventricular depolarisation). The conduction flows from the bundle of His through the left and right bundle branches to end at the Purkinje fibres (the QRS complex represents ventricular depolarisation). By convention, the first downwards deflection of the QRS complex is labelled Q; the first upwards deflection labelled R; a further downward deflection after the R wave is labelled S. There is then a transient period in which no electrical current can pass through the myocardium before repolarisation (ST segment). Finally, the ventricles repolarise to their normal 'resting' electrical state (T wave). The QT interval represents the total time taken for ventricular depolarisation and repolarisation. Measurement of the amplitude, duration and deflection direction can provide valuable information related to cardiac structure and electrical conduction.

Physically active individuals and athletes participating in regular intensive exercise often present with training-related changes in their ECG related to structural adaptation and an increased vagal tone (Sharma et al., 2018). Increased vagal tone means athletes commonly present with sinus bradycardia and sinus arrhythmia with less common markers including junctional escape or ectopic atrial rhythms, first-degree atrioventricular (AV) block and Mobitz Type I second-degree AV block. Other training-related changes include QRS voltage criteria consistent with left ventricular (LV) and right ventricular (RV) hypertrophy (LVH and RVH, respectively), early repolarisation and incomplete right bundle branch block (RBBB) (Table 4.3.1). Knowledge of training-related changes helps accurate differentiation of physiological and pathological changes in the ECG. Accurate diagnosis allows targeted intervention (true positive) as well as the avoidance of unnecessary disqualification from competition and the subsequent physiological, psychological and financial implications (false positive). The 'International recommendations for electrocardiographic interpretation in athletes', published in 2018, provides physicians with clear diagnostic support (see Figure 4.3.2; Sharma et al., 2018).

Resting transthoracic echocardiogram (ECHO)

ECHO is an inexpensive and widely available cardiac assessment technique. The process of ECHO data collection and analysis is complex but provides the observer with quantitative information on cardiac structure, function and mechanics as well as blood flow within the heart. A dedicated cardiac ultrasound system, transducer (or 'probe') and analysis software are required with various vendors and models commercially available.

ECHO can provide information on training-related adaptation in cardiac structure, function and mechanics within athletic individuals. The pioneering work of Morganroth et al. (1975) utilised ECHO in highly trained athletes. This research gave rise to the widely cited and accepted 'Morganroth's Hypothesis' which suggests that athletes have an increased cardiac mass in response to exercise training

Table 4.3.1 Training-related ECG changes

	Definitions
Sinus bradycardia	30–60 beats/min
Sinus arrythmia	Heart rate variation with respiration: increased rate during inspiration and decreased rate during expiration
Ectopic atrial rhythm	P waves are a different morphology to sinus P wave
Junction escape rhythm	QRS rate is faster than resting P wave or sinus rate and typically <100 beats/min with narrow QRS complex
Increased QRS voltage criteria	Isolated QRS voltage criteria for LVH (SV1 + RV5 or RV6 >3.5 mV) or RVH (RV1 + SV5 or SV6 >1.1 mV)
Incomplete RBBB	rSR' pattern in V1 and a qRS pattern in V6 with a QRS duration <120 ms
Early repolarisation	J-point elevation, ST-segment elevation, J waves, or terminal QRS slurring in the inferior and/or lateral leads
First-degree AV block	PR interval 200–400 ms
Mobitz type I second-degree AV block	Progressive lengthening of the PR interval until there is a non-conducted P wave with no QRS complex; the first PR interval after the dropped beat is shorter than the last conducted PR interval

AV, atrioventricular; ECG, 12-lead electrocardiogram; LVH, left ventricular hypertrophy; RBBB, right bundle branch block; RVH, right ventricular hypertrophy.

Source: Adapted from Sharma et al. (2018).

but that the structural adaptation resulting in this increase in mass is dependent upon the type of exercise stimulus; with isotonic (endurance) exercise responsible for a balanced increase in LV volume and wall thickness whilst isometric (strength) exercise promotes an increase in LV wall thickness only, termed eccentric and concentric hypertrophy respectively. It is now recognised that sporting discipline, training volume, ethnicity, body size, gender and age are all factors that impact physiological cardiac adaptation (Brown et al., 2017). Further to its application in athletic populations, ECHO can be used to evaluate the cardiac adaptation response to exercise, nutrition, supplements or performance-enhancing drugs through observational or interventional studies. ECHO can also be used in cardiac pre-participation screening alongside the ECG. Multimodality cardiac assessments including ECG, ECHO and stress ECHO can evaluate risk at primary and secondary care; identify and differentiate physiological and pathological cardiac adaptation; and manage future sporting participation in at-risk athletes (Oxborough et al., 2018; Pelliccia et al., 2018).

A comprehensive ECHO examination uses two-dimensional (2D), Doppler, tissue Doppler imaging (TDI) and colour Doppler modalities (Figure 4.3.3). The incorporation of a range of modalities makes ECHO a highly sensitive and specific investigative tool. The majority of ECHO images are produced using conventional 2D echocardiography which provides a cross-sectional view of the heart represented by the grey-scale images characteristic of ultrasound. Doppler

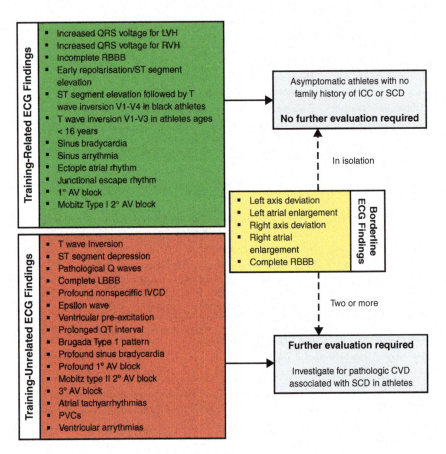

Figure 4.3.2 International consensus standards for electrocardiographic interpretation in athletes. AV, atrioventricular block; CVD, cardiovascular disease; ECG, electrocardiogram; ICC, inherited cardiac conditions; IVCD, intra-ventricular conduction delay; LBBB, left bundle branch block; LVH, left ventricular hypertrophy; RBBB, right bundle branch block; RVH, right ventricular hypertrophy; PVC, premature ventricular contraction; SCD, sudden cardiac death.

Source: Adapted from Sharma et al. (2018).

ultrasound utilises the Doppler effect to provide quantitative data on the direction and velocity of blood flow between cardiac chambers and in major vessels. TDI uses the Doppler principle to assess systolic and diastolic myocardial tissue velocities. Colour Doppler provides a superimposed visual (colour) representation of blood flow direction and velocities.

Speckle tracking echocardiography (STE) is a novel ECHO technique that assesses myocardial wall deformation (Johnson et al., 2019). STE provides a quantitative measure of regional and global myocardial deformation during the cardiac cycle

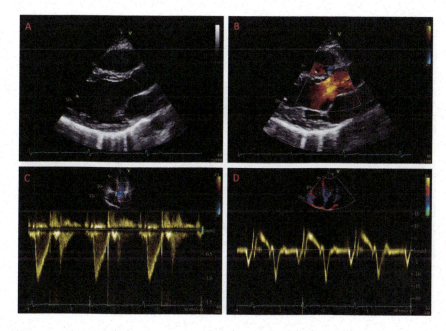

Figure 4.3.3 Echocardiographic modalities. A) Two-dimensional; B) colour Doppler; C) Doppler; and D) tissue Doppler.

providing information on longitudinal, circumferential and radial strain and strain rate as well as rotation and torsion mechanics. There are four main ECHO 'windows' (or probe sites) utilised in a comprehensive ECHO assessment; the left parasternal, apical, subcostal and suprasternal windows. Each of these windows provides one or more views of the heart.

Left parasternal window

The left parasternal window is located at the third or fourth intercostal space on the left sternal edge. The left parasternal long axis view (PLAX) is obtained with the probe placed at the left parasternal window with the probe reference (a small light, dot or edge present on one side of the probe) directed towards the participant's right shoulder. Colour Doppler is used to assess blood flow across the mitral valve (MV) and aortic valve (AV). Measurements of LV dimensions; and posterior and interventricular septal wall thickness allow the calculation of LV mass and relative wall thickness (RWT) to determine LV geometry (Figures 4.3.4 and 4.3.5). Further measurements include the left ventricular outflow tract (LVOT), aortic root, right ventricular outflow tract (RVOT) and left atrial (LA) dimensions (Figure 4.3.4).

The parasternal short axis view (PSAX) is obtained by rotating the probe ~90 degrees clockwise from the PLAX until the reference is pointing towards

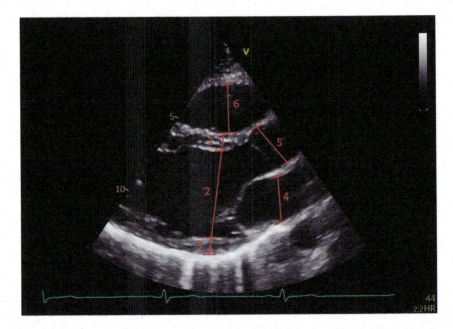

Figure 4.3.4 **PLAX** view and measurements including 1) LV interventricular septum thickness; 2) LV end-diastolic dimension; 3) LV posterior wall thickness; 4) LA dimension; 5) Sinus of Valsalva; 6) RVOT PLAX dimension. LA, left atrium; LV, left ventricle; PLAX, parasternal long axis view; RVOT, right ventricular outflow tract.

the participant's left shoulder. This view is taken at four levels including the AV, MV (base), papillary muscle (PM, mid-cavity) and apical level which are obtained by a combination of tilting and translation (sweeping) of the probe to optimise visualisation of the cavity and structures (Figure 4.3.6). The PSAX views provide a comprehensive evaluation of LV wall thickness. Colour Doppler at the MV and AV level provides a visual assessment of the blood flow through the valves and potential interatrial septal defects. Doppler at the pulmonary valve (PV) provides blood flow velocity. Further measures of RVOT dimensions can be taken at the AV level (Figure 4.3.6). STE in the PSAX at the MV, PM and apical level can be used to quantify LV circumferential, radial and rotational mechanics.

Apical window

The apical window is located at the fifth to seventh intercostal space on the mid-axillary line with the participant lying slightly more supine. The apical four-chamber view (A4CH) is obtained by placing the probe at the apex with the reference pointing towards the participant's left side or towards the bed (Figure 4.3.7). Ejection fraction, a ubiquitous measure of LV systolic function, is calculated from biplane (A4CH and A2CH) volumetric measures of the LV at end-diastole and

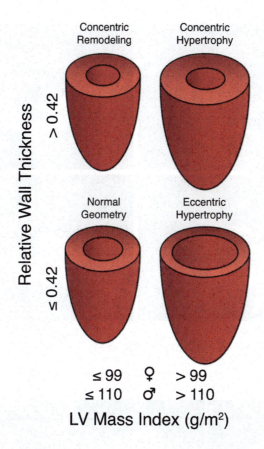

<figure>Concentric Remodeling | Concentric Hypertrophy

Normal Geometry | Eccentric Hypertrophy

Relative Wall Thickness > 0.42 / ≤ 0.42

≤ 99 ♀ > 99
≤ 110 ♂ > 110

LV Mass Index (g/m²)</figure>

Figure 4.3.5 LV geometry determined by LV mass index and relative wall thickness. LV, left ventricle.

Source: Adapted from Harkness et al. (2020).

end-systole. Biplane LA volume is measured using a similar approach. LV septal and lateral TDI provides measures of early diastolic, late diastolic and systolic myocardial velocities (Figure 4.3.8). Doppler and colour Doppler at the MV provide visualisation and measurement of LV inflow blood velocities (Figure 4.3.9).

From the A4CH view, anterior angulation of the probe presents the AV and aortic root; this is the apical five-chamber view (A5CH, Figure 4.3.9). Doppler and colour Doppler at the LVOT and AV provide LV outflow blood velocities (Figure 4.3.9).

The apical two-chamber view (A2CH) is obtained by rotating ~60 degrees counter-clockwise from the A4CH with the probe reference directed towards the participant's left shoulder (Figure 4.3.7). Further rotation 60 degrees counter-clockwise presents the A3CH (Figure 4.3.7). Colour Doppler can be used to assess LV inflow and outflow. STE of the apical views quantifies LV longitudinal strain.

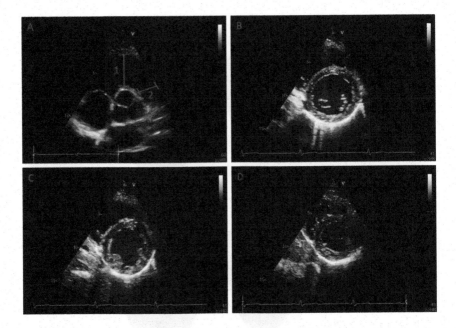

Figure 4.3.6 PSAX views A) AV; B) MV; C) PM; and D) apical level. RVOT dimensions 1) proximal and 2) distal. AV, aortic valve; MV, mitral valve; PM, papillary muscle; PSAX, parasternal short axis view; RVOT, right ventricular outflow tract.

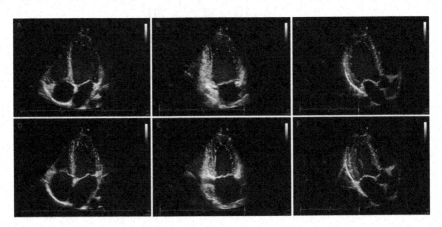

Figure 4.3.7 Apical views at end-diastole A) A4CH; B) A2CH; C) A3CH and end-systole; D) A4CH; E) A2CH; F) A3CH. A2CH, apical two-chamber view; A3CH, apical three-chamber view; A4CH, apical four-chamber view.

To optimally assess the right heart, a modified A4CH view (A4CH$_{RV}$) is required. From the A4CH lateral and superior translation and medial angulation, bring the right heart to the centre of the screen giving a more representative view of the right heart chambers (Figure 4.3.10). RV diameter and length as well as RA area

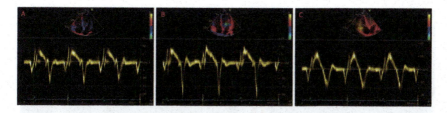

Figure 4.3.8 TDI at the A) LV septum; B) LV lateral wall; and C) RV wall. LV, left ventricle; RV, right ventricle; TDI, tissue Doppler imaging.

Figure 4.3.9 A) LV inflow Doppler; B) A5CH two-dimensional; and C) LVOT Doppler. A5CH, apical five-chamber view; AV, aortic valve; LV, left ventricle; LVOT, left ventricular outflow tract.

can be measured. Measurements of RV function include TDI of the RV free wall, tricuspid annular plane systolic excursion (TAPSE) and fractional area change (FAC; calculated from end-systolic and end-diastolic RV area measurements). STE can be used to quantify RV longitudinal strain.

Subcostal window

The subcostal window is obtained with the participant in the supine position with his or her knees bent to allow the abdominal muscles to relax. The probe is placed under the xiphoid pointing anteriorly towards the heart. The subcostal four-chamber view (S4CH) is obtained at the subcostal window with the probe reference directed towards the participant's left (Figure 4.3.11). Due to the proximity and alignment of the RV free wall to the probe, this is a good view to measure RV wall thickness. The subcostal short axis view (SSAX) is obtained by rotating the probe 90 degrees counter-clockwise until the inferior vena cava (IVC) is visible (Figure 4.3.11).

Suprasternal window

The suprasternal window is obtained with the participant in the supine position with the neck extended. The suprasternal window is located at the suprasternal notch. To obtain the aortic view in the suprasternal window, place the probe in the suprasternal notch and angled down into the chest with the reference directed roughly

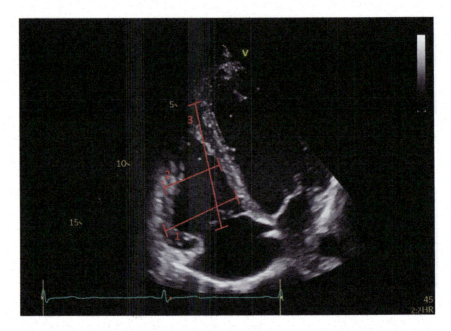

Figure 4.3.10 A4CH$_{RV}$ view with measurements 1) RVD1 (basal); 2) RVD2 (mid-cavity); and 3) RVD3 (length). A4CH$_{RV}$, right ventricular-focussed apical four-chamber view; RVD, right ventricular dimension.

Figure 4.3.11 A) Subcostal four-chamber view; B) subcostal short axis view; C) suprasternal notch view.

towards the participant's left ear. The aortic arch should be in view with both the ascending and descending aorta visible. Doppler and colour Doppler provide visualisation and measurement of descending aortic blood flow velocities (Figure 4.3.11).

It is important to interpret ECHO measurements in context of the multiple facets of the participant's demographics (age, sex, body size) as well as activity levels. BSE reference values are representative of a normal healthy individual. Athletes and regular sports participants often present with cardiac adaptation in response to frequent strenuous physical exertion commonly referred to as 'athlete's heart' (Prior and La Gerche, 2012). Athletic cardiac adaptation affects all four chambers of the heart with common markers including an increase in cardiac chamber size, wall thickness, mass and alterations in function and mechanics (Beaumont et al., 2017; Brown et al.,

2017). Therefore, specific guidelines for the interpretation of ECHO in athletes are required (Oxborough et al., 2018). It is important to note that even with guidelines tailored especially for the athlete, ambiguous cases can arise requiring further assessment. Table 4.3.2 presents BSE normative values and athletic reference ranges.

Table 4.3.2 Left and right heart echocardiographic parameters

	Normal (Male)	Athlete Upper Limit (Male)	Normal (Female)	Athlete Upper Limit (Female)
LV dimensions				
LVIDd (mm)	37–56	64	35–51	57
LVIDs (mm)	22–41		20–37	
IVSd (mm)	6–12	13	5–11	
LVPWd (mm)	6–12	13	6–12	
LV mass				
LVMI (g/m²)	440–110		33–99	
LV mass (g)	72–219	263	51–173	243
LV and LA volumes				
LVEDVi (mL/m²)	30–79		29–70	
LVESVi (mL/m²)	9–31		8–27	
LVEDV (mL)	53–156		46–121	
LVESV (mL)	15–62		13–47	
EF (%)	≥55%		≥55%	
LA (mL)	<34		<34	
RV and RA indexed values				
RVd area (cm²/m²)	≤13.6		≤12.6	
RA area (cm²/m²)	≤11		≤11	
RV and RA absolute values				
RVOT proximal (mm)	24–44	44	20–42	
RVOT distal (mm)	16–29	41	14–28	
RVD1 (basal; mm)	26–47	49	22–43	
RVD2 (mid-cavity; mm)	19–42	44	17–35	
RVD3 (length; mm)	55–87	92	51–80	
RV wall thickness	≤5		≤5	
RA area (cm²)	≤22		≤19	
RV function				
FAC (%)	≥30		≥35	

Abbreviations: d, end-diastole; EF, ejection fraction; FAC, fractional area changes; IVS, interventricular septum thickness; LA, left atrium; LV, left ventricle; LVEDV, left ventricular end diastolic volume; LVESV, left ventricular end systolic volume; LVID, left ventricular internal dimension; LVMI, left ventricular mass index; LVPW, left ventricular posterior wall thickness; RA, right atrium; RV, right ventricle; RVD, right ventricular dimension; RVOT, right ventricular outflow tract; s, end-systole. Normal cut-off values adapted from Harkness et al. (2020); Oxborough et al. (2018); Zaidi et al. (2020).

Stress transthoracic echocardiogram

Exercise stress ECHO is an inexpensive and widely available cardiac investigative technique used to assess cardiac function, contractile reserve and mechanics in response to exercise stress and can be applied in a range of research and clinical situations. In research, stress ECHO can be used to evaluate the acute cardiac response to physical exertion and to observe physiological alterations in the athlete's response to exercise stimulus (contractile reserve). Clinically, stress ECHO can aid differential diagnosis in 'difficult' or grey-zone pre-participation screening cases. Although there is limited data regarding exercise stress ECHO and contractile reserve in heathy athletes, Millar et al. (2020) demonstrated its application in the differentiation of asymptomatic patients with dilated cardiomyopathy (DCM) from 'grey-zone' athletes with LV enlargement and borderline low EF (<55%). Millar et al. (2020) observed that a failure to increase LV EF by >11% from baseline to peak exercise was a marker of impaired contractile reserve. Furthermore, although considerable attention is given to SCD in young athletes (<35 years), the risk is greater in older athletes (>35 years), with coronary artery disease (CAD) the leading cause of SCD in this age group (Marijon et al., 2015). Stress ECHO is commonly used to assess CAD in a clinical setting. During the investigation, the heart is subdivided into myocardial segments with a grading system used to compare resting myocardial function and the response to exercise to provide an indication of regions of dysfunction resulting from possible ischaemia due to an underlying CAD.

The exercise stress protocol is optimally completed on a semi-recumbent cycle ergometer. This method provides the optimal position for image collection because the participant is lying in a similar position to a resting ECHO, allowing the heart to drop closer to the chest wall. A ramp protocol is common practice with the participant working at cadence of ~60 revolutions per minute with the resistance increasing by a pre-set load at either a specific time point such as every 2–3 minutes or incrementally in order to reach a target heart rate to mimic low-, moderate- or high-intensity training zones. Images can be gathered at baseline, during exercise and post exercise during the recovery period. The commonly acquired images include the PLAX, PSAX at the MV, PM and apical levels and the apical views including the A4CH, A2CH and A3CH. It is important to gather optimal images at baseline and replicate these images during stress. On completion of the exercise protocol and image acquisition, the observer should visually inspect the corresponding resting, exercise and recovery images side by side. Further to visual inspection, quantification of LV EF and RV FAC provides information on contractile reserve in athletic individuals. Doppler and TDI provide assessment of myocardial systolic and diastolic function in response to exercise. STE can be used to quantify regional and global strain and strain rate at rest, during exercise and recovery for each cardiac chamber.

Conclusion

The 12-lead ECG and the resting and stress ECHO are investigative techniques employed to assess cardiac electrical conduction, structure, function and mechanics at rest, during exercise and in recovery. These techniques are accessible and frequently encountered in sports and exercise science to assess populations across the entire spectrum of physical activity from elite athletes to sedentary clinical patients. Multi-modality cardiac assessment is indispensable for the evaluation of physiological and pathological cardiac phenotypes and can be employed in exercise, drug and clinical interventions.

References

Beaumont, A., Grace, F., Richards, J., Hough, J., Oxborough, D. and Sculthorpe, N. (2017). Left ventricular speckle tracking-derived cardiac strain and cardiac twist mechanics in athletes: A systematic review and meta-analysis of controlled studies. *Sports Medicine*, 47(6), 1145–1170. https://doi.org/10.1007/s40279-016-0644-4

Brown, B., Somauroo, J., Green, D. J., Wilson, M., Drezner, J., George, K. and Oxborough, D. (2017). The complex phenotype of the Athlete's heart: Implications for preparticipation screening. *Exercise and Sport Sciences Reviews*, 45(2), 96–104. https://doi.org/10.1249/JES.0000000000000102

Harkness, A., Ring, L., Augustine, D. X., Oxborough, D., Robinson, S. and Sharma, V. (2020). Normal reference intervals for cardiac dimensions and function for use in echocardiographic practice: A guideline from the British Society of Echocardiography. *Echo Research and Practice*, 7(1), G1–G18. https://doi.org/10.1530/ERP-19-0050

Johnson, C., Kuyt, K., Oxborough, D. and Stout, M. (2019). Practical tips and tricks in measuring strain, strain rate and twist for the left and right ventricles. *Echo Research and Practice*, 6(3), R87–R98. https://doi.org/10.1530/ERP-19-0020

Marijon, E., Uy-Evanado, A., Reinier, K., Teodorescu, C., Narayanan, K., Jouven, X., Gunson, K., Jui, J. and Chugh, S. S. (2015). Sudden cardiac arrest during sports activity in middle age. *Circulation*, 131(16), 1384–1391. https://doi.org/10.1161/CIRCULATIONAHA.114.011988

Millar, L. M., Fanton, Z., Finocchiaro, G., Sanchez-Fernandez, G., Dhutia, H., Malhotra, A., Merghani, A., Papadakis, M., Behr, E. R., Bunce, N., Oxborough, D., Reed, M., O'Driscoll, J., Tome Esteban, M. T., D'Silva, A., Carr-White, G., Webb, J., Sharma, R. and Sharma, S. (2020). Differentiation between athlete's heart and dilated cardiomyopathy in athletic individuals. *Heart*, 106(14). https://doi.org/10.1136/heartjnl-2019-316147

Morganroth, J., Maron, B. J., Henry, W. L. and Epstein, S. E. (1975). Comparative left ventricular dimensions in trained athletes. *Annals of Internal Medicine*, 82(4). https://doi.org/10.7326/0003-4819-82-4-521

Oxborough, D., Augustine, D., Gati, S., George, K., Harkness, A., Mathew, T., Papadakis, M., Ring, L., Robinson, S., Sandoval, J., Sarwar, R., Sharma, S., Sharma, V., Sheikh, N., Somauroo, J., Stout, M., Willis, J. and Zaidi, A. (2018). A guideline update for the practice of echocardiography in the cardiac screening of sports participants: A joint policy statement from the British Society of Echocardiography and Cardiac Risk in the Young. *Echo Research and Practice*, 5(1), G1–G10. https://doi.org/10.1530/erp-17-0075

Pelliccia, A., Caselli, S., Sharma, S., Basso, C., Bax, J. J., Corrado, D., D'Andrea, A., D'Ascenzi, F., Di Paolo, F. M., Edvardsen, T., Gati, S., Galderisi, M., Heidbuchel, H., Nchimi, A., Nieman, K., Papadakis, M., Pisicchio, C., Schmied, C., Popescu, B. A., . . . Lancellotti, P. (2018). European Association of Preventive Cardiology (EAPC) and European Association of Cardiovascular Imaging (EACVI) joint position statement: Recommendations for the indication and interpretation of cardiovascular imaging in the evaluation of the athlete's he. *European Heart Journal*, 39(21), 1949–1969. https://doi.org/10.1093/eurheartj/ehx532

Prior, D. L. and La Gerche, A. (2012). The athlete's heart. *Heart*, 98(12), 947–955. https://doi.org/10.1136/heartjnl-2011-301329

Sharma, S., Drezner, J. A., Baggish, A., Papadakis, M., Wilson, M. G., Prutkin, J. M., La Gerche, A., Ackerman, M. J., Borjesson, M., Salerno, J. C., Asif, I. M., Owens, D. S., Chung, E. H., Emery, M. S., Froelicher, V. F., Heidbuchel, H., Adamuz, C., Asplund, C. A., Cohen, G., . . . Corrado, D. (2018). International recommendations for electrocardiographic interpretation in athletes. *European Heart Journal*, 39(16), 1466–1480. https://doi.org/10.1093/eurheartj/ehw631

Steeds, R. P., Wheeler, R., Bhattacharyya, S., Reiken, J., Nihoyannopoulos, P., Senior, R., Monaghan, M. J. and Sharma, V. (2019). Stress echocardiography in coronary artery disease: A practical guideline from the British Society of Echocardiography. *Echo Research and Practice*, 6(2), G17–G33. https://doi.org/10.1530/ERP-18-0068

Wharton, G., Steeds, R., Allen, J., Phillips, H., Jones, R., Kanagala, P., Lloyd, G., Masani, N., Mathew, T., Oxborough, D., Rana, B., Sandoval, J., Wheeler, R., O'Gallagher, K. and Sharma, V. (2015). A minimum dataset for a standard adult transthoracic echocardiogram: A guideline protocol from the British Society of echocardiography. *Echo Research and Practice*, 2(1), G9–G24. https://doi.org/10.1530/ERP-14-0079

Zaidi, A., Knight, D. S., Augustine, D. X., Harkness, A. A., Oxborough, D., Pearce, K., Ring, L., Robinson, S., Stout, M., Willis, J., Sharma, V. and The Education Committee of the British Society of Echocardiography. (2020). Echocardiographic assessment of the right heart in adults: A practical guideline from the British Society of Echocardiography. *Echo Research and Practice*, 7(1), G19–G41. https://doi.org/10.1530/ERP-19-0051

4.4 Methods in exercise immunology

Nicolette C. Bishop and Neil P. Walsh

Introduction

Keeping those who are physically active free from infectious illness is a major priority for athletes to be able to reach their performance potential. Absence from training due to illness is a key contributor in athlete underperformance (Raysmith and Drew, 2016) and respiratory infections are a particular issue (Walsh et al., 2011a). It is undoubtable that a high-performance environment can provide an ideal opportunity for pathogen transmission (for example, through close contact with others, long-haul travel and less-than-ideal hygiene practices such as sharing drinks bottles, towels and utensils). This phenomenon is more prevalent in endurance and team sports than sprint and power events (Timpka et al., 2017) and has been associated with the negative impact of physiological and psychological stress on immune function (Walsh et al., 2011b). As such, there is much interest in methods for monitoring infection burden (incidence, symptom severity and duration) and assessing immune function in this population.

Considerations before testing

Unlike other aspects of performance testing, there is no current standard or established exercise protocol to challenge immune function. An individual's immune response to an acute exercise challenge, be it interval, continuous, aerobic or power, is transient and depends on several aspects, not least the intensity and duration of the test itself. In this regard, responses to acute exercise protocols on their own, while useful for investigating mechanisms for research, will not provide much meaningful data on the integrity of an individual's immune defences and therefore risk for infection. It is the response at rest that is more useful in this situation, and this will depend on current training status, training volume and any underlying medical conditions. To add a further layer of complexity, there is not an established one-stop *in vivo* or *in vitro* outcome measure of immune status that is easily applicable to athletes because testing is often in field settings. As such, outcome measures tend to focus on particular aspects of immune function and one often chooses a measurement tool(s) according to convenience, practicality and cost. Added to this, most immune functions exhibit a circadian rhythm and so for monitoring purposes tests must be performed at the same time of day. Immune

DOI: 10.4324/9781003045267-31

outcome measures are also notoriously variable, both within and between individuals. For this reason, when assessing immune function in athletes, an individualised (rather than cohort) approach is best, whereby one gains some indication of what is 'normal' for that individual over time. This way, deviations are easier to pick up and allow alterations to training to be made to minimise the risk of developing an infection, or at the very least, to reduce the severity and duration of symptoms allowing a faster return to training.

Given the multitude of ways of assessing infection symptoms and immune function, many of which are beyond the scope of this chapter, here we describe key considerations and processes of data collection, and suggest common methods of analysis and interpretation considered valid within the field of exercise immunology. We present relevant information in three subsections: assessing illness and infection, assessing mucosal immune function and assessing systemic immune function. For a detailed discussion of the methods suggested, readers are directed to the International Society of Exercise Immunology Consensus Statements (Walsh et al., 2011b; Bermon et al., 2017).

Assessing illness and infection

Monitoring symptoms of respiratory infections is usually performed using subjective self-report of either unstandardised health logs, standardised symptom questionnaires or physician assessment of common cold. Swab testing of the oral mucosa (inside the mouth and back of the throat) can be performed and assessed using polymerase chain reaction techniques to amplify the presence of viral DNA, and allows detection of the specific viral strains, but this is costly and requires specific expertise. It is also common practice now to assess for the presence of allergy because this causes similar symptoms to respiratory infections but would require a different management strategy.

Collecting symptom data

There are two main standardised questionnaires used by exercise immunologists: the Jackson Common Cold Questionnaire (Jackson et al., 1958) and the Wisconsin Upper Respiratory Symptom Survey (WURSS; www.fammed.wisc.edu/wurss/). These are designed to be completed daily and many sports incorporate modified versions of these into a training log for their own purposes. The Jackson Questionnaire was developed from the symptoms experienced by over 1,000 volunteers in the 6 days after nasal inoculation with nasal common cold secretions collected from donors. It incorporates 8 clinical symptoms: sneezing, headache, feeling generally unwell, runny nose, blocked nose, sore throat, cough and chilliness. These 8 symptoms are scored on a 4-point scale from 0 (no symptom) to 3 (severe symptom) and summed to determine a total daily symptom score.

Table 4.4.1 summarises an example of a completed Jackson Questionnaire and associated scoring. Jackson's criteria for a common cold included a total symptom score of ≥14 during the six-day monitoring period and a 'yes' answer to the dichotomous question, 'Do you think you are suffering from a common cold?' For

Table 4.4.1 Case study example of a completed Jackson Common Cold Questionnaire

1 Do you think you are suffering from a common cold *today?*

         [X] YES   [ ] NO

2 For each sign of illness, please cross *one* box that describes how you feel *today*:

	Not at All (0)	*Mild (1)*	*Moderate (2)*	*Severe (3)*	*Score*
Sneezing			X		2
Headache			X		2
Feeling generally unwell		X			1
Runny nose		X			1
Blocked nose	X				0
Sore throat			X		2
Cough	X				0
Chilliness	X				0
				Total score	8

The original Jackson criteria for a common cold included a total symptom score of ≥ 14 during the six-day monitoring period and a 'yes' answer to the dichotomous question, 'Do you think you are suffering from a common cold? However, in a practical sense, confirming a common cold after six-day reporting is not helpful because most athletes will be recovering after this time. Instead, we suggest that a reasonable practical recommendation is a total symptom score of ≥ 6 on two consecutive days (equating to three moderate or two severe symptoms each day) and a 'yes' answer to the dichotomous question, 'Do you think you are suffering from a common cold?'

the early detection of a common cold, a total symptom score of ≥ 6 on two consecutive days (equating to three moderate or two severe symptoms each day) and a 'yes' answer to the dichotomous question is a reasonable practical recommendation. Common cold duration is recorded as the number of consecutive days with total symptom score ≥ 6; peak symptom severity and total symptom score for each episode are also frequently reported. The International Society of Exercise Immunology consensus statements provide important guidance for exercise both during and after respiratory infection (Walsh et al., 2011a; Bermon et al., 2017).

The WURSS is also widely used by researchers and practitioners. It was developed and validated against the Jackson Questionnaire, physician-verified common cold incidence and nasal inoculation with rhinovirus in ~400 participants (Barrett et al., 2002, 2005, 2006). It also considers the impact of common cold symptoms on an individual's quality-of-life measures. In addition to the original 44-question version there is also a 21-question validated version, and influenza-like illness symptoms of headache, body aches and fever are included on a 24-question version. The WURSS is longer than the 8-question Jackson Questionnaire, so it is worth considering the time burden of daily completion if looking to use one of these questionnaires on a longer-term basis. Additionally, an 11-question version and a version specifically for children are currently being validated.

Assessing mucosal immune function

Immune markers in mucosal secretions, particularly saliva and tears, are of interest to exercise immunologists, particularly those working in the field environment. The process involved in collecting these fluids is non-invasive, convenient, practical and low-cost. The statistic that as many as 95% of all infections are thought to be initiated at the mucosal surfaces (Bosch et al., 2002) highlights the important role mucosal immunity plays in defence against opportunistic infections such as the common cold.

Salivary secretory IgA (s-IgA) production is the major effector function of the mucosal immune system and acts with innate mucosal defences such as defensins, alpha-amylase, lactoferrin and lysozyme to provide the 'first line of defence' against pathogens and antigens presented at the mucosa. Falls in secretion rate of salivary markers of mucosal immunity have been implicated as a potential risk factor for subsequent episodes of respiratory infection in athletes; however, concentration and secretion of saliva markers are notoriously open to several influences, not the least of which are the time of day, not taking hydration or saliva flow into consideration, and unwittingly stimulating saliva flow through sight or smell of food when collecting the sample; these factors change the composition of the saliva as well as the volume. Moreover, concentrations of mucosal markers of immune function are highly varied both within and between individuals. For this reason, to assess meaningful changes in mucosal immunity, the normal healthy (i.e., in the absence of infection) range for an individual must first be established. This is best assessed using weekly sample collection.

Collecting saliva samples

Saliva samples are usually collected 'passively', either via cotton swab or by dribbling into a sterile tube. Passive collection into cotton swabs is used to minimise the risk of gingival bleeding that is sometimes associated with the expectoration method of saliva collection. However, care is needed to ensure that the sample volume is optimal since there are issues with the reliability of s-IgA determination from cotton swab collections in sample volumes of less than 200 μl and more than 2 ml (Li and Gleeson, 2004). Furthermore, s-IgA concentrations from cotton swabs are often lower than those collected by passive dribbling (Strazdins et al., 2005). The choice of collection method may also depend on the participant population; studies of children and the elderly may prefer to use swab collections because they are rated positively for both comfort and acceptability compared with passive dribbling (Strazdins et al., 2005). Larger sterile tubes are useful for those with limited hand mobility.

The volume of saliva is also a key consideration and should be accounted for. Concentrations of antimicrobial proteins are diluted in higher volumes of saliva, giving an artefactual lower concentration. Likewise, a decrease in saliva volume will concentrate the proteins, giving higher values. Saliva volume can be accounted for by either collecting a fixed volume of saliva in a graduated tube (e.g., 1 ml), or by measuring the volume of saliva collected over a fixed period of time (e.g., 2 min). A standard protocol for collecting saliva samples is provided below; this can also be used for the collection of saliva for hormone analysis. Analysis of saliva antimicrobial proteins can be performed using commercially available Enzyme Linked Immunosorbent Assays (ELISAs); these are widely available for s-IgA, lysozyme, lactoferrin, defensins and α-amylase.

Protocol for collecting saliva samples using the passive dribble method

1 Provide the participant with a small (approximately 100 ml) cup of plain water to wash mouth and remove any contaminants two to five minutes prior to collection;
2 Give the participant the unopened sterile screw-top tube and ask him or her to unscrew the lid;
3 Ask the participant to swallow to empty the mouth and sit with head tilted slightly forward;
4 Ask participant to make minimal facial movement and expectorate saliva as it collects under the tongue every 20 seconds either for the duration of a timed collection (normally two minutes) or until the 1 ml of saliva is collected, as marked on the tube;
5 If using a timed collection, the end of the collection period the participant must expectorate any saliva in the mouth into the collection tube, replace the tube lid and pass the closed tube to you;
6 Store the saliva samples at −20°C or −80°C for analysis; and
7 When analysing, thaw completely at room temperature. When defrosted, centrifuge for 2 min at 12,000 rpm in a microcentrifuge and use the clear supernatant in your analysis.

Assessing systemic immune function

There are a multitude of methods to assess both innate (non-specific, first line of defence) and adaptive (specific response) immune cell phenotypes and functions; however, the majority are not practical or feasible to be used in a field setting. For this reason, we only summarise key techniques here; a detailed overview of methods is provided in Bermon et al. (2017).

Immune cell numbers

Basic assessment of numbers of total immune cells (white blood cells or leukocytes) and the differential count of the key cells (neutrophils, lymphocytes, monocytes) can be derived from a full blood count in EDTA-treated whole blood using a haematology analyser. If you don't have an analyser in your institution, many hospital pathology labs offer this service.

Flow cytometry

More detailed assessment of immune cell types and their receptors can be determined using flow cytometry. This is a method of single-cell analysis, whereby the cell population is suspended in a clear saline solution and funnelled through a nozzle to create a stream of single cells. The cells flow past a set of laser sources and as the light hits each cell it is scattered in different directions; this gives an indication of the cell morphology. Light scattered in a forward direction ('forward scatter') gives an indication of cell size; bigger cells will cause more scattering. Light scattered sideways ('side scatter') gives an indication of volume of cytoplasmic granules inside the cell. The degree of scattering is detected, converted into an electrical signal, and visualised by the cytometer software; hence, populations of cells with similar properties are clustered together. Because the three main circulating immune cell types (neutrophils, monocytes and lymphocytes) differ in size and granularity, plotting forward scatter against side scatter allows the identification of these different cell populations (Figure 4.4.1). Specific cell subpopulations within these populations can be subsequently identified by 'tagging' receptors on the surface of the cells using fluorescent emitting chemicals (fluorochromes) joined

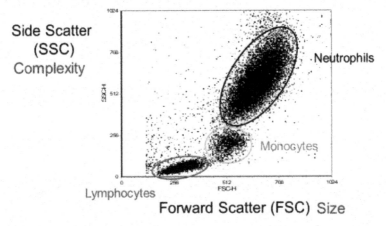

Cell Type	Size (Forward Scatter, FSC)	Complexity 'granularity' (Side Scatter, SSC)
Lymphocytes	small	Low
Monocytes	medium	Low
Neutrophils	medium-large	High

Figure 4.4.1 Cell morphology can be used to identify the three main immune cell populations in whole blood. Forward scatter (FSC) gives an indication of size and side scatter (SSC) gives an indication of a cell's internal complexity. The cytometer plots FSC against SSC to provide a visual image of the three distinctive white blood cell populations.

to antibodies which then bind to cell surface receptors. Once excited by the laser, each fluorochrome emits light at a specific wavelength and is gathered by the flow cytometer's detectors.

Do not be put off by state-of-the-art flow cytometers; simple and useful information can be gathered using just a few cell markers and this technique is more accessible than ever with several bench-top analysers now available – some even have an automated set-up. Flow cytometer manufacturers (e.g., Becton Dickinson, Beckman Coulter, Bio-Rad) provide excellent advice and training.

Immune cell functional responses

In vitro measures of systemic immune function rely on challenging immune cells with a stimulus (e.g., a plant-derived mitogen, a vaccine or other antigen) designed to elicit a response that closely mimics the response *in vivo*. This can be in whole blood or in cells separated from the blood and by incubating them in the presence of a synthetic media enriched in serum (typically fetal calf serum; FCS) or from a human participant. Using the participant's serum (autologous serum) can provide very useful information about how the immune cells might respond when challenged *in vivo*. Often the cell supernatant is collected before and after stimulation to provide information about soluble mediators (e.g., cytokines important in antiviral defence) that have been synthesised and released by the cells. The cells themselves can be harvested and changes in cell surface receptor expression assessed using flow cytometry. Alternatively, there are many techniques based on this principle that can be used to assess other cell functions, including cell proliferation (e.g., Nieman et al., 1995; Bishop et al., 2005), the ability of cytotoxic cells to attack target cells and/or the ability of phagocytic cells to engulf foreign particles (Meaney et al., 2016).

Conclusion

In this chapter we have outlined key approaches and methods of data collection and analysis used in exercise immunology. There are a multitude of methods performed in research settings but assessing symptoms and mucosal immune function are probably most useful and feasible for practical and field settings. In these situations, frequent resting collections are needed (e.g., daily symptoms, weekly saliva) to gain the most meaningful data and several need to be taken to standardise longitudinal saliva collections. This will provide practical data to prompt early management intervention to maintain athlete health and facilitate a swift return to training.

References

Barrett, B., Brown, R., Mundt, M., Safdar, N., Dye, L., Maberry, R. and Alt, J. (2005). The Wisconsin Upper Respiratory Symptom Survey is responsive, reliable, and valid. *Journal of Clinical Epidemiology*, 58(6), 609–617.

Barrett, B., Brown, R., Voland, R., Maberry, R. and Turner, R. (2006). Relations among questionnaire and laboratory measures of rhinovirus infection. *European Respiratory Journal*, 28(2), 358–363.

Barrett, B., Locken, K., Maberry, R., Schwamman, J., Brown, R., Bobula, J. and Stauffacher, E. A. (2002). The Wisconsin Upper Respiratory Symptom Survey (WURSS): A new research instrument for assessing the common cold. *Journal of Family Practice*, 51(3), 265.

Bermon, S., Castell, L. M., Calder, P. C., Bishop, N. C., Blomstrand, E., Mooren, F. C., Krüger, K., Kavazis, A. N., Quindry, J. C., Senchina, D. S., Nieman, D. C., Gleeson, M., Pyne, D. B., Kitic, C. M., Close, G. L., Larson-Meyer, D. E., Marcos, A., Meydani, S. N., Wu, D., Walsh, N. P. and Nagatom, R. (2017). Consensus statement immunonutrition and exercise. *Exercise Immunology Review*, 23, 8–50.

Bishop, N. C., Walker, G. J., Bowley, L. A., Evans, K. F., Molyneux, K., Wallace, F. A. and Smith, A. C. (2005). Lymphocyte responses to influenza and tetanus toxoid in vitro following intensive exercise and carbohydrate ingestion on consecutive days. *Journal of Applied Physiology*, 99(4), 1327–1335.

Bosch, J. A., Ring, C., de Geus, E. J., Veerman, E. C. and Amerongen, A. V. (2002). Stress and secretory immunity. *International Review of Neurobiology*, 52, 213–253.

Jackson, G. G., Dowling, H. F., Spiesman, I. G. and Boand, A. V. (1958). Transmission of the common cold to volunteers under controlled conditions: I. The common cold as a clinical entity. *American Medical Association Archives of Internal Medicine*, 101(2), 267–278.

Li, T. L. and Gleeson, M. (2004). The effect of collection methods on unstimulated salivary immunoglobulin A, total protein, amylase and cortisol. *Bulletin of Physical Education*, 36, 17–30.

Meaney, M. P., Nieman, D. C., Henson, D. A., Jiang, Q. and Wang, F. Z. (2016). Measuring granulocyte and monocyte phagocytosis and oxidative burst activity in human blood. *Journal of Visualized Experiments*, 115, 54264.

Nieman, D. C., Brendle, D., Henson, D. A., Suttles, J., Cook, V. D., Warren, B. J., Butterworth, D. E., Fagoaga, O. R. and Nehlsen-Cannarella, S. L. (1995). Immune function in athletes versus nonathletes. *International Journal of Sports Medicine*, 16(5), 329–333.

Raysmith, B. and Drew, M. (2016). Performance success or failure is influenced by weeks lost to injury and illness in elite Australian track and field athletes: A 5-year prospective study. *Journal of Science and Medicine in Sport*, 19(10), 778–783.

Strazdins, L., Meyerkort, S., Brent, V., D'Souza, R. M., Broom, D. H. and Kyd, J. M. (2005). Impact of saliva collection methods on sIgA and cortisol assays and acceptability to participants. *Journal of Immunological Methods*, 307(1–2), 167–171.

Timpka, T., Jacobsson, J., Bargoria, V., Périard, J. D., Racinais, S., Ronsen, O., Halje, K., Andersson, C., Dahlström, Ö., Spreco, A., Edouard, P. and Alonso, J. M. (2017). Preparticipation predictors for championship injury and illness: Cohort study at the Beijing 2015 International Association of Athletics Federations World Championships. *British Journal of Sports Medicine*, 51(4), 271–276.

Walsh, N. P., Gleeson, M., Pyne, D. B., Nieman, D. C., Dhabhar, F. S., Shephard, R. J., Oliver, S. J., Bermon, S. and Kajeniene, A. (2011a). Position statement. Part two: Maintaining immune health. *Exercise Immunolology Review*, 17, 64–103.

Walsh, N. P., Gleeson, M., Shephard, R. J., Gleeson, M., Woods, J. A., Bishop, N. C., Fleshner, M., Green, C., Pedersen, B. K., Hoffman-Goetz, L., Rogers, C. J., Northoff, H., Abbasi, A. and Simon, P. (2011b). Position statement. Part one: Immune function and exercise. *Exercise Immunology Review*, 17, 6–63.

4.5 Skeletal muscle biopsy

Techniques and applications

Richard A. Ferguson and Natalie F. Shur

Introduction and background

The successful use of the percutaneous needle biopsy technique has formed an integral part of human skeletal muscle research for many years. Originally described by Duchenne (Charriere and Duchenne, 1865), it was not until the introduction of a new type of percutaneous biopsy needle by Jonas Bergström (1962) that the technique became an important tool, initially in clinical medicine but more recently for biochemical, physiological, nutritional, cellular and molecular research within the sport and exercise sciences. Indeed, Bergström and his colleague Eric Hultman, both Scandinavian physician scientists, were instrumental in performing some of the pioneering studies in human exercise metabolism using the muscle biopsy technique (Figure 4.5.1), frequently using themselves as participants (Bergström and Hultman, 1966). Following a sabbatical at the Karolinska Institute in Sweden, Richard H. T. Edwards (1971), a British physician later famed for his research into muscular dystrophy, brought this technique to the United Kingdom.

The Bergström needle consists of two cylinders. The outer one is 3–5 mm in diameter with an aperture near the tip. The sharp inner trochar cuts the tissue and a sample enters the aperture. One subsequently removes the tissue sample by pushing it out with a metal rod. Using suction significantly increases muscle tissue yield to over 200 mg (Evans et al., 1982; Hennessey et al., 1997; Tarnopolsky et al., 2011). Sample yield and relative discomfort of the procedure relates to the sharpness of the inner trochar, which one should replace if it becomes blunt. Many studies require multiple samples to be taken in a single experimental session (e.g., pre- and post-exercise); therefore, care must be taken to ensure repeated samples on the same leg are taken from different incisions at least 2.5 cm apart. Whilst some aspects of muscle metabolism may still be influenced (impaired ATP and glycogen resynthesis for several days; Constantin-Teodosiu et al., 1996) confounding changes in muscle transcription responses are not elicited (Murton et al., 2014).

Whilst the Bergström needle seems to be the most common method used, other percutaneous needles are available. The micro-biopsy device is a variant of a spring-loaded one-handed automated biopsy and utilises a disposable core biopsy needle (e.g., Bard Magnum™, TSK Acecut™). The advantage of the micro-biopsy

DOI: 10.4324/9781003045267-32

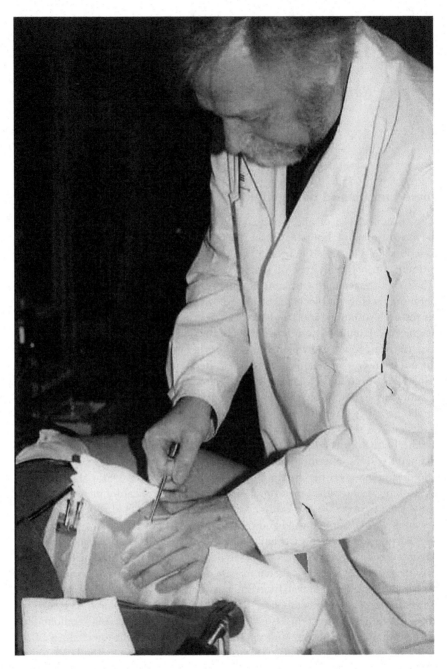

Figure 4.5.1 Professor Eric Hultman performing a muscle biopsy of the vastus lateralis using a Bergström needle.

technique is that a smaller incision (2–3 mm) is required. Alternatively, an insertion cannula can be used for biopsy needle placement, rather than making an incision. This method has been described as a 'less invasive' method that results in lower levels of discomfort (Hayot et al., 2005); therefore, in certain patient populations such as the frail, comorbid or sarcopenic, it may be better tolerated. The disadvantage of the micro-biopsy technique, however, is that it has a reduced yield (~20 mg) compared to Bergström, necessitating multiple passes depending on outcome measures. Smaller yields may make subsequent analyses more difficult, although previous studies have demonstrated that if the yield is sufficient, the micro-biopsy technique is equivalent to Bergström for laboratory analyses including enzymatic activity and fibre-type distribution (Hayot et al., 2005).

Muscle biopsies can also be obtained using a conchotome forceps, which opens with a scissor grip and was originally designed for ear, nose and throat (ENT) interventions. Advantages of the conchotome are a more exact placement of the instrument and less disruption of the biopsy sample, important for histology/ histochemical analyses. Disadvantages include increased trauma to surrounding tissues and higher bleeding rates.

Muscle biopsy procedure

The biopsy procedure itself is relatively simple. One should check the participant for contraindications including bleeding diatheses, current anticoagulant or anti-platelet medication, immunosuppression, active infection, musculoskeletal abnormalities such as local trauma and allergy to local anaesthetic: one must obtain written informed consent. The most common site for human muscle biopsies is the vastus lateralis since it is generally the largest muscle of the quadriceps femoris, it is a major locomotory muscle and it is easily accessed. The optimal site for vastus lateralis biopsy is the distal portion of the muscle, between ½ and ¾ of the length from the greater trochanter to the lateral epicondyle, just anterior to the iliotibial band, where the risk of hitting a major nerve or blood vessel is lowest (Chen et al., 2019). Other sites include the gastrocnemius (e.g., Morton et al., 2009), soleus (e.g., Harridge et al., 1996), biceps femoris (e.g., Evangelidis et al., 2017), biceps brachii (e.g., Venturelli et al., 2015), triceps brachii (Harridge et al., 1996) and deltoid (e.g., Costill et al., 1985).

Under sterile conditions, one injects local anaesthetic (typically 1% lidocaine without adrenaline) subcutaneously, which infiltrates over the superficial muscle fascia. Ideally, one should avoid infiltration of local anaesthetic into the muscle since this can potentially interfere with outcome measures: in practice, however, infiltration might occur without ultrasound guidance. After about 2 minutes, one makes a 4–5 mm incision through the skin, which continues through the superficial muscle fascia. One then advances a biopsy needle gently through the skin incision and uses it to locate the incision in the fascia. Once located, the needle is gently but firmly advanced into the muscle 1–2 cm beyond the fascia (some resistance is usually felt). The participant is likely to feel a pressure sensation ('discomfort' rather than a 'sharp pain') and the muscle will occasionally twitch. At this point, the inner trochar is pulled back enough to open the cutting aperture and an assistant applies suction. The needle is firmly closed and with suction maintained, one obtains two or three further samples: rotation of the needle may occur between each sample. For micro-biopsies, follow the same preparatory steps as with the Bergström needle, although it is not necessary to continue the incision through the superficial muscle fascia. With a micro-biopsy sample, one inserts a needle through the incision and advances it through the muscle fascia into the belly of the muscle. The device is then triggered and a sample taken. Multiple passes would occur, whereby the needle angle changes to ensure one samples fresh muscle. For biopsies using a conchotome, after local anaesthetic infiltration, a 5 mm skin incision is made and continued through the superficial muscle fascia. The closed jaws of the one insert the conchotome into the muscle, with the long axis of the jaws parallel to the muscle fibres. Subsequently, the jaws are opened, advanced and closed over the muscle and then rotated 180 degrees and withdrawn (Dietrichson et al., 1987).

In all cases, once the biopsy needle is removed, firm and direct pressure is applied to the biopsy site; ice may also be applied. This pressure is maintained for a minimum of 5 minutes, or longer if there is persistent bleeding/oozing. The incision can be closed using sterile Steri-Strips™ ensuring opposition of the two wound edges. Then a sterile gauze is applied over the top of the site of an incision for further protection and a compression bandage used, thereafter, to maintain pressure for 12 hours. Written aftercare advice is given to the participant, including details of wound care (ensuring the incision is kept clean and dry), information about performing exercise and to take simple painkillers such as paracetamol if discomfort is excessive.

Muscle tissue treatment after collection

Muscle tissue can be prepared in several ways depending on the subsequent analysis. For measurement of muscle metabolites, gene expression, mRNA/protein content and enzyme activity, the tissue is quickly snap-frozen in liquid nitrogen and subsequently stored at $-80°C$ until analysis. In the case of analysis of high-energy phosphates, the time taken between the muscle sampling and snap-freezing should be rapid (and can be as quick as 3 sec; Hultman and Sjöholm, 1983). One may perform subsequent assays on homogenised samples. One may also conduct fibre-type specific analysis on single fibres, micro-dissected from freeze-dried samples. Despite being very time consuming, one section of the dissected fibre is analysed for fibre type using acid-labile myofibrillar ATPase histochemistry (Essen et al., 1975), SDS-PAGE for myosin heavy chain isoform determination (Sant'Ana Pereirra et al., 1995) or, more recently, a dot blotting method based on Western blotting techniques (Christiansen et al., 2019). The remaining fibre fragment, or pooled samples of the same fibre type, are then analysed for the metabolites, gene transcripts or proteins of interest.

The preparation of tissue for histology/histochemical analysis requires preservation of tissue architecture and cell morphology; therefore, prompt and adequate embedding and/or fixation is essential. The three main methods of embedding tissue for sectioning are paraffin wax, optimal cutting temperature (OCT) compound (e.g., Tissue-Tek ™) and resin, each with its own benefits and weaknesses. Excess blood, fat and connective tissue are removed prior to mounting, in most cases with OCT, on either cork or an appropriate mould. This is carefully but rapidly frozen in liquid nitrogen-cooled isopentane, which prevents the formation of ice crystals, and subsequently stored at −80°C until analysis.

If fresh tissue is required, the sample is simply placed into the appropriate buffer/medium (Dulbecco's Modified Eagle's Medium [DMEM] for cell culture; or 'BIOPS' for mitochondrial respiration) prior to further processing. Examination of the contractile properties of single fibres is also possible (Bottinelli et al., 1996) whereby the sample is immediately placed in skinning solution prior to microdissection of single fibres and subsequent analysis of force-velocity and energetic characteristics.

Risks and safety aspects

The muscle biopsy method is a safe procedure. Overall, the complication rate for biopsies is generally reported to be in the range of 0.1–4% (for summary table see Chen et al., 2019). Normally, after a biopsy, participants experience a day or two of localised stiffness, but mobility is not affected. Indeed, for athletic populations, training should not be impaired and it may be recommended to perform light physical exercise the day after the procedure. The incision should be kept dry and any potential sources of infection should be avoided. The incision heals after about 10 days and a small scar is visible that fades over time. On occasions, a small lump of scar tissue may form under the site of the incision, but this normally disappears within two to three months. The risks of local skin infection or a deeper wound infection are extremely rare and ensuring good clinical practice in maintaining sterility throughout the procedure minimises this risk. There is a risk of bleeding within the muscle or beneath the fatty layer of the skin next to the muscle, evident from swelling or extensive bruising. Rarely, haematomas may form, limiting the range of motion of the muscles for a few weeks. Altered sensation or numbness of an area of skin (paraesthesia) adjacent to the biopsy scar may occur which is caused by injury to a small sensory nerve branch. There is a very low risk of damage to a small motor nerve branch to the muscle, which may result in partial atrophy and subsequent weakness of the muscle. This will not be initially obvious, but will become apparent after several months. Although this may be cosmetically visible, this complication will not influence day-to-day activities.

Because muscle biopsies are an invasive clinical procedure, only trained and experienced practitioners should perform the technique: individuals performing such a procedure should be indemnified. Best practice should include appropriate clinical supervision and/or oversight with an established pathway for medical follow-up should any complications arise.

Acknowledgements

We would like to thank Professor Paul L. Greenhaff and Professor Kenny Smith for supplying some of the images.

References

Bergström, J. (1962). Muscle electrolytes in man: Determined by neutron activation analysis on needle biopsy specimens: A study on normal subjects, kidney patients, and patients with chronic diarrhaea. *Scandinavian Journal of Clinical Laboratory Investigation*, 14(110), Suppl. 68.

Bergström, J. and Hultman, E. (1966). Muscle glycogen synthesis after exercise: An enhancing factor localized to the muscle cells in man. *Nature*, 210(5033), 309–310.

Bottinelli, R., Canepari, M., Pellegrino, M. A. and Reggiani, C. (1996). Force-velocity properties of human skeletal muscle fibres: Myosin heavy chain isoform and temperature dependence. *Journal of Physiology*, 495(2), 573–586.

Charriere, M. and Duchenne, G. B. (1865). Emporte piece histologique. *Bulletin of the Academy of Medicine*, 30, 1050–1051.

Chen, X. S., Abbey, A., Bharmal, S., Harris, E., Hudson, L., Krinner, E., Langan, A., Maling, J., Nijran, H., Street, C. and Wooley, B. R. (2019). Neurovascular structures in human vastus lateralis muscle and the ideal biopsy site. *Scandinavian Journal of Medicine and Science in Sports*, 29(4), 504–514.

Christiansen, D., MacInnis, M. J., Zacharewicz, E., Xu, H., Frankish, B. P. and Murphy, R. M. (2019). A fast, reliable, and sample-sparing method to identify fibre types of single muscle fibres. *Scientific Reports*, 9, 6473.

Constantin-Teodosiu, D., Casey, A., Short, A. H., Hultman, E. and Greenhaff, P. L. (1996). The effect of repeated muscle biopsy sampling on ATP and glycogen resynthesis following exercise in man. *European Journal of Applied Physiology*, 73(1–2), 186–190.

Costill, D. L., Fink, W. J., Hargreaves, M., King, D. S., Thomas, R. and Fielding, R. (1985). Metabolic characteristics of skeletal muscle during detraining from competitive swimming. *Medicine and Science in Sports and Exercise*, 17(3), 339–343.

Dietrichson, P., Coakley, J., Smith, P. E., Griffiths, R. D., Helliwell, T. R. and Edwards, R. H. (1987). Conchotome and needle percutaneous biopsy of skeletal muscle. *Journal of Neurology, Neurosurgery and Psychiatry*, 50(11), 1461–1467.

Edwards, R. H. (1971). Percutaneous needle-biopsy of skeletal muscle in diagnosis and research. *The Lancet*, 298(7724), 593–595.

Essen, B., Jansson, E., Henriksson, J., Taylor, A. W. and Saltin, B. (1975). Metabolic characteristics of fibre types in human skeletal muscle. *Acta Physiologia Scandinavica*, 95, 153–165.

Evangelidis, P. E., Massey, G. J., Ferguson, R. A., Wheeler, P. C., Pain, M. T. and Folland, J. P. (2017). The functional significance of hamstrings composition: Is it really a "fast" muscle group? *Scandinavian Journal of Medicine and Science in Sports*, 27, 1181–1189.

Evans, W. J., Phinney, S. D. and Young, V. R. (1982). Suction applied to a muscle biopsy maximizes sample size. *Medicine and Science in Sports and Exercise*, 14, 101–102.

Harridge, S. D., Bottinelli, R., Canepari, M., Pellegrino, M. A., Reggiani, C., Esbjörnsson, M. and Saltin, B. (1996). Whole-muscle and single-fibre contractile properties and myosin heavy chain isoforms in humans. *Pflügers Archiv*, 432(5), 913–920.

Hayot, M., Michaud, A., Koechlin, C., Caron, M. A., Leblanc, P., Préfaut, C. and Maltais, F. (2005). Skeletal muscle microbiopsy: A validation study of a minimally invasive technique. *Europeab Respiratory Journal*, 25(3), 431–440.

Hennessey, J. V., Chromiak, J. A., Della Ventura, S., Guertin, J. and MacLean, D. B. (1997). Increase in percutaneous muscle biopsy yield with a suction enhancement technique. *Journal of Applied Physiology*, 82, 1739–1742.

Hultman, E. and Sjöholm, H. (1983). Energy metabolism and contraction force of human skeletal muscle in situ during electrical stimulation. *Journal of Physiology*, 345, 525–532.

Morton, J. P., Croft, L., Bartlett, J. D., Maclaren, D. P., Reilly, T., Evans, L., McArdle, A. and Drust, B. (2009). Reduced carbohydrate availability does not modulate training-induced heat shock protein adaptations but does upregulate oxidative enzyme activity in human skeletal muscle. *Journal of Applied Physiology*, 106(5), 1513–1521.

Murton, A. J., Billeter, R., Stephens, F. B., Des Etages, S. G., Graber, F., Hill, R. J., Marimuthu, K. and Greenhaff, P. L. (2014). Transient transcriptional events in human skeletal muscle at the outset of concentric resistance exercise training. *Journal of Applied Physiology*, 116(1), 113–125.

Sant'Ana Pereira, J. A., Wessels, A., Nijtmans, L., Moorman, A. F. and Sargeant, A. J. (1995). New method for the accurate characterization of single human skeletal muscle fibres demonstrates a relation between mATPase and MyHC expression in pure and hybrid fibre types. *Journal of Muscle Research and Cell Motility*, 16(1), 21–34.

Tarnopolsky, M. A., Pearce, E., Smith, K. and Lach, B. (2011). Suction-modified Bergström muscle biopsy technique: Experience with 13,500 procedures. *Muscle and Nerve*, 43, 717–725.

Venturelli, M., Saggin, P., Muti, E., Naro, F., Cancellara, L., Toniolo, L., Tarperi, C., Calabria, E., Richardson, R. S., Reggiani, C. and Schena, F. (2015). In vivo and in vitro evidence that intrinsic upper- and lower-limb skeletal muscle function is unaffected by ageing and disuse in oldest-old humans. *Acta Physiologica*, 215(1), 58–71.

Part V

5.1 Exercise testing in obesity

David Broom, Matthew Capehorn and Anna Myers

Obesity is defined by the World Health Organization (WHO) as abnormal or excessive fat accumulation that may impair health (WHO, 2010). Put simply, the development of obesity results from a chronic positive energy balance in which daily energy intake (from food and drinks) exceeds energy expenditure (from the body's metabolism and physical activity) resulting in the accumulation of fat mass. The complex aetiology of obesity is beyond the scope of this chapter, so the reader is directed to the obesity systems map (Government Office for Science, 2007).

Once considered a problem only in high-income countries, obesity is dramatically on the rise in low- and middle-income countries. Based on Health Survey for England data, the percentage of men and women with obesity is 26% and 29%, respectively (NHS Digital, 2020), with similar prevalence in Scotland, Wales and Ireland.

Measurement and classification of obesity

Classifying weight status and potentially obesity is important to determine whether an individual is at risk of developing health problems and to monitor changes over time in response to weight loss strategies such as diet and/or exercise.

There are a number of different methods for measuring obesity-related outcomes, each with strengths and limitations. The most common is body mass index (BMI) due its ease of calculation from height and body mass. Other measures include waist circumference to measure central obesity, which is more indicative of greater risk of non-communicable disease than total body fat percentage.

A variety of body composition measurement techniques can be used ranging from easily accessible methods such as bioelectrical impedance and skinfold thickness (see Surface Anthropometry chapter) to more sophisticated measures such as magnetic resonance imaging or dual energy X-ray absorptiometry (see Use of DEXA chapter).

Body mass index (BMI)

Despite flaws due to muscle being denser than fat and body fat distribution, BMI is a globally accepted proxy measure used to classify obesity in adults. BMI is

DOI: 10.4324/9781003045267-34

calculated as a person's body mass in kilograms divided by the square of height in meters (kg/m^2). For detailed guidance on the measurement of body mass and height, see Surface Anthropometry chapter.

The WHO classify an individual as being with obesity if BMI is ≥30 kg/m^2. Other categories are as follows:

- $\geq30-35$ kg/m^2 – class I obesity
- $35-40$ kg/m^2 – class II obesity
- $40+$ kg/m^2 – class III obesity

A BMI >40 kg/m^2 is often referred to as severe and/or complex obesity depending on comorbidities.

Waist circumference (WC)

If measured accurately, WC can provide a direct correlation to expected levels of visceral adiposity. WC is measured halfway between the bottom rib and the anterior superior iliac spine (the top of the hip). Following a deep inhalation, the measurement is taken on exhalation with the tape measure parallel to the ground. WC is categorised into sex-specific risk thresholds as follows: for men: Desirable = <94 cm, High = $\geq94-102$ cm, Very high = >102 cm; and for women: Desirable = <80 cm, High = $\geq80-88$ cm, Very high = >88 cm

Body fat composition analysis

Body fat percentages of $>32\%$ for women and $>25\%$ for men are indicative of obesity (Hamdy and Khardori, 2021). There are multiple tools available to measure body composition and body fat percentage with varying validity and reliability and for further details please see related chapters.

Obesity-related complications and comorbidities

Obesity is associated with multiple comorbidities so it is important for practitioners to screen for other long-term conditions and proceed appropriately. For example, 14% of men and 10% of women with a very high waist circumference (>102 cm and >88 cm respectively) have either diagnosed or undiagnosed type 2 diabetes (NHS Digital, 2020).

Metabolic syndrome is the medical term for a combination of diabetes, high blood pressure (hypertension) and central obesity, all of which puts the person at greater risk of cardio-renal metabolic disease. Evidence also suggests that people with obesity are 14 times more likely to develop knee osteoarthritis (Arthritis Research Campaign, 2020). People with obesity may have a range of comorbidities; therefore, the reader is encouraged to read related chapters on these.

Physical fitness and functional assessment

Whilst it is not the purpose of this chapter to promote the benefits of exercise for weight management *per se*, the authors stress the importance of its inclusion in any well-rounded weight loss programme. It is therefore important to establish baseline fitness and function to complement weight loss goals. Frequent fitness and functional assessments are necessary for monitoring purposes.

Considerations prior to the physical fitness and function assessment

People with obesity may have body image issues so should be encouraged to arrive in comfortable attire and loose-fitting clothing if desired. Physical activity is safe for the majority of adults but the Physical Activity Readiness Questionnaire (PAR-Q) is designed to identify the small number of adults who should seek medical advice before changing the amount of physical activity they do. The PAR-Q is the minimum screening tool that should be completed prior to conducting an exercise test with people with obesity. However, practitioners are encouraged to consider a more comprehensive pre-physical function assessment depending on comorbidities. This may include:

1   A detailed medical history and information about medications, e.g., anti-hypertensive medications or anti-diabetic agents that may carry risks of hypoglycaemia.
2   Blood tests to ascertain blood glucose and lipid concentrations.
3   Measurement of blood pressure.
4   Physical activity, sedentary behaviour and diet.

If screening highlights that the participant is being prescribed medication, the practitioner should check for known side effects. The participant should be well hydrated, having not fasted for a prolonged period (approximately ≥4 hours) unless requested. Practitioners should highlight the location of the changing facilities and the toilet in case of faecal urgency.

Practitioners should be prepared to provide choice of mode of activity if possible, and before undertaking any aerobic exercise, functional, strength, muscular endurance or flexibility testing, a warm-up should be undertaken before more intensive exertion. Warm-up should include all the essential elements such as mobility exercises, pulse raiser and stretching.

Aerobic exercise tests

Submaximal exercise tests

There are a number of submaximal aerobic graded exercise tests that are suitable for people with obesity, like the Siconolfi step test; however, the Astrand Rhyming cycle test is commonly used due to being non-weight bearing. This test predicts maximal oxygen uptake ($\dot{V}O_2$max) from a 'steady state' heart rate obtained while cycling on a Monark ergometer at a known workload. Since it is not a test requiring maximum exertion it is considered suitable to assess individuals classified as being moderate risk without the presence of a doctor with the requirement that the exercise intensity remains below 6 METS or 60% $\dot{V}O_2$max (approximately 70% maximum heart rate). Instructions are as follows but for detailed guidance see Astrand and Ryhming (1954):

1   Determine the mass of your participant and record his or her age;
2   Adjust the seat height and handlebars on the Monark cycle;
3   Attach a heart rate monitor and check that it is working;
4   Instruct the participant to pedal at 50 rev·min^{-1} and then set the power output;
5   Single cradles on Monark cycles weigh 0.5 kg and double cradles weigh 1 kg. Begin by setting a 1 kg mass for females (cradle only = 50 W) and 1.5 kg mass for males (cradle + 0.5 kg = 75 W);
6   The participant then exercises for 6 minutes or for 7 minutes if a steady state heart rate has not been reached. Monitor the heart rate during the last 15 s of each minute of exercise;
7   Check that the heart rate is at or above 120 beats·min^{-1} after the first minute and consider if it is likely to be within the appropriate age-dependent heart rate range after 6 minutes of exercise is completed. If not within the desired range adjust the intensity accordingly;
8   The average heart rates recorded at the end of the fifth and sixth minutes are used to estimate $\dot{V}O_2$max and should not vary by more than 5 beats·min^{-1};
9   If the heart rate in the fifth and sixth minutes differ by more than 5 beats· min^{-1} continue exercising for a further minute using data from the last 15 seconds of the sixth and seventh minute as previous;
10   $\dot{V}O_2$max max can only be estimated if the final heart rate is in the range indicated in Table 5.1.1; and
11   Use the Astrand and Ryhming (1954) nomogram to obtain the predicted $\dot{V}O_2$max value.

Table 5.1.1. Age-related maximum and minimum heart rates for the Astrand-Ryhming Test (Astrand and Ryhming 1954)

Age Range (Years)	Heart Rate Range (Beats Per Minute)	
	Min	Max
15–20	120	160
21–30	120	152
31–40	120	144
41–50	120	136
51–60	120	128

Maximal exercise tests

Maximal tests involving ramp protocols using treadmills or cycle ergometers can be used. Rowing ergometers can also be used, but positioning may be difficult in those with extremely high BMIs.

If a person with obesity presents with knee osteoarthritis, it is advisable to use a non-weight bearing mode of activity such as the cycle ergometer. If they present with diabetes (and potentially foot ulcers) then submaximal testing and other functional tests are advisable due to the reduced likelihood of exacerbating symptoms.

Functional testing

Physical function tests, e.g., chair sit-to-stand and timed up-and-go, can be completed (see Chapter 5.10 Older Adults) and may be preferable to those extremely deconditioned and/or low in confidence.

Strength and muscular endurance testing

Strength and muscular endurance testing can be completed using free weights or fixed resistance machines, though practitioners should consider the ergonomic design and seat size. Body weight muscular endurance tests such as the push-up test and others requiring transitional changes from the floor such as the partial curl-up test are not contraindicated. However, practitioners should consider participant comfort and ability, particularly in people with extremely high BMIs.

Flexibility testing

Flexibility testing can be undertaken but should not be prioritised considering the likely goal of any exercise programme for people with obesity is weight loss and increasing fitness.

Considerations during physical function assessment

Due to potential low baseline fitness, practitioners must consider the relative intensity of the test since even normal daily tasks, such as walking extended distances, can be more difficult for people with obesity due to increased body mass. Rate of perceived exertion (RPE) and vital signs such as heart rate should be monitored frequently. Heart rate should not be used in people with obesity who are hypertensive and using heart rate-lowering medication (e.g., beta blockers).

On initiation of a fitness test, it may become apparent that it is not appropriate due to mobility issues or being too difficult, so the practitioner should take decisive action if the person is showing signs of discomfort, which can be ascertained by frequent verbal checks. Additionally, ensure adequate room ventilation and hydration, and therefore availability of fluid, during any test. A towel should be available for excessive sweating and a fan for cooling if desired.

Considerations following physical function assessment

A cool-down should be undertaken following any exertive test and should include all typical elements such as pulse lowering and stretching. The person with obesity should be monitored after the test, fluid should be available that contains a high-glycaemic, fast-acting carbohydrate source – particularly if type 2 diabetes is a comorbidity, and in this instance, blood glucose should also be monitored. It is important to be sensitive to test outcomes and encourage participation in future testing to ensure effective exercise and physical activity programming.

Summary of important considerations for exercise testing

The following are examples of key considerations when preparing for and undertaking exercise and physical activity testing based on the authors' experience of working with people with obesity:

- Check readiness and willingness to undertake testing;
- Identify barriers and any anxiety or body image issues, and support the person to overcome them;
- Identify any previous negative experiences of any particular type of activity and raise confidence as demanded;
- If possible, minimise sensations of displeasure. Adherence to testing or a program of physical activity is a pre-requisite for success, and people usually avoid activities they find overly aversive;
- Carefully consider if the participant has low physical work capacity due to excess body mass as well as poor joint mobility and balance. Lower intensity, i.e., submaximal testing may be more achievable for those with a very high BMI but do not immediately stereotype into gentler activities to avoid stigma;
- Repeated testing to monitor changes and suitable adaptions to the exercise program should occur regularly to ensure success. If rapport is established, openly discuss flatulence and/or faecal urgency to prepare for any events and potential embarrassment;
- Support and educate participants to understand their responses to exertion and exercise – what is 'normal' for them?
- To manage expectations, make it clear that everyone is different, and achievements in testing and responses to a physical activity program will vary;
- Take the opportunity to educate participants that exercise-induced reductions in body mass will vary between individuals due to numerous behavioural and physiological factors. Identifying and reinforcing that inter-individual differences exist will help to manage expectations to promote a better understanding of weight loss; and
- Inform your participant that as a result of physical activity, health outcomes will be improving even in the absence of weight loss.

Conclusion

Exercise scientists and practitioners must draw on their learning and experience because there is no 'one size fits all' methodology when performing exercise or physical activity testing in people with obesity. When working with people with obesity, a person-centred approach is essential and the implementation of and choice of any test depends on factors including previous experience, enjoyment and confidence. There are many important factors that practitioners must take into account when undertaking physical activity and exercise testing. Notwithstanding, the best type of exercise or physical activity for losing weight or preventing weight gain is the one that people will actually do and this should be reflected in the testing.

References

Arthritis Research Campaign. (2020). *Osteoarthritis and Obesity: A Report by the Arthritis Research Campaign*. London: Author.

Astrand, P. O. and Ryhming, I. (1954). A nomogram for calculation of aerobic capacity (physical fitness) from pulse rate during sub-maximal work. *Journal of Applied Physiology*, 7, 218–221.

Government Office for Science. (2007). *Foresight–Tackling Obesities: Future Choices and Obesity Systems Atlas*. London: Author.

Hamdy, O. and Khardori, R. (2021). *Obesity*. https://emedicine.medscape.com/article/123702-overview#a2 (accessed 8 April 2021).

NHS Digital. (2020). *Statistics on Obesity, Physical Activity and Diet, England*. London: Author.

WHO. (2010). *Obesity*. www.who.int/news-room/facts-in-pictures/detail/6-facts-on-obesity (accessed 8 April 2021).

5.2 Exercise testing in cardiovascular disease

Victoria S. Sprung, John P. Buckley and David L. Oxborough

Cardiovascular disease (CVD) provides one of the biggest challenges to exercise and health professionals in the UK, and worldwide. This is primarily due to the scale of the problem as well as the diversity and complexity of these diseases. It is well known that CVD is the most common pathology in 'Westernised' societies. The British Heart Foundation data compendium, published in April 2020, detailed that 7.6 million people live with CVD in the UK. In terms of mortality rate, CVD accounted for ~168,000 deaths in the UK which represented 25% of all deaths and ~46,000 of which were deemed premature (recorded in individuals under 75 years of age) in 2020 (British Heart Foundation, 2021). Further, CVD accounts for one-third of deaths worldwide. Coronary artery disease (CAD) accounts for the greatest proportion of CVD-related deaths, and risk factors including hypertension, cigarette smoking, diabetes mellitus or glucose intolerance, hypercholesterolaemia and obesity are the top six causes of death globally (Wong, 2014). CVD cases constitute a huge medical burden to the National Health Service (NHS) because they are often progressive and impose a life-long burden of intervention and treatment that require the investment of time, labour, drug therapy and other broader cost implications. The most prominent and greatest amount of treatment in CVD is linked to acquired atheromatic diseases leading to ischaemic conditions and infarctions of the myocardium or the brain. Electrical conductance disorders (e.g., arrhythmias) and myocardial dysfunction (e.g., ventricular heart failure) often result from these.

The umbrella term of CVD is an oversimplification of an exceptionally diverse set of pathologies. It should be acknowledged that any disease of the central or peripheral circulatory system is covered in the collective term 'CVD'. These include congenital, inherited and acquired diseases which, when broadly categorised, form the three main groups of CVD.

Congenital, inherited and acquired heart disease

The term 'congenital' refers to an inborn (existing at birth) defect affecting the heart and proximal blood vessels. Some of the more common congenital cardiovascular defects include pulmonary stenosis, septal defects and aortic coarctation.

DOI: 10.4324/9781003045267-35

Congenital cardiovascular defects are present in about 1% of live births and represent the most common congenital malformations in new-borns. The majority of congenital cardiovascular diseases obstruct blood flow in the heart or proximal vessels, or cause an abnormal pattern of blood flow through the heart. The natural history of congenital cardiovascular defects is incompletely understood. Amongst the possible candidates for causative factors are heredity, viral infections (e.g., rubella), certain conditions affecting multiple organs (e.g., Down's syndrome), some prescription drugs and over-the-counter medicines, as well as alcohol and recreational drugs.

The term 'inherited' refers to diseases that have a genetic origin and are often familial (diseases that run in families). Inherited heart diseases are disorders of the DNA code (known as 'mutations') of specific genes, and examples include cardiomyopathies such as hypertrophic cardiomyopathy and dilated cardiomyopathy. The process of inheritance depends upon whether the gene is dominant or recessive and the number of affected siblings in a family will depend upon the penetrance and the chromosome within which the abnormal gene resides. Although an individual may be a carrier (i.e., positive genotype), they may not always express a positive phenotype.

Acquired heart disease covers a broad spectrum of CVD that can be attributable to lifestyle and environment (although some genetic component may be present) and develop over a more prolonged period. Specifically, these diseases, such as CAD, valve disease, hypertensive remodelling and heart failure are not present at birth and normally manifest themselves in mid- to later life. We now possess a degree of knowledge related to the development of acquired heart disease as well as some of the key risk factors including hypertension, hyperlipidaemia, physical inactivity, obesity and smoking. Due to their prevalence and impact upon lifestyle, socioeconomics and morbidity/mortality statistics, acquired CVDs are at the core of the health-related roles now fulfilled by appropriately trained sport and exercise scientists.

Exercise testing in cardiac disorders

One increasingly common intervention to aid prevention and improve outcomes of CVD is physical activity (Thomas et al., 2003; Cobiac and Scarborough, 2017). A structured approach when attempting to increase levels of physical activity generally begins with the assessment of aspects of cardiovascular health (structure and function; Chapter 4.3) as well as the determination of an individual's cardiorespiratory fitness, normally performed via maximal and/or symptom limited incremental treadmill or cycle ergometry. In rehabilitative practice however, for pragmatic and access purposes, submaximal field-based shuttle walking/running, cycling and step tests are used (see Chapter 3.12 for basic principles). The understanding of cardiovascular health and physical performance capabilities is required to determine prognosis, risk stratification and functional capability measures, from which guidance for treatment and surgery, physical activity and exercise prescription can be made. This chapter cannot cover all tests associated with

CVD patients but a range of exercise tests that have been employed to assess (or estimate) cardiovascular performance capacity will be reviewed. In this section we wish to move forward from just a standard graded exercise tolerance test (Corra et al., 2004) and detail other methods of assessment of cardiovascular performance capacity that may include tests that are submaximal in nature and/or may be functionally relevant (Olsson et al., 2005). When selecting the mode of exercise test utilised, the test purpose and patient preference should also be considered (Fletcher et al., 2013).

Exercise testing in congenital, inherited and acquired heart disease

Careful consideration regarding the nature of the underlying CVD is crucial in the safe management of exercise testing, and indeed exercise prescription, in all patients (American Thoracic Society, & American College of Chest Physicians, 2003). Specific concerns in congenital and inherited heart disease are related to the variety of structural and/or functional alterations of the heart or proximal vessels and an abnormal cardiovascular response to exercise is expected. The abnormalities associated with congenital and inherited CVD, as well as the issues related to acquired CVD, affect (i) the electrical conduction through the heart; (ii) the functional capacity of the heart; and (iii) the function of the peripheral vasculature. As noted in the next section, respiratory responses to exertion can provide important prognostic and diagnostic information in relation to cardiac function. In all patients with cardiac disease, the impact of drug therapy on exercise tolerance and physiological response to exercise should also be considered, particularly those associated with chronotropic and inotropic function. Further, exercise stress testing in extremely sedentary patients may not yield maximum values for various physiological parameters. The use of gas exchange response during testing in these patients may be a valuable addition in the diagnosis of the condition, evaluation of exercise capacity and subsequent prescription of exercise (Whyte et al., 1999; Lainchbury and Richards, 2002). Contraindications to exercise (Table 5.2.1) should be carefully evaluated and, given the increased potential for adverse outcome, particularly during maximal exercise testing, appropriate steps should be taken to avoid incidents including modification of protocols and availability of appropriately trained individuals. Due to the range of observed abnormalities, integrated cardiopulmonary stress testing, including simultaneous 12-lead ECG, blood pressure and gas exchange during and post exercise (for a minimum of 10 minutes), is recommended in most cases, particularly for hospital-based clinical assessment (Myers et al., 1998, 2000).

Cardiopulmonary exercise test

The ideal exercise test employed in the clinical environment for patients with, or suspected of having, CVD is the integrated cardiopulmonary exercise test (CPET); however, not all centres have this capacity. The American College of Sports Medicine (ACSM, 2021) describes the value of this assessment in terms of

Table 5.2.1 Absolute and relative contraindications for CPET; adapted from American Thoracic Society (ATS)/American College of Chest Physicians (ACCP) (2003), Perioperative Exercise Testing and Training Society (POETTS) (2018) and American Heart Association (AHA) CPET guidelines (2010)

Absolute Contraindications	Relative Contraindications
• Acute myocardial infarction (3–5 days)	• Untreated left main stem coronary stenosis
• Unstable angina	• Asymptomatic severe aortic stenosis
• Uncontrolled/symptomatic arrhythmia	• Severe untreated arterial hypertension at rest (>200 mmHg [systolic], >120 mmHg [diastolic])
• Acute right-sided heart failure	• Tachyarrhythmias or bradyarrhythmias
• Uncontrolled heart failure	• Hypertrophic cardiomyopathy
• Syncope	• Significant pulmonary hypertension
• Active endocarditis	• Untreated thrombosis of the lower extremity
• Acute myocarditis or pericarditis	• Acute symptomatic pulmonary embolus (2 weeks)
• Symptomatic severe aortic stenosis	
• Suspected dissecting/leaking aortic aneurysm	
• Arterial desaturation at rest (<85%)	• Abdominal aortic aneurysm >8.0 cm

Testing for patients with absolute contraindications should be discussed with an appropriate clinician in terms of risks/benefits of testing. Patients with relative contraindications should receive direct supervision from a physician.

determining the presence of significant heart disease, and specifically CAD (2020). However, practitioners should exercise caution if utilising this assessment for diagnostic purposes, for which imaging is generally recommended. In patients with known heart disease, such tests are useful for assessing functional tolerance (e.g., anginal thresholds), progress of rehabilitation, influence of drug administration and other important issues (Levett et al., 2018). To this end, CPET is complimentary to define prognosis (Kokkinos et al., 2008; Kodama et al., 2009), determine risk stratification (Williams et al., 2004) and estimate functional capabilities of patients, which enables objective development of physical activity programmes. It is normal for the test to be treadmill-based, for the greatest cardiovascular work, and be continuous with exercise intensity progression achieved by staged changes in speed, incline or both. Other clinical laboratory-based tests may use stepping or cycling protocols, but the treadmill test remains the 'gold standard'.

Generally speaking, stepwise protocols for CPET are most commonly used in CVD patients. CPET protocols with large stage increments in energy requirements display a weaker relationship between peak oxygen consumption ($\dot{V}O_2$peak) and work rate. The Bruce/modified Bruce (1971) and individualised ramp protocols, which involve only modest increases in energy requirements per stage, are therefore recommended (Table 5.2.2). Patients should take their medications as usual, with the exception of beta-blockers (avoided 24 hours prior to the assessment), and are encouraged to exercise until volitional fatigue in the absence of symptoms or other indicators of ischaemia. The use of handrails during the exercise test is discouraged. Results are expressed relative to body weight (ml/kg/min).

Table 5.2.2 Stepwise increments of the modified Bruce Protocol (Reed et al., 2019)

Stage	Speed (mph)	Grade (%)	Duration (min)
1	1.7	0	3
2	1.7	5	3
3	1.7	10	3
4	2.5	12	3
5	3.4	14	3
6	4.2	15	3
7	5.0	15	3

Peak exercise time is recorded in minutes. Peak oxygen consumption is calculated as the highest consecutive 15-second period of gas exchange data occurring in the last minute before volitional exhaustion. Physiological criteria for assessment of $\dot{V}O_2$peak includes a levelling of $\dot{V}O_2$peak and/or a respiratory exchange ratio of ≥ 1.15 combined with a maximal heart rate at least 90% of the age-predicted maximal estimation (220 − age) (ACSM, 2021).

Alternative outcome measures of a cardiopulmonary stress test

In recent decades, other measures from an exercise test have been associated with prognosis, such as chronotropic response (Cole et al., 1999; Morshedi-Meibodi et al., 2002), oxygen uptake efficiency (Das et al., 2020) and $\dot{V}E/\dot{V}CO_2$ (Sayegh et al., 2021). These measures in addition to a simple $\dot{V}O_2$peak are invaluable, especially in clinical practice wherein patients rarely achieve a true maximum.

Assessment of functional capacity

There are now several valid and reliable exercise test alternatives to a maximal treadmill test that may be used, with appropriate considerations for the patient and the disease, in a broader range of exercise settings. Tests of exercise capacity or tolerance are often conducted outside the clinical laboratory (e.g., phase III and IV cardiac rehabilitation in gyms/exercise physiology laboratories) and thus come more within the direct remit of sport and exercise scientists. Over the last two decades, significant interest has arisen in tests of functional capacity that more closely reflect activities of habitual daily lifestyle (Arena et al., 2007). Most interest has been focussed on a variety of walking tests, and these have been used to assess functional capacity or to predict clinical outcomes/events (Girish et al., 2001), including protocols such as walks for time, walks for distance and shuttle walks.

Walking tests

The incremental shuttle walk test (ISWT) is a maximal test that closely correlates with laboratory generated data (Singh et al., 1994). The test was initially developed with patients who had respiratory disease (Singh et al., 1992), but has more recently been used in a variety of CVD populations including stroke (Wittink et al., 2020), heart failure (Polgar et al., 2020) and CAD (Gayda et al., 2003). The ISWT has been determined to be safe and reproducible in the assessment of patients engaged in cardiac rehabilitation programmes (Jolly et al., 2008). In heart failure patients, a shuttle walk test accurately predicted event-free survival at one year (Morales et al., 2000) and predicted $\dot{V}O_2$peak (Morales et al., 1999). Furthermore, research from Gayda and colleagues (2003) reported that using the validated 20 m shuttle walk test in patients with CAD yielded a maximal walking pace that was not dissimilar to maximal treadmill speed. More recent research evidence points to the utility of walking-based exercise tests in which patients self-select their speed and thus are more reflective of daily living, such as the six-minute walk test (Holland et al., 2014) for which patients are given standardised instruction to walk as far as possible in six minutes along a flat corridor.

Accurate heart rate (HR) measurement is vital during testing. Although this can be obtained via palpation, the experience/technique of the practitioner acutely impacts the accuracy of this measurement; it is recommended therefore that an ECG or validated HR monitor be utilised.

As far back as 1996, researchers have identified that the shuttle walk is easy to administer, requires little equipment and produces a symptom-limited maximal performance (Payne and Skehan, 1996). Green et al. (2001) provided evidence to support the reliability of the shuttle walk test, and described a closer relationship between treadmill $\dot{V}O_2$peak and distance ambulated in the shuttle walk test, compared with the six-minute walk test. Details regarding execution of submaximal walk, cycle and step tests and the use of HR and perceived exertion can be found in Chapters 3.9 and 3.12.

Summary of knowledge and future directions

When working with clinical populations, it is always important to know where the boundaries of our roles and competencies lie with respect to the patient, the disease and the assessments employed. It is likely that our work in these scenarios will evolve alongside important developments in our understanding of CVDs and their prevention, detection and treatment. It is incumbent on the sport and exercise science practitioner to be familiar with an ever-changing literature base related to CVD. Specifically, we should endeavour to keep abreast of advancing literature related to new methods of assessment, as well as data pertaining to the accuracy and quality of any estimated or measured outcomes.

References

ACSM. (2021). In G. Liguori, Y. Feito, C. Fountaine, and B. A. Roy (eds.), *ACSM's Guidelines for Exercise Testing and Prescription* (11th ed.). Philadelphia, PA: Lippincott Williams & Wilkins.

American Thoracic Society, & American College of Chest Physicians (2003). ATS/ACCP statement on cardiopulmonary exercise testing. *American Journal of Respiratory and Critical Care Medicine*, 167(2), 211–277. https://doi.org/10.1164/rccm.167.2.211.

Arena, R., Myers, J., Williams, M. A., Gulati, M., Kligfield, P., Balady, G. J., Collins, E., Fletcher, G., American Heart Association Committee on Exercise, R., Prevention of the Council on Clinical, C. and American Heart Association Council on Cardiovascular, N. (2007). Assessment of functional capacity in clinical and research settings: A scientific statement from the American Heart Association Committee on Exercise, Rehabilitation, and Prevention of the Council on Clinical Cardiology and the Council on Cardiovascular Nursing. *Circulation*, 116(3), 329–343.

British Heart Foundation. (2021). *Heart & Circulatory Disease Statistics 2021*. https://www.bhf.org.uk/what-we-do/our-research/heart-statistics/heart-statistics-publications/cardiovascular-disease-statistics-2021 (accessed 26 October 2021).

Bruce, R. A. (1971). Exercise testing of patients with coronary heart disease: Principles and normal standards for evaluation. *Annals of Clinical Research*, 3(6), 323–332.

Cobiac, L. J. and Scarborough, P. (2017). Translating the WHO 25x25 goals into a UK context: The PROMISE modelling study. *BMJ Open*, 7(4), e012805.

Cole, C. R., Blackstone, E. H., Pashkow, F. J., Snader, C. E. and Lauer, M. S. (1999). Heart-rate recovery immediately after exercise as a predictor of mortality. *New England Journal of Medicine*, 341(18), 1351–1357.

Corra, U., Mezzani, A., Bosimini, E. and Giannuzzi, P. (2004). Cardiopulmonary exercise testing and prognosis in chronic heart failure: A prognosticating algorithm for the individual patient. *Chest*, 126(3), 942–950.

Das, B. B., Godoy, A., Kadish, T. and Niu, J. (2020). Maximal versus sub-maximal effort during cardiopulmonary exercise testing in adults with congenital heart disease: Outcome analysis of short-term cardiac-related events. *Cardiology in the Young*, 1–6.

Fletcher, G. F., Ades, P. A., Kligfield, P., Arena, R., Balady, G. J., Bittner, V. A., Coke, L. A., Fleg, J. L., Forman, D. E., Gerber, T. C., Gulati, M., Madan, K., Rhodes, J., Thompson, P. D., Williams, M. A., American Heart Association Exercise, Cardiac Rehabilitation, and Prevention Committee of the Council on Clinical Cardiology, Council on Nutrition, Physical Activity and Metabolism, Council on Cardiovascular and Stroke Nursing, and Council on Epidemiology and Prevention. (2013). Exercise standards for testing and training: A scientific statement from the American Heart Association. *Circulation*, 128(8), 873–934.

Gayda, M., Choquet, D., Temfemo, A. and Ahmaidi, S. (2003). Cardiorespiratory fitness and functional capacity assessed by the 20-meter shuttle walking test in patients with coronary artery disease. *Archives of Physical Medicine and Rehabilitation*, 84(7), 1012–1016.

Girish, M., Trayner, E., Jr., Dammann, O., Pinto-Plata, V. and Celli, B. (2001). Symptom-limited stair climbing as a predictor of postoperative cardiopulmonary complications after high-risk surgery. *Chest*, 120(4), 1147–1151.

Green, D. J., Watts, K., Rankin, S., Wong, P. and O'Driscoll, J. G. (2001). A comparison of the shuttle and 6 minute walking tests with measured peak oxygen consumption in patients with heart failure. *Journal of Science and Medicine in Sport*, 4(3), 292–300.

Holland, A. E., Spruit, M. A., Troosters, T., Puhan, M. A., Pepin, V., Saey, D., McCormack, M. C., Carlin, B. W., Sciurba, F. C., Pitta, F., Wanger, J., MacIntyre, N., Kaminsky, D. A., Culver, B. H., Revill, S. M., Hernandes, N. A., Andrianopoulos, V., Camillo, C. A., Mitchell, K. E., Lee, A. L., Hill, C. J. and Singh, S. J. (2014). An official European Respiratory Society/American Thoracic Society technical standard: Field walking tests in chronic respiratory disease. *European Respiratory Journal*, 44(6), 1428–1446.

Jolly, K., Taylor, R. S., Lip, G. Y., Singh, S. and Committee, B. S. (2008). Reproducibility and safety of the incremental shuttle walking test for cardiac rehabilitation. *International Journal of Cardiology*, 125(1), 144–145.

Kodama, S., Saito, K., Tanaka, S., Maki, M., Yachi, Y., Asumi, M., Sugawara, A., Totsuka, K., Shimano, H., Ohashi, Y., Yamada, N. and Sone, H. (2009). Cardiorespiratory fitness as a quantitative predictor of all-cause mortality and cardiovascular events in healthy men and women: A meta-analysis. *JAMA*, 301(19), 2024–2035.

Kokkinos, P., Myers, J., Kokkinos, J. P., Pittaras, A., Narayan, P., Manolis, A., Karasik, P., Greenberg, M., Papademetriou, V. and Singh, S. (2008). Exercise capacity and mortality in black and white men. *Circulation*, 117(5), 614–622.

Lainchbury, J. G. and Richards, A. M. (2002). Exercise testing in the assessment of chronic congestive heart failure. *Heart*, 88(5), 538–543.

Levett, D. Z. H., Jack, S., Swart, M., Carlisle, J., Wilson, J., Snowden, C., Riley, M., Danjoux, G., Ward, S. A., Older, P. and Grocott, M. P. W. (2018). Perioperative cardiopulmonary exercise testing (CPET): Consensus clinical guidelines on indications, organization, conduct, and physiological interpretation. *British Journal of Anaesthesia*, 120, 484–500. https://doi.org/10.1016/j.bja.2017.10.020

Morales, F. J., Martinez, A., Mendez, M., Agarrado, A., Ortega, F., Fernandez-Guerra, J., Montemayor, T. and Burgos, J. (1999). A shuttle walk test for assessment of functional capacity in chronic heart failure. *American Heart Journal*, 138(2 Pt 1), 291–298.

Morales, F. J., Montemayor, T. and Martinez, A. (2000). Shuttle versus six-minute walk test in the prediction of outcome in chronic heart failure. *International Journal of Cardiology*, 76(2–3), 101–105.

Morshedi-Meibodi, A., Larson, M. G., Levy, D., O'Donnell, C. J. and Vasan, R. S. (2002). Heart rate recovery after treadmill exercise testing and risk of cardiovascular disease events (The Framingham Heart Study). *American Journal of Cardiology*, 90(8), 848–852.

Myers, J., Gullestad, L., Vagelos, R., Do, D., Bellin, D., Ross, H. and Fowler, M. B. (1998). Clinical, hemodynamic, and cardiopulmonary exercise test determinants of survival in patients referred for evaluation of heart failure. *Annals of Internal Medicine*, 129(4), 286–293.

Myers, J., Gullestad, L., Vagelos, R., Do, D., Bellin, D., Ross, H. and Fowler, M. B. (2000). Cardiopulmonary exercise testing and prognosis in severe heart failure: 14 mL/kg/min revisited. *American Heart Journal*, 139(1 Pt 1), 78–84.

Olsson, L. G., Swedberg, K., Clark, A. L., Witte, K. K. and Cleland, J. G. (2005). Six minute corridor walk test as an outcome measure for the assessment of treatment in randomized, blinded intervention trials of chronic heart failure: A systematic review. *European Heart Journal*, 26(8), 778–793.

Payne, G. E. and Skehan, J. D. (1996). Shuttle walking test: A new approach for evaluating patients with pacemakers. *Heart*, 75(4), 414–418.

Polgar, O., Nolan, C. M., Barker, R. E., Patel, S., Walsh, J. A. and Man, W. D. (2020). Incorporating Patients with Chronic Heart Failure (CHF) into Pulmonary Rehabilitation (PR): A Propensity Matched Analysis. *ERS International Congress 2020 abstracts*. doi: 10.1183/13993003.congress-2020.892.

Reed, J. L., Cotie, L. M., Cole, C. A., Harris, J., Moran, B., Scott, K., Terada, T., Buckley, J. P. and Pipe, A. L. (2019). Submaximal exercise testing in cardiovascular rehabilitation settings (BEST study). *Frontiers in Physiology*, 10, 1517.

Sayegh, A. L. C., Silva, B. M., Ferreira, E. V., Ramos, R. P., Fisher, J. P., Nery, L. E., Ota-Arakaki, J. S. and Oliveira, R. K. (2021). Clinical utility of ventilatory and gas exchange evaluation during low-intensity exercise for risk stratification and prognostication in pulmonary arterial hypertension. *Respirology*, 26(3), 264–272.

Singh, S. J., Morgan, M. D., Hardman, A. E., Rowe, C. and Bardsley, P. A. (1994). Comparison of oxygen uptake during a conventional treadmill test and the shuttle walking test in chronic airflow limitation. *European Respiratory Journal*, 7(11), 2016–2020.

Singh, S. J., Morgan, M. D., Scott, S., Walters, D. and Hardman, A. E. (1992). Development of a shuttle walking test of disability in patients with chronic airways obstruction. *Thorax*, 47(12), 1019–1024.

Thomas, N. E., Baker, J. S. and Davies, B. (2003). Established and recently identified coronary heart disease risk factors in young people: The influence of physical activity and physical fitness. *Sports Medicine*, 33(9), 633–650.

Whyte, G. P., Sharma, S., George, K. and McKenna, W. J. (1999). Exercise gas exchange responses in the differentiation of pathologic and physiologic left ventricular hypertrophy. *Medicine and Science in Sports and Exercise*, 31(9), 1237–1241.

Williams, M., Balady, G., Carlson, J., Comoss, P., Humphrey, R., Lounsbury, P., Roitman, J. and Southard, D. (2004). *AACVPR Guidelines for Cardiac Rehabilitation and Secondary Prevention Programs*. Champaign, IL: Human Kinetics.

Wittink, H., Blatter, T., Outermans, J., Volkers, M., Westers, P. and Verschuren, O. (2020). Feasibility, reproducibility and validity of the 10 meter shuttle test in mild to moderately impaired people with stroke. *Plos One*, 15(10), e0239203.

Wong, N. D. (2014). Epidemiological studies of CHD and the evolution of preventive cardiology. *Nature Reviews Cardiology*, 11(5), 276.

5.3 Exercise testing in diabetes

Rob C. Andrews, Parth Narendran and Emma Cockcroft

Introduction

Diabetes is a group of metabolic diseases that are characterised by elevated levels of blood glucose (hyperglycaemia) due to defects in insulin secretion, insulin action or both. Approximately 422 million people worldwide have diabetes and 1.6 million annual deaths are attributed to diabetes. In the UK, just under 4 million people are diagnosed with diabetes, with a further 6 million being at high risk of developing the condition.

The classic symptoms of untreated diabetes are unintended weight loss, polyuria (increased urination) and polydipsia (increased thirst). Numerous tests can help diagnose diabetes (see Table 5.3.1). In a patient with no symptoms, two diagnostic tests are required to make the diagnosis, whereas in a symptomatic individual only one test is required. In practice, the simplest way to confirm a diagnosis is with an HbA1c test, which does not require an individual to fast.

Diabetes is due to either the insulin making cells of the pancreas (β-cells) not producing enough insulin, or the cells of the body not responding properly to the insulin produced (insulin resistance). Diabetes can be classified into four general categories (American Diabetes Association, 2021), as follows:

1   Type 1 diabetes (T1D) accounts for about 8% of cases of diabetes and is due to autoimmune destruction of the insulin-making cells of the pancreas

Table 5.3.1 Exercise and diabetes

Table 5.3.1 Criteria for the Diagnosis of Diabetes

FBG ≥ 7.0 mmol/L (126 mg/dL). Fasting is defined as no calorie intake for at least 8 hours.
2h PG ≥ 11.1 mmol/L (200 mg/dL) during OGTT. The test should be performed using a glucose load containing the equivalent of 75 g anhydrous glucose dissolved in water.
HbA1c ≥ 48 mmol/mol (6.5%). The test should be performed in an accredited laboratory
In a patient with classic symptoms of hyperglycaemia a random plasma glucose ≥ 11.1 mmol/L (200 mg/dL).
FPG, fasting plasma glucose; OGTT, oral glucose tolerance test; 2h PG, two-hour plasma glucose; HbA1c, glycated haemoglobin

DOI: 10.4324/9781003045267-36

(β-cells) leading to absolute insulin deficiency and the need for lifelong insulin treatment.

2   Type 2 diabetes (T2D) accounts for about 90% of cases and begins with insulin resistance. As the disease progresses, a lack of insulin may develop. Initially, treatment starts with diet and exercise, followed by glucose-lowering drugs. About one third of patients with T2D will require insulin treatment as their diabetes progresses.

3   Gestational diabetes (GDM) is diagnosed in the second or third trimester of pregnancy in someone not known to have diabetes before becoming pregnant.

4   Other types of diabetes account for 2% of cases and include different types of monogenic diabetes, cystic fibrosis-related diabetes and diabetes caused by rare syndromes.

Use of exercise tests

Diabetic patients can complete an exercise test for several reasons: to evaluate physical capacity, to help with a training prescription, to evaluate exercise-related symptoms and to obtain medical clearance for specific events or high-intensity training. Patients can also undergo such tests for research purposes, for example, to test a specific dietary regimen or to explore how an exercise regimen has affected fitness.

Screening and contraindications

Over time, the hyperglycaemia associated with diabetes can lead to damage to the heart, blood vessels, eyes, kidneys and nerves. For this reason, additional questions will need to be asked and greater care taken in the examination when screening someone with diabetes for an exercise test.

As with individuals without diabetes, the absolute and relative contraindications to exercise testing due to CVD (e.g., acute myocardial infarction, unstable angina, acute pulmonary embolism) and uncontrolled hypertension are the same for people with diabetes (Fletcher et al., 2013). There are only two absolute contractions specific to people with diabetes. The first is brittle diabetes control with frequent high and low glucose (hypoglycaemia) excursions that place the individual at risk of having low glucose or high glucose during the exercise test; the second is severe retinopathy that increases the risk of retinal detachment and/or vitreous haemorrhage during the exercise test (Colberg et al., 2010).

The presence of autonomic neuropathy, damage to nerves that manage everyday body functions such as blood pressure, heart rate and sweating, will require adaptions. Autonomic neuropathy reduces the ability of the heart to increase the heart rate adequately and this will mean that termination criteria based on heart rate reserve or theoretical maximum heart rate will need to be adapted. Additional care during and after a test will also need to be taken because autonomic neuropathy may lead to postural hypotension and unpredictable absorption of carbohydrate, due to delayed gastric emptying, which can increase the risk of hypoglycaemia (Colberg et al., 2010).

Diabetic kidney disease (nephropathy) is not a contraindication, but blood electrolytes should be measured prior to exercise to ensure potassium is not high, particularly in people with end-stage renal failure who are undergoing dialysis (Colberg et al., 2010). The presence of diabetic neuropathy will require adaptions to me made. Treadmill or walking tests should be avoided in people with foot deformities, unhealed foot ulcers or amputations (Colberg et al., 2010).

If one has any doubt about whether a participant should conduct an exercise test, the participant should seek informed medical advice from the doctor who takes care of his or her diabetes. If no contraindications exist and the test goes ahead, the participant should be carefully prepared to avoid complications.

Preparing the participant

Overall glucose control affects performance in exercise tests (see the section later in this chapter, Interpretation and training zones). Considering this, good diabetes control should be encouraged in the weeks prior to an exercise test. Similarly, in studies that look at the effect of different diets or exercise regimens on performance of exercise tests, each arm of the study should have a comparable glucose control both before and after an intervention.

During an exercise test, a participant should be able to perform to maximal capacity, reach an exercise intensity to be able to access metabolic function (e.g., lactate threshold), avoid counter-regulatory mechanisms and not have to stop the test due to hyperglycaemia or hypoglycaemia.

When people without diabetes exercise, changes in insulin and counter-regulatory hormone secretion occur, which are dependent on the type and nature of exercise. These changes facilitate an increase in liver glucose production which matches skeletal muscle glucose uptake during exercise (Stokes et al., 2013).

People with T1D

In people with T1D, fuel regulation is difficult because the insulin level does not fall in response to exercise and there may be impaired secretion or action of counter-regulatory hormones, making normal fuel regulation difficult. After activity, the inability of the pancreas to increase insulin and reduced blood concentrations of counter-regulatory hormones can hamper recovery and adaptation to exercise. This means that hypoglycaemia both during and following exercise becomes a significant risk. Furthermore, hyperglycaemia prior to, and following, some types of exercise can also be problematic (Riddell et al., 2017). It is important to note that different modalities have differing effects on blood glucose during and after exercise. In general, aerobic-type exercise increases glycaemia, anaerobic exercise tends to increase glycaemia and mixed (anaerobic and aerobic) exercise is associated with glucose stability. There is high individual variability in blood glucose response to exercise; thus, one must consider each patient's prior experience.

There are several approaches to minimising the risk of hypoglycaemia during or after an exercise test (see Figure 5.3.1). Subcutaneous injections of insulin

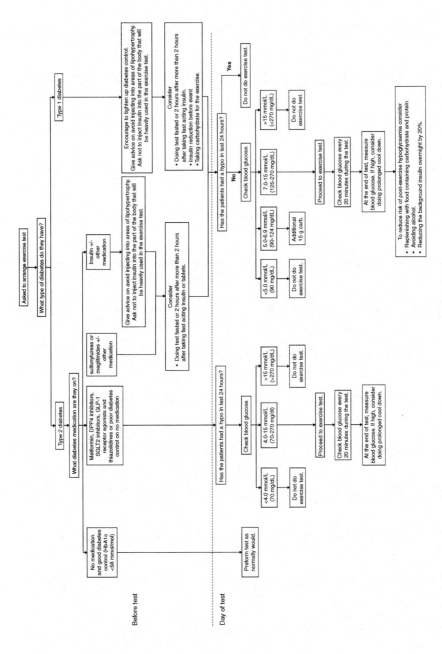

Figure 5.3.1 Flowsheet for preparing and carrying out an exercise test in patients with diabetes.

should avoid areas of lipohypertrophy, because this can result in variation in insulin absorption. Patients should also avoid injecting into the part of the body engaged in performing an exercise test, such as avoiding injection into legs for a cycling test. This is because there will be increased blood flow to these body parts, and this results in faster insulin absorption at the start of exercise and greater risk of hypoglycaemia.

The timing of an exercise test is important when considering hypoglycaemia prevention. Conducting the test first thing in the morning, before breakfast for example, may be a novel approach to preventing hypoglycaemia. Results from a recent laboratory study showed that exercising fasting (either high-intensity interval exercise or continuous moderate-intensity exercise) for less than 45 minutes maintained a stable blood glucose with no increased risk of hypoglycaemia over the 24-hour period following exercise (Scott et al., 2019a). The reproducibility of the achieved plasma glucose concentration is better when exercising fasted compared to exercising after eating (Biankin et al., 2003). If the test cannot be done fasted, then in line with standard practice in individuals without diabetes, it should be completed more than two hours after a main meal, because this is the point when there is the lowest amount of fast-acting insulin (or bolus insulin that is taken before/with meals). There is also a differential impact of morning or afternoon exercise on subsequent hypoglycaemic events, with less incidence of hypoglycaemia with morning exercise compared with afternoon (Gomez et al., 2015). For optimum test-retest comparisons, patients should complete exercise testing at the same time of day, with replication of pre-test regimen.

If the exercise test cannot be conducted fasted or more than two hours after taking fast-acting insulin, then patients can take carbohydrate or adjust their insulin regimen to limit their risk of hypoglycaemia. A simple strategy to prevent hypoglycaemia is to replace the amount of carbohydrate used during exercise via oral supplementation. Doing this should mean that the glucose remains stable across the exercise. For moderate-intensity activity, $0.5 \text{ g·kg}^{-1}\text{·hr}^{-1}$ should be used, and for high-intensity activity, $1 \text{ g·kg}^{-1}\text{·hr}^{-1}$ should be used (Riddell et al., 2017). To prevent a large glucose rise at the start and then a fall across the duration of the exercise, carbohydrate should be ingested every 20 minutes and should be received in the form of high-glycaemic, rapidly digested and absorbed carbohydrates. Most people tend to use glucose-based products but there is emerging evidence that the addition of fructose or isomaltose can help to protect against hypoglycaemia (Scott et al., 2019b). If more than 90 grams per hour are needed, then a combination of carbohydrates will be needed because the gut cannot absorb more than 90 grams per hour of glucose. Using carbohydrate will influence the composition of any pulmonary gas exchange samples collected as well as affecting lactate production. This would impair the outcome as well as test-retest comparison of cardiopulmonary exercise tests. Therefore, for these short-duration tests, insulin adjustment is preferred.

Adjusting insulin dose is another strategy that could be utilised and may negate the need to consume extra carbohydrate. The approach used will depend on the insulin treatment regimen (multiple daily injections [MDI] or pump). When an exercise test occurs within 90 minutes postprandial, pre-meal insulin bolus reductions have been successful in reducing exercise-induced hypoglycaemia (Campbell et al., 2013). A simple starting point is to reduce the amount of insulin given by 50%. These techniques work for patients using MDI or a pump. A further strategy available for those using insulin pump therapy is to temporarily reduce basal (background) insulin for the exercise period by ~80% starting 40 minutes prior to exercise and finishing at the end of exercise (Roy-Fleming et al., 2019).

Whether a patient adjusts his or her insulin regimen or takes carbohydrates for the exercise test will depend on what has happened previously with his or her glucose when doing the nature (i.e., mode, modality, intensity and duration) of exercise planned. It also depends on what a patient's glucose concentration is at the start of the test (see the following). Tactics for managing the patient's glucose before, during and after a scheduled exercise test should be discussed with a healthcare professional who is responsible for managing the patient's diabetes.

People with T2D

In people with T2D, changes in insulin and counter-regulatory hormone secretion are normal during exercise. If glucose concentration is initially high, this will initially fall during exercise, but normal adaptations will occur as glucose concentration falls into the normal range. Hypoglycaemia is rare and only tends to occur when patients are on insulin or agents that increase its secretion (sulfonylureas or meglitinides). The risk of hypoglycaemia with the other diabetes medications such as biguanides, DPP4 inhibitors, SGLT2 inhibitors, GLP-1 receptor agonists and thiazolidines is low (see Figure 5.3.1).

For patients on insulin, sulfonylureas or meglitinides, the risk of developing hypoglycaemia is reduced when an exercise test occurs in a fasted state, or at least 2 hours postprandial. Alternatively, on the day of the exercise test, a patient could simply miss his or her morning dose of the sulfonylureas or meglitinides. For patients on insulin, we do not recommend reduction of insulin dosage, unless the patient has experienced a hypoglycaemic event during exercise that forms the basis of a proposed exercise test. Whether carbohydrate supplementation is required on the day of an exercise test will largely depend on the blood glucose concentration at the start of the test (see the following).

Exercise test protocol and supervision

There are no specific protocols for patients with diabetes, so researchers or clinicians must design and implement any test protocol according a patient's needs (Fletcher et al., 2013). For individuals with T1D, if possible, a total testing time that does not exceed 45 minutes of continuous exercise including warm-up and cool-down times will reduce the risk of hypoglycaemia. A qualified health professional must be involved in administering supervised exercise tests: in addition to having knowledge of exercise testing, such an individual must be trained in emergency first aid, including cardiopulmonary resuscitation. The person supervising the test should also know the patient's specific hypoglycaemic symptoms, be able to conduct and interpret capillary blood tests and know how to treat hypoglycaemia. For individuals on no diabetes medication and with good diabetes control (HbA1c less than 58 mmol·mol^{-1}), the test can be conducted as normal (see Figure 5.3.1).

Before the test

A hypoglycaemia event within the previous 24 hours is a contraindication to doing the exercise test because of the substantially increased risk of a more serious hypoglycaemic episode during the test (Galassetti and Riddell, 2013). Before starting an exercise test, at least two blood glucose readings, separated 10 minutes apart, should be taken so that a starting (resting) blood glucose concentration is established. These measures allow one to ascertain the both the magnitude and direction of blood glucose changes. This will determine whether any other adjustments are required prior to starting exercise (see Figure 5.3.1). The test will have to be postponed for individuals on insulin, sulfonylureas or meglitinides if blood glucose concentration is <5 mmol·l^{-1} (90 mg·dl^{-1}) because even a rapid correction of glycaemia will still impair counter-regulatory mechanisms. If the blood glucose is 5.0 to 6.9 mmol·L^{-1} (90–124 mg·dL^{-1}) then T1D patients and T2D patients on insulin, sulfonylureas or meglitinides will need to take 15 grams of carbohydrate (see Figure 5.3.1). If the glucose is 7–15 mmol·l^{-1} (126–270 mg·dl^{-1}) then it is safe to start the test (Riddell et al., 2017). If glucose is >15 mmol·l^{-1} (>270 mg·dl^{-1}) then the test will have to be postponed because intense exercise may exaggerate hyperglycaemia and induce ketosis or worsen it if already present (Riddell et al., 2017). For patients on biguanides, DPP4 inhibitors, SGLT2 inhibitors, GLP-1 receptor agonists and thiazolidines, the exercise test should not be performed if glucose is less than 4.0 mmol·L^{-1} (70 mg·dL^{-1} or greater than 15 mmol·l^{-1} (270 mg·dl^{-1}). If a patient's glucose concentration lies between these two readings, s/he can undertake an exercise test.

During the test

During a maximal exercise test, one should monitor blood pressure (BP), heart rate (HR) and information from an electrocardiogram. Patients with autonomic disturbance have abnormal BP and HR responses to exercise, so they should have these monitored for all types of exercise tests. One should measure blood glucose concentration every 20 minutes, but the use of continuous glucose or flash glucose monitor readings tend to have a 10–15-minute delay during exercise. If glucose falls below a concentration 4 mmol·l^{-1} (70 mg·dl^{-1}), a test will have to be stopped and carbohydrates given in line with usual management of hypoglycaemia.

After the test

Post-exercise hypotension is more common in people with diabetes, so after the test the participant should recover in the sitting position for at least 15–20 minutes or until cardiovascular values have returned to, or near to, pre-exercise levels. Blood glucose concentration should also be monitored during the immediate recovery period and on a frequent basis for 24 hours after a test. People with T2D rarely have problems with their glucose after exercise tests. People with T1D can suffer with both hyperglycaemia and hypoglycaemia after exercise. Hyperglycaemia is more common after intense exercise, particularly if insulin concentrations fall. A patient can modify this response by performing a prolonged cool-down, since this will facilitate the disposal of excess amounts of blood glucose. Late-onset post-exercise hypoglycaemia relates to a natural repletion of hepatic and muscle glycogen stores. Such episodes are associated mostly with intense and prolonged exercise, but can also occur following physical function assessments, especially those that require patients to perform a battery of tests in quick succession. Replenishing with food containing carbohydrate and protein, avoiding alcohol and reducing the background insulin overnight by 20% can all protect against post-exercise hypoglycaemia (Riddell et al., 2017).

Interpretation and training zones

Although some studies have shown that poor glycaemic control can affect training response to exercise (Baldi et al., 2010), exercise performance in a cardiopulmonary exercise test (Moser et al., 2017) and heart rate dynamics during exercise tests (Moser et al., 2018a), the interpretation of exercise test outcomes should be completed as usual. This is because there are no studies, to our knowledge, that have compared exercise test outcomes in people with and without diabetes while at the same time being able to control for training modalities or habitual physical activity. Caution should be taken in using relative percentages of maximum values (e.g., HRmax or $\dot{V}O_2$max) to prescribe exercise intensities since this may push individuals with diabetes to exercise at an intensity that is too high, inducing different training effects than those desired (Moser et al., 2018b). In addition, one must exercise care when comparing effects of interventions in patients with T2D on different diabetes medications: there is emerging evidence that some diabetes medication can augment the effect of exercise training on exercise tolerance (Eckstein et al., 2019).

Conclusions

Diabetes is not a contraindication to carrying out an exercise test. A thorough screening is required and includes the search for potential risks for hypoglycaemia and complications that may require adaption of the exercise test. The key aspect to obtaining valid data is planning to avoid glycaemic excursions in participants taking insulin therapy or insulin secretagogues. An important consideration in performing exercise tests is consistency in approach to pre-exercise preparation, in terms of insulin dose, carbohydrate intake and glycaemic control. A consistent approach to pre-exercise preparation will give greater reliability in test-retest comparisons.

References

American Diabetes Association. (2021). 2. Classification and diagnosis of diabetes: Standards of medical care in diabetes-2021. *Diabetes Care*, 44, S15–S33.

Baldi, J. C., Cassuto, N. A., Foxx-Lupo, W. T., Wheatley, C. M. and Snyder, E. M. (2010). Glycemic status affects cardiopulmonary exercise response in athletes with type I diabetes. *Medicine and Science in Sports and Exercise*, 42, 1454–1459.

Biankin, S. A., Jenkins, A. B., Campbell, L. V., Choi, K. L., Forrest, Q. G. and Chisholm, D. J. (2003). Target-seeking behavior of plasma glucose with exercise in type 1 diabetes. *Diabetes Care*, 26, 297–301.

Campbell, M. D., Walker, M., Trenell, M. I., Jakovljevic, D. G., Stevenson, E. J., Bracken, R. M., Bain, S. C. and West, D. J. (2013). Large pre- and postexercise rapid-acting insulin reductions preserve glycemia and prevent early- but not late-onset hypoglycemia in patients with type 1 diabetes. *Diabetes Care*, 36, 2217–2224.

Colberg, S. R., Sigal, R. J., Fernhall, B., Regensteiner, J. G., Blissmer, B. J., Rubin, R. R., Chasan-Taber, L., Albright, A. L. and Braun, B. (2010). Exercise and type 2 diabetes. *Diabetes Care*, 33, 2692.

Eckstein, M. L., Williams, D. M., O'Neil, L. K., Hayes, J., Stephens, J. W. and Bracken, R. M. (2019). Physical exercise and non-insulin glucose-lowering therapies in the management of Type 2 diabetes mellitus: A clinical review. *Diabetic Medicine*, 36, 349–358.

Fletcher, G. F., Ades, P. A., Kligfield, P., Arena, R., Balady, G. J., Bittner, V. A., Coke, L. A., Fleg, J. L., Forman, D. E., Gerber, T. C., Gulati, M., Madan, K., Rhodes, J., Thompson, P. D. and Williams, M. A. (2013). Exercise standards for testing and training: A scientific statement from the American Heart Association. *Circulation*, 128, 873–934.

Galassetti, P. and Riddell, M. C. (2013). Exercise and type 1 diabetes (T1DM). *Comprehensive Physiology*, 3, 1309–1336.

Gomez, A. M., Gomez, C., Aschner, P., Veloza, A., Muñoz, O., Rubio, C. and Vallejo, S. (2015). Effects of performing morning versus afternoon exercise on glycemic control and hypoglycemia frequency in type 1 diabetes patients on sensor-augmented insulin pump therapy. *Journal of Diabetes Science and Technology*, 9, 619–624.

Moser, O., Eckstein, M. L., Mccarthy, O., Deere, R., Bain, S. C., Haahr, H. L., Zijlstra, E. and Bracken, R. M. (2017). Poor glycaemic control is associated with reduced exercise performance and oxygen economy during cardio-pulmonary exercise testing in people with type 1 diabetes. *Diabetology and Metabolic Syndrome*, 9, 93.

Moser, O., Eckstein, M. L., Mccarthy, O., Deere, R., Bain, S. C., Haahr, H. L., Zijlstra, E., Heise, T. and Bracken, R. M. (2018a). Heart rate dynamics during cardio-pulmonary exercise testing are associated with glycemic control in individuals with type 1 diabetes. *PLoS One*, 13, e0194750.

Moser, O., Tschakert, G., Mueller, A., Groeschl, W., Eckstein, M. L., Koehler, G., Bracken, R. M., Pieber, T. R. and Hofmann, P. (2018b). Different heart rate patterns during cardio-pulmonary exercise (CPX) testing in individuals with type 1 diabetes. *Frontiers in Endocrinology*, 9, 585.

Riddell, M. C., Gallen, I. W., Smart, C. E., Taplin, C. E., Adolfsson, P., Lumb, A. N., Kowalski, A., Rabasa-Lhoret, R., McCrimmon, R. J., Hume, C., Annan, F., Fournier, P. A., Graham, C., Bode, B., Galassetti, P., Jones, T. W., Millán, I. S., Heise, T., Peters, A. L., Petz, A. and Laffel, L. M. (2017). Exercise management in type 1 diabetes: A consensus statement. *The Lancet Diabetes Endocrinology*, 5, 377–390.

Roy-Fleming, A., Taleb, N., Messier, V., Suppère, C., Cameli, C., Elbekri, S., Smaoui, M. R., Ladouceur, M., Legault, L. and Rabasa-Lhoret, R. (2019). Timing of insulin basal rate reduction to reduce hypoglycemia during late post-prandial exercise in adults with type 1 diabetes using insulin pump therapy: A randomized crossover trial. *Diabetes and Metabolism*, 45, 294–300.

Scott, S. N., Cocks, M., Andrews, R. C., Narendran, P., Purewal, T. S., Cuthbertson, D. J., Wagenmakers, A. J. M. and Shepherd, S. O. (2019a). Fasted high-intensity interval and moderate-intensity exercise do not lead to detrimental 24-hour blood glucose profiles. *The Journal of Clinical Endocrinology and Metabolism*, 104, 111–117.

Scott, S. N., Anderson, L., Morton, J. P., Wagenmakers, A. J. M. and Riddell, M. C. (2019b). Carbohydrate restriction in type 1 diabetes: A realistic therapy for improved glycaemic control and athletic performance? *Nutrients*, May 7;11(5), 1022.

Stokes, K. A., Gilbert, K. L., Hall, G. M., Andrews, R. C. and Thompson, D. (2013). Different responses of selected hormones to three types of exercise in young men. *European Journal of Applied Physiology*, 113, 775–783.

5.4 Exercise testing in chronic kidney disease

Pelagia Koufaki, Sharlene Greenwood and
Jamie H. Macdonald

Introduction

Chronic kidney disease (CKD) is a term that represents disorders affecting the kidney structure and function for >3 months. One classifies the severity of CKD using different thresholds of decreased glomerular filtration rate (GFR) (Levin and Stevens, 2014; Table 5.4.1).

A transition into CKD-5 coincides with a progressive derangement and dysfunction of multiple body systems with manifestation of disorders affecting physical, cognitive and psychosocial well-being. The partial or complete loss of kidney function necessitates some form of renal replacement therapy (RRT) to maintain life. Haemodialysis (HD) and peritoneal dialysis (PD) are the principal dialysis techniques used to remove excess fluid and waste products from the body, but kidney transplantation (KTx) is the preferred treatment (Koufaki and Mercer, 2007).

Chronic kidney disease is becoming a global health problem and a significant independent risk factor for increased mortality, morbidity and disability from noncommunicable diseases. A global estimated prevalence of CKD sits at 9.1%, with the largest proportion of people being in CKD stages 2–4 (GBD Chronic Kidney Disease Collaboration, 2020). In the UK, about 7% of the adult population presents with CKD-3–5 (Health Survey for England, 2017).

A framework for physical function assessment in CKD

According to the World Health Organization, physical health can be characterised and assessed by *symptoms experienced*, such as pain, fatigue, breathlessness, stiffness

Table 5.4.1 Classification of CKD stage based on severity of kidney function impairment

CKD Stage	GFR (ml/min/1.73m2)	Kidney Function
CKD-1	>90	Normal or high
CKD-2	60–89	Mildly decreased
CKD-3a	45–59	Mildly to moderately decreased
CKD-3b	30–44	Moderately to severely decreased
CKD-4	15–29	Severely decreased
CKD-5	<15	Kidney failure

DOI: 10.4324/9781003045267-37

and *physical function indicators*, such as participation in physical activities (PA) and one's perceived ability and/or 'objectively' measured capacity to conduct a variety of physical tasks ranging from self-care (activities of daily living [ADL]) to more challenging activities that require increasing degrees of mobility, balance, strength or endurance. In the interests of standardising research and practice relating to physical function, one should adopt the International Classification and terminology employed by the Framework of Functioning, Disability and Health (ICF; Koufaki and Mercer, 2009).

This approach advocates that physical function assessments should be 'grouped' according to their ability to describe:

a   *Physiological impairment* at the level of *Body Structures* and *Functions* (often achieved in relation to physical function via exercise tolerance testing)
b   *Function limitations* of the individual, at the level of *Activities* and primarily described via objective physical performance tests (PPT)
c   *Disability* (*Participation*) experiences of the individual within their social-cultural and environmental context largely via self-reported functional status assessments)

The consensus amongst researchers in the field of renal rehabilitation and health professionals involved in the clinical management of people with CKD is that physical dysfunction and inactivity are severe and prevalent in all ages and CKD stages, compared to normative data (Painter and Marcus, 2013). Deterioration of physical function starts early in the disease process and may result in the rapid onset of severe frailty and disability. There has been a growing interest in incorporating appropriate measures of physical function in clinical practice and a number of reviews have summarised the evidence reflecting the value of these in predicting event-free survival, better mental health and less frequent hospitalisations for patients with better physical function (Kallenberg et al., 2016; Jassal et al., 2016; MacKinnon et al., 2018; Johansen et al., 2019; Yang et al., 2020).

The specific domain and protocol for physical function assessment will mainly depend on the primary purpose of the assessment (diagnostic, exercise training prescription, risk stratification). All assessment tools should satisfy standards of clinimetric utility (validity, reliability, responsiveness) and patient safety (Supplementary Table 5.4.1 and Table 5.4.2)

Physiological impairment

Peak exercise capacity

The most commonly reported measures of integrated cardiorespiratory exercise capacity are $\dot{V}O_2$ peak, peak power output and time to exhaustion, obtained from a graded exercise tolerance test using either a treadmill or a cycle ergometer protocol (Koufaki and Mercer, 2007). Peak exercise capacity measures provide valuable information on the upper limits of integrated cardiorespiratory physiology. However, that information may not necessarily reflect the ability of patients

Table 5.4.2 Recommended 'menu' of physical function assessment tools based on current available research and practice-based evidence on safety, feasibility, validity, research and clinical utility characteristics for use in people in all stages of CKD. If good practice is followed, the available literature and experience suggests that assessment of the patient with CKD is both safe, feasible and informative. An online full version of this table with references can be found in supplementary materials and accessed via: www.routledge.com/9780367489847

Physical Function Domain	Measurement Outcomes (what to report)	End Points (when to terminate physical function testing)	SEM, MDC90–95, CV% (considered true change if exceeding these limits)	Clinical Anchors for Risk Stratification and Interpretation (associated with worse outcome)	Comments
		Physiological Impairment			
Incremental cycle protocols / Incremental treadmill protocols	• Time at peak (min) • Peak power output (watts) • $\dot{V}O_2$ peak (ml/min/kg) • RPP at exhaustion [SBP (mmHg) x HR (bpm)]/1000	• $\dot{V}O_2$ plateau – no further increases with increasing work rate • RER>1.2	$\dot{V}O_2$ peak SEM: 1 MDC: 2.8 CV: 5% $\dot{V}O_2$ at VT/LT SEM: 0.9 CV%: 6.7	$\dot{V}O_2$ peak <17.5ml/min/kg $\dot{V}O_2$ at VT <40% of $\dot{V}O_2$ peak or <11 ml/min/kg	• Same indices could be reported at a defined submaximal level of exercise such as at the VT or LT.
Incremental shuttle walk test	• Distance (m) and speed (m.sec^{-1}) • BP/HR • Angina scales • RPE scales • $\dot{V}O_2$ at VT or at LT	• No increases in BP with increasing workload • BP> 220/110 mmHg • Symptoms such as dizziness, angina, lack of responsiveness to oral and/or visual signs • Patient's request • Equipment failure			• Familiarisation sessions should be provided. • Proper and adequate warm-up and cool-down should be provided.
Absolute dynamic muscle strength	Max weight lifted in a continuous fashion; once, (1-RM), three times (3-RM) or 5 times (5-RM)	• Patient's request • Inability to continue	SEM: 2.3 MDC: 6.4		• Familiarisation sessions may be required. • Whole-body and muscle-group-specific warm-up sessions are required.

(*Continued*)

Table 5.4.2 (Continued)

Physical Function Domain	Measurement Outcomes (what to report)	End Points (when to terminate physical function testing)	SEM, MDC90–95, CV% (considered true change if exceeding these limits)	Clinical Anchors for Risk Stratification and Interpretation (associated with worse outcome)	Comments
Relative dynamic muscle strength	Max number of repetitions performed at % of RM				• Cut-off points for frailty phenotype. • Cut-off points for sarcopenia.
Hand-grip strength	$kg.m.s^{-1}$ or max kg achieved		SEM: 1.5 MDC: 3.4	Men < 30 kg Women <20 kg	• 2–3 consecutive measurements of hand-grip should be attempted and results should be averaged.
Function Limitations					
Incremental shuttle walk	• Distance (m) • BP/HR • Angina scales • RPE scales	• Patient's request • Inability to continue due to adverse symptom development	SEM: 7–47 MDC: 20–110	<50m	• Familiarisation sessions should be provided. • Quick and inexpensive. • Minimum interference and inconvenience for patient. • Normative data available. • Gait speed stands out as the best single screening outcome for physical frailty.
Six-minute walk test Gait speed over 3, 4 or 7 metres Three-minute timed up-and-go mobility Sit-to-stand transfers	Distance (m) Gait speed $(m.s^{-1})$ Total time in sec Time (sec) it takes to complete 5 (STS-5) or 10 (STS-10) complete transfers OR STS-60 (total number of complete STS transfers achieved in 60 sec)		6MWT SEM: 28 MDC: 66.3–77 SEM: 0.8–2.2 MDC: 2–5.2 STS-5 CV%: 15.1 SEM: 2.7 MDC: 7.5 STS-60 CV%: 12.8 SEM: 1.3–3.5 MDC: 4–8.3	<350–400 metres walked <0.6 m/sec >10–12 sec STS5 >13.7	

Disability (Activities of Daily Living [ADL])

Measure	Score	Threshold	Notes
Physical Component Score (PCS) from Short-Form 36 Health Survey (SF36-SF) or from Kidney Disease Quality of Life (KDQOL)	Physical Component Score (0–100)	PCS<25 10 point decrease/ increase in PCS	• Composite score made up of a range of perceived physical abilities for ADL and symptoms. • KDQOL also reports on a range of symptoms and burden specific to kidney disease. • Normative data available. • Widely used in the CKD population.
DASI index	Total score from 0–58.2	SEM: 3–3.95 MDC: 8.5–9.2	• All widely used in various chronic conditions and limited DASI, KATZ data exist in CKD. • All subject to ceiling effects by higher-functioning patients. • Extremely limited data exist on test-retest reproducibility.
KATZ index	Total score from 0–6	<19.2 4: moderate impairment 2: severe impairment	

BP: Blood Pressure; HR: Heart Rate; RPE: Ratings of Perceived Exertion; RM: Repetition Maximum; DASI: Duke Activity Status Index; SEM: Standard Error of Measurement defined as test-retest variability in measurement score with 68% confidence intervals; MDC: Minimal Detectable Change defined as SEM with 90–95% confidence intervals; CV%: MDC converted to % variation score; VT: Ventilatory Threshold; LT: Lactate Threshold; RER: Respiratory Exchange Ratio; RPP: Rate Pressure Product.

to perform ADL. Functional independence is also associated with the ability to sustain tasks without experiencing fatigue and this may be more easily derived from submaximal exercise tests. Measurement and/or estimation of $\dot{V}O_2$ at a metabolic threshold using pulmonary (whole body) gas exchange data during the execution of an incremental test is feasible, exhibits good reproducibility and is strongly associated with better survival (Ting et al., 2014).

The incremental shuttle walk test (ISWT; Singh et al., 1994) is a feasible alternative, and information can establish upper and submaximal limits of exercise tolerance. If combined with integrated cardiopulmonary testing using gas exchange systems, it serves the same purpose as cycle or treadmill protocols. The ISWT has also be used to estimate $\dot{V}O_2$peak, with an adjusted equation recommended (Xenophontos et al., 2019).

Neuromuscular function

Although muscle mass and function are related, they can also vary independently. Muscle function can change in the absence of significant changes in muscle mass and/or changes are not always linear, as we observe from exercise intervention studies. Although measures of muscle mass are necessary to classify sarcopenia, muscle function outcomes such as strength are needed to determine the risk of physical frailty and functional disability (Carerro et al., 2016). In the last decade, a significant volume of evidence has emerged on the predictive value of handgrip strength (Leal et al., 2011) for mortality (Isoyama et al., 2014) and hospitalisation outcomes (Chan et al., 2019), with handgrip strength showing superior predictive value over indices of muscle mass, sarcopenia and sarcopenic obesity (Table 5.4.2).

Function limitations

Physical performance tests that imitate and reflect ADL are recommended for assessing this domain. Batteries of physical performance tests such as the Short Physical Performance Battery (SPPB) have been reported (Yang et al., 2020). The SPPB is composed of performance components of standing balance, chair rise (STS-5) and gait speed that are aggregated to produce a scoring range from 0 (worst) to 12 (best); however, changes in the total score are largely determined by alterations in gait speed and/or STS performance (Chen et al., 2010). Because a single test is usually simpler to conduct and more time-efficient, and it carries superior prognostic value (Yang et al., 2020), we propose the following tests and outcomes.

Walking ability tests and gait speed

Maintaining walking ability is important for active living and life participation, considering that walking is the most accessible form of mobility. Gait speed stands out as the most consistent and discriminatory outcome for health-related outcomes (Johansen et al., 2019). Gait speed <0.6 m/sec and inability to complete a walk of 4.57 m was associated with an increased risk of death, and difficulties with

ADL were more prevalent in the subgroup with gait speed <0.6 m/sec (Kutner et al., 2015). Each 0.1 m/sec decrement in gait speed was associated with a 17% increased risk of death in the same HD patients (Kutner et al., 2015) and with 26% increased risk in CKD-2–4 over a period of 2 to 3 years (Roshanravan et al., 2013).

Distance walked over 6 minutes (6MWT) of <350 m has been associated with a 3 times higher risk of death over 3 years in pre-dialysis patients (Roshanravan et al., 2013). Torino et al., (2014) reported that a 20 m increase in distance covered during a 6MWT was associated with a reduced risk of 11% for all-cause death and 4% for all-cause hospitalisations in HD. Similarly, a 1 sec slower timed up-and-go performance (TUAG) was associated with 8% increased risk of death (Roshanravan et al., 2013), and absolute scores of >10 s, or inability to complete the test, was associated with a 7-fold increased likelihood of ADL disability in elderly CKD-5 patients (Cook and Jassal, 2008).

Lower limb muscle strength and function

Sit-to-stand performance tests (STS) are commonly used in practice and research settings and several variations of the test exist (Table 5.4.2 and Koufaki and Mercer, 2007). Lower STS30 was associated with a 35% reduced risk of major adverse cardiovascular events and 16% reduced risk of all-cause hospitalisation over a period of 29 months in CKD-2–5 patients (Tsai et al., 2017).

Disability

Disability is defined as one's inability to perform normal ADL within a given socio-cultural context (Koufaki and Mercer, 2009). Practitioners frequently use questionnaires to obtain information about the extent of ADL disability. Although questionnaires have the advantage of ease of administration, low cost and minimal resource utilisation, it is worth noting that self-rated physical function might overestimate the extent of physical dysfunction in comparison to objectively measured physical performance, which may result in higher prevalence estimations of frailty and functional disability (Painter and Roshanravan, 2013).

Lower and declining e-GFR is associated with higher odds of presenting with and developing ADL disabilities (Kurella et al., 2004). Practice-based evidence from the Dialysis Outcomes and Practice Patterns Study (DOPPS) shows that about 79% of the assessed population present with significant difficulties with routine daily tasks, as opposed to about 30% prevalence of functional dependencies in the general population of similar age. In the UK, 48% of the HD population report severe functional dependencies (Jassal et al., 2016). For the most commonly used questionnaires capturing physical function and ADL in CKD, refer to Table 5.4.2.

Summary

A case already exists for the regular assessment and promotion of physically active life styles to enhance clinical management of the CKD patient and alleviate

248   *Koufaki, Greenwood, Macdonald*

disability symptoms (Guideline Development Group, 2015). Accurate and regular assessment of physical function is key for supporting the clinical implementation of care management guidance. Routine monitoring of physical function can help to characterise prognosis and/or adverse clinical risks, while monitoring progress towards optimised levels of well-being for a given individual. Sharing this information with those concerned will help motivate patients to become more actively engaged with PA in an attempt to maintain or further enhance physical function (Koufaki et al., 2015).

References

Carrero, J. J., Johansen, K. L., Lindholm, B., et al. (2016). Screening for muscle wasting and dysfunction in patients with chronic kidney disease. *Kidney International*, 90(1), 53–66.

Chan, W., Chin, S. H., Whittaker, A. C., et al. (2019). The associations of muscle strength, muscle mass, and adiposity with clinical outcomes and quality of life in prevalent kidney transplant recipients. *Journal of Renal Nutrition*, 29(6), 536–547.

Chen, J. L. T., Godfrey, S., Ng, T. T., et al. (2010). Effect of intra-dialytic, low-intensity strength training on functional capacity in adult haemodialysis patients: A randomized pilot trial. *Nephrology, Dialysis, Transplantation*, 25(6), 1936–1943.

Cook, C. W. L. and Jassal, S. V. (2008). Functional dependencies among the elderly on hemodialysis. *Kidney International*, 73, 1289–1295.

Guideline Development Group. (2015). Clinical practice guideline on management of patients with diabetes and chronic kidney disease stage 3b or higher (eGFR <45 mL/min). *Nephrology, Dialysis, Transplantation*, 30(Suppl. 2), ii1–ii142. doi: 10.1093/ndt/gfv100

GBD Chronic Kidney Disease Collaboration. (2020). Global, regional, and national burden of chronic kidney disease, 1990–2017: A systematic analysis for the global burden of disease study 2017. (2020). *Lancet*, 395 North American Edition (10225), 709–733. doi: 10.1016/S0140-6736(20)30045-3

Isoyama, N., Qureshi, A. R., Avesani, C. M., et al. (2014). Comparative associations of muscle mass and muscle strength with mortality in dialysis patients. *Clinical Journal of the American Society of Nephrology: CJASN*, 9(10), 1720–1728.

Jassal, S. V., Karaboyas, A., Comment, L. A., et al. (2016). Functional dependence and mortality in the international Dialysis Outcomes and Practice Patterns Study (DOPPS). *American Journal of Kidney Diseases*, 67(2), 283–292.

Johansen, K. L., Delgado, C., Kaysen, G. A., et al. (2019). Frailty among patients receiving hemodialysis: Evolution of components and associations with mortality. *Journals of Gerontology Series A: Biological Sciences & Medical Sciences*, 74(3), 380–386.

Kallenberg, M. H., Kleinveld, H. A., Dekker, F. W., et al. (2016). Functional and cognitive impairment, frailty, and adverse health outcomes in older patients reaching ESRD: A systematic review. *Clinical Journal of the American Society of Nephrology*, 11(9), 1624–1639.

Koufaki, P. and Mercer, T. (2007). Exercise assessment for people with end stage renal disease. In E. Winter, A. Jones, R. C. Davison, P. D. Bromley and T. H. Mercer (eds.), *BASES Sport and Exercise Physiology Testing Guidelines Exercise and Clinical Testing*, p. 28. Oxon: Routledge.

Koufaki, P. and Mercer, T. (2009). Assessment and monitoring of physical function for people with CKD. *Advances in Chronic Kidney Disease*, 16(6), 410–419.

Koufaki, P., Greenwood, S., Painter, P., et al. (2015). The BASES expert statement on exercise therapy for people with chronic kidney disease. *Journal of Sports Sciences*, 33(18), 1902.

Kurella, M., Ireland, C., Hlatky, M. A., et al. (2004). Physical and sexual function in women with chronic kidney disease. *American Journal of Kidney*, 43(5), 868–876.

Kutner, N. G., Zhang, R., Huang, Y., et al. (2015). Gait speed and mortality, hospitalization, and functional status change among hemodialysis patients: A US renal data system special study. *American Journal of Kidney Diseases*, 66(2), 297–304.

Leal, V. O., Mafra, D., Fouque, D., et al. (2011). Use of handgrip strength in the assessment of the muscle function of chronic kidney disease patients on dialysis: A systematic review. *Nephrology, Dialysis, Transplantation*, 26(4), 1354–1360.

Levin, A. and Stevens, P. E. (2014). Summary of KDIGO 2012 CKD guideline: Behind the scenes, need for guidance, and a framework for moving forward. *Kidney International*, 85(1), 49–61.

MacKinnon, H. J., Wilkinson, T. J., Clarke, A. L., et al. (2018). The association of physical function and physical activity with all-cause mortality and adverse clinical outcomes in non-dialysis chronic kidney disease: A systematic review. *Therapeutic Advances in Chronic Disease*, 9(11), 209–226.

Painter, P. and Marcus, R. L. (2013). Assessing physical function and physical activity in patients with CKD. *Clinical Journal of the American Society of Nephrology*, 8(5), 861–872.

Painter, P. and Roshanravan, B. (2013). The association of physical activity and physical function with clinical outcomes in adults with chronic kidney disease. *Current Opinion in Nephrology and Hypertension*, 22(6), 615–623.

Roshanravan, B., Robinson-Cohen, C., Patel, K. V., et al. (2013). Association between physical performance and all-cause mortality in CKD. *Journal of the American Society of Nephrology (JASN)*, 24(5), 822–830.

Singh, S. J., Morgan, M. D., Hardman, A. E., et al. (1994). Comparison of oxygen uptake during a conventional treadmill test and the shuttle walking test in chronic airflow limitation. *The European Respiratory Journal*, 7(11), 2016–2020.

Ting, S. M. S., Iqbal, H., Kanji, H., et al. (2014). Functional cardiovascular reserve predicts survival pre-kidney and post-kidney transplantation. *Journal of the American Society of Nephrology (JASN)*, 25(1), 187–195.

Torino, C., Manfredini, F., Bolignano, D., et al. (2014). Physical performance and clinical outcomes in dialysis patients: A secondary analysis of the EXCITE trial. *Kidney & Blood Pressure Research*, 39(2–3), 205–211.

Tsai, Y., Chen, H., Hsiao, S., et al. (2017). Association of physical activity with cardiovascular and renal outcomes and quality of life in chronic kidney disease. *PloS One*, 12(8).

Xenophontos, S., Wilkinson, T. J., Gould, D. W., et al. (2019). Peak aerobic capacity from incremental shuttle walk test in chronic kidney disease. *Journal of Renal Care*, 45(3), 185–192.

Yang, D., Robinson, R., Selinski, C., et al. (2020). Physical function in kidney transplantation: Current knowledge and future directions. *Current Transplantation Reports*, 7, 46.

5.5 Exercise testing in chronic lung disease

Oliver J. Price, Karl Sylvester, Joanna Shakespeare and Mark A. Faghy

Cardiopulmonary exercise testing (CPET) is utilised in the assessment of lung disease patients to (i) identify the cause of exercise limitation and quantify the degree of impairment, (ii) determine prognosis and/or monitor recovery, (iii) inform and evaluate the efficacy of treatment interventions and (iv) assess pre-operative risk (Palange et al., 2018). This chapter provides an overview of recent advances in CPET measurement and interpretation in the context of chronic lung disease.

Obstructive vs. restrictive disorders

Lung disease affects one in five people and is a leading cause of morbidity and mortality in the UK (*Taskforce for Lung Health*, 2018). Broadly, lung diseases can be classified into obstructive (e.g., asthma and chronic obstructive pulmonary disease [COPD]) or restrictive disorders (e.g., interstitial lung disease [ILD]). In reality, however, patients often present with comorbidities such as asthma/COPD overlap syndrome (ACOS) and/or cardiovascular disease. Specifically, obstructive lung disease is typically characterised by a reduction in forced expiratory volume in one second (FEV_1) to forced vital capacity (FVC) ratio (FEV_1/FVC) but with normal relaxed vital capacity (VC). In severe obstructive lung diseases, increases in measured residual volume (RV) are evident, as a consequence of early airway closure and gas trapping and an increase in functional residual capacity (FRC) due to dynamic hyperinflation. In contrast, restrictive lung disease is characterised by a reduction in lung volume, either due to a reduction in the ability of the lungs to expand (e.g., ILD) or the inability to generate the force required to allow sufficient lung expansion (e.g., respiratory muscle weakness) (see Maynard et al. [2020], West and Luks [2015] and Association for Respiratory Technology and Physiology [ARTP] [2020a] for a detailed overview of respiratory physiology and lung function assessment).

It is often necessary to stress the respiratory system to detect any underlying pathology that may not be evident using static measurements. Thus, CPET is a useful addition to identify factors associated with limited exercise capacity and to quantify the extent of impairment when co-existing respiratory and cardiac disease is suspected.

DOI: 10.4324/9781003045267-38

CPET modality and equipment set-up

CPET can be conducted on a treadmill or static cycle ergometer. Treadmill walking is specific to the demands of daily living and thus patients are typically more familiar with this activity. It is recognised that breathlessness or 'dyspnoea' is the most common limiting factor during treadmill-based CPET, whereas leg discomfort (particularly for unaccustomed or deconditioned individuals) is greater when cycling (O'Donnell et al., 2016). Despite this, cycling is often considered preferable since workload can be quantified and controlled more effectively and is more convenient for in-test measurements such as blood sampling or electrocardiogram (ECG) which is susceptible to motion artefact.

Risk assessment, quality control and pre-test procedures

To optimise health and safety and mitigate against the risk of a severe adverse event (estimated to occur in approximately 2–5 per 100,000 tests), several absolute and relative contraindications should be considered before assessment (Table 5.5.1). To ensure valid and reliable pre- and in-test measurements (see Chapter 4.6, Respiratory Gas Analysis), it is recommended that flow sensors are calibrated using a standard-volume 3 L syringe between at least three flow ranges (i.e., 2 $L \cdot s^{-1}$, 4–6 $L \cdot s^{-1}$, 8 $L \cdot s^{-1}$) (Porszasz et al., 2018). Pre-test instructions, test phases and in-test measurements are detailed in Table 5.5.2.

Infection control

It is important to minimise direct contact between lung disease patients in both clinical practice and research trials to reduce the potential for cross-infection. Technical staff should practice good hand hygiene at all times and sufficient time should be allocated to disinfect equipment (i.e., respiratory tubing, facemasks, handgrips etc.), decontaminate surfaces and allow room aeration between tests. For a detailed overview, see the recent ARTP infection control guideline statement (ARTP, 2020b).

Test protocol and in-test measurements

The most recent systematic appraisal of evidence concerning the standardisation of CPET in chronic lung disease suggests that the optimal protocol consists of a resting phase lasting at least 3 minutes, followed by a 3-minute (2-minute for severely impaired patients) unloaded phase, an 8–12-minute incremental phase with work rate increased linearly every minute, followed by a recovery phase of at least 2–3 minutes (i.e., total testing time is approximately 20 minutes in duration) (Radtke et al., 2019).

Resting phase

The resting phase provides an opportunity to obtain baseline measurements of heart rate (HR), blood pressure (BP), oxygen saturation (SpO_2), ECG, minute

Table 5.5.1 Absolute and relative contraindications

Absolute Contraindications

Cardiovascular Conditions (Uncontrolled):

- Acute myocardial infarction
- Coronary stenosis
- Unstable angina
- Moderate to severe stenotic valvular heart disease
- Symptomatic uncontrolled arrhythmias (including atrial fibrillation with uncontrolled ventricular rate)
- Severe untreated arterial hypertension
- Syncope tachyarrhythmias or bradyarrhythmias
- Active endocarditis
- High-degree atrioventricular block
- Acute myocarditis or pericarditis
- Hypertrophic cardiomyopathy
- Uncontrolled heart failure
- Suspected dissecting aneurysm
- Deep venous thrombosis of lower limbs

Respiratory Conditions (Uncontrolled):

- Pulmonary embolism
- Pulmonary oedema
- Severe pulmonary arterial hypertension
- Uncontrolled asthma

Non-Cardiorespiratory Conditions (Uncontrolled – Affected by Exercise):

- Infection
- Renal failure
- Thyrotoxicosis
- Acute bleeding
- Electrolyte abnormalities
- Advanced or complicated pregnancy

Relative Contraindications

- Resting oxygen saturation (SpO_2) <85%
- Orthopaedic impairment that compromises exercise performance (e.g., musculoskeletal injury etc.)
- Psychiatric disorders (i.e., mental or cognitive impairment impacting ability to co-operate)
- >2 mm ST depression if symptomatic or 4 mm if asymptomatic or >1 mm ST elevation
- Significant arrhythmias causing symptoms or haemodynamic compromise
- Fall in systolic blood pressure >20 mmHg from the highest value during the test
- Hypertension >230 mmHg systolic (200 mmHg in the presence of a AAA); >120 mmHg diastolic

Definitions of abbreviations: SpO_2 oxygen saturation; AAA, aortic abdominal aneurysm.

Table 5.5.2 Pre-test instructions, test phases and in-test measurements

Pre-Test Instructions

- Advise to avoid eating for at least two hours before testing.
- Advise to avoid strenuous exercise for at least 24 hours before testing.
- Advise to avoid caffeine on the day of the test.
- Advise to avoid smoking for at least eight hours before testing.
- Advise to wear comfortable clothing and appropriate shoes suitable for exercise.
- Provide patients with a layman's overview of the test (i.e., discuss incremental workload and in-test measurements. Highlight that shortness of breath +/– degree of leg discomfort is an expected response with the increasing workload but will resolve rapidly on exercise cessation).
- Advise patients to work near to maximal capacity or volitional exhaustion.
- Unless screening for suspected EIB,patients prescribed bronchodilators should administer his or her inhaler therapy at least 10 minutes before testing.

Pre-Test Measurements

- Calibrate flow sensor and the gas analysers of the metabolic cart before the test.
- Obtain verbal or written consent (clinical practice and research trials, respectively).
- Conduct physical examination and record resting vital signs (i.e., HR, ECG, SpO_2, BP, body temperature).
- Measure blood glucose in patients with diabetes mellitus to mitigate against the risk of hypoglycaemia. Severe hypoglycaemia (blood glucose <2.8 $mmol.L^{-1}$ or 50 $mg.dL^{-1}$) or hyperglycaemic event requiring assistance in the past 24 hours is a contraindication for exercise testing.
- Baseline pulmonary function assessment via spirometry (forced flow-volume loop).
- Resting arterial or capillary blood gas measurements can be obtained if pulmonary gas exchange abnormalities are to be expected and non-invasive estimation of oxygenation is considered inadequate.

Test Phases

- Resting phase: 3 minutes
- Unloaded phase: 3 minutes (2 minutes in severely impaired patients)
- Incremental exercise phase: 1 minutes (ramp vs. minute-by-minute incremental protocol)
- Recovery phase: 2–3 minutes (unloaded pedalling)

In-Test Measurements

- Breath-by-breath respiratory gas exchange (continuous recording)
- HR, ECG, SpO_2 (continuous recording)
- BP (2-min intervals)
- RPE – 0–10 modified Borg scale – dyspnoea and leg discomfort (2-min intervals)
- IC manoeuvres (2-min intervals)
- Arterial or capillary blood gases (close to test termination or immediately post exercise)

Definitions of abbreviations: EIB, exercise-induced bronchoconstriction; HR, heart rate; ECG, electrocardiogram, SpO_2, oxygen saturation; BP, blood pressure; RPE, rating of perceived exertion; IC, inspiratory capacity.

ventilation ($\dot{V}_E$), gas exchange variables, arterial blood gas sampling (selected cases) and inspiratory capacity (IC) manoeuvres to evaluate operational lung volumes (particularly relevant in obstructive lung disease).

Unloaded phase

The unloaded phase should be completed against a workload of 0–10 W during cycling or the lowest speed on a treadmill (e.g., 1.0–1.6 km.h^{-1}). This phase allows the patient to warm up and to become familiar with the equipment and permits the assessment of baseline $\dot{V}O_2$.

Incremental exercise phase

Ramp and minute-by-minute workload increments are acceptable methods and provide comparable results when the total duration of the exercise test is the same. It is important to note that workload increments should be individually calculated according to patient characteristics (i.e., paediatric vs. adult populations) and disease sub-types and severity (Radtke et al., 2019). In-test measurements include continuous breath-by-breath respiratory gas exchange, HR, ECG, SpO_2 and BP, RPE (dyspnoea and leg discomfort) and IC manoeuvres at 2-minute intervals (Table 5.5.2). For a detailed overview of acceptable treadmill and cycling-based protocols, predicted workload equations, reference values and technical considerations, see Palange et al. (2018). It is important to routinely check that the patient is feeling well and prepared to continue the test and offer verbal encouragement as required. For repeat assessments, it is recommended that methods are replicated to permit direct comparisons between tests.

Recovery phase

The recovery phase should consist of unloaded pedalling at a reduced cadence (approximately 30 revolutions per minute) or very slow walking for cycling and treadmill-based CPET, respectively. This phase is important for safety reasons but also permits evaluation of recovery times following pulmonary rehabilitation and exercise training programmes (Puente-Maestu et al., 2016).

Test interpretation

Interpretation begins by evaluating $\dot{V}O_2max$ and the anaerobic threshold. In lung disease, it is unlikely that a true $\dot{V}O_2max$ will be achieved, and thus the 'peak' $\dot{V}O_2$ is often reported with a value <85% or below the lower limit of normal (LLN) suggesting exercise limitation. Exercise efficiency is expressed as the slope of the relationship between $\dot{V}O_2$ and work rate and is linear (10.3 ml·min^{-1}·W^{-1}) in healthy individuals. A decreased slope (<8.3 ml·min^{-1}·W^{-1}) indicates inadequate oxygen delivery to the exercising skeletal muscle or reduced oxygen uptake by the mitochondria, such as in a metabolic myopathy. In lung disease, the anaerobic threshold can fall to <40% predicted $\dot{V}O_2$ with values of 40–50% typically seen in deconditioned individuals. As expected, lung disease typically results in ventilatory rather than cardiovascular limitation at peak exercise and thus parameters such as the ventilatory equivalents for carbon dioxide ($\dot{V}E / \dot{V}CO_2$) and oxygen ($\dot{V}E / \dot{V}CO_2$) and end-tidal carbon dioxide levels ($P_{ET}CO_2$) can be evaluated to determine gas exchange abnormalities (for a detailed schematic of CPET test interpretation, see Figure 5.5.1).

Typical pattern of response in obstructive lung disease

Exercise intolerance in patients with obstructive lung disease is usually related to an inability to increase $\dot{V}E$ sufficiently and to maintain gas exchange at higher exercise intensities. Inefficient ventilation is a consequence of airflow obstruction and increases dead space (V_D/V_T) and $\dot{V}E / \dot{V}CO_2$. Dynamic hyperinflation often occurs which increases end expiratory lung volume (EELV) and is characterised by a fall in IC with increasing workload.

Typical pattern of response in restrictive lung disease

A reduced ventilatory reserve is common in patients with restrictive lung disease with decreased tidal volumes and increased breathing frequency. Increased ventilatory demand is a consequence of increased dead space ventilation (V_D/V_T), inefficient ventilation ($\dot{V}E / \dot{V}CO_2$) and hypoxia. Significant reductions in SpO_2 are common and are often the cause of exercise cessation.

Reporting

CPET results should consider four key areas: (i) patient information (i.e., name, date of birth, date of the test, patient's characteristics and the reason(s) for test referral), (ii) technical report, which defines the protocol and work rate increments, (iii) response to incremental exercise and the reasons for terminating the test and (iv) summary in which the technical report and cardio-respiratory responses are discussed within the context of the patient. Further information concerning reporting (including templates) are provided by Radtke et al. (2019). It is important to recognise that 'normative' reference values used for interpretation must be relevant to the mode of exercise undertaken (e.g., treadmill vs. cycle ergometer). Several reference equations are currently available; however, all have limitations which have the potential to impact differential diagnosis and prognosis (Waterfall et al., 2020). Accordingly, there remains an urgent need to establish up-to-date reference ranges akin to those recently generated for other lung function parameters by the Global Lung Function Initiative (GLI) (Quanjer et al., 2012).

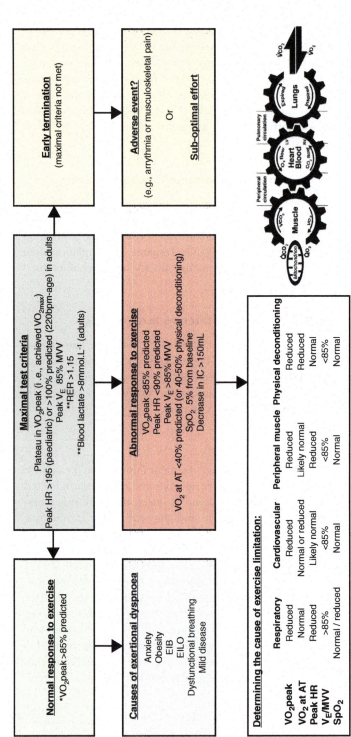

Early termination
(maximal criteria not met)

Adverse event?
(e.g., arrythmia or musculoskeletal pain)

Or

Sub-optimal effort

Maximal test criteria
Plateau in VO_2peak (i.e., achieved VO_{2max})
Peak HR >195 (paediatric) or >100% predicted (220ppm-age) in adults
Peak V_E 85% MVV
**RER >1.15
**Blood lactate >8mmol.L^{-1} (adults)

Abnormal response to exercise
VO_2peak <85% predicted
Peak HR <90% predicted
Peak V_E >85% MVV
VO_2 at AT <40% predicted (or 40-50% physical deconditioning)
SpO_2 5% from baseline
Decrease in IC >150mL

Normal response to exercise
*VO_2peak >85% predicted

Causes of exertional dyspnoea
Anxiety
Obesity
EIB
EILO
Dysfunctional breathing
Mild disease

Determining the cause of exercise limitation:

	Respiratory	Cardiovascular	Peripheral muscle	Physical deconditioning
VO_2peak	Reduced	Reduced	Reduced	Reduced
VO_2 at AT	Normal	Normal or reduced	Likely normal	Reduced
Peak HR	Reduced	Likely normal	Reduced	Normal
V_E/MVV	>85%	<85%	<85%	<85%
SpO_2	Normal / reduced	Normal	Normal	Normal

Figure 5.5.1 Schematic detailing test interpretation.

*dependent on selected CPET reference values; **not to be used in isolation as a maximal test criterion.

Definition of abbreviations: $\dot{V}O_2$peak, peak oxygen uptake; $\dot{V}O_{2max}$, maximal oxygen uptake; HR, heart rate; VE, minute ventilation; RER, respiratory exchange ratio; EIB, exercise-induced bronchoconstriction; EILO, exercise-induced laryngeal obstruction; SpO_2, oxygen saturation; IC, inspiratory capacity; MVV, maximal voluntary ventilation.

References

ARTP. (2020a). *ARTP Statement on Pulmonary Function Testing 2020*. www.artp.org.uk/News/artp-statement-on-pulmonary-function-testing-2020.

ARTP. (2020b). *Covid19 Infection Control Issues for Lung Function*. www.artp.org.uk/News/covid19-infection-control-issues-for-lung-function.

Maynard, R. L., Pearce, S. J., Nemery, B., Wagner, P. D., Cooper, B. G. and Fers, F. (2020). *Cotes' Lung Function*. Hoboken, NJ: Wiley Online Library.

O'Donnell, D. E., Elbehairy, A. F., Faisal, A., Webb, K. A., Neder, J. A. and Mahler, D. A. (2016). Exertional dyspnoea in COPD: The clinical utility of cardiopulmonary exercise testing. *European Respiratory Society*. https://err.ersjournals.com/content/25/141/333?utm_source=TrendMD&utm_medium=cpc&utm_campaign=European_Respiratory_Review_TrendMD_0.

Palange, P., Laveneziana, P., Neder, J. A. and Ward, S. A. (Eds.). (2018). *Clinical Exercise Testing* (Vol. 80). Sheffield, UK: European Respiratory Society. doi: 10.1183/2312508X. erm8018. ISBN: 978-1-84984-096-5

Porszasz, J., Stringer, W. and Casaburi, R. (2018). Equipment, measurements and quality control. *Clinical Exercise Testing (ERS Monograph): Sheffield, European Respiratory Society*, 59–81.

Puente-Maestu, L., Palange, P., Casaburi, R., Laveneziana, P., Maltais, F., Neder, J. A., O'Donnell, D. E., Onorati, P., Porszasz, J. and Rabinovich, R. (2016). Use of exercise testing in the evaluation of interventional efficacy: An official ERS statement. *European Respiratory Journal*, 47(2), 429–460.

Quanjer, P. H., Stanojevic, S., Cole, T. J., Baur, X., Hall, G. L., Culver, B. H., Enright, P. L., Hankinson, J. L., Ip, M. S. M., Zheng, J., Stocks, J. and ERS Global Lung Function Initiative. (2012). Multi-ethnic reference values for spirometry for the 3–95-yr age range: The global lung function 2012 equations. *The European Respiratory Journal*, 40(6), 1324–1343. https://doi.org/10.1183/09031936.00080312

Radtke, T., Vogiatzis, I., Urquhart, D. S., Laveneziana, P., Casaburi, R. and Hebestreit, H. (2019). *Standardisation of Cardiopulmonary Exercise Testing in Chronic Lung Diseases: Summary of Key Findings from the ERS Task Force*. Sheffield, UK: European Respiratory Society.

Taskforce for Lung Health. (2018, November 27). British Lung Foundation. www.blf.org.uk/taskforce/plan.

Waterfall, J. L., Burns, P., Shackell, D., Pepke-Zaba, J., Oates, K. E. and Sylvester, K. P. (2020). The risks of applying normative values in paediatric cardiopulmonary exercise testing: A case report. *ERJ Open Research*, 00333–02020. https://doi.org/10.1183/23120541.00333-2020

West, J. and Luks, A. (2015). *West's Respiratory Physiology*. https://blackwells.co.uk/bookshop/product/Wests-Respiratory-Physiology-by-John-B-West-author-Andrew-Luks-author/9781496310118.

5.6 Exercise testing in breast and prostate cancer

John M. Saxton and Ruth Ashton

Cancer, a growing concern

Cancer is a generic term for a large group of complex diseases, in which cells of the body grow and divide in an uncontrolled way. In more advanced disease, uncontrolled cellular growth invades and destroys neighbouring tissues and metastasises via the blood or lymphatic system to other sites. Data from Cancer Research UK (Cancer Research UK Cancer Incidence Statistics, 2017) and the World Cancer Research Fund (World Cancer Research Fund Cancer Statistics, 2017) show that there are over 350,000 new cases of cancer in the UK every year. Globally, breast cancer is the most commonly occurring cancer in women (World Cancer Research Fund Breast Cancer Statistics, 2018) and prostate cancer is the second most frequently occurring cancer in men, after lung cancer (Rawla, 2019). These cancers are amongst the most commonly researched in the scientific literature, and it is increasingly becoming acknowledged that physical activity (PA) and structured exercise has an important role to play in the care of breast and prostate cancer patients.

The cancer journey

Cancer is most commonly treated with some combination of surgery, radiotherapy and/or chemotherapy initially, though hormone therapies, immunotherapy and stem-cell transplant are other treatments that may be offered. After the primary treatment phase, an increasing number of patients are entering a recovery/rehabilitation phase, with the aim of regaining full or acceptable levels of health and physical function. However, a proportion of these patients will experience recurrent disease or will develop second primary tumours and will enter the treatment cycle again. For patients not eligible for curative treatments, the treatment phase becomes a palliative end-of-life phase.

Cancer survival rates are increasing in the UK due to well-established screening programmes and more effective treatments. Recent data shows that 78% of female breast cancer patients and 84% of prostate cancer patients are now living for at least 10 years after diagnosis (Cancer Research UK Cancer Survival Statistics,

DOI: 10.4324/9781003045267-39

2010–2011). Yet despite these promising figures, cancer and its treatments can have a profound effect on physiological function. Studies have reported a decline in cardiopulmonary fitness (Steins Bisschop et al., 2012) and skeletal muscle function (Christensen et al., 2014) in cancer survivors which is likely to be at least partly attributable to the deconditioning effects of inactivity and cancer-related fatigue (Prinsen et al., 2013). However, physiological changes associated with the disease process, the adverse effects of chemotherapy and hormone therapies on body composition and cardiometabolic risk and the effects of surgery on skeletal muscle function are other important factors contributing to impaired physiological function in cancer survivors.

Testing in people with breast or prostate cancer

Overview

Current guidance recommends the comprehensive assessment of all components of health-related physical fitness in cancer patients, including cardiopulmonary fitness, muscular strength and endurance, body composition and flexibility, while also considering cancer-specific impairments and/or functional limitations (Campbell et al., 2019). Where limited resources preclude sophisticated physiological testing (i.e., maximal cardiopulmonary exercise test [CPET] under medical supervision, availability of isokinetic dynamometry etc.), standardised submaximal functional fitness tests have been used to assess cardiopulmonary fitness (e.g., Balke submaximal exercise test, six-minute walk test [6MWT] etc.) and muscular strength and function (e.g. hand-held dynamometry, repeated biceps curls against a standardised resistance, sit-to-stand test etc.). However, one-repetition maximum strength testing is also considered to be safe for breast and prostate cancer patients who do not exhibit bone metastases (Campbell et al., 2019).

Safety considerations

Exercise is safe for cancer survivors who are in a stable condition. Current guidance has removed the requirement for medical clearance in those at low risk of cardiovascular events, on the basis that it is an unnecessary barrier to participation (Campbell et al., 2019). However, medical clearance is more likely to be needed for patients undergoing primary treatment or longer-term adjuvant therapies and should include a detailed history and physical examination of cardiac, pulmonary, neurological and musculoskeletal signs and symptoms. The PAR-Q+ and ePAR-med-X have been recommended as useful screening tools to determine whether medical clearance (including a symptom-limited CPET with 12-lead ECG) is required (Jones et al., 2010). Excellent articles providing guidance on how to identify and manage a broad range of cancer-specific exercise contraindications have been published and serve as useful reference documents (Campbell et al., 2019; Mina et al., 2018; Stefani, 2017).

Pre-treatment physiological and functional testing

Physiological testing is increasingly being used pre-operatively for risk stratifying patients prior to high-risk intra-abdominal cancer surgery (Thomas et al., 2019). Pre-operative risk stratification, including CPET, assessment of frailty and pre-operative exercise (pre-habilitation), is also gaining credence as a means of improving the short-term safety and long-term effectiveness of urological surgery (Cui et al., 2017). The use of pre-operative risk stratification in the breast cancer care setting has received relatively less attention, although pre-habilitation studies have focussed on restoring impaired shoulder function (Flores and Dwyer, 2014; Yang et al., 2018).

During and after breast cancer treatment

Women with non-metastatic breast cancer usually undergo surgical treatment (mastectomy, reconstructive surgery or breast-conserving surgery) followed by radiotherapy and/or chemotherapy and, depending on tumour type, hormone or targeted therapies. Impaired shoulder mobility and strength sometimes compounded by ipsilateral lymphoedema (arm-swelling), are common on the treated side and may still be present after five years (Sagen et al., 2009). There is also evidence of impaired trunk flexion/extension and reduced abdominal muscle strength after breast reconstruction surgery (Atisha and Alderman, 2009) and so the sit-and-reach test may be a useful assessment tool here (Langhammer and Stanghelle, 2015). A more generalised loss of skeletal muscle function has also been reported after adjuvant treatment (Klassen et al., 2017) and sarcopenia may be present in a proportion of women, irrespective of body weight. An observational study of over 3,000 newly diagnosed breast cancer patients reported a 34% incidence of sarcopenia, with low skeletal muscle quality being present in 37% of the patients (Caan et al., 2018). Reduced cardiopulmonary exercise capacity has also been reported in breast cancer patients, particularly after adjuvant treatment which can be readily examined by conducting a CPET (Peel et al., 2014). In addition, the cardiotoxic effects of chemotherapy and radiotherapy and adverse impact of anti-HER2 targeted therapy on left ventricular cardiac function are well-reported treatment side effects (Lenneman and Sawyer, 2016). Finally, chemotherapy and hormone therapies for breast cancer predispose women to an increased risk of osteopenia and osteoporosis (Fornusek and Kilbreath, 2017). Refer to Table 5.6.1 for an overview of physiological and functional fitness tests which take into consideration common breast cancer-specific impairments and functional limitations.

During and after prostate cancer treatment

Although minimally invasive robot-assisted radical prostatectomy is widely available and is associated with fewer intra-operative and post-operative complications (Trinh et al., 2012), there can still be considerable long-term morbidity (Barry et al., 2012; Capogrosso et al., 2019). Recovery of physical functioning and quality

Table 5.6.1 Recommended health-related fitness dimensions to be assessed in cancer patients (Campbell et al., 2019), with specific reference to breast and prostate cancer-specific physiological impairments and functional limitations

Health-Related Fitness Dimension and Common Assessment Methods	Breast Cancer-Specific Considerations	Prostate Cancer-Specific Considerations
Cardiopulmonary fitness CPET, with 12-lead ECG Submaximal testing, e.g., modified Balke treadmill protocol (Aadland et al., 2017); Bruce Ramp treadmill protocol (Kaminsky and Whaley, 1998); 6MWT (Schmidt et al., 2013)	Screening for patients at moderate to high risk of cardiovascular events (Steins Bisschop et al., 2012) Reduced cardiopulmonary exercise capacity, particularly after adjuvant treatment (Peel et al., 2014) Cardiotoxic effects of chemotherapy/ radiotherapy/anti-HER2 therapy (Lenneman and Sawyer, 2016)	Screening for patients at moderate to high risk of cardiovascular events (Steins Bisschop et al., 2012) Impaired cardiopulmonary exercise capacity (Wall et al., 2014) Impaired physical functioning (Litwin et al., 1999) (Gonzalez et al., 2016)
Muscular strength 1RM strength Isokinetic dynamometry Sit-to-stand (Langhammer and Stanghelle, 2015) Grip strength Biceps curl test (Langhammer and Stanghelle, 2015)	Impaired upper- and lower-limb strength (Klassen et al., 2017) Impaired shoulder and abdominal strength (Sagen et al., 2009; Atisha and Alderman, 2009)	Impaired upper- and lower-limb strength (Gonzalez et al., 2016) Impaired physical functioning (Litwin et al., 1999) (Gonzalez et al., 2016)
Body composition Body mass Waist circumference DXA Skin-fold measures (Jackson and Pollock, 1978) Mid-upper-arm circumference (Jensen et al., 1981)	Excess body fat at diagnosis and weight gain during/ after treatment (Cecchini et al., 2016) Loss of skeletal muscle mass/sarcopenia (Caan et al., 2018) Reduced bone mineral density (Fornusek and Kilbreath, 2017) Lymphoedema (DiSipio et al., 2013)	Reduced upper- and lower-limb skeletal muscle mass (Singh et al., 2017) Reduced upper- and lower-limb skeletal muscle mass (Singh et al., 2017) Reduced bone mineral density (Berruti et al., 2002) Increased body weight, BMI and body fat (Haseen et al., 2010) Reduced skeletal muscle mass (Haseen et al., 2010)
Flexibility Goniometry Sit-and-reach test/ back scratch test (Langhammer and Stanghelle, 2015)	Impaired shoulder flexibility on the involved side (Flores and Dwyer, 2014; Sagen et al., 2009) Impaired trunk flexibility after breast reconstruction	

Table 5.6.1 (Continued)

Health-Related Fitness Dimension and Common Assessment Methods	Breast Cancer-Specific Considerations	Prostate Cancer-Specific Considerations
Other		
Cardiometabolic risk markers	Increased cardiometabolic risk in survivors (Lohmann et al., 2017)	Increased risk of cardiovascular morbidity in (Ashton et al., 2019; Saigal et al., 2007)
Left ventricular cardiac function	Cardiotoxic effects of chemotherapy/radiotherapy/anti-HER2 therapy (Lenneman and Sawyer, 2016)	
Neurological function; static and dynamic balance	CIPN in women treated with taxane-based chemotherapy agents (Stefani, 2017)	
Patient-reported outcomes	Core outcome set for breast cancer-specific side effects (Ong et al., 2017)	Core outcome set for prostate cancer-specific side effects (Morgans et al., 2015; MacLennan et al., 2017)

CPET: cardiopulmonary exercise test; ECG: electrocardiography; 6MWT: six-minute walk test distance; 1RM: one repetition maximum; DXA: dual-energy X-ray absorptiometry.

of life after radical prostatectomy often has a protracted time-course, with only 23–38% of patients recovered to baseline levels of physical, mental and social functioning by three months post surgery, increasing to 71–82% at six months post surgery (Litwin et al., 1999). However, 66–73% of men still report experiencing sexual and urinary functional impairments six months after surgery (Litwin et al., 1999). Recent cross-sectional data suggest that a substantial proportion of men treated with radical prostatectomy (an average of 11.7 months previously) were at increased risk of suffering a cardiovascular-related event within the next 10–15 years (Ashton et al., 2019). A recent small-scale study reported a reduction in upper- and lower-limb strength, accompanied by decreases in lean body mass, following radical prostatectomy (Singh et al., 2017).

Men with locally advanced and metastatic disease are routinely treated with androgen deprivation therapy (ADT). The physical side effects of ADT include reduced bone mineral density, with evidence of osteopenia and osteoporosis (Berruti et al., 2002), and a decrease in skeletal muscle mass (Smith et al., 2012) which can be examined using dual-energy X-ray absorptiometry. Furthermore, adverse effects of ADT on body composition, and particularly body fat accumulation and increased abdominal obesity (Braga-Basaria et al., 2006), could underpin reported associations with metabolic syndrome (Braga-Basaria et al., 2006) and increased risk of cardiovascular morbidity (Saigal et al., 2007). There is also evidence of reduced muscular strength and self-reported physical functioning (Gonzalez et al., 2016) and low cardiopulmonary exercise capacity in men receiving ADT, with the latter equating to the 10th–15th percentile of age-matched healthy controls (Wall et al., 2014). Refer to Table 5.6.1 for an overview of physiological and functional fitness tests which take into consideration these common prostate cancer-specific impairments and functional limitations.

Conclusions

Surgical risk stratification and assessing the impact of those treatment interventions on cancer recovery outcomes and late effects of treatment are all examples of how physiological/functional testing is now being used in cancer care pathways. In addition, core outcome sets have been developed for assessing the health impacts of commonly experienced side effects in breast and prostate cancer which adversely impact health-related quality of life (Ong et al., 2017; Morgans et al., 2015; MacLennan et al., 2017). These patient-reported outcomes (not considered in this chapter) are important for assessing the severity of physical and psychosocial symptoms and should be used alongside physiological and functional testing to gain a more complete understanding of the cancer treatment experience and response to therapeutic interventions.

References

Aadland, E., Solbraa, A. K., Resaland, G. K., Steene-Johannessen, J., Edvardsen, E., Hansen, B. H. and Anderssen, S. A. (2017). Reference values for and cross-validation of time to exhaustion on a modified Balke protocol in Norwegian men and women. *Scandanavian Journal of Medicine and Science in Sports*, 27, 1248–1257.

Ashton, R. E., Tew, G. A., Robson, W. A., Saxton, J. M. and Aning, J. J. (2019). Cross-sectional study of patient-reported fatigue, physical activity and cardiovascular status in men after robotic-assisted radical prostatectomy. *Support Care Cancer*, 27, 4763–4770.

Atisha, D. and Alderman, A. K. (2009). A systematic review of abdominal wall function following abdominal flaps for postmastectomy breast reconstruction. *Annals of Plastic Surgery*, 63, 222–230.

Barry, M. J., Gallagher, P. M., Skinner, J. S. and Fowler Jr., F. J. (2012). Adverse effects of robotic-assisted laparoscopic versus open retropubic radical prostatectomy among a nationwide random sample of medicare-age men. *Journal of Clinical Oncology*, 30, 513–518.

Berruti, A., Dogliotti, L., Terrone, C., Cerutti, S., Isaia, G., Tarabuzzi, R., Reimondo, G., Mari, M., Ardissone, P., De, L. S., Fasolis, G., Fontana, D., Rossetti, S. R. and Angeli, A. (2002). Changes in bone mineral density, lean body mass and fat content as measured by dual energy x-ray absorptiometry in patients with prostate cancer without apparent bone metastases given androgen deprivation therapy. *Journal of Urology.*, 167, 2361–2367.

Braga-Basaria, M., Dobs, A. S., Muller, D. C., Carducci, M. A., John, M., Egan, J. and Basaria, S. (2006). Metabolic syndrome in men with prostate cancer undergoing long-term androgen-deprivation therapy. *Journal of Clinical Oncology*, 24, 3979–3983.

Caan, B. J., Cespedes Feliciano, E. M., Prado, C. M., Alexeeff, S., Kroenke, C. H., Bradshaw, P., Quesenberry, C. P., Weltzien, E. K., Castillo, A. L., Olobatuyi, T. A. and Chen, W. Y. (2018). Association of muscle and adiposity measured by computed tomography with survival in patients with nonmetastatic breast cancer. *Journal of the American Medical Association Oncology*, 4, 798–804.

Campbell, K. L., Winters-Stone, K. M., Wiskemann, J., May, A. M., Schwartz, A. L., Courneya, K. S., Zucker, D. S., Matthews, C. E., Ligibel, J. A., Gerber, L. H., Morris, G. S., Patel, A. V., Hue, T. F., Perna, F. M. and Schmitz, K. H. (2019). Exercise guidelines for cancer survivors: Consensus statement from international multidisciplinary roundtable. *Medicine & Science in Sports & Exercise*, 51, 2375–2390.

Cancer Research UK Cancer Incidence Statistics. (2017). www.cancerresearchuk.org/health-professional/cancer-statistics/incidence#heading-Zero (accessed 29 September 2020).

Cancer Research UK Cancer Survival Statistics. (2010–2011).

Capogrosso, P., Vertosick, E. A., Benfante, N. E., Eastham, J. A., Scardino, P. J., Vickers, A. J. and Mulhall, J. P. (2019). Are we improving erectile function recovery after radical prostatectomy? Analysis of patients treated over the last decade. *European Urology*, 75, 221–228.

Cecchini, R. S., Swain, S. M., Costantino, J. P., Rastogi, P., Jeong, J. H., Anderson, S. J., Tang, G., Geyer Jr., C. E., Lembersky, B. C., Romond, E. H., Paterson, A. H. and Wolmark, N. (2016). Body mass index at diagnosis and breast cancer survival prognosis in clinical trial populations from NRG oncology/NSABP B-30, B-31, B-34, and B-38. *Cancer Epidemiological, Biomarkers and Prevention*, 25, 51–59.

Christensen, J. F., Jones, L. W., Andersen, J. L., Daugaard, G., Rorth, M. and Hojman, P. (2014). Muscle dysfunction in cancer patients. *Annals of Oncology*, 25, 947–958.

Cui, H. W., Turney, B. W. and Griffiths, J. (2017). The preoperative assessment and optimization of patients undergoing major urological surgery. *Current Urology Reports*, 18, 54.

DiSipio, T., Rye, S., Newman, B. and Hayes, S. (2013). Incidence of unilateral arm lymphoedema after breast cancer: A systematic review and meta-analysis. *The Lancet Oncology*, 14, 500–515.

Flores, A. M. and Dwyer, K. (2014). Shoulder impairment before breast cancer surgery. *Journal of Womens Health and Physical Therapy*, 38, 118–124.

Fornusek, C. P. and Kilbreath, S. L. (2017). Exercise for improving bone health in women treated for stages I-III breast cancer: A systematic review and meta-analyses. *Journal of Cancer Survivors*, 11, 525–541.

Gonzalez, B. D., Jim, H. S. L., Small, B. J., Sutton, S. K., Fishman, M. N., Zachariah, B., Heysek, R. V. and Jacobsen, P. B. (2016). Changes in physical functioning and muscle strength in men receiving androgen deprivation therapy for prostate cancer: A controlled comparison. *Support Care Cancer*, 24, 2201–2207.

Haseen, F., Murray, L. J., Cardwell, C. R., O'sullivan, J. M. and Cantwell, M. M. (2010). The effect of androgen deprivation therapy on body composition in men with prostate cancer: Systematic review and meta-analysis. *Journal of Cancer Survivor*, 4, 128–139.

Jackson, A. S. and Pollock, M. L. (1978). Generalized equations for predicting body density of men. *British Journal of Nutrition*, 40, 497–504.

Jensen, T. G., Dudrick, S. J. and Johnston, D. A. (1981). A comparison of triceps skinfold and upper arm circumference measurements taken in standard and supine positions. *The Journal of Parenteral and Enteral Nutrition*, 5, 519–521.

Jones, L. W., Eves, N. D. and Peppercorn, J. (2010). Pre-exercise screening and prescription guidelines for cancer patients. *The Lancet Oncology*, 11, 914–916.

Kaminsky, L. A. and Whaley, M. H. (1998). Evaluation of a new standardized ramp protocol: The BSU/Bruce Ramp protocol. *Journal of Cardiopulmonary Rehabilitation*, 18, 438–444.

Klassen, O., Schmidt, M. E., Ulrich, C. M., Schneeweiss, A., Potthoff, K., Steindorf, K. and Wiskemann, J. (2017). Muscle strength in breast cancer patients receiving different treatment regimes. *Journal of Cachexia, Sarcopenia and Muscle*, 8, 305–316.

Langhammer, B. and Stanghelle, J. K. (2015). The senior fitness test. *Journal of Physiotherapy*, 61, 163.

Lenneman, C. G. and Sawyer, D. B. (2016). Cardio-oncology: An update on cardiotoxicity of cancer-related treatment. *Circulation Research*, 118, 1008–1020.

Litwin, M. S., Mcguigan, K. A., Shpall, A. I. and Dhanani, N. (1999). Recovery of health related quality of life in the year after radical prostatectomy: Early experience. *Journal of Urology*, 161, 515–519.

Lohmann, A. E., Ennis, M., Taylor, S. K. and Goodwin, P. J. (2017). Metabolic factors, anthropometric measures, diet, and physical activity in long-term breast cancer survivors: Change from diagnosis and comparison to non-breast cancer controls. *Breast Cancer Research and Treatment*, 164(2), 451–460.

MacLennan, S., Williamson, P. R., Bekema, H., Campbell, M., Ramsay, C., N'Dow, J., MacLennan, S., Vale, L., Dahm, P., Mottet, N., Lam, T. and Group, C. S. (2017). A core outcome set for localised prostate cancer effectiveness trials. *British Journal of Urology International*, 120, E64–E79.

Mina, D. S., Langelier, D., Adams, S. C., Alibhai, S. M. H., Chasen, M., Campbell, K. L., Oh, P., Jones, J. M. and Chang, E. (2018). Exercise as part of routine cancer care. *The Lancet Oncology*, 19, e433–e436.

Morgans, A. K., Van Bommel, A. C., Stowell, C., Abrahm, J. L., Basch, E., Bekelman, J. E., Berry, D. L., Bossi, A., Davis, I. D., De Reijke, T. M., Denis, L. J., Evans, S. M., Fleshner, N. E., George, D. J., Kiefert, J., Lin, D. W., Matthew, A. G., McDermott, R., Payne, H., Roos, I. A., Schrag, D., Steuber, T., Tombal, B., Van Basten, J. P., Van Der Hoeven, J. J., Penson, D. F. and Advanced Prostate Cancer Working Group of The International Consortium for Health Outcomes, M. (2015). Development of a standardized set of patient-centered outcomes for advanced prostate cancer: An international effort for a unified approach. *European Urology*, 68, 891–898.

Ong, W. L., Schouwenburg, M. G., Van Bommel, A. C. M., Stowell, C., Allison, K. H., Benn, K. E., Browne, J. P., Cooter, R. D., Delaney, G. P., Duhoux, F. P., Ganz, P. A., Hancock, P., Jagsi, R., Knaul, F. M., Knip, A. M., Koppert, L. B., Kuerer, H. M., McLaughlin, S., Mureau, M. A. M., Partridge, A. H., Reid, D. P., Sheeran, L., Smith, T. J., Stoutjesdijk, M. J., Vrancken Peeters, M., Wengstrom, Y., Yip, C. H. and Saunders, C. (2017). A standard set of value-based patient-centered outcomes for breast cancer: The International Consortium for Health Outcomes Measurement (ICHOM) initiative. *Journal of the American Medical Association Oncology*, 3, 677–685.

Peel, A. B., Thomas, S. M., Dittus, K., Jones, L. W. and Lakoski, S. G. (2014). Cardiorespiratory fitness in breast cancer patients: A call for normative values. *Journal of the American Heart Association*, 3, e000432.

Prinsen, H., Hopman, M. T., Zwarts, M. J., Leer, J. W., Heerschap, A., Bleijenberg, G. and Van Laarhoven, H. W. (2013). Maximal exercise performance in patients with postcancer fatigue. *Support Care in Cancer*, 21, 439–447.

Rawla, P. (2019). Epidemiology of prostate cancer. *World Journal of Oncology*, 10, 63–89.

Sagen, A., Karesen, R., Sandvik, L. and Risberg, M. A. (2009). Changes in arm morbidities and health-related quality of life after breast cancer surgery: A five-year follow-up study. *Acta Oncologica*, 48, 1111–1118.

Saigal, C. S., Gore, J. L., Krupski, T. L., Hanley, J., Schonlau, M. and Litwin, M. S. (2007). Androgen deprivation therapy increases cardiovascular morbidity in men with prostate cancer. *Cancer*, 110, 1493–1500.

Schmidt, K., Vogt, L., Thiel, C., Jäger, E. and Banzer, W. (2013). Validity of the six-minute walk test in cancer patients. *International Journal of Sports Medicine*, 34, 631–636.

Singh, F., Newton, R. U., Baker, M. K., Spry, N. A., Taaffe, D. R., Thavaseelan, J. and Galvão, D. A. (2017). Feasibility of presurgical exercise in men with prostate cancer undergoing prostatectomy. *Integrative Cancer Therapies*, 16, 290–299.

Smith, M. R., Saad, F., Egerdie, B., Sieber, P. R., Tammela, T. L., Ke, C., Leder, B. Z. and Goessl, C. (2012). Sarcopenia during androgen-deprivation therapy for prostate cancer. *Journal of Clinical Oncology*, 30, 3271–3276.

Stefani, L., Galanti, G. and Klika, R. (2017). Clinical implementation of exercise guidelines for cancer patients: Adaptation of ACSM's guidelines to the Italian model. *Journal of Functional Morphology and Kinesiology*, 2(1), 4.

Steins Bisschop, C. N., Velthuis, M. J., Wittink, H., Kuiper, K., Takken, T., Van Der Meulen, W. J., Lindeman, E., Peeters, P. H. and May, A. M. (2012). Cardiopulmonary exercise testing in cancer rehabilitation: A systematic review. *Sports Medicine*, 42, 367–379.

Thomas, G., Tahir, M. R., Bongers, B. C., Kallen, V. L., Slooter, G. D. and Van Meeteren, N. L. (2019). Prehabilitation before major intra-abdominal cancer surgery: A systematic review of randomised controlled trials. *European Journal of Anaesthesiology*, 36, 933–945.

Trinh, Q. D., Sammon, J., Sun, M., Ravi, P., Ghani, K. R., Bianchi, M., Jeong, W., Shariat, S. F., Hansen, J., Schmitges, J., Jeldres, C., Rogers, C. G., Peabody, J. O., Montorsi, F., Menon, M. and Karakiewicz, P. I. (2012). Perioperative outcomes of robot-assisted radical prostatectomy compared with open radical prostatectomy: Results from the nationwide inpatient sample. *European Urology*, 61, 679–685.

Wall, B. A., Galvao, D. A., Fatehee, N., Taaffe, D. R., Spry, N., Joseph, D. and Newton, R. U. (2014). Maximal exercise testing of men with prostate cancer being treated with androgen deprivation therapy. *Medicine & Science in Sports & Exercise*, 46, 2210–2215.

World Cancer Research Fund Breast Cancer Statistics. (2018).

World Cancer Research Fund Cancer Statistics. (2017). www.wcrf-uk.org/uk/preventing-cancer/cancer-preventability-statistics?gclid=EAIaIQobChMI37DzwcD96wIViql3Ch3NCAzbEAAYASAAEgJiOPD_BwE (accessed 29 September 2020).

Yang, A., Sokolof, J. and Gulati, A. (2018). The effect of preoperative exercise on upper extremity recovery following breast cancer surgery: a systematic review. *International Journal of Rehabilitation Research*, 41, 189–196.

5.7 Exercise testing in peripheral arterial disease

Amy Harwood, Edward Caldow and Gabriel Cucato

Peripheral arterial disease (PAD) or peripheral vascular disease is the process of atherosclerosis that causes the arteries that carry blood away from the heart to other parts of the body to become narrow and hardened, and leads to obstruction or occlusion of arterial blood flow (Ouriel, 2001). The most common type of PAD is lower extremity PAD that causes reduced blood flow to the legs and the feet, which will be the focus of this chapter.

PAD is a common condition and it is estimated that the global prevalence is approximately 237 million (Song et al., 2019). It can be symptomatic or asymptomatic, with approximately three asymptomatic patients for every one symptomatic patient (Norgren et al., 2007). It affects approximately 3% of those aged under 50, rising to around 20% in those over 70 years of age (Song et al., 2019). The manifestation and development of PAD is complex and multifactorial, with a number of 'modifiable' (e.g., smoking) and 'non-modifiable' (age, sex etc.) risk factors contributing to risk of disease and progression (Shammas, 2007). The 'classic' symptomatic manifestation of PAD is intermittent claudication (IC), characterised by a cramp-like pain, ache or burning sensation in the buttock, thigh or calf region during physical activity and relieved by rest (Morley et al., 2018). Generally, the site of pain can provide an indication of the site of disease (i.e., location of stenosis) (Morley et al., 2018). The pain is caused by an exercise-induced ischemia, whereby there is an imbalance between oxygen demand and supply at the muscle level (Meru et al., 2006). IC is associated with significant reductions in walking capabilities, quality of life and physical activity levels (Lane et al., 2017; Gerage et al., 2019).

This chapter will cover the diagnosis and classification of PAD and appropriate clinical measurements to determine disease severity. It will also outline appropriate exercise testing measures and clinical outcomes that can be measured and reported for patients with PAD.

Diagnosis of PAD

PAD diagnosis is established via patient history and general, clinical and lower-limb examinations. It is confirmed via Doppler assessment of the ankle brachial pressure index (ABPI or ABI). The ABPI is defined as the ratio of systolic blood pressure

DOI: 10.4324/9781003045267-40

Table 5.7.1 Fontaine and Rutherford classifications for peripheral arterial disease (Hardman et al., 2014)

Fontaine		Rutherford		
Stage	Clinical	Grade	Category	Clinical
I	Asymptomatic	0	0	Asymptomatic
IIA	Mild claudication	I	1	Mild claudication
IIB	Moderate–severe claudication	I	2	Moderate claudication
		I	3	Severe claudication
III	Ischemic rest pain	II	4	Ischemic rest pain
IV	Ulceration or gangrene	III	5	Minor tissue loss
		III	6	Major tissue loss

measured in the ankle to that in the arm (brachial artery). The ABPI has good sensitivity and specificity and can provide information regarding disease severity (Aboyans et al., 2012). In addition to Doppler assessment, there are a number of imaging modalities that can provide anatomical localisation of disease. Duplex ultrasound assessment is widely regarded as the 'gold-standard' imaging modality (Anderson et al., 2013). Other imaging modalities such as magnetic resonance or computerised tomographic angiography are often used prior to surgical intervention rather than for diagnostic purposes. To classify patients, a combination of clinical examination, diagnostic testing and exercise testing can be utilised (Table 5.7.1).

Ankle brachial pressure index

To accurately measure ABPI, patients should be in the supine position and rest for 5 to 10 minutes (Aboyans et al., 2012). An appropriately sized blood pressure cuff should be used at the arm and the ankle to measure systolic blood pressure. The recommended width of the cuff should be at least 40% of the limb circumference (Pickering et al., 2005). A small amount of electro-conductive ultrasound gel should be placed at the measurement sites; namely the brachial, posterior tibial and dorsalis pedis arteries. Anatomically, the posterior tibial artery can be palpated behind the medial malleolus and the dorsalis pedis can be palpated between the first and second metatarsal bones. A hand-held 8–10 MHz Doppler ultrasound probe is placed at each site to detect any audible pulsatile blood flow. The blood pressure cuff should then be inflated above the pressure level where the audible signal is no longer detected and then slowly released until the signal returns. The pressure at which the signal returns should be recorded. This process is repeated at each site and in both lower limbs. The ABPI is calculated by taking the highest systolic pressure in the lower limb and dividing it by the highest systolic pressure in the arms. A normal reading should be equal to or slightly higher than the systolic pressure in the arm, equating to a ratio of around 1.0 (a full interpretation of all values is shown in Table 5.7.2). It should be noted that in some patients, a pulse may not be detectable at both sites in the foot. In such cases, a single measure

Table 5.7.2 Interpretation of the ankle brachial pressure index (Aboyans et al., 2012; Ko and Bandyk, 2013)

ABPI	Interpretation
>1.4	Falsely elevated due to calcification. Further assessment needed via toe-pressure measurement.
1.0–1.4	Normal.
0.91–0.99	Borderline. Need to obtain exercise treadmill testing if exercise-induced calf pain is present.
<0.9	Abnormal, indication of peripheral arterial disease.
0.7–0.9	Mild peripheral arterial disease.
0.4–0.7	Moderate peripheral arterial disease. Typical ABPI range in patients with intermittent claudication.
<0.4	Severe peripheral arterial disease. Critical limb ischaemia when associated with systolic toe pressure <30 mmHg, rest pain or non-healing ulcers.

of either the posterior tibial or dorsalis pedis artery is acceptable. Some patients with long-standing diabetes or other disorders may have vascular calcification, causing falsely elevated systolic pressures due to non-compressible arteries. Non-compressible values are defined as an ABPI >1.4 or systolic ankle pressure (>250 mmHg). In this situation, a toe-brachial pressure index is required to provide an accurate measurement (Norgren et al., 2007). An ABPI value less than 0.4 in the presence of other signs and symptoms can be associated with critical limb ischaemia, defined as severe pain at rest and/or the presence of gangrene and ulcers (Gerhard-Herman et al., 2017).

Exercise testing in patients with peripheral arterial disease

ABPI is an important diagnostic test; however, it is a poor predictor of walking performance (Parmenter et al., 2010) and in some cases, patients may have PAD but a normal ABPI at rest. Exercise testing should therefore be used to support the diagnosis of PAD. It should also be used for the assessment of functional impairment. Exercise testing outcome measures for patients with PAD typically comprise pain-free walking distance (PFWD) and/or time (defined as the walking distance or time when patients report the first experience of pain, aching or burning in calves or buttocks) and maximum walking distance (MWD) and/or time (defined as the walking distance or time when patients cannot continue due to maximal pain). Patients may also report a 'claudication pain score' during exercise testing ranging from 1 = no pain, up to 5 = severe pain (or a 0 to 4 scale in some clinical practices).

Treadmill walking protocols for patients with peripheral arterial disease

Walking capacity is considered an important clinical outcome in PAD and treadmill tests can be used to assess the impact of the disease on functional impairment and the efficacy of clinical therapeutic interventions. Two different treadmill protocols are often used in PAD: constant-load (single-stage) and graded (multi-stage). Constant-load treadmill tests are performed at a single work rate with a variation of 2 to 4 km/h and 10–12% for speed and grade, respectively. Graded protocols are performed at the same speed but with variation on treadmill grade at predetermined intervals. Common protocols include Hiatt (3.2 km/h and 3.5% increase in grade every 3 min) (Hiatt et al., 1988) and the Gardner/Skinner protocol (3.2 km/h and 2% increase in grade every 2 min) (Gardner et al., 1991).

Conducting the exercise test

Treadmill walking exercise tests must be performed under standardised conditions. Patients should be asked to refrain from any exercise and avoid smoking cigarettes and drinking alcohol for at least 24 hours before the test. It is also important to make sure that patients are familiarised with a treadmill before conducting a formal test for analysis to reduce the learning effect. During the test, patients must be instructed to walk until maximal levels of claudication pain (self-reported using the aforementioned scale). If patients terminate for other reasons, this should be recorded since it is not a true reflection of MWD. It is also good practice to cover the stopwatch and face of the treadmill. Additionally, patients should not hold onto the treadmill other than for very light support. Because patients with PAD often have additional comorbidities and systemic atherosclerosis, electrocardiogram and blood pressure monitoring during maximal treadmill exercise tests are recommended to enhance patient safety and help to detect possible coexisting cardiovascular diseases.

Constant-load vs. graded treadmill exercise testing

Constant-load protocols are easier to perform because a programmable treadmill is not required. However, they present low reliability with coefficients of variation of 30% to 45% for PFWD and MWD, respectively (Hiatt et al., 2014). This is typically due to the heterogeneity of clinical characteristics of PAD patients, with some unable to walk 50 m whereas others have minimal physical activity restrictions (able to walk more >1 km with low levels of pain). Moreover, constant-load protocols that employ low speed (e.g., 2.0 km/h) and without grade commonly result in a longer PFWD. Constant-load protocols are also more affected by a learning effect with an increase in walking distance ranging from 25% to 100% for the MWD over a two-week period (Hiatt et al., 2014).

In contrast, graded treadmill tests present better reliability compared to continuous protocols with a coefficient of variation for PFWD of 15% and 12% for MWD. In addition, graded treadmill tests are less affected by a learning effect (Brass et al., 2006). Thus, despite both treadmill exercise protocols being considered useful, the graded test better reflects the mechanism of the walking impairment in PAD, is more reliable and is suitable across a wide range of PAD severity.

Alternative walking assessments

Although treadmill-based exercise tests can establish maximum walking capacity, evidence has demonstrated there is only a moderate correlation between tread-mill outcomes, self-reported walking distance and free-living activity (measured through pedometer, activity monitoring or global positioning systems) (Nasr et al., 2002; Gernigon et al., 2014; Clarke et al., 2013). Therefore, alternative approaches such as the six-minute walk test (6MWT) and GPS device-based test-ing can be used.

Six-minute walk test (6MWT)

As described in both the cardiac and respiratory chapters, the 6MWT is a well-validated and low-cost test that is utilised across a range of different clinical popu-lations. An excellent test-retest reliability has been shown for six-minute walking distance (6MWD) in patients with PAD, with a correlation coefficient of 0.90 (p<0.001) and a coefficient of variation of 8.9% with testing performed one to two weeks apart (McDermott et al., 2008). Change in 6MWD can be used to predict mortality and mobility loss in patients with PAD, and clinically meaningful changes in the 6MWD have been defined (Sandberg et al., 2020). As with all test-ing procedures, a protocol such as that provided by the American Thoracic Soci-ety needs to be strictly followed, e.g., standardised walking course and consistency of encouragement provided during the test (Holland et al., 2014).

Global positioning system (GPS) recorders

A measure of 'real-life' outdoor walking can be undertaken via the use of GPS recorders. Patients are given a GPS recorder and instructed to walk on a pre-defined course. The walking course should be flat, with minimal barriers that would cause the individual to stop or pause for any other reason than PAD-related symptoms (e.g., road crossings). Therefore, athletics tracks and local parks are good options. The duration of the walk should be between 40 and 60 minutes, with at least 30 minutes of consistent data. Patients should walk at a habitual pace and continue until limited by maximal walking pain. Patients should then resume walking either when the pain has subsided completely, or when they feel able to walk again. The GPS device should have a function (i.e., button press) that allows patients to record the point of initial onset of claudication and the maximal pain so that PFWD and MWD can be measured. GPS devices can also record total walking distance, MWD between bouts of walking, average walking speed and average duration of stops between bouts (Gernigon et al., 2015).

Research has shown that GPS recorders have a good coefficient of variation for reliability and for accuracy when compared with known walking distances (Abraham et al., 2012). There are a range of GPS recorders available (including smartphone apps) and they can be easily worn (e.g., on waistband, on wrist or in a backpack) during outdoor walking (Nordanstig et al., 2014).

Cardiopulmonary exercise testing

Cardiopulmonary exercise testing (CPET) provides an integrated assessment and quantification of the cardiorespiratory system at rest and under submaximal and maximal exercise. In patients with PAD, studies have demonstrated that ventilatory threshold and peak oxygen uptake are significantly reduced (50% lower compared to non-PAD patients) (Bauer et al., 2004) and are moderately correlated to walking performance (Womack et al., 1998). In addition, oxygen uptake kinetics are also impaired and related to exercise intolerance in PAD (Bauer et al., 1999).

For patients with PAD, cycling should be considered the primary modality for CPET, since it minimises the impact of body mass and represents a relatively low load placed on the calf muscles during exercise. It can therefore establish a maximum value without inducing leg symptoms. Studies have demonstrated that cycle ergometry incurs a similar cardiovascular and metabolic response as treadmill walking (Tuner et al., 2008) and allows for better quality electrocardiogram traces and measurement of blood pressure, which would aid in the detection of coexisting cardiac conditions (Fletcher et al., 2013).

Arm-cranking may also be suitable, given that patients can perform the test without inducing claudication symptoms. Although in healthy individuals, peak oxygen uptake for arm-cranking is typically lower compared to cycle ergometry (around 70%), in PAD the values are similar (Bauer et al., 2004). The test should be performed on a specific arm ergometer or modified from an existing stationary cycle ergometer by replacing the pedals with handles and mounting the unit on a table at shoulder height. The protocol should start with a 2-minute warm-up against no resistance followed by work rate increments of 7 $W \cdot min^{-1}$, at a cranking rate of 50–60 $rev \cdot min^{-1}$ until maximal volitional exertion (Tew et al., 2009).

Peripheral blood flow and skeletal muscle oxygenation

In addition to ABPI, near-infrared light spectroscopy (NIRS) can be used to non-invasively measure lower-limb haemodynamics (Hamaoka et al., 2007). NIRS measures the saturation of haemoglobin by oxygen from the differential absorption by oxymyoglobin and deoxyhaemoglobin of monochromatic light spectrum emitted by laser beams at characteristic wavelengths. In PAD patients, a sensor is attached to the skin on the medial portion of gastrocnemius muscle in the leg with the lowest ABPI to monitor the oxygen muscle saturation in real-time at rest, during and after an exercise test.

Studies have demonstrated that PAD patients present a sudden fall in muscle oxygen saturation at the beginning of the exercise and present lower values compared to age-matched controls during treadmill walking (Andrade-Lima et al., 2018). Additionally, muscle oxygen saturation parameters are strongly associated with objective and subjective measurement of walking capacity (Gardner et al., 2008, 2020) and are sensitive to changes in peripheral circulation and skeletal muscle oxygenation after exercise interventions in PAD (Tew et al., 2009; Monteiro et al., 2019).

In addition to NIRS, transcutaneous oxygen pressure (TcpO$_2$) can be used to measure local oxygen pressure in patients with PAD. TcpO$_2$ uses light from a green LED to excite the sensor spots in the matrix layer of the skin to emit fluorescence. If the sensor spot encounters an oxygen molecule, the excess energy is transferred, quenching the fluorescence signal (Abraham et al., 2018). The degree of quenching correlates to the partial pressure of oxygen in the matrix, which is in dynamic equilibrium with oxygen in the sample.

TcpO$_2$ can be measured at proximal and distal areas related to the arterial stenosis. Probes are positioned on the chest as a reference and in one or more areas of the lower limbs (buttocks, thigh and calves). TcpO$_2$ is measured at rest and during a constant treadmill test (2.0 / 3.2 km at 10% grade). During exercise, the drop of oxygen pressure is calculated (the absolute change in TcpO$_2$ from rest at each of the limb probes minus changes from rest values from the chest reference probe). For the interpretation, previous studies showed that a drop of 15 mmHg is the optimal cut-off point to discriminate normal from abnormal haemodynamics in both the buttock and calf levels (Abraham et al., 2018, 2020).

Summary

Patients with PAD typically have a reduced functional capacity, physical activity levels, walking ability and cardiorespiratory fitness. Once patients have been clinically assessed and diagnosed with PAD, there are several exercise tests that can be used to assess functional status and to monitor any improvements following an exercise, lifestyle or surgical intervention. Primary outcomes of interest include pain-free walking distance and maximum walking distance. These can be obtained via graded treadmill testing, six-minute walking distance or community-based walking assessments via the use of GPS or accelerometers. In addition to walking assessments, cardiorespiratory fitness can be measured used cycling or arm-cranking protocols. Finally, lower-limb haemodynamics may be monitored using near-infrared light spectroscopy or transcutaneous oxygen pressure. For all of these testing modalities, practitioners need to ensure they strictly adhere to protocols to ensure that tests are valid and reliable.

References

Aboyans, V., Criqui, M. H., Abraham, P., Allison, M. A., Creager, M. A., Diehm, C., et al. (2012). Measurement and interpretation of the ankle-brachial index: a scientific statement from the American Heart Association. *Circulation*, 126(24), 2890–2909.

Abraham, P., Gu, Y., Guo, L., Kroeger, K., Ouedraogo, N., Wennberg, P., et al. (2018). Clinical application of transcutaneous oxygen pressure measurements during exercise. *Atherosclerosis*, 276, 117–123.

Abraham, P., Noury-Desvaux, B., Gernigon, M., Mahé, G., Sauvaget, T., Leftheriotis, G., et al. (2012). The inter- and intra-unit variability of a low-cost GPS data logger/receiver to study human outdoor walking in view of health and clinical studies. *PLoS One*, 7(2), e31338.

Abraham, P., Ramondou, P., Hersant, J., Sempore, W. Y., Feuilloy, M. and Henni, S. (2020). Investigation of arterial claudication with transcutaneous oxygen pres. *Trends in Cardiovascular Medicine*.

Anderson, J. L., Halperin, J. L., Albert, N. M., Bozkurt, B., Brindis, R. G., Curtis, L. H., et al. (2013). Management of patients with peripheral artery disease (compilation of 2005 and 2011 ACCF/AHA guideline recommendations): A report of the American College of Cardiology Foundation/American Heart Association Task Force on Practice Guidelines. *Circulation*, 127(13), 1425–1443.

Andrade-Lima, A., Cucato, G. G., Domingues, W. J. R., Germano-Soares, A. H., Cavalcante, B. R., Correia, M. A., et al. (2018). Calf muscle oxygen saturation during 6-minute walk test and its relationship with walking impairment in symptomatic peripheral artery disease. *Annals of Vascular Surgery*, 52, 147–152.

Bauer, T. A., Brass, E. P., Nehler, M., Barstow, T. J. and Hiatt, W. R. (2004). Pulmonary $\dot{V}O_2$ dynamics during treadmill and arm exercise in peripheral arterial disease. *Journal of Applied Physiology* (Bethesda, Md: 1985), 97(2), 627–634.

Bauer, T. A., Regensteiner, J. G., Brass, E. P. and Hiatt, W. R. (1999). Oxygen uptake kinetics during exercise are slowed in patients with peripheral arterial disease. *Journal of Applied Physiology* (Bethesda, Md: 1985), 87(2), 809–816.

Brass, E. P., Anthony, R., Cobb, F. R., Koda, I., Jiao, J. and Hiatt, W. R. (2006). The novel phosphodiesterase inhibitor NM-702 improves claudication-limited exercise performance in patients with peripheral arterial disease. *Journal of the American College of Cardiology*, 48(12), 2539–2545.

Clarke, C. L., Holdsworth, R. J., Ryan, C. G. and Granat, M. H. (2013). Free-living physical activity as a novel outcome measure in patients with intermittent claudication. *European Journal of Vascular and Endovascular Surgery*, 45(2), 162–167.

Fletcher, G. F., Ades, P. A., Kligfield, P., Arena, R., Balady, G. J., Bittner, V. A., et al. (2013). Exercise standards for testing and training: A scientific statement from the American Heart Association. *Circulation*, 128(8), 873–934.

Gardner, A. W., Montgomery, P. S., Wang, M. and Shen, B. (2020). Association between calf muscle oxygen saturation with ambulatory function and quality of life in symptomatic patients with peripheral artery disease. *Journal of Vascular Surgery*, 72(2), 632–642.

Gardner, A. W., Parker, D. E., Webb, N., Montgomery, P. S., Scott, K. J. and Blevins, S. M. (2008). Calf muscle hemoglobin oxygen saturation characteristics and exercise performance in patients with intermittent claudication. *Journal of Vascular Surgery*, 48(3), 644–649.

Gardner, A. W., Skinner, J. S., Cantwell, B. W. and Smith, L. K. (1991). Progressive vs single-stage treadmill tests for evaluation of claudication. *Medicine & Science in Sports & Exercise*, 23(4), 402–408.

Gerage, A. M., Correia, M. A., Oliveira, P. M. L., Palmeira, A. C., Domingues, W. J. R., Zeratti, A. E., et al. (2019). Physical activity levels in peripheral artery disease patients. *Arquivos Brasileiros de Cardiologia*, 113(3), 410–416.

Gerhard-Herman, M. D., Gornik, H. L., Barrett, C., Barshes, N. R., Corriere, M. A., Drachman, D. E., et al. (2017). AHA/ACC guideline on the management of patients with lower extremity peripheral artery disease: Executive summary: A report of the American College of Cardiology/American Heart Association Task Force on Clinical Practice Guidelines. *Circulation*, 135(12), e686–e725.

Gernigon, M., Le Faucheur, A., Fradin, D., Noury-Desvaux, B., Landron, C., Mahe, G., et al. (2015). Global positioning system use in the community to evaluate improvements in walking after revascularization: A prospective multicenter study with 6-month follow-up in patients with peripheral arterial disease. *Medicine*, 94(18), e838.

Gernigon, M., Le Faucheur, A., Noury-Desvaux, B., Mahe, G., Abraham, P. and Post, G. P. S. S. C. G. (2014). Applicability of global positioning system for the assessment of walking ability in patients with arterial claudication. *Journal of Vascular Surgery*, 60(4), 973–81.

Hamaoka, T., McCully, K., Quaresima, V., Yamamoto, K. and Chance, B. (2007). Near-infrared spectroscopy/imaging for monitoring muscle oxygenation and oxidative metabolism in healthy and diseased humans. *Journal of Biomedical Optics*, 6, 062105.

Hardman, R. L., Jazaeri, O., Yi, J., Smith, M. and Gupta, R. (2014). Overview of classification systems in peripheral artery disease. *Seminars in Interventional Radiology*, 31(4), 378–388.

Hiatt, W. R., Nawaz, D., Regensteiner, J. G. and Hossack, K. F. (1988). The evaluation of exercise performance in patients with peripheral vascular disease. *Journal of Cardiopulmonary Rehabilitation*, 8(12), 525–532.

Hiatt, W. R., Rogers, R. K. and Brass, E. P. (2014). The treadmill is a better functional test than the 6-minute walk test in therapeutic trials of patients with peripheral artery disease. *Circulation*, 130(1), 69–78.

Holland, A. E., Spruit, M. A., Troosters, T., Puhan, M. A., Pepin, V., Saey, D., et al. (2014). An official European Respiratory Society/American Thoracic Society technical standard: field walking tests in chronic respiratory disease. *European Respiratory Journal*, 44(6), 1428–1446.

Ko, S. H. and Bandyk, D. F. (2013). Interpretation and significance of ankle-brachial systolic pressure index. *Seminars in Vascular Surgery*, 26(2–3), 86–94.

Lane, R., Harwood, A., Watson, L. and Leng, G. C. (2017). Exercise for intermittent claudication. *Cochrane Database of Systematic Reviews*, 12, CD000990.

McDermott, M. M., Ades, P. A., Dyer, A., Guralnik, J. M., Kibbe, M. and Criqui, M. H. (2008). Corridor-based functional performance measures correlate better with physical activity during daily life than treadmill measures in persons with peripheral arterial disease. *Journal of Vascular Surgery*, 48(5), 1231–1237, 7 e1.

Meru, A. V., Mittra, S., Thyagarajan, B. and Chugh, A. (2006). Intermittent claudication: An overview. *Atherosclerosis*, 187(2), 221–237.

Monteiro, D. P., Ribeiro-Samora, G. A., Britto, R. R. and Pereira, D. A. G. (2019). Effects of modified aerobic training on muscle metabolism in individuals with peripheral arterial disease: a randomized clinical trial. *Scientific Reports*, 9(1), 15966.

Morley, R. L., Sharma, A., Horsch, A. D. and Hinchliffe, R. J. (2018). Peripheral artery disease. *BMJ*, 360, j5842.

Nasr, M. K., McCarthy, R. J., Walker, R. A. and Horrocks, M. (2002). The role of pedometers in the assessment of intermittent claudication. *European Journal of Vascular and Endovascular Surgery*, 23(4), 317–320.

Nordanstig, J., Taft, C., Hensäter, M., Perlander, A., Osterberg, K. and Jivegård, L. (2014). Improved quality of life after 1 year with an invasive versus a noninvasive treatment strategy in claudicants: One-year results of the Invasive Revascularization or Not in Intermittent Claudication (IRONIC) trial. *Circulation*, 130(12), 939–947.

Norgren, L., Hiatt, W. R., Dormandy, J. A., Nehler, M. R., Harris, K. A., Fowkes, F. G., et al. (2007). Inter-society consensus for the management of peripheral arterial disease (TASC II). *Journal of Vascular Surgery*, 45(Suppl S), S5–67.

Ouriel, K. (2001). Peripheral arterial disease. *Lancet*, 358(9289), 1257–1264.

Parmenter, B. J., Raymond, J. and Fiatarone Singh, M. A. (2010). The effect of exercise on haemodynamics in intermittent claudication: A systematic review of randomized controlled trials. *Sports Medicine*, 40(5), 433–447.

Pickering, T. G., Hall, J. E., Appel, L. J., Falkner, B. E., Graves, J., Hill, M. N., et al. (2005). Recommendations for blood pressure measurement in humans and experimental animals: part 1: Blood pressure measurement in humans: a statement for professionals from the Subcommittee of Professional and Public Education of the American Heart Association Council on High Blood Pressure Research. *Circulation*, 111(5), 697–716.

Sandberg, A., Cider, A., Jivegard, L., Nordanstig, J., Wittboldt, S. and Back, M. (2020). Test-retest reliability, agreement, and minimal detectable change in the 6-minute walk test in patients with intermittent claudication. *Journal of Vascular Surgery*, 71(1), 197–203.

Shammas, N. W. (2007). Epidemiology, classification, and modifiable risk factors of peripheral arterial disease. *Vascular Health and Risk Management*, 3(2), 229–234.

Song, P., Rudan, D., Zhu, Y., Fowkes, F. J. I., Rahimi, K., Fowkes, F. G. R., et al. (2019). Global, regional, and national prevalence and risk factors for peripheral artery disease in 2015: An updated systematic review and analysis. *Lancet Global Health*, 7(8), e1020–e1030.

Tew, G., Nawaz, S., Zwierska, I. and Saxton, J. M. (2009). Limb-specific and cross-transfer effects of arm-crank exercise training in patients with symptomatic peripheral arterial disease. *Clinical Science (London, England: 1979)*, 117(12), 405–413.

Tuner, S. L., Easton, C., Wilson, J., Byrne, D. S., Rogers, P., Kilduff, L. P., et al. (2008). Cardiopulmonary responses to treadmill and cycle ergometry exercise in patients with peripheral vascular disease. *Journal of Vascular Surgery*, 47(1), 123–130.

Womack, C. J., Hyman, B. A. and Gardner, A. W. (1998). Prediction of peak oxygen consumption in patients with intermittent claudication. *Angiology*, 49(8), 591–598.

5.8   Exercise testing in children

Craig Williams, Melitta McNarry and Keith Tolfrey

Specific physiological testing guidelines for children and young people should be established instead of adopting those for adults due to age-specific ethics consider-ations, including the ability to provide informed consent; differences in body size, with implications for the appropriate methodological approaches and physiological interpretations; and the impact of growth and maturation on exercise responses.

We delimit the definition of a child or young person as anyone who has not reached his or her 18th birthday. These guidelines are recommendations for valid and reliable techniques in measuring physical and physiological parameters in children and young people and can be adopted for the purpose of testing in a sport and/or research context. Readers are firstly directed to the supplementary material on 'participation of the child in a project'.

Assessment of maturation

Techniques for assessing biological maturity range in practicality, accuracy, required expertise, ethical viability and their ability to capture the continuous nature of this process that all young people experience (Malina et al., 2004). Two methods common to exercise physiology are the use of secondary sexual characteristics (Tanner, 1962) and the estimation of age at peak height velocity (maturity offset; Mirwald et al., 2002). The different stages of sexual maturity can be self-assessed by children and adolescents, with varying degrees of accuracy and reliability (Matsudo and Matsudo, 1994; Taylor et al., 2001), or by a clinician, which is invasive and unlikely to be popu-lar with study participants. This categorises the individual into one of five maturity levels ranging from prepubertal to adult maturation (see supplementary material).

Use of maturity offset is increasingly common in the paediatric literature due to only requiring measures of stature, body mass, leg length and chronological age, subsequently used in sex-specific regression equations available online (www.apps. usask.ca/kin-growthutility/phv_ui.php). The accuracy of the original equations has been questioned, with the equations subsequently simplified and updated for boys and girls (Moore et al., 2015):

$$\text{Girls' maturity offset (years from PHV)} = -7.709133 + (0.0042232 \times (\text{age} \times \text{height})); R^2 = 0.898, \text{SEE} = 0.528$$

DOI: 10.4324/9781003045267-41

Boys' maturity offset (years from PHV) = -7.999994 + (0.0036124 (age $\times$
height)); R^2 = 0.896, SEE = 0.542

Concerns about the accuracy of this technique in exercise-trained young people and those who are early or late maturers (Koziel and Malina, 2018) are also
acknowledged. For a more detailed overview, please refer to Malina (2017).

Anthropometry and body composition

The size, location and rates of change of skeletal muscle and adipose tissue
are frequently measured or estimated in paediatric exercise physiology. Use
of advanced technologies, such as quantitative magnetic resonance imaging
(qMRI), dual energy X-ray absorptiometry (DXA), air displacement plethysmography (ADP), ultrasound and bioelectric impedance analysis (BIA) are more
prevalent in contemporary laboratories; they all require considerable expertise and expense to obtain meaningful, consistent and accurate measurements
within a paediatric population that is growing, developing and maturing (Simoni
et al., 2020).

Critical to the use and understanding of these data are population-specific
software derived from studies conducted with young people, which must at least
take into account maturity, age, sex and ethnic differences in fat-free mass (Fomon
et al., 1982). The meticulous measurement of body mass, stature, skinfolds and
circumferences (Cameron, 2012) is vital, again with adjustments to ensure their
interpretation reflects population-specific differences (see Chapter 3.4 Surface
Anthropometry).

Sex, maturity and ethnic specific equations have been published to estimate
percent body fat (%BF) from skinfolds (e.g., Wendel et al., 2017), which are sample
specific and should be used with caution because of changes in tissue density during childhood (Roemmich et al., 1997). Nevertheless, the prediction equations can
be used if an estimation of percent body fat is desired, provided the participant
characteristics match those in Table 5.8.1.

If body composition is the primary research outcome, qMRI, DXA or ADP
is recommended (see Chapter 4.2 Applications of DEXA), but for secondary outcomes, field-based estimations can be used judiciously if they are well
matched to the population characteristics and the validity is available in the
literature.

Laboratory-based exercise tests

Ergometry

Cycle ergometer or treadmill tests are most common in children. Most children
report being more comfortable on a cycle ergometer than a treadmill (LeMura
et al., 2001) and the quality of the data obtained for measures subject to movement artefact, such as electrocardiograms and blood pressure, is superior during

Table 5.8.1 Sex, maturity and ethnic specific equations for estimation of percent body fat (%BF) from skinfolds

	Non-African American	*African American*
2-Skinfold prediction equations		
Boys		
Tanner 1–3	(13.12×log Sum 2SF) −15.46×log Height) + 64.58	(14.73×log Sum 2SF) −10.55×log Height) + 64.82
Tanner 4–5	(13.12×log Sum 2SF) −13.27×log Height) + 50.92	(14.73×log Sum 2SF) −25.95×log Height) + 110.54
All[a]	(14.28×log Sum 2SF) −21.50×log Height) + 90.69	(14.28×log Sum 2SF) −19.23×log Height) + 78.29
Girls		
All	(13.95×log Sum 2SF) −18.09×log Height) + 77.17	(13.95×log Sum 2SF) −18.09×log Height) + 75.40
4-Skinfold prediction equations		
Boys		
Tanner 1–3	(12.41×log Sum 4SF) −16.90×log Height) + 66.78	(14.68×log Sum 4SF) −16.90×log Height) + 58.32
Tanner 4–5	(12.41×log Sum 4SF) −16.90×log Height) + 64.94	(14.68×log Sum 4SF) −16.90×log Height) + 58.32
All[a]	(12.74×log Sum4) −21.47×Log Height) + 87.82	(14.68×log Sum 4SF) −21.47×log Height) + 79.82
Girls		
All	(13.99×log Sum 4SF) −21.42×Log Height) + 85.65	(13.99×log Sum 4SF) −14.69×log Height) + 51.04

[a] Simplified equation that does not require Tanner staging; Tanner = secondary sexual characteristic levels of biological maturity; sum 2SF = sum of triceps and subscapular skinfolds; sum 4SF = sum of triceps, biceps, subscapular and suprailiac skinfolds; log = natural logarithm

cycle-based exercise (Takken et al., 2017). However, children may prematurely stop cycle tests due to local peripheral muscle fatigue, potentially limiting true maximal efforts. Conversely, despite its greater commonality with habitual movements, some children may adopt an unnatural gait on a treadmill and hold the handrail which should be strongly discouraged since it alters physiological responses (Ellestad, 2003).

Mostly due to differences in posture and the exercising muscle mass, cycle and treadmill exercise results are not directly comparable, with treadmill exercise eliciting a greater maximal oxygen uptake ($\dot{V}O_2$max), stroke volume, heart rate and cardiac output (Forbregd et al., 2019). Recently, a wider range of ergometers have been used in children, including rowing ergometers, arm cranks and swim benches. Whilst beneficial regarding sport-specificity, it is important that any ergometers used are appropriately adapted for children and that the load is accurately applied and measured to enable the interpretation.

Aerobic performance (cardiorespiratory fitness)

The criterion measure of aerobic performance is $\dot{V}O_2$max using specialised respiratory gas analysis equipment (see Chapter 3.7 Respiratory Gas Analysis). Following suitable preliminary pilot work with a sub-sample of the target population and familiarisation, our experience has supported a comfortable fixed treadmill speed or cycling cadence for the young person, with progressive increments in gradient or resistive load, respectively, until running or cycling cannot be sustained (i.e., volitional exhaustion). Paediatric exercise test considerations may include more extensive familiarisation with the ergometers and laboratory environment, appreciation of the young person's size – particularly for treadmill safety rails or harnesses and cycle-ergometer seat and handlebar height and crank length – and expired gas mouthpieces and facemasks. The timing of the increments will depend on whether other measures are required (heart rate or blood lactate) and if these need to demonstrate a physiological steady state (e.g., 1 or ≥ 3 min) (Zakrzewski and Tolfrey, 2012). Until quite recently, $\dot{V}O_2$max was expressed as peak $\dot{V}O_2$ for young people who did not demonstrate a plateau in oxygen consumption at the volitional termination of exercise, supported by secondary physiological measures (e.g., maximal heart rate or respiratory exchange ratio). However, this has been challenged with the suggestion that an extra 'verification' exercise bout be completed at a constant work rate in excess (110% $\pm$ 5%) of the final work rate from the initial test protocol (Barker et al., 2011). Finally, despite Tanner's (1949) warning to exercise physiologists not to adjust $\dot{V}O_2$max using a ratio scaling technique with total body mass (i.e., $mL \cdot kg^{-1} \cdot min^{-1}$) because it was 'theoretically fallacious', this practice has still continued although the limitations have recently been reiterated (Armstrong and Welsman, 2020). Time will tell whether active muscle mass or even total fat-free mass will be used as recommended. For readers looking for exemplar protocols for measuring $\dot{V}O_2$ max:

- Treadmill – fixed speed (preferred comfortable jogging 5–12 $km \cdot h^{-1}$) with 1% gradient increases each minute; alternatively increases in gradient only increased once maximum running speed is obtained.
- Cycling – fixed cadence (preferred comfortable pace 50–80 $revs \cdot min^{-1}$) with 10 to 25 W increases each minute.
- Faster cadences can offset lighter loads when cycling to avoid local muscular fatigue in the legs.

Anaerobic performance testing

Anaerobic testing protocols for children are less well developed than aerobic tests with no 'gold-standard' measure (Ingle and Tolfrey, 2013) and significant variations in methodologies used. The most widely used measure remains the Wingate test, commonly conducted on a cycle ergometer for 30 s, although other exercise modalities and test durations can be used (Chia et al., 1997; McNarry et al.,

2011). The Wingate test allows the determination of peak power, mean power and fatigue index. These power metrics are influenced by the load applied; a load of 75 g and 45 g·kg⁻¹ body mass are recommended for lower- and upper-body Wingate tests, respectively. A rolling start is advisable to avoid issues with overcoming flywheel inertia which are likely to be greater in younger and/or smaller children. A limitation of the Wingate test is that it is not a truly anaerobic test, with a significant aerobic contribution that depends on the exercise modality, age and training status (Chia et al., 1997; McNarry et al., 2011).

More recently, the 30 m overground sprint has been used as a measure of anaerobic performance, requiring participants to complete up to three all-out sprints from a standing start, with the force-velocity-power relationship subsequently derived. Whilst reported to be reliable and applicable to sporting contexts in children (Runacres et al., 2019), the associated biomechanical model is not overly accessible for practitioners.

Isokinetic strength testing

Isokinetic dynamometry is the gold-standard method of assessing muscle strength (Santos et al., 2013), with the knee the most widely studied joint due to ease of evaluation and the knee extensor strength potentially representing total strength of the lower extremities (Muñoz-Bermejo et al., 2019). Provided appropriate standards are followed to ensure the correct positioning and stabilising of the child, isokinetic dynamometry is safe (Fagher et al., 2016) and allows the investigation of a range of angular velocities during both eccentric and concentric movements (Iga et al., 2006). There is little consensus regarding the optimal testing protocol, although a familiarisation session is essential. A variety of velocities have been used, ranging from 60–180°·s⁻¹, with up to 90 s rest periods between efforts and 3–10 maximal efforts typically utilised.

Field testing for fitness/performance

Field-based tests offer indirect estimations of health- and skill-related physical fitness in a manner that is easier and less expensive to administer than laboratory tests and is appropriate for population-level studies (Tabacchi et al., 2019). There are numerous physical fitness testing batteries, with the EUROFIT being most widely used in children, for which both norm and criterion referenced scales are available (Kemper and Mechelen, 1996). Criterion referenced scales provide levels that all children are expected to achieve rather than percentile values for each test, which can result in inappropriate peer-comparisons that fail to account for the influence of growth and maturation. Whilst field-based tests are potentially useful for large cohort studies, it is important to highlight that such tests do not provide equivalent information to physiological tests in a laboratory. Indeed, there has been significant controversy regarding field-based tests in recent years regarding their validity and reliability (Armstrong and Welsman, 2019; Tomkinson et al., 2019).

References

Armstrong, N. and Welsman, J. (2019). Twenty-metre shuttle run: (mis)representation, (mis) interpretation and (mis)use. *British Journal of Sports Medicine*, 53(19), 1199.

Armstrong, N. and Welsman, J. (2020). Traditional and new perspectives on youth cardio-respiratory fitness. *Medicine and Science in Sports and Exercise*, 52, 2563–2573.

Barker, A. R., Williams, C. A., Jones, A. M. and Armstrong, N. (2011). Establishing maximal oxygen uptake in young people during a ramp cycle test to exhaustion. *British Journal of Sports Medicine*, 45, 498–503.

Cameron, N. (2012). The measurement of human growth. In N. Cameron and B. Bogin (eds.), *Human Growth and Development* (2nd ed.), pp. 487–513. Cambridge, USA: Academic Press.

Chia, M., Armstrong, N. and Childs D. (1997). The assessment of children's anaerobic performance using modifications of the Wingate Anaerobic Test. *Pediatric Exercise Science*, 9(1), 80–89.

Ellestad, M. (2003). *Stress Testing*. Oxford: Oxford University Press.

Fagher, K., Fritzson, A. and Drake, A. M. (2016). Test-retest reliability of isokinetic knee strength measurements in children aged 8 to 10 years. *Sports Health*, 8(3), 255–259.

Fomon, S. J., Haschke, F., Ziegler, E. E. and Nelson, S. E. (1982). Body composition from birth to age 10 years. *American Journal of Clinical Nutrition*, 35, 1169–1175.

Forbregd, T. R., Aloyseus, M. A., Berg, A. and Greve, G. (2019). Cardiopulmonary capacity in children during exercise testing: The differences between treadmill and upright and supine cycle ergometry. *Frontiers in Physiology*, 10, 1440.

Iga, J., George, K., Lees, A. and Reilly, T. (2006). Reliability of assessing indices of isokinetic leg strength in pubertal soccer players. *Pediatric Exercise Science*, 18(4), 436–445.

Ingle, L. and Tolfrey, K. (2013). The variability of high intensity exercise tests in pre-pubertal boys. *International Journal of Sports Medicine*, 34(12), 1063–1069.

Kemper, H. C. G. and Mechelen, W. V. (1996). Physical fitness testing of children: A European perspective. *Pediatric Exercise Science*, 8(3), 201–214.

Koziel, S. M. and Malina, R. M. (2018). Modified maturity offset prediction equations: validation in independent longitudinal samples of boys and girls. *Sports Medicine*, 48, 221–236.

LeMura, L. M., von Duvillard, S. P., Cohen, S. L., Root, C. J., Chelland, S. A., Andreacci, J., et al. (2001). Treadmill and cycle ergometry testing in 5- to 6-year-old children. *European Journal of Applied Physiology*, 85(5), 472–478.

Malina, R. M. (2017). Assessment of biological maturation. In N. Armstrong and W. van Mechelen (eds.), *Oxford Textbook of Children's Sport and Exercise Medicine* (3rd ed.), pp. 3–11. Oxford, UK: Oxford University Press.

Malina, R. M., Bouchard, C. and Bar-Or, O. (2004). *Growth, Maturation and Physical Activity* (2nd ed.). Champaign, USA: Human Kinetics.

Matsudo, S. M. M. and Matsudo, V. K. R. (1994). Self-assessment and physician assessment of sexual maturation in Brazilian boys and girls: Concordance and reproducibility. *American Journal of Human Biology*, 6, 451–455.

McNarry, M. A., Welsman, J. R. and Jones, A. M. (2011). The influence of training and maturity status on girls' responses to short-term, high-intensity upper- and lower-body exercise. *Applied Physiology of Nutrition and Metabolism*, 36(3), 344–352.

Mirwald, R. L., Baxter-Jones, A. D., Bailey, D. A. and Beunen, G. P. (2002). An assessment of maturity from anthropometric measurements. *Medicine and Science in Sports and Exercise*, 34, 689–694.

Moore, S. A., McKay, H. A., Macdonald, H., Nettlefold, L., Baxter-Jones, A. D., Cameron, N., & Brasher, P. M. (2015). Enhancing a somatic maturity prediction model. *Medicine and Science in Sports and Exercise*, 47(8), 1755–1764. https://doi.org/10.1249/MSS.0000000000000588

Muñoz-Bermejo, L., Pérez-Gómez, J., Manzano, F., Collado-Mateo, D., Villafaina, S. and Adsuar, J. C. (2019). Reliability of isokinetic knee strength measurements in children: A systematic review and meta-analysis. *PLoS One*, 14(12), e0226274.

Rabelo, M., Nunes, G. S., da Costa Amante, N. M., de Noronha, M. and Fachin-Martins, E. (2016). Reliability of muscle strength assessment in chronic post-stroke hemiparesis: A systematic review and meta-analysis. *Top Stroke Rehabilitation*, 23(1), 26–36.

Roemmich, J. N., Clark, P. A., Weltman, A. and Rogol, A. D. (1997). Alterations in growth and body composition during puberty: I. Comparing multicompartment body composition models. *Journal of Applied Physiology*, 83, 927–935.

Runacres, A., Bezodis, N. E., Mackintosh, K. A. and McNarry, M. A. (2019). The reliability of force-velocity-power profiling during over-ground sprinting in children and adolescents. *Journal of Sports Sciences*, 37(18), 2131–2137.

Santos, A. N., Pavão, S. L., Avila, M. A., Salvini, T. F. and Rocha, N. A. (2013). Reliability of isokinetic evaluation in passive mode for knee flexors and extensors in healthy children. *Brazilian Journal of Physical Therapy*, 17(2), 112–120.

Simoni, P., Guglielmi, R. and Gómez, M. P. A. (2020). Imaging of body composition in children. *Quantitative Imaging in Medicine and Surgery*, 10, 1661–1671.

Tabacchi, G., Lopez Sanchez, G. F., Nese Sahin, F., Kizilyalli, M., Genchi, R., Basile M., et al. (2019). Field-based tests for the assessment of physical fitness in children and adolescents practicing sport: A systematic review within the ESA program. *Sustainability*, 11(24), 7187.

Takken, T., Bongers, B. C., van Brussel, M., Haapala, E. A. and Hulzebos, E. H. J. (2017). Cardiopulmonary exercise testing in pediatrics. *Annual American Thoracic Society*, 14(Supp. 1), S123–S128.

Tanner, J. M. (1949). Fallacy of per-weight and per-surface area standards and their relation to spurious correlation. *Journal of Applied Physiology*, 2, 1–15.

Tanner, J. M. (1962). *Growth of Adolescents* (2nd ed.). Oxford, UK: Blackwell Scientific.

Taylor, S. J. C., Whincup, P. H., Hindmarsh, P. C., Lampe, F., Odoki, K. and Cook, D. G. (2001). Performance of a new pubertal self-assessment questionnaire: A preliminary study. *Paediatric and Perinatal Epidemiology*, 15, 88–94.

Tomkinson, G. R., Lang, J. J., Léger, L. A., Olds, T. S., Ortega, F. B., Ruiz, J. R., et al. (2019). Response to criticisms of the 20 m shuttle run test: Deflections, distortions and distractions. *British Journal of Sports Medicine*, 53(19), 1200–1201.

Wendel, D., Weber, D., Leonard, M. B., Magge, S. N., Kelly, A., Stallings, V. A., Pipan, M. Stettler, N. and Zemel, B. S. (2017). Body composition estimation using skinfolds in children with and without health conditions affecting growth and body composition. *Annals of Human Biology*, 44, 108–120.

Zakrzewski, J. K. and Tolfrey, K. (2012). Comparison of fat oxidation over a range of intensities during treadmill and cycling exercise in children. *European Journal of Applied Exercise Physiology*, 112, 163–171.

5.9 Exercise testing in older adults

Matt W. Hill and Michael J. Price

Researchers define the term 'older adult' as being over the age of 65 years (Orimo et al., 2006). Individuals of the same chronological age demonstrate distinct reductions in cardiovascular, pulmonary, musculoskeletal, metabolic and neurological functioning (Khan et al., 2017). However, the observation that individuals do not age at the same rate has led to the concept of physiological (or biological) ageing, which specifically relates to compromised function. The progressive degenerative adaptations noted earlier compromise physical capacities, including muscle strength, balance, mobility and endurance, which can profoundly affect the ability to perform everyday activities. As such, the execution of activities of daily living (e.g., ascending and descending stairs or rising from a chair) can be close to their maximal capabilities (Hortobágyi et al., 2003). Understanding the effects of biological ageing on physiological function at rest and during exercise is crucial to inform researchers and practitioners of how to perform physiological assessments in older adults. This chapter presents recommendations for exercise testing in older adults with an emphasis on functional evaluation.

Maximal and submaximal cardiopulmonary exercise testing

Maximum or peak oxygen consumption ($\dot{V}O_2$max / $\dot{V}O_2$peak) declines with advancing age at a rate of ~10% per decade after 25 years of age and ~15% between 50 and 75 years of age (Hawkins and Wiswell, 2003). The requirement of exercising to volitional exhaustion when assessing $\dot{V}O_2$max often leads to concerns regarding patient safety. However, making subtle adjustments to an exercise testing protocol improves tolerance, comfort and safety when maximally testing older adults.

Exercise mode

In older adults, researchers typically conduct exercise stress testing and prescribed training using a treadmill or cycle ergometer. If balance and mobility are limited, seated exercise (i.e., arm-crank ergometry) provides a safe and well-tolerated alternative for older adults. Values of $\dot{V}O_2$peak during seated arm-crank ergometry

DOI: 10.4324/9781003045267-42

are ~20% lower than those during leg cycling, primarily due to the smaller volume of exercising muscle mass (Hill et al., 2018). With an unconditioned state, peripheral muscle fatigue is a prominent factor causing early test termination during both arm-crank ergometry and leg cycling. If using a treadmill, a safety harness attached to an overhead suspension arm is essential, and a handrail may be required.

Speed and grade increases

Initial workloads for arm and leg cycling should be light (e.g., 25 W and 50 W, respectively) and increments should be small (e.g., 5 $W \cdot min^{-1}$ and 10 $W \cdot min^{-1}$, respectively; Hill et al., 2018). The initial speed for treadmill testing should be between 2.0–4.0 $km.h^{-1}$ with a grade of 0%. Increasing grade rather than speed may need to be considered according to walking confidence and ability. For example, grade could be increased by 1% every minute or 2% every 2 minutes at a constant speed of 3.0 $km.h^{-1}$. If submaximal data are not required, then a steady but slow increase in both speed and grade is most appropriate.

End criteria

End-of-test criteria for achieving $\dot{V}O_2max$ / $\dot{V}O_2peak$ should be adjusted in older adults. Although the variability of maximal heart rate precludes its use as a criterion for maximal effort in older adults, where appropriate, the Tanaka age adjusted-prediction equation should be used (208–0.7 × age; Tanaka et al., 2001). Subtracting 20 $beats \cdot min^{-1}$ from this equation should provide a reasonable estimate for arm cycling (Hill et al., 2016). Typically, blood lactate concentrations of >3.5 (females) and >4.0 (males) $mmol \cdot L^{-}1$, and an RER of >1.0 should be expected for adults over the age of 65 years.

Submaximal exercise protocols to predict $\dot{V}O_2max$ that incorporate walking, cycling or stepping are useful when laboratory equipment or physician supervision is unavailable. Submaximal tests are typically guided by heart rate responses to one or more submaximal workloads and a regression equation used to predict $\dot{V}O_2max$ (see Noonan and Dean, 2000 for a review). Test selection depends on generic factors, such as the accuracy and precision required, equipment available, type of predictive parameter, safety and supervision, as well as population-specific factors, including functional limitation, disability, primary and secondary pathologies, mobility, balance and cognitive limitations, age, weight, nutritional status and the use of assistive walking aids.

Assessing functional fitness in older adults

The majority of studies evaluating the functional capacity of older adults utilise a battery of strength, endurance and functional tests. Normative values for the following tests are shown in Table 5.9.1.

Table 5.9.1 Typical values for key outcome variables in older adults

Outcome	Sex/Age	Norm Values/Range	Reference
Peak oxygen uptake	Men and women *65–66 years*		
	Cycle ergometry	23 ml.kg.$^{-1}$min.$^{-1}$	Hill et al. (2018)
	Arm-crank ergometry	17 ml.kg.$^{-1}$min.$^{-1}$	
	Men *66–68 years*		
	Cycle ergometry	29–31 ml.kg.$^{-1}$min.$^{-1}$	Pogliaghi et al. (2006)
	Arm-crank ergometry	22–24 ml.kg.$^{-1}$min.$^{-1}$	
30 s arm curl test (# reps)	Men *60–64 years* *65–69 years* *70–74 years* *75–79 years*	16–22 15–21 14–21 13–19	Jones and Rikli (2002)
	Women *60–64 years* *65–69 years* *70–74 years* *75–79 years*	13–19 12–18 12–17 11–17	
Six-minute walk test (m)	Years 60–69 years 70–79 years 80–89 years	571 (380–782) 460–609 m 442–578 m 316–507 m	Casanova et al. (2011) Bohannon et al. (2007)
Five times sit-to-stand (sec)	60–69 years 70–79 years 80–89 years	11.4 s 12.6 s 14.8 s	Bohannon (2006)
Grip strength (kg)	*65–69 years* Men Right hand Left hand	 41.7 (35.4–47.9) 38.2 (32.0–44.4)	Bohannon et al. (2006)
	Women Right hand Left hand	 25.6 (22.5–28.8) 22.9 (19.6–26.2)	
	70–74 years Mean hand Left hand	 38.2 (32.0–44.5) 36.2 (30.3–42.1)	
	Women Right hand Left hand	 24.2 (20.7–27.8) 22.5 (19.1–25.8)	
	75+ years Men Right hand Left men	 28.0 (12.7–31.0) 29.8 (24.8–34.7)	
	Women Right hand Left hand	 18.0 (16.0–19.9) 16.4 (14.7–18.1)	

Muscular strength and endurance

Arm curl test

Upper body strength and endurance are crucial for executing many activities of daily living. The 30 s arm curl test is widely used to measure muscle strength of the upper extremities. The test records the number of elbow flexions and extensions performed with a dumbbell (women ~2.5 kg; men ~3.5 kg) in 30 s. The participant is seated on a straight-backed chair without arm rests and feet flat on the floor, holding the weight in the dominant hand at the side of the body in the fully extended elbow position. The elbow should be braced against the side of the body to stabilise the upper arm. If dumbbells are unavailable, containers filled with sand (e.g., milk cartons) are acceptable. The total number of repetitions performed with good form in 30 s is recorded. Arm curls greater than halfway through the range of movement at the end of 30 s are counted as complete repetitions.

Grip strength

Maximal grip strength is widely used for the measurement of muscle strength and has been suggested as a biomarker of ageing (Sayer and Kirkwood, 2015). Low grip strength is consistently associated with poor outcomes, including care dependence, all-cause and disease-specific mortality, falls, fractures and hospitalisation. Variable procedures and cut-off points are evident for the older adult population, so we recommend that practitioners use a standardised measurement protocol (e.g., the Southampton protocol; Roberts et al., 2011). Briefly, a handgrip strength dynamometer is gripped with flexed fingers and base of the thumb with the participant seated, elbow at side and hand in a neutral position. Participants should be encouraged to squeeze as hard as possible for 3–5 s. The highest reading of three attempts is recorded.

Chair sit-to-stand performance

The ability to rise out of a chair independently is an essential part of daily living in older adults. Researchers use the sit-to-stand manoeuvre as a measure of lower limb strength (most notably the quadriceps femoris) in older adults, but several variations of this test exist. Protocols assessing the time it takes to perform a given number of sit-to-stand repetitions (usually 5) are subject to 'floor' effects, i.e., some lower-functioning older adults might not be able to complete five attempts and, therefore, do not get a score assigned. Testing the maximal number of repetitions over a pre-defined period, typically 30 or 60 s, should overcome this issue. Participants are instructed to sit down on a chair (recommended dimensions: height ~45 cm, width ~50 cm and depth ~40 cm) with arms folded across the chest and feet shoulder width apart. The chair back should be placed against a wall to prevent movement. At the signal 'go', participants are required to stand up fully with complete knee and hip extension and sit down fully as quickly and/or as many times as possible, with participants verbally encouraged throughout the test. The score is the total number of stands performed correctly (full standing position attained and fully seated between stands) in the pre-defined time or the amount of time taken to achieve the desired number of repetitions. During timed tests, if a participant is standing more than halfway, this should be counted as a full repetition.

Aerobic capacity

Six-minute walk test

Walking is a fundamental prerequisite to quality of life and independent living. A variety of walking tests exist, including timed-based tests (e.g., 6-minute, 9-minute and 12-minute walk tests), fixed-distance tests (e.g., half-mile and 2 km walk test) and velocity-based tests (e.g., incremental shuttle walk test). However, as a valid, reliable, readily available and well-tolerated method, the 6-minute walk test is the most extensively researched and best established alternative measure of aerobic capacity in older adults and is more reflective of activities of daily living than the other walk tests. For this test, a 20–60 m walkway or flat 50 m rectangular course (20 m × 5 m) is marked off in 5 m segments with cones and chairs, for resting, positioned at various locations along the course. Because courses may differ in design, due to the testing space available, consistency across testing sessions is important. Participants walk as fast as they can around the course, covering as much distance as possible in the 6-minute time limit. The distance walked is recorded to the nearest meter. Participants should give the impression that they could not have gone any farther. The timed 6-minute walk test has a good correlation with a direct measure of $\dot{V}O_2max$ (r = 0.59; Zhang et al., 2017).

Balance and mobility

Balance control can be subdivided into four categories (Table 5.9.2): static steady-state balance (i.e., maintaining a steady position while standing), dynamic steady-state balance (i.e., maintaining a steady position while walking), proactive balance (i.e., anticipation of a predicted postural disturbance, such as leaning or reaching) and reactive balance (i.e., compensation of an unpredicted postural disturbance) (Shumway-Cook and Woollacott, 2007). Balance performance is often viewed as a 'general ability', suggesting that the various types of balance are interlinked. Contrary to this view, these components represent very different subsets of our balance repertoire (Kiss et al., 2018). The ideal balance screening measurement should be quick and simple to administer, provide easily interpretable results and be adequately sensitive to reveal emerging deterioration in balance control. Functional assessments of balance are easy to use, do not require expensive equipment, are usually quick to administer and are predictive of falls. However, these assessments are typically subjective, show ceiling and/or floor effects, are somewhat rudimentary and usually lack the ability to capture balance impairment at its early phase. In a laboratory setting, researchers explore postural stability using objective measures of posturography. Advantages of this approach over functional assessments include the avoidance of subjective scoring systems and a greater sensitivity

Table 5.9.2 Common tests of balance in older adults

Balance Component	Specific Tests
Static steady-state balance	• Centre of pressure movements during quiet bipedal standing (manipulations that render the task more challenging, such as reducing the size of the base of support, closing the eyes or standing on a compliant surface) • Ability to stand for a pre-defined length of time (usually up to 60 s) on one leg
Dynamic steady-state balance	• Ability to stand for a pre-defined length of time (usually up to 30 s) on a free moving platform • Heel-to-toe beam walking time • Fast and comfortable gait speed • Instrumented gait analysis
Proactive balance	• Multi-directional functional reach test • Timed up-and-go test • Star Excursion Balance Test/Y Balance Test • Step test, rapid step test and four-square step test • Limits of stability test (force platform) • Forward or lateral jump time to stabilisation (i.e., Dynamic Postural Stability Index)
Reactive balance	• Standing in a bipedal or unipedal stance and responding to a platform perturbation • Reactive stepping during gait in response to surface perturbations using movable platforms, treadmills or walkways with tripping obstacles or sudden speed changes • Balance recovery using a tether release protocol

to small changes. However, assessment of quiet stance using posturography lacks ecological validity, often demonstrates substantial inter- and intra-participant variability, requires expensive equipment and may not adequately stress an individual's postural control system. Thus, this test represents a relatively small subset of our balance repertoire.

References

Bohannon, R. W. (2006). Reference values for the five-repetition sit-to-stand test: A descriptive meta-analysis of data from elders. *Perceptual and Motor Skills*, 103(1), 215–222.

Bohannon, R. W. (2007). Six-minute walk test: A meta-analysis of data from apparently healthy elders. *Topics in Geriatric Rehabilitation*, 23(2), 155–160.

Bohannon, R. W., Peolsson, A., Massy-Westropp, N., Desrosiers, J. and Bear-Lehman, J. (2006). Reference values for adult grip strength measured with a Jamar dynamometer: A descriptive meta-analysis. *Physiotherapy*, 92(1), 11–15.

Casanova, C., Celli, B. R., Barria, P., Casas, A., Cote, C., De Torres, J. P., . . . Aguirre-Jaime, A. (2011). The 6-min walk distance in healthy subjects: Reference standards from seven countries. *European Respiratory Journal*, 37(1), 150–156.

Hawkins, S. A. and Wiswell, R. A. (2003). Rate and mechanism of maximal oxygen consumption decline with aging. *Sports Medicine*, 33(12), 877–888.

Hill, M., Oxford, S., Duncan, M. and Price, M. (2018). Arm-crank training improves postural stability and physical functioning in older people. *Experimental Gerontology*, 113, 218–227.

Hill, M., Talbot, C. and Price, M. (2016). Predicted maximal heart rate for upper body exercise testing. *Clinical Physiology and Functional Imaging*, 36(2), 155–158.

Hortobágyi, T., Mizelle, C., Beam, S. and DeVita, P. (2003). Old adults perform activities of daily living near their maximal capabilities. *The Journals of Gerontology Series A: Biological Sciences and Medical Sciences*, 58(5), M453–M460.

Jones, C. J. and Rikli, R. E. (2002). Measuring functional. *The Journal on Active Aging*, 1(24–30).

Khan, S. S., Singer, B. D. and Vaughan, D. E. (2017). Molecular and physiological manifestations and measurement of aging in humans. *Aging Cell*, 16(4), 624–633.

Kiss, R., Schedler, S. and Muehlbauer, T. (2018). Associations between types of balance performance in healthy individuals across the lifespan: A systematic review and meta-analysis. *Frontiers in Physiology*, 9, 1366.

Noonan, V. and Dean, E. (2000). Submaximal exercise testing: Clinical application and interpretation. *Physical Therapy*, 80(8), 782–807.

Orimo, H., Ito, H., Suzuki, T., Araki, A., Hosoi, T. and Sawabe, M. (2006). Reviewing the definition of "elderly". *Geriatrics & Gerontology International*, 6(3), 149–158.

Pogliaghi, S., Terziotti, P., Cevese, A., Balestreri, F. and Schena, F. (2006). Adaptations to endurance training in the healthy elderly: Arm cranking versus leg cycling. *European Journal of Applied Physiology*, 97(6), 723–731. https://doi.org/10.1007/s00421-006-0229-2

Roberts, H. C., Denison, H. J., Martin, H. J., Patel, H. P., Syddall, H., Cooper, C. and Sayer, A. A. (2011). A review of the measurement of grip strength in clinical and epidemiological studies: towards a standardised approach. *Age and Ageing*, 40(4), 423–429.

Sayer, A. A. and Kirkwood, T. B. (2015). Grip strength and mortality: A biomarker of ageing?. *Lancet* (London, England), 386(9990), 226–227.

Shumway-Cook, A. and Woollacott, M. H. (2007). *Motor Control: Translating Research into Clinical Practice*. Philadelphia, Baltimore: Lippincott Williams & Wilkins.

Tanaka, H., Monahan, K. D. and Seals, D. R. (2001). Age-predicted maximal heart rate revisited. *Journal of the American College of Cardiology*, 37(1), 153–156.

Zhang, Q., Lu, H., Pan, S., Lin, Y., Zhou, K. and Wang, L. (2017). 6MWT performance and its correlations with $\dot{V}O2$ and handgrip strength in home-dwelling mid-aged and older Chinese. *International Journal of Environmental Research and Public Health*, 14(5), 473.

5.10 Exercise testing in females

Kirsty M. Hicks, Anthony C. Hackney, Michael Dooley and Georgie Bruinvels

Practitioners often pay close attention to the effect of circadian, diurnal and ultra-dian rhythms on exercise and health in athletes. However, in female athletes, the menstrual cycle, which is an infradian rhythm, is sometimes overlooked. The menstrual cycle is an essential biological rhythm during which ovarian sex hormones, specifically oestrogen and progesterone, fluctuate. These hormones exert biological effects on several body systems, including the reproductive, immune, cardiovascular, neuromuscular and musculoskeletal systems (e.g., Enns and Tiidus, 2010; Ansdell et al., 2019). Consequently, the cyclical pattern of changes in hormonal concentrations can result in a plethora of systemic physiological-psychological alterations, which can affect exercise responses. Despite these potential effects, most practitioners do not consider the influence of the menstrual cycle. Therefore, this chapter presents a systematic framework for working with female athletes, by providing insight into the implementation and interpretation of screening and monitoring tools (Figure 5.10.1). Screening tools, including questionnaires and/or interviews, are designed to obtain medical and family history, and identify any pre-existing conditions and risks which might precede medical conditions. Monitoring, conversely, is a systematic, continuous process of collecting and analysing data to detect changes from the individual's 'baseline'.

The menstrual cycle

Menstrual cycle length is calculated from the first day of a menstrual bleed to the first day of the next menstrual bleed. Due to large inter- and intra-individual variability, the length of a menstrual cycle can range from 21 to 35 days. Consistent deviations from this range might indicate an irregularity (e.g., <21 days polymenorrhoea, >35 days oligomenorrhoea). Hormonal fluctuations throughout the menstrual cycle create three distinct hormonal milieu: the early follicular (low oestrogen and progesterone), late follicular (high oestrogen and low progesterone) and the mid-luteal (high oestrogen and high progesterone) phases. However, significant hormonal shifts occur when transitioning between phases, which might be symptomatic. Another essential time point is ovulation, a fundamental marker of a eumenorrheic cycle, which occurs approximately 36 hours following the surge in luteinising hormone.

DOI: 10.4324/9781003045267-43

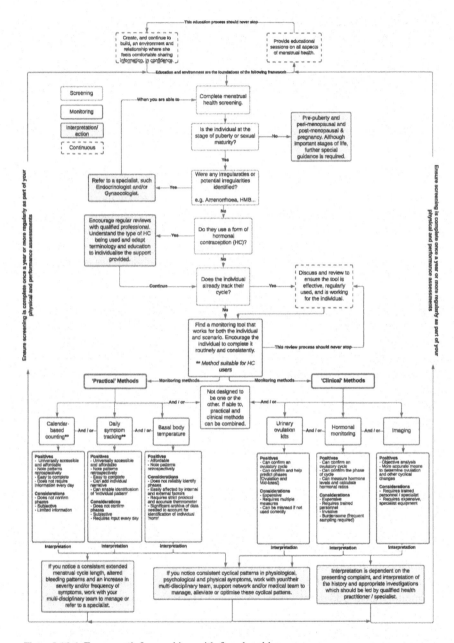

Figure 5.10.1 Framework for working with female athletes.

The fluctuations in sex hormones can be altered by pregnancy, chronological age and use of hormonal contraceptives. Although puberty, pregnancy and menopause are vital stages of the female lifespan, they are beyond the scope of this chapter. Secondary to birth control, hormonal contraceptives are used by both recreational and elite athletes to manipulate the menstrual cycle and manage dysfunction or unwanted symptoms. Approximately 50% of elite female athletes use a form of hormonal contraceptive. Of note, the extent and process by which hormonal contraceptives alter fluctuations in sex hormones must be understood, because it varies substantially with each type, and even brand, of hormonal contraceptive (Elliott-Sale et al., 2020).

Screening

Screening can be used for the identification, and prevention, of medical issues. It is also for establishing performance-related implications. There are a range of different symptoms and irregularities that females of a reproductive age can experience, such as amenorrhoea (no periods), heavy menstrual bleeding and premenstrual symptoms. Information regarding whether these might be present, and if action is required (e.g., referral to specialist), can be obtained through menstrual history screening. This can be done through a questionnaire and/or an interview. The screening process will also highlight the potential need for and focus of education, in addition to identifying the best form(s) of monitoring. As a minimum, screening should be repeated once a year. The frequency can be increased if indicated by history or monitoring (e.g., amenorrhoea).

Monitoring

Monitoring day-to-day physical, physiological and psychological changes across the menstrual cycle can provide insight into menstrual health and identify any potential perturbations. There are multiple methods of monitoring, some of which provide more discernment than others, but typically at a greater financial and logistical cost.

Practical methods are easy and affordable to implement. Calendar-based counting is the simplest tool, only requiring logging bleed days. From this data, menstrual cycle length can be calculated alongside bleeding patterns. Calendar-based counting is also required to support other monitoring tools (e.g., basal body temperature, urinary ovulation kits). If appropriate, calendar-based counting can be modified to narrate physical, physiological, pathological and psychological symptoms, e.g., cervical mucus, breast tenderness, menstrual cramps, bloating, mood, fatigue and physical performance. Over time (>3 cycles), consistent monitoring can be used, retrospectively and preemptively, to identify menstrual patterns and associations. Unfortunately, due to the subjective nature of these monitoring tools, physiological confirmation of menstrual phases and/or ovulation is not possible. Alternatively, tracking basal body temperature can infer ovulation and, with calendar-based counting, menstrual phases. Twenty-four hours prior to ovulation, basal body temperature reaches its thermal nadir, followed by a 0.2–0.5°C post-ovulatory rise, which plateaus and then returns preceding menstruation.

Clinical monitoring methods can provide further insight into menstrual health, pathology and performance associations. In tandem with calendar-based counting, urinary ovulation can be used to confirm an ovulatory cycle. Generally, about five days before predicted ovulation, the individual tests her urine daily, until the luteinising hormone surge preceding ovulation is detected. Hormonal concentrations can be measured directly or indirectly through body fluid. Knowing the concentration of these hormones can allow for specific phase verification and detect hormonal deficiencies which could indicate menstrual irregularities such as luteal phase deficiency, and prompt further investigations. This could include a physical examination by appropriately trained and qualified practitioners.

Interpretation

For practical monitoring methods, at least three months of menstrual cycle monitoring is required to establish a 'baseline'. From this archive of data, irregularities such as heavy menstrual bleeding, amenorrhoea, or premenstrual symptoms can be identified. If menstrual irregularities are identified, a multi-disciplinary team approach should be applied with potential referral to specialist. If patterns of or associations between hormonal changes and physical performance and/or readiness are observed (e.g., mood changes, fatigability or clumsiness), a multi-disciplinary team approach should also be applied.

Considerations

As noted, the menstrual cycle can be manipulated via hormonal contraceptives. Users of hormonal contraceptives still experience cyclical symptoms and underlying bleeding irregularities; therefore, screening, monitoring and appropriate management in these female athletes remain important. Furthermore, practitioners should be mindful that hormonal contraceptives use might mask an underlying pathology. Not all tools are suitable for all types, and brands of hormonal contraceptives; consequently, terminology, screening and monitoring tools should be individualised, and appropriate for her choice of hormonal contraceptive.

Performance testing

Performance tests are often carried out several times per season/year to monitor progression, evaluate changes in performance, identify the athletes' strengths and weaknesses and facilitate individualisation of training programs. These tests should be standardised to minimise variation and support the detection of 'true' changes in performance. Whilst many female athletes cite unwanted symptoms associated with specific times in their menstrual cycle, which might affect perceived readiness and ability to perform, to date, research is inconclusive on the effect of the menstrual cycle on performance *per se*. A large literature review reported that, on average, performance across the menstrual cycle is trivially reduced during the early follicular phase compared with other phases of the menstrual cycle (McNulty et al., 2020). Thus, to further standardise female athlete testing, it is recommended that the menstrual cycle phase is recorded, and, when possible, replicated for the next performance test(s). If an aim is to establish any potential effect of an individual's menstrual cycle on her performance, systematic monitoring over at least three cycles is needed along with appropriate verification of phases. While specific forms of hormonal contraception aim to create a more stable hormone milieu, the physiological-psychological response remains variable between individuals; therefore, this should still be taken into consideration when conducting performance test(s). Monitoring and screening procedures can facilitate the inclusion of the menstrual cycle and hormonal contraceptive use to standardise testing procedures. Currently, there is not enough evidence to recommend specific types of performance tests to be conducted at certain phases of the menstrual cycle, since athletes must be able to perform on any day of the cycle.

Summary

The menstrual cycle can affect physical readiness and highlight potential health issues; therefore, screening menstrual history and monitoring changes in the menstrual cycle are imperative actions when providing support to all female athletes. Due to large intra- and inter-variability in the menstrual cycle and the common use of hormonal contraceptives, the screening and monitoring tools and subsequent interpretation must be tailored to the individual. The implementation and progression of this process needs to be accompanied by ongoing education. When conducting performance tests, it is recommended that the individual's phase of the menstrual cycle or the use of, and response to, hormonal contraception, is captured and, when possible, replicated. Definitions and terminology were omitted from this chapter due to space; however, it is imperative that practitioners take the time to understand and use correct terminology and definitions (see Elliott-Sale et al. [2020] and Hackney [2016] for recommendations).

References

Ansdell, P., et al. (2019). Menstrual cycle-associated modulations in neuromuscular function and fatigability of the knee extensors in eumenorrheic women. *Journal of Applied Physiology*, 126(6), 1701–1717, 12.

Elliott-Sale, K. J., McNulty, K. L., Ansdell, P., Goodall, S., Hicks, K. M., Thomas, K., Swinton, P. A., Dolan, E. (2020). The effects of oral contraceptives on exercise performance in women: A systematic review and meta-analysis. *Sports Medicine* 50, 1785–1812. https://doi.org/10.1007/s40279-020-01317-5

Enns, D. and Tiidus, P. (2010). The influence of estrogen on skeletal muscle. *Sports Medicine*, 40(1), 41–58.

Hackney, A. C. (ed.). (2016). *Sex Hormones, Exercise and Women: Scientific and Clinical Aspects*. Springer.

McNulty, K. L., et al. (2020). The effects of menstrual cycle phase on exercise performance in eumenorrheic women: A systematic review and meta-analysis. *Sports Medicine*, 1–15.

5.11 Exercise testing in pregnancy

Victoria L. Meah, Amal Hassan, Lin Foo,
Christoph Lees and Marlize de Vivo

Pregnancy represents a period of profound physiological adaptation, which is required to support fetal development without compromising maternal health (Figure 5.11.1). The multi-system adaptations of gestation present unique considerations for physical activity.

The current national guidelines for physical activity during pregnancy recommend accumulating 150 minutes of moderate-intensity activity per week and performing strengthening activities twice per week (Department of Health & Social Care, 2019a, 2019b). When pregnant individuals meet these recommendations, regular physical activity can improve maximal oxygen consumption ($\dot{V}O_2$max) by 2.77 ml·kg^{-1}·min^{-1} (Cai et al., 2020) and provide significant clinical benefits. These include reduced odds of preeclampsia, gestational hypertension, gestational diabetes (Davenport et al., 2018c), antenatal depression (Davenport et al., 2018a) and excessive gestational weight gain (Ruchat et al., 2018) without any increased risk of miscarriage (Davenport et al., 2019a), preterm delivery or adverse fetal outcomes (Davenport et al., 2018b).

It is long established that low $\dot{V}O_2$max predicts all-cause mortality in the general population. Although comprehensive investigations are required, data that supports $\dot{V}O_2$max as an indicator of pregnancy health and a therapeutic avenue to improve maternal-fetal outcomes is emerging (Lane-Cordova et al., 2018; Whitaker et al., 2018; Ohuchi et al., 2013; Bisson et al., 2014). Standardisation of exercise testing during pregnancy is important to facilitate wider research data homogeneity and maintain safety standards with this population. This chapter will focus on practical considerations for exercise testing during pregnancy.

Screening

All healthy pregnant individuals without complications are encouraged to meet current physical activity guidelines, whilst those with obstetric or general medical complications are encouraged to receive additional monitoring and/or specialist support to remain active. In pregnant individuals with certain conditions, acute and chronic physical activity may pose significant risks to maternal and/or fetal health (Meah et al., 2020). The Get Active for Pregnancy questionnaire is a screening tool that can be used to identify these contraindications to prenatal physical activity (Canadian Society for Exercise Physiology, 2021).

DOI: 10.4324/9781003045267-44

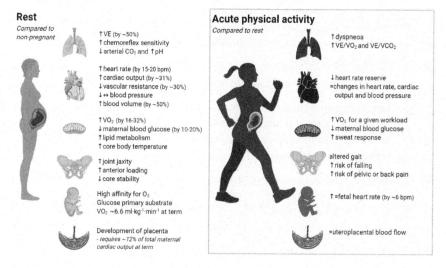

Figure 5.11.1 Physiological adaptation to healthy pregnancy at rest, and altered responses or considerations for acute, submaximal physical activity in pregnant individuals.

VE, minute ventilation; CO2, carbon dioxide; $\dot{V}O2$, oxygen consumption; O2, oxygen; VCO2, carbon dioxide production. Created with BioRender.com.

Participants must be fully informed of the purpose, procedures, risks and benefits, as well as their rights and expectations prior to completing the protocol. Practitioners should ensure they have highlighted the pregnancy-specific risks and should inform participants of how adverse events and/or clinically meaningful results (e.g., resting blood pressure above 140/90 mmHg) will be handled. Practitioners should collect maternity healthcare provider contact details, as well as maintain records of consent and other documentation. Pregnant participants should be encouraged to inform their maternity healthcare provider of any exercise testing or research that they are participating in, so that on-going advice regarding physical activity can be tailored to complications that may later develop.

Exercise testing

Pre-test considerations

Practitioners should prepare to complete an exercise test with a pregnant participant by:

- Ensuring pre-activity screening is completed.
- Ensuring an ambient environment with additional options for cooling, because:

  - Pregnant participants may have a lower sweat threshold.

- There are concerns regarding maternal hyperthermia in the first trimester and adverse fetal outcomes. These risks are unsubstantiated with moderate-vigorous physical activity in the second or third trimesters in ambient (Davenport et al., 2019b) and temperate environments (Ravanelli et al., 2019).

- Ensuring a team of qualified and experienced personnel, including:

  - Exercise professional with relevant experience and/or accredited qualifications for antenatal physical activity.
  - Maternity healthcare provider with expertise in fetal monitoring for higher-risk participants.

- Creating clear health and safety protocols for risk mitigation and dealing with adverse events, such as falls, syncope, nausea or vomiting, or participant identification of reasons to cease exercise (Table 5.11.1).

In addition to usual pre-test procedures, pregnant participants should prepare to complete an exercise test by:

- Avoiding eating a heavy meal for 3 hours prior to the test, instead eating a small snack containing 30–50 g of carbohydrate 1 hour prior to the test.
- Wearing comfortable, light clothing with a supportive bra.
- Emptying her bladder immediately prior to the test to reduce the risk of urinary incontinence during activity.

Upon arrival for the exercise test, the practitioner should:

- Determine an individual's capability and preparedness by considering her activity background (i.e., exercise history), current physical activity status and intentions to engage in physical activity for the remainder of her pregnancy.

Table 5.11.1 Physical reasons to stop antenatal activity and consult a healthcare provider

Persistent excessive shortness of breath prior to exertion or following exertion, which does not resolve on rest
Severe chest pain
Regular and painful uterine contractions
Vaginal bleeding
Persistent loss of fluid from the vagina indicating rupture of the membranes
Persistent dizziness or faintness that does not resolve on rest
Abdominal pain
Amniotic fluid leakage indicating rupture of membranes
Headache
Muscle weakness affecting balance
Calf pain or swelling

Adapted from Mottola et al. (2018) and American College of Obstetricians and Gynecologists (2020).

This can be achieved through exploratory questions, validated questionnaires and/or objective measures, although prior planning would be required for the latter. Such profiling of pregnant individuals allows practitioners to adapt tests accordingly (e.g., intensity, mode etc.) and allows for tailored advice and feedback (De Vivo, 2017).

- Confirm that the participant is aware of the signs to cease exercise (Table 5.11.1).
- Obtain details of medication use and be aware of potential effects on responses to exercise.
- Identify musculoskeletal injuries or complaints (e.g., pelvic girdle pain, lower back pain) to offer modifications to exercise test modality.
- Inquire about hypotension in pregnancy (e.g., excessive fatigue or pre-syncopal symptoms) to identify any heightened risks of syncope during or upon cessation of activity.
- Confirm pre-exercise blood glucose is >4 mmol/L to prevent hypoglycaemia because of exercise (Hordern et al., 2012):

  - If pre-exercise blood glucose is ≤4 mmol/L, blood glucose can be increased through eating a snack prior to the test.

- Confirm that resting heart rate and blood pressure are <100 bpm and <140/90 mmHg, respectively:

  - Measurements should be made following >5 minutes of quiet, calm rest in a comfortable position (i.e., not resting on the exercise equipment) with an appropriately sized blood pressure cuff and automated sphygmomanometer that has been validated for use in pregnancy.
  - If resting heart rate or blood pressure is higher than these cut-off values, measurements should be repeated after a further 5 minutes of rest.
  - If values remain elevated after this additional rest, the participant should not complete the exercise test and should be referred to her maternity healthcare provider for clinical evaluation.

Modality of exercise

Pregnancy results in hormonally mediated increases in joint laxity and changes to axial, thoracic, pelvic and lower-limb biomechanics, which shift the centre of gravity forwards, thus focussing load on the anterior chain. This can contribute to the experience of musculoskeletal pain in day-to-day life, as well as during and following physical activity. Up to three quarters of pregnant individuals suffer from low back and/or pelvic girdle pain (Weis et al., 2018). Exercise modality should be adjusted to reduce the risk of worsening an individual's musculoskeletal pain simply because of participating. If any pregnant individual does suffer from musculoskeletal pain, practitioners should offer non-weight bearing options (e.g., recumbent cycle) where possible.

Changes to the centre of gravity alongside decreased abdominal strength, increased fluid retention in the lower limbs and increased joint laxity contribute to impaired balance during pregnancy, and individuals therefore have higher risks of falling (Mei et al., 2018). Falls, which can result in placental abruption, membrane rupture or fetal trauma, present the greatest risk of harm during physical activity for otherwise healthy individuals. All testing protocols and equipment should be chosen to specifically reduce this risk.

Pregnant individuals are more likely to use handrails when exercising on a treadmill; however, this can artificially improve performance. Encouragement for light touching for balance and not holding for support should be provided (Wowdzia and Davenport, 2020).

Maximal exercise testing

Maximal exercise testing is not recommended unless completed in highly supervised settings (Bo et al., 2016). Although previous publications have utilised maximal protocols, pregnant individuals rarely achieve $\dot{V}O_2max$, as per established attainment criteria (Hesse et al., 2018).

Peak aerobic capacity

Suggested peak tests in pregnancy include the Bruce treadmill or ramp/cycling protocols to volitional fatigue (e.g., 3-minute warm-up at 30 W, followed by increments of 20 W/minute). Apprehension of strenuous activity, general fatigue and decreased lung capacity with advancing gestation, pregnancy symptoms and lack of familiarity with procedures may reduce performance in peak tests.

Submaximal exercise testing

Submaximal exercise testing is preferred during pregnancy. For laboratory-based tests, previous research has utilised established (e.g., modified Balke treadmill or YMCA cycle protocols) and researcher-developed step/ramp protocols to predetermined intensity thresholds. For the latter, calculation of a target threshold heart rate using heart rate reserve is recommended, since this accommodates for changes in resting heart rate across gestation (Meah et al., 2018).

Prediction of $\dot{V}O_2peak$ during pregnancy through submaximal exercise testing is not without limitations. Specifically, resting $\dot{V}O_2$ increases during pregnancy, however, resting heart rate increases to a greater extent. The assumed linear relationship of $\dot{V}O_2$ and heart rate may be altered in pregnant individuals and as a result, the accuracy of estimating maternal $\dot{V}O_2peak$ using a heart rate-$\dot{V}O_2$ extrapolation may be reduced (Lotgering et al., 1992). It should be noted that less than 15% of individuals meet physical activity guidelines during pregnancy (Evenson and Wen, 2011); therefore, a broad range of fitness levels should be expected.

Field-based submaximal protocols could be integrated in a clinical setting, mainly for risk prediction for how a pregnant individual may cope with exertional strain of labour, or in risk stratification of certain disorders linked with cardiovascular compromise such as preeclampsia. However, these protocols have not been validated in pregnant populations. The six-minute walk test has been shown to be a feasible test in late gestation, and some reference ranges for walking distance have been reported (Dennis et al., 2019). Step and walking-based test performance may also be reduced in pregnancy due to changes in gait (Mei et al., 2018), and this may be further impacted by the presence of low back or pelvic girdle pain.

Maternal monitoring

In laboratory-based tests, the following measures should be taken at minimum:

- Continuous heart rate – intensity can be identified using Table 5.11.2.
- Blood pressure – pre-, during and post-exercise at minimum (continuous where possible).
- Talk test – individuals exercising at a comfortable intensity can maintain a conversation. If not possible, the intensity may be reduced.

    - The Rating of Perceived Exertion can be used for a subjective measure of participant effort, however, there is a poor correlation to exercising heart rate in pregnant populations and targets require adjustment (da Silva et al., 2020).

- Peripheral oxygen saturation – with a reading of <80% as a reason for test cessation.

Fetal monitoring

In otherwise healthy pregnancy, acute exercise does not adversely affect fetal heart rate or uteroplacental blood flow (Skow et al., 2019). However, adverse fetal responses to maternal exercise, including fetal heart rate decelerations (drop by 15 bpm from baseline), fetal bradycardia (<100 bpm ≥3 minutes), fetal tachycardia (>160 bpm) and reduced uteroplacental blood flow can occur in individuals

Table 5.11.2 Heart rate ranges and corresponding intensities of physical activity in individuals with uncomplicated pregnancies

Maternal Age (years)	Intensity	Heart Rate Range (beats·min^{-1})
<29	Light	102–124
	Moderate *	125–146
	Vigorous **	147–169
≥30	Light	101–120
	Moderate *	121–141
	Vigorous **	142–162

* Moderate-intensity physical activity is equivalent to 40%–59% heart rate reserve.
** Vigorous-intensity physical activity is equivalent to 60%–80% heart rate reserve. There is limited evidence regarding physical activity at the upper end of the vigorous-intensity HR ranges; pregnant clients wishing to be active at this intensity (or beyond) should consult their healthcare professional.
Adapted from Mottola et al. (2018).

with placental insufficiency and/or intrauterine growth restriction (Ertan et al., 2004; Nabeshima et al., 1997; Rafla, 1999; Chaddha et al., 2005; Rauramo, 1987). These responses are rare in pre-screened pregnant individuals; however, submaximal exercise tests including higher-risk pregnancies (e.g., maternal age >35 years, classified as obese, previous history of growth restriction, preeclampsia or other pregnancy-complications) should include fetal monitoring. This should be completed by a suitably trained individual using ultrasound or fetal heart cardiotocography. Care should be taken to ensure quality recording without maternal movement artefact.

Exercise testing should be stopped if any adverse responses are noted (fetal distress or umbilical or uterine blood flow <50% of baseline measurement) and conservative measures such as putting the participant into a left lateral tilt position could be carried out. Continued monitoring until values return to normal is essential. Adverse responses are considered transient if less than three minutes in duration and do not require follow-up; however, prolonged observations may be suggestive of complications and participants should be referred to their healthcare provider.

Post-test considerations

Following an adequate cool-down, pregnant participants should rest in a comfortable seated position for a minimum of 5 minutes until heart rate and blood pressure are close to resting values (within 10 bpm/mmHg and not exceeding pre-exercise cut-offs). Attenuated recovery could be indicative of poor cardiovascular health and/or fitness (Dennis et al., 2019). Pregnant participants should rehydrate during recovery and practitioners should monitor for pre-syncopal symptoms. Post-exercise blood glucose levels should be checked, intervening (e.g., reclining, offering a carbohydrate-rich snack) when and if necessary.

Reporting and results

The application of results from exercise tests in pregnant participants are currently limited to research settings (e.g., individualised prescription for physical activity interventions; risk prediction and associations), although the clinical relevance of cardiorespiratory fitness in pregnancy health is a promising area of research.

When reporting outcomes of exercise tests, it is recommended that:

- All maternal monitoring measures should be reported (i.e., heart rate, blood pressure, peripheral oxygen saturation, subjective measure of exertion).
- When $\dot{V}O_2$peak is estimated, this parameter should be reported in absolute values (L/min) due to changes in body habitus during pregnancy.
- Adverse responses during or following exercise are detailed in academic publications.
- Modifications to tests should be detailed to inform future protocols.

Clinical considerations

During pregnancy, exercise testing places acute, additional demands on maternal physiology. Although comprehensive investigations to determine normative values are required, dysfunctional responses to such tests may indicate placental insufficiency and/or impaired cardiovascular reserve, and may predict or identify the development of complications prior to diagnosis of overt disease. Consequently, pregnant individuals with adverse responses to exercise tests could be considered at-risk patients and could receive increased support from healthcare providers.

Although exercise testing in pregnant individuals has been completed for decades, methodological inconsistencies and a lack of validated protocols have created barriers to the effective application of this work from a clinical perspective. At present, there is no evidence-based application of exercise test results for pregnant individuals. While some of the aforementioned tests could be completed in a clinical setting, the onus for exercise testing during pregnancy should not be placed upon already over-burdened healthcare providers (De Vivo and Mills, 2019). Maternity healthcare professionals are not solely responsible for imparting evidence-based messages regarding physical activity. To fully support and promote physical behaviour during and beyond pregnancy, there is a need to have multi-disciplinary consistency and coordination between clinicians and exercise physiologists (Mills et al., 2020).

As part of holistic care during pregnancy, healthcare providers should feel confident in promoting and providing informed advice with regards to benefit, types and duration of physical activity that is safe in pregnancy. When advice is provided, pregnant individuals are three times more likely to be active during gestation (Nascimento et al., 2015). However, as little as 9% of pregnant individuals receive accurate, evidence-based advice on physical activity from their healthcare provider (Hayman et al., 2020).

A large barrier to physical activity includes uncertainty amongst end users and obstetric care providers as to whether being active may increase the risk of harm to the fetus. Concerns over harms have not been substantiated by research (Davenport et al., 2019a, 2018b, 2018c, 2019b) and risks of not engaging in physical activity are not adequately emphasised.

References

American College of Obstetricians and Gynecologists. (2020). Committee opinion, number 804: Physical activity and exercise during pregnancy and the postpartum period. *Obstetrics and Gynecology*, 135, e178–e188.

Bisson, M., Rheaume, C., Bujold, E., Tremblay, A. and Marc, I. (2014). Modulation of blood pressure response to exercise by physical activity and relationship with resting blood pressure during pregnancy. *Journal of Hypertension*, 32, 1450–1457; discussion 1457.

Bo, K., Artal, R., Barakat, R., Brown, W., Davies, G. A., Dooley, M., Evenson, K. R., Haakstad, L. A., Henriksson-Larsen, K., Kayser, B., Kinnunen, T. I., Mottola, M. F., Nygaard, I., Van Poppel, M., Stuge, B. and Khan, K. M. (2016). Exercise and pregnancy in recreational and elite athletes: 2016 evidence summary from the IOC expert group meeting, Lausanne: Part 1-exercise in women planning pregnancy and those who are pregnant. *British Journal of Sports Medicine*, 50, 571–589.

Cai, C., Ruchat, S. M., Sivak, A. and Davenport, M. H. (2020). Prenatal exercise and cardiorespiratory health and fitness: A meta-analysis. *Medicine & Science in Sports & Exercise*, 52, 1538–1548.

Canadian Society for Exercise Physiology. (2021). *Get Active for Pregnancy Questionnaire*. www. csep.ca/getactivequestionnaire-pregnancy/CSEP-PATH_GAQ_P_Guidelines.pdf (accessed 5 May 2021).

Chaddha, V., Simchen, M. J., Hornberger, L. K., Allen, V. M., Fallah, S., Coates, A. L., Roberts, A., Wilkes, D., Schneiderman-Walker, J., Jaeggi, E. and Kingdom, J. C. P. (2005). Fetal response to maternal exercise in pregnancies with uteroplacental insufficiency. *American Journal of Obstetrics and Gynecology*, 193, 995–999.

da Silva, D. F., Mohammad, S., Hutchinson, K. A. and Adamo, K. B. (2020). Cross-validation of ratings of perceived exertion derived from heart rate target ranges recommended for pregnant women. *International Journal of Exercise Science*, 13, 1340–1351.

Davenport, M. H., Kathol, A. J., Mottola, M. F., Skow, R. J., Meah, V. L., Poitras, V. J., Jaramillo Garcia, A., Gray, C. E., Barrowman, N., Riske, L., Sobierajski, F., James, M., Nagpal, T., Marchand, A. A., Slater, L. G., Adamo, K. B., Davies, G. A., Barakat, R. and Ruchat, S. M. (2019a). Prenatal exercise is not associated with fetal mortality: A systematic review and meta-analysis. *British Journal of Sports Medicine*, 53, 108–115.

Davenport, M. H., Mccurdy, A. P., Mottola, M. F., Skow, R. J., Meah, V. L., Poitras, V. J., Jaramillo Garcia, A., Gray, C. E., Barrowman, N., Riske, L., Sobierajski, F., James, M., Nagpal, T., Marchand, A. A., Nuspl, M., Slater, L. G., Barakat, R., Adamo, K. B., Davies, G. A. and Ruchat, S. M. (2018a). Impact of prenatal exercise on both prenatal and postnatal anxiety and depressive symptoms: A systematic review and meta-analysis. *British Journal of Sports Medicine*, 52, 1376–1385.

Davenport, M. H., Meah, V. L., Ruchat, S. M., Davies, G. A., Skow, R. J., Barrowman, N., Adamo, K. B., Poitras, V. J., Gray, C. E., Jaramillo Garcia, A., Sobierajski, F., Riske, L., James, M., Kathol, A. J., Nuspl, M., Marchand, A. A., Nagpal, T. S., Slater, L. G., Weeks, A., Barakat, R. and Mottola, M. F. (2018b). Impact of prenatal exercise on neonatal and childhood outcomes: A systematic review and meta-analysis. *British Journal of Sports Medicine*, 52, 1386–1396.

Davenport, M. H., Ruchat, S. M., Poitras, V. J., Jaramillo Garcia, A., Gray, C. E., Barrowman, N., Skow, R. J., Meah, V. L., Riske, L., Sobierajski, F., James, M., Kathol, A. J., Nuspl, M., Marchand, A. A., Nagpal, T. S., Slater, L. G., Weeks, A., Adamo, K. B., Davies, G. A., Barakat, R. and Mottola, M. F. (2018c). Prenatal exercise for the prevention of gestational diabetes mellitus and hypertensive disorders of pregnancy: A systematic review and meta-analysis. *British Journal of Sports Medicine*, 52, 1367–1375.

Davenport, M. H., Yoo, C., Mottola, M. F., Poitras, V. J., Jaramillo Garcia, A., Gray, C. E., Barrowman, N., Davies, G. A., Kathol, A., Skow, R. J., Meah, V. L., Riske, L., Sobierajski, F., James, M., Nagpal, T. S., Marchand, A. A., Slater, L. G., Adamo, K. B., Barakat, R. and Ruchat, S. M. (2019b). Effects of prenatal exercise on incidence of congenital anomalies and hyperthermia: a systematic review and meta-analysis. *British Journal of Sports Medicine*, 53, 116–123.

Dennis, A. T., Salman, M., Paxton, E., Flint, M., Leeton, L., Roodt, F., Yentis, S. and Dyer, R. A. (2019). Resting hemodynamics and response to exercise using the 6-minute walk test in late pregnancy: An international prospective multicentre study. *Anesthesia and Analgesia*, 129, 450–457.

Department of Health & Social Care. (2019a). *UK Chief Medical Officers' Physical Activity Guidelines*. https://assets.publishing.service.gov.uk/government/uploads/system/uploads/attachment_data/file/832868/ukchief-medical-officers-physical-activity-guidelines.pdf (accessed 5 May 2021).

Department of Health & Social Care. (2019b). *Physical Activity in Pregnancy Infographic Guidance*. https://assets.publishing.service.gov.uk/government/uploads/system/uploads/attachment_data/file/829894/5-physical-activity-for-pregnant-women.pdf (accessed 5 May 2021).

De Vivo, M. (2017). *Predicting and Understanding Physical Activity Behaviour during Pregnancy: A Multiphase Investigation*. Ph.D., Canterbury Christ Church University, UK.

De Vivo, M. and Mills, H. (2019). "They turn to you first for everything": Insights into midwives' perspectives of providing physical activity advice and guidance to pregnant women. *BMC Pregnancy Childbirth*, 19, 462.

Ertan, A. K., Schanz, S., Tanriverdi, H. A., Meyberg, R. and Schmidt, W. (2004). Doppler examinations of fetal and uteroplacental blood flow in AGA and IUGR fetuses before and after maternal physical exercise with the bicycle ergometer. *Journal of Perinatal Medicine*, 32, 260–265.

Evenson, K. R. and Wen, F. (2011). Prevalence and correlates of objectively measured physical activity and sedentary behavior among US pregnant women. *Preventative Medicine*, 53, 39–43.

Hayman, M., Reaburn, P., Alley, S., Cannon, S. and Short, C. (2020). What exercise advice are women receiving from their healthcare practitioners during pregnancy? *Women Birth*, 33, e357–e362.

Hesse, C. M., Tinius, R. A., Pitts, B. C., Olenick, A. A., Blankenship, M. M., Hoover, D. L. and Maples, J. M. (2018). Assessment of endpoint criteria and perceived barriers during maximal cardiorespiratory fitness testing among pregnant women. *Journal of Sports Medicine and Physical Fitness*, 58, 1844–1851.

Hordern, M. D., Dunstan, D. W., Prins, J. B., Baker, M. K., Singh, M. A. and Coombes, J. S. (2012). Exercise prescription for patients with type 2 diabetes and pre-diabetes: a position statement from Exercise and Sport Science Australia. *Journal of Science and Medicine in Sport*, 15, 25–31.

Lane-Cordova, A. D., Carnethon, M. R., Catov, J. M., Montag, S., Lewis, C. E., Schreiner, P. J., Dude, A., Sternfeld, B., Badon, S. E., Greenland, P. and Gunderson, E. P. (2018). Cardiorespiratory fitness, exercise haemodynamics and birth outcomes: The coronary artery risk development in young adults study. *British Journal of Obstetrics and Gynecology*, 125, 1127–1134.

Lotgering, F. K., Struijk, P. C., Van Doorn, M. B. and Wallenburg, H. C. (1992). Errors in predicting maximal oxygen consumption in pregnant women. *Journal of Applied Physiology (1985)*, 72, 562–567.

Meah, V. L., Backx, K., Davenport, M. H. and International Working Group on Maternal, H. (2018). Functional hemodynamic testing in pregnancy: Recommendations of the International Working Group on Maternal Hemodynamics. *Ultrasound, Obstetrics and Gynecology*, 51, 331–340.

Meah, V. L., Davies, G. A. and Davenport, M. H. (2020). Why can't I exercise during pregnancy? Time to revisit medical 'absolute' and 'relative' contraindications: Systematic review of evidence of harm and a call to action. *British Journal of Sports Medicine*, 54(23), 1395–1404.

Mei, Q., Gu, Y. and Fernandez, J. (2018). Alterations of pregnant gait during pregnancy and post-partum. *Scientific Reports*, 8, 2217.

Mills, H., Atkinson, L., Olander, E., Smith, D., Hayes, L., Currie, S., Newham, J., Foster, C. and De Vivo, M. (2020). Bump start needed: Linking guidelines, policy and practice in promoting physical activity during and beyond pregnancy. *British Journal of Sports Medicine*, 54, 764–765.

Mottola, M. F., Davenport, M. H., Ruchat, S. M., Davies, G. A., Poitras, V. J., Gray, C. E., Jaramillo Garcia, A., Barrowman, N., Adamo, K. B., Duggan, M., Barakat, R., Chilibeck, P., Fleming, K., Forte, M., Korolnek, J., Nagpal, T., Slater, L. G., Stirling, D. and Zehr, L. (2018). 2019 Canadian guideline for physical activity throughout pregnancy. *British Journal of Sports Medicine*, 52, 1339–1346.

Nabeshima, Y., Sasaki, J., Mesaki, N., Sohda, S. and Kubo, T. (1997). Effect of maternal exercise on fetal umbilical artery waveforms: The comparison of IUGR and AFD fetuses. *Journal of Obstetrics & Gynaecology Research*, 23, 255–259.

Nascimento, S. L., Surita, F. G., Godoy, A. C., Kasawara, K. T. and Morais, S. S. (2015). Physical activity patterns and factors related to exercise during pregnancy: A cross sectional study. *PLoS One*, 10, e0128953.

Ohuchi, H., Tanabe, Y., Kamiya, C., Noritake, K., Yasuda, K., Miyazaki, A., Ikeda, T. and Yamada, O. (2013). Cardiopulmonary variables during exercise predict pregnancy outcome in women with congenital heart disease. *Circulation Journal*, 77, 470–476.

Rafla, N. M. (1999). The effect of maternal exercise on umbilical artery velocimetry waveforms in intrauterine growth retardation. *Journal of Obstetrics and Gynaecology*, 19, 469–473.

Rauramo, I. (1987). Effect of short-term physical exercise on foetal heart rate and uterine activity in normal and abnormal pregnancies. *Annales Chirurgiae et Gynaecologiae*, 76, 274–279.

Ravanelli, N., Casasola, W., English, T., Edwards, K. M. and Jay, O. (2019). Heat stress and fetal risk: Environmental limits for exercise and passive heat stress during pregnancy: A systematic review with best evidence synthesis. *British Journal of Sports Medicine*, 53, 799–805.

Ruchat, S. M., Mottola, M. F., Skow, R. J., Nagpal, T. S., Meah, V. L., James, M., Riske, L., Sobierajski, F., Kathol, A. J., Marchand, A. A., Nuspl, M., Weeks, A., Gray, C. E., Poitras, V. J., Jaramillo Garcia, A., Barrowman, N., Slater, L. G., Adamo, K. B., Davies, G. A., Barakat, R. and Davenport, M. H. (2018). Effectiveness of exercise interventions in the prevention of excessive gestational weight gain and postpartum weight retention: A systematic review and meta-analysis. *British Journal of Sports Medicine*, 52, 1347–1356.

Skow, R. J., Davenport, M. H., Mottola, M. F., Davies, G. A., Poitras, V. J., Gray, C. E., Jaramillo Garcia, A., Barrowman, N., Meah, V. L., Slater, L. G., Adamo, K. B., Barakat, R. and Ruchat, S. M. (2019). Effects of prenatal exercise on fetal heart rate, umbilical and uterine blood flow: A systematic review and meta-analysis. *British Journal of Sports Medicine*, 53, 124–133.

Weis, C. A., Barrett, J., Tavares, P., Draper, C., Ngo, K., Leung, J., Huynh, T. and Landsman, V. (2018). Prevalence of low back pain, pelvic girdle pain, and combination pain in a pregnant ontario population. *Journal of Obstetrics and Gynaecology Canada*, 40, 1038–1043.

Whitaker, K. M., Ingram, K. H., Appiah, D., Nicholson, W. K., Bennett, W. L., Lewis, C. E., Reis, J. P., Schreiner, P. J. and Gunderson, E. P. (2018). Prepregnancy fitness and risk of gestational diabetes: A longitudinal analysis. *Medicine & Science in Sports & Exercise*, 50, 1613–1619.

Wowdzia, J. B. and Davenport, M. H. (2020). Cardiopulmonary exercise testing during pregnancy. *Birth Defects Research*, 113(3), 248–264.

5.12 Exercise testing in heart failure

Eric J. Stöhr, Lauren K. Truby, Veli Topkara, Gordon McGregor and Mark J. Haykowsky

Introduction

Cardiovascular disease remains one of the biggest challenges to healthcare professionals in the United Kingdom and worldwide. Prior to the medical progress of the last century, a major challenge was to improve the treatment of acute cardiovascular events and increase the chance of survival of sick patients. As technologies, biomedical sciences and pharmacological developments have progressed, life expectancy has increased, creating an ageing population with an increasing burden of chronic disease. One such disease is heart failure, with a worrying prevalence and incidence that is rising exponentially (Savarese and Lund, 2017; Benjamin et al., 2019). Comprehensive exercise testing plays an important role in quantifying the manifestations of the disease and understanding its progression over time. In this chapter, the most relevant knowledge on the role of cardiopulmonary exercise testing (CPET) in heart failure is summarised, key methodological aspects are discussed, the importance of careful interpretation of CPET data is highlighted and areas of future work are proposed.

Definitions and clinical thresholds

Historically, heart failure was a disease of 'low cardiac output', associated with the poor contractile function that was clinically identified via a low ejection fraction (EF). Accordingly, the disease was called heart failure with reduced ejection fraction (*HFrEF*), a terminology that remains today. Because the focus of the label 'HFrEF' was on the output of the heart (i.e., systolic function), the identification of '*diastolic* dysfunction' or '*diastolic* heart failure' received the term heart failure with *preserved* ejection fraction (*HFpEF*). However, it has long been recognised that this dichotomous categorisation is not all-encompassing, and systolic and diastolic dysfunction often co-exist, particularly in the advanced state of the disease. Whether HFrEF progresses from HFpEF remains a matter of debate, although the consensus is moving towards the view that the underlying pathophysiology of HFrEF and HFpEF is different (Louridas and Lourida, 2016; Upadhya and Kitzman, 2020). The recent addition of a new category called heart failure with mid-range ejection

DOI: 10.4324/9781003045267-45

fraction (*HFmrEF*) highlights the complexity of the clinical presentations of this disease (Branca et al., 2020). Importantly, these categories are based upon the ejection fraction at rest, which may present some serious limitations, as discussed in more detail later.

Independent of cardiac output and ejection fraction (which helps to define the previously mentioned categories), heart failure patients are also described and categorised by their symptoms. This is reflected in the commonly used New York Heart Association (NYHA) classification shown in Table 5.12.1. Importantly, limitations in *physical activity* play a central role in those definitions.

Practitioners use cardiopulmonary exercise testing (CPET) to determine the maximal physical *capacity* of patients. Typical measurements during a CPET include the assessment of ventilation measurements obtained from the 'Wassermann 9 plot', including minute ventilation (VE, $L·min^{-1}$); oxygen consumption ($\dot{V}O_2$, $mL·kg^{-1}·min^{-1}$); carbon dioxide production ($\dot{V}CO_2$, $mL·kg^{-1}·min^{-1}$); workload (W); arterial (or mixed venous) oxygenation (SaO_2, %); heart rate (HR, $beats·min^{-1}$); blood pressure (BP, mmHg); and lactate ($mMol·L^{-1}$). Other parameters are derived from a combination of these, for example, the $VE/\dot{V}CO_2$ slope, the oxygen uptake efficiency slope (OUES), the respiratory exchange ratio (RER, derived from $\dot{V}O_2/\dot{V}CO_2$), or the ratio between skeletal muscle $\dot{V}O_2$ and microvascular or mixed venous PO_2 (Wasserman, 1990; Arena et al., 2008; Dhakal et al., 2015; Alba et al., 2016; Malhotra et al., 2016; Poole et al., 2018). In addition, 'personalized O_2 pathway analysis [that requires the measurement of convective O_2 delivery and skeletal muscle O_2 diffusion] identifies patients most likely to benefit from treating a specific defect; however, the system properties of O_2 transport favour treating multiple defects at once, as with exercise training' (Houstis et al., 2018). At present, $\dot{V}O_2max$ is used as an important clinical threshold to determine the eligibility for heart transplant (Mancini et al., 1991). Although small differences exist between countries and institutions, a $\dot{V}O_2max$ that is 50% below predicted as well as ≤ 14 ml/kg/min is typically considered an

Table 5.12.1 New York Heart Association (NYHA) classification of heart failure

NYHA Class	Patient Symptoms
I	*No limitation* of physical activity. Ordinary physical activity does not cause undue fatigue, palpitation, dyspnoea (shortness of breath).
II	*Slight limitation* of physical activity. Comfortable at rest. Ordinary physical activity results in fatigue, palpitation, dyspnoea (shortness of breath).
III	*Marked limitation* of physical activity. Comfortable at rest. Less than ordinary activity causes fatigue, palpitation, or dyspnoea.
IV	*Unable to carry on* any physical activity without discomfort. Symptoms of heart failure at rest. If any physical activity is undertaken, discomfort increases.

Note: Information retrieved from the American Heart Association (AHA) website www.heart.org/en/health-topics/heart-failure/what-is-heart-failure/classes-of-heart-failure (accessed 30th of September 2020).

essential criterion to list a patient on the heart transplant registry (Mancini and Lietz, 2010).

In some circumstances, it may also be advisable to measure indices of cardiac function not just at rest but also during exercise, a process also referred to as 'exercise echocardiography'. Specific exercise-related echocardiographic parameters play an emerging role in the evaluation of heart failure (Guazzi et al., 2017). In brief, data that reveal the functional reserve of the heart such as the 'identification of a basic role of RV [right ventricular] to pulmonary circulation uncoupling in determining the flattening of the $\Delta \dot{V}O_2/\Delta WR$ relationship' (Guazzi et al., 2017) are considered of great value. Several other morphological, functional and valvular parameters – including the diastolic index of mitral inflow to early myocardial relaxation, E/e' – can be obtained that may significantly increase the diagnostic accuracy of the patient (see Figure 4 in Guazzi et al., 2017). Other indicators of systolic and diastolic cardiac function may also be obtained during exercise echocardiography, including cardiac output and novel parameters of myocardial deformation such as longitudinal strain and twist (Stöhr and Samuel, 2020).

The value of exercise testing

Common symptoms and physical presentations of heart failure include dyspnoea, fatigue and peripheral and/or pulmonary oedema (Crawford, 2010; Pieske et al., 2020). A hallmark indicator of heart failure is also a reduced exercise capacity, indicating that heart failure is a disease of reduced oxygen availability/consumption. However, the reasons for a reduced exercise capacity and the diagnosis of heart failure can differ significantly between patients. Therefore, 'cardiopulmonary exercise testing may be the singular most important risk stratification test in patients with advanced heart failure' (Truby and Rogers, 2020). In agreement with this sentiment, recent studies have revealed the complex interplay between central (cardiac and/or pulmonary) and peripheral (arterial or skeletal muscle) factors that may cause a reduced physical capacity in heart failure patients.

Dhakal et al. (2015) showed that HFpEF patients had a reduced $\dot{V}O_2$ (13.9 ml/kg/min) that was only marginally higher than HFrEF patients (12.1 ml/kg/min), emphasising that $\dot{V}O_2$max can be drastically low regardless of the ejection fraction. Together with further invasive measurements, the findings from this study suggest a reduced ability for O_2 uptake at the level of the peripheral organs (see Figure 5.12.1). Similarly, Houstis et al. (2018) concluded that a reduced cardiac output was not the only possible reason for an impaired exercise capacity in HF, and that the skeletal musculature plays an important role in some individuals. These observations add evidence to the pool of possible factors that may impact exercise capacity, including reduced oxygenation within the pulmonary system (detected by a reduced SaO_2 during exercise testing), and a reduced delivery of blood flow from the weakened left and/or right ventricles (detected by a reduced cardiac output during exercise testing).

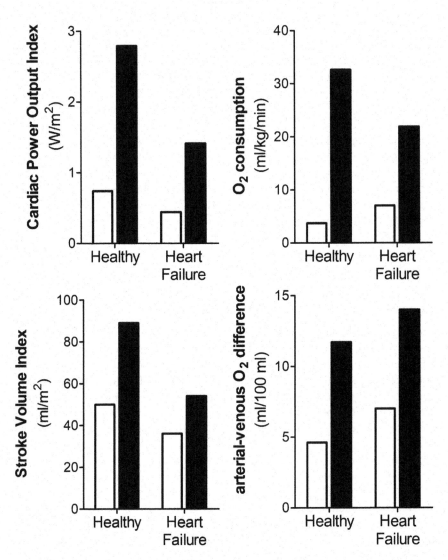

Figure 5.12.1 The contributions to exercise limitations in heart failure. Cardiac power output, stroke volume and $\dot{V}O_2$ were lower in heart failure (HF) patients and increased less from rest (¨) to peak exercise (n). In contrast, the arterial-venous oxygen (A-v O_2) difference was higher in HF patients, although the increase from rest to peak exercise was comparable to healthy controls.

Note: *: $p < 0.05$ compared with controls.

Source: The figure has been modified from the original presented in McCoy et al. (2017), distributed in accordance with the terms of the Creative Commons Attribution (CC BY 4.0) licence. The original figure also contains data from patients with diabetes, stroke and mitochondrial disease.

Whatever an individual patient's main cause of heart failure, CPET and exercise echocardiography can identify:

1 whether exercise capacity is indeed reduced, indicating a problem with the delivery and/or utilisation of substrates via aerobic and/or anaerobic metabolic pathways;
2 the biological origins of the reduced exercise capacity;
3 the progression of the disease over time;
4 the presence of exercise-induced cardiac rhythm disorders, and wall motion abnormalities suggestive of arrhythmia or coronary artery disease;
5 the eligibility for advanced heart failure therapies including heart transplant or left ventricular assist device (LVAD) support; and
6 the success of heart failure therapies, including the exercise capacity of transplant and LVAD recipients (Loyaga-Rendon et al., 2015; Haykowsky et al., 2018).

Methodological considerations

Valuable clinical information requires sound measurements that are precise (valid) and repeatable (reliable) so that comparisons within one person over time, as well as against clinical criteria, can be made with confidence. The following section in relation to exercise testing in heart failure emphasises those factors that deserve the most attention. Reduced quality in these areas has the greatest chance of compromising the value of the clinical data.

Standardising exercise protocols

Determining the best exercise protocol for a clinical CPET is of great importance and consultation of statements by professional organisations is essential (Durstine, 2016). Although reference values exist for most protocols, some generic issues when choosing the best exercise protocol for a CPET deserve brief mention. For example, testing patients for their maximal aerobic capacity (as reflected by $\dot{V}O_2max$) requires a protocol that allows for a valid and reliable assessment of aerobic energy systems. Not every protocol is similarly effective in this regard, and keen readers and practitioners are advised to spend time determining the best protocol from the guidelines provided by leading societies such as BASES or the American College of Sports Medicine (American College of Sports Medicine, 2006; Winter, 2007). It is well known that different CPET protocols can generate different $\dot{V}O_2max$, which may be further complicated in the cardiac patient (Beltrami et al., 2012; Smirmaul et al., 2013).

In some instances, the typical continuously increasing exercise intensity may be adjusted to a discontinuous, ramp or step-wise protocol, and the readers of this chapter are directed to excellent descriptions of the different protocols that are available (Fletcher et al., 2013; Durstine, 2016). Equally, a brief warm-up may influence the overall performance of the patient and reduce the risk of adverse events during the CPET. This further emphasises the importance of carefully designing and preparing the exact protocol for each patient, and that 'studies assessing [$\dot{V}O_2$max] verification phases in different patient populations are still warranted' (Bogaty et al., 2003; Schaun, 2017). Despite careful designs, investigators performing exercise tests must be prepared for sudden changes in the patient's physiology, symptoms or performance. For example, some patients may not be able to exercise beyond the initial warm-up stage (even during unloaded cycling), reflecting the limited capacity and potentially rendering the CPET results unusable or inconclusive.

Exercise echocardiography

For the more detailed evaluation of coronary artery disease (including the coronary distribution or the location of possible ischaemia), structural heart disease like valve stenosis/regurgitation or congenital defects and an estimation of pulmonary artery pressures during exertion, a supine exercise echocardiography test may be indicated in addition to the CPET (Pellikka et al., 2007). Specific echocardiography training is required for the correct acquisition and analysis of ultrasound images of the heart, in particular when acquiring sensitive images for the analysis of myocardial deformation (Stöhr and Samuel, 2020). Although prestigious publications currently state that echocardiographic images acquired during exercise 'must be obtained within 1 to 2 minutes (preferably <1 minute) after exercise because inducible wall motion abnormalities resolve rapidly after stress' (Fletcher et al., 2013), it is imperative to keep in mind that the overall physiological state of the patient changes *instantly* with the cessation of exercise (Laughlin, 1999; Stöhr and Samuel, 2020). Therefore, any parameters obtained 1–2 minutes *after* exercise will not be representative of the patient's stress state during exercise. Similarly, it is important to note that the protocols for a standard CPET may differ from those of an exercise echocardiography protocol, mostly due to the logistical reasons associated with acquiring high-quality, standardised echocardiographic images during exercise (Stöhr and Samuel, 2020).

Monitoring vital non-primary parameters

While the primary parameters of the CPET relate to the oxygen delivery and uptake of the heart failure patient, comorbidities in this population are prevalent. Accordingly, further monitoring during the CPET is essential. One should acquire a clean 12-lead electrocardiogram (ECG) before, during and after the CPET. Further, abnormally high or low blood pressure during exercise may not only be indicative of heart failure, but may also present an acute risk to the patient. Therefore, systolic and diastolic BP should be monitored before, during and in the recovery phase from the CPET (American College of Sports Medicine, 2006). Exercise practitioners may implement additional monitoring strategies according to an individual patient's medical history and current symptoms.

Interpretation of data

Recent data clearly suggest that multiple biological systems are affected in patients with heart failure. Consequently, the term 'heart failure' is somewhat misleading because the interpretation of test results must consider the integrative (patho-) physiology of multiple organ systems. Data, such as those mentioned in the previous sections, are a stark reminder that a reduced cardiac output, or a low $\dot{V}O_2$max, may not just be symptomatic of impaired cardiac function. Even if cardiac output and $\dot{V}O_2$max were significantly lower than expected during an exercise test, the causes for the overall limitation in maximal exercise capacity may vary between individuals. For example, patients may stop an exercise test because of pulmonary restriction or skeletal muscle 'fatigue', thus not being able to achieve a true maximal cardiac output or $\dot{V}O_2$max. Since the instruction to the patient is to exercise until 'volitional fatigue', it is also conceivable that the brain may play a role in exercise cessation, either due to biological or motivational limitations. Consequently, it is important to interpret the collective data, including the values obtained at rest, to make a final judgement on the meaning of the CPET results. Similarly, the interpretation of exercise echo data requires knowledge of whole-body metabolic responses as well as other generic cardiac measurements.

For cardiac exercise physiologists and medical personnel, data obtained during a CPET can indicate the source of functional limitation in which compromised values of exercise capacity and/or $\dot{V}O_2$max are noted. For example, a severe cardiac compromise may result in an abnormally low blood pressure as well as a low $\dot{V}O_2$max (Il'giovine et al., 2018), while pulmonary restrictions may be reflected in a reduced arterial oxygen saturation at rest or as 'exercise-induced arterial hypoxaemia' (Wasserman et al., 1997). Muscle fatigue or deconditioning may be indicated by an unusually early exercise cessation, for example, when the highest heart rate remains clearly below the predicted value, the maximal RER is below 1 or lactate is below the anticipated values for a maximal effort. Equally, some heart failure patients have an elevated lactate at rest and an RER that exceeds 1. Together with signs of exercise oscillatory ventilation, EOV (Dhakal and Lewis, 2016), these observations reflect the altered ventilatory drive and metabolic state that may also link to a reduced physical capacity. For similar reasons, the ventilatory anaerobic threshold (VAT) is often difficult to determine, in particular with the V-slope method. Other reasons for a low maximal exercise performance may include the presence of an iliocaval venous stenosis (Morris et al., 2020), emphasising the need to carefully examine the patient and consider multiple origins for the limited physical capacity.

Future directions

Researchers, in time, will learn much more about the origins and progression of heart failure and, importantly, how exercise science can contribute to the improvement of our knowledge and understanding of the disease. Specific areas of interest may include investigations into the longitudinal progression of heart failure to determine the potential overlap between HFpEF, HFmrEF and HFpEF, as well as the improved understanding of the role of exercise training in alleviating heart failure symptoms. Moreover, the recent successes in pharmacological and left ventricular assist device (LVAD) therapies have shown great promise, but patients still have significant limitations in their physical capacity (Mehra et al., 2019; Jarcho, 2020). Therefore, exercise science will continue to play a key role in heart disease, even under the most extreme conditions (Stöhr, 2019; Stöhr and McDonnell, 2020).

References

Alba, A. C., Adamson, M. W., MacIsaac, J., Lalonde. S. D., Chan, W. S., Delgado, D. H. and Ross, H. J. (2016). The added value of exercise variables in heart failure prognosis. *Journal of Cardiac Failure*, 22, 492–497.

American College of Sports Medicine. (2006). *ACSM's Guidelines for Exercise Testing and Prescription*. Philadelphia, PA; London: Lippincott Williams & Wilkins.

Arena, R., Myers, J., Abella, J., Peberdy, M. A., Bensimhon, D., Chase, P. and Guazzi, M. (2008). The ventilatory classification system effectively predicts hospitalization in patients with heart failure. *Journal of Cardiopulmonary Rehabilitation and Prevention*, 28, 195–198.

Beltrami, F. G., Froyd, C., Mauger, A. R., Metcalfe, A. J., Marino, F. and Noakes, T. D. (2012). Conventional testing methods produce submaximal values of maximum oxygen consumption. *British Journal of Sports Medicine*, 46, 23–29.

Benjamin, E. J., Muntner, P., Alonso, A., Bittencourt, M. S., Callaway, C. W., Carson, A. P., Chamberlain, A. M., Chang, A. R., Cheng, S., Das, S. R., Delling, F. N., Djousse, L., Elkind, M. S. V., Ferguson, J. F., Fornage, M., Jordan, L. C., Khan, S. S., Kissela, B. M., Knutson, K. L., Kwan, T. W., Lackland, D. T., Lewis, T. T., Lichtman, J. H., Longenecker, C. T., Loop, M. S., Lutsey, P. L., Martin, S. S., Matsushita, K., Moran, A. E., Mussolino, M. E., O'Flaherty, M., Pandey, A., Perak, A. M., Rosamond, W. D., Roth, G. A., Sampson, U. K. A., Satou, G. M., Schroeder, E. B., Shah, S. H., Spartano, N. L., Stokes, A., Tirschwell, D. L., Tsao, C. W., Turakhia, M. P., Van Wagner, L. B., Wilkins, J. T., Wong, S. S., Virani, S. S., American Heart Association Council on E, Prevention Statistics C and Stroke Statistics S. (2019). Heart disease and stroke statistics-2019 update: A report from the American Heart Association. *Circulation*, 139, e56–e528.

Bogaty, P., Poirier, P., Boyer, L., Jobin, J. and Dagenais, G. R. (2003). What induces the warm-up ischemia/angina phenomenon: Exercise or myocardial ischemia? *Circulation*, 107, 1858–1863.

Branca, L., Sbolli, M., Metra, M. and Fudim, M. (2020). Heart failure with mid-range ejection fraction: Pro and cons of the new classification of heart failure by European Society of Cardiology guidelines. *European Society of Cardiology Heart Failure*, 7, 381–399.

Crawford, M. H. (2010). *Cardiology*. London: Mosby.

Dhakal, B. P. and Lewis, G. D. (2016). Exercise oscillatory ventilation: Mechanisms and prognostic significance. *World Journal of Cardiology*, 8, 258–266.

Dhakal, B. P., Malhotra, R., Murphy, R. M., Pappagianopoulos, P. P., Baggish, A. L., Weiner, R. B., Houstis, N. E., Eisman, A. S., Hough, S. S. and Lewis, G. D. (2015). Mechanisms of exercise intolerance in heart failure with preserved ejection fraction: The role of abnormal peripheral oxygen extraction. *Circulation: Heart Failure*, 8, 286–294.

Durstine, J. L. (2016). *ACSM's Exercise Management for Persons with Chronic Diseases and Disabilities*. Leeds: Human Kinetics.

Fletcher, G. F., Ades, P. A., Kligfield, P., Arena, R., Balady, G. J., Bittner, V. A., Coke, L. A., Fleg, J. L., Forman, D. E., Gerber, T. C., Gulati, M., Madan, K., Rhodes, J., Thompson, P. D., Williams, M. A., American Heart Association Exercise CR, Prevention Committee of the Council on Clinical Cardiology CoNPA, Metabolism CoC, Stroke N, Council on E and Prevention. (2013). Exercise standards for testing and training: A scientific statement from the American Heart Association. *Circulation*, 128, 873–934.

Guazzi, M., Bandera, F., Ozemek, C., Systrom, D. and Arena, R. (2017). Cardiopulmonary exercise testing: What is its value? *Journal of the American College of Cardiology*, 70, 1618–1636.

Haykowsky, M. J., Halle, M. and Baggish, A. (2018). Upper limits of aerobic power and performance in heart transplant recipients: Legacy fffect of prior endurance training. *Circulation*, 137, 650–652.

Houstis, N. E., Eisman, A. S., Pappagianopoulos, P. P., Wooster, L., Bailey, C. S., Wagner, P. D. and Lewis, G. D. (2018). Exercise intolerance in heart failure with preserved ejection fraction: Diagnosing and ranking its causes using personalized O2 pathway analysis. *Circulation*, 137, 148–161.

Il'giovine, Z. J., Solomon, N., Devore, A. D., Wojdyla, D., Patel, C. B. and Rogers, J. G. (2018). Blood pressure response during cardiopulmonary exercise testing in heart failure. *Medicine & Science in Sports & Exercise*, 50, 1345–1349.

Jarcho, J. A. (2020). More evidence for SGLT2 inhibitors in heart failure. *New England Journal of Medicine*, 383, 1481–1482.

Laughlin, M. H. (1999). Cardiovascular response to exercise. *American Journal of Physiology*, 277, S244–S259.

Louridas, G. E. and Lourida, K. G. (2016). Heart failure in patients with preserved ejection fraction: Questions concerning clinical progression. *Journal of Cardiovascular Development and Disease*, 3.

Loyaga-Rendon, R. Y., Plaisance, E. P., Arena, R. and Shah, K. (2015). Exercise physiology, testing, and training in patients supported by a left ventricular assist device. *Journal of Heart, Lung and Transplantation*, 34, 1005–1016.

Malhotra, R., Bakken, K., D'Elia, E. and Lewis, G. D. (2016). Cardiopulmonary exercise testing in heart failure. *Journal of the American College of Cardiology Heart Failure*, 4, 607–616.

Mancini, D. M., Eisen, H., Kussmaul, W., Mull, R., Edmunds, L. H., Jr. and Wilson, J. R. (1991). Value of peak exercise oxygen consumption for optimal timing of cardiac transplantation in ambulatory patients with heart failure. *Circulation*, 83, 778–786.

Mancini, D. M. and Lietz, K. (2010). Selection of cardiac transplantation candidates in 2010. *Circulation*, 122, 173–183.

McCoy, J., Bates, M., Eggett, C., Siervo, M., Cassidy, S., Newman, J., Moore, S. A., Gorman, G., Trenell, M. I., Velicki, L., Seferovic, P. M., Cleland, J. G. F., MacGowan, G. A., Turnbull, D. M. and Jakovljevic, D. G. (2017). Pathophysiology of exercise intolerance in chronic diseases: The role of diminished cardiac performance in mitochondrial and heart failure patients. *Open Heart Journal*, 4, e000632.

Mehra, M. R., Uriel, N., Naka, Y., Cleveland, J. C., Jr., Yuzefpolskaya, M., Salerno, C. T., Walsh, M. N., Milano, C. A., Patel, C. B., Hutchins, S. W., Ransom, J., Ewald, G. A., Itoh, A., Raval, N. Y., Silvestry, S. C., Cogswell, R., John, R., Bhimaraj, A., Bruckner, B. A., Lowes, B. D., Um, J. Y., Jeevanandam, V., Sayer, G., Mangi, A. A., Molina, E. J., Sheikh, F., Aaronson, K., Pagani, F. D., Cotts, W. G., Tatooles, A. J., Babu, A., Chomsky, D., Katz, J. N., Tessmann, P. B., Dean, D., Krishnamoorthy A., Chuang, J., Topuria, I., Sood, P., Goldstein, D. J. and Investigators M & the MI. (2019). A fully magnetically levitated left ventricular assist device: Final report. *New England Journal of Medicine*, 380, 1618–1627.

Morris, R. I., Sobotka, P. A., Balmforth, P. K., Stöhr, E. J., McDonnell, B. J., Spencer, D., O'Sullivan, G. J. and Black, S. A. (2020). Iliocaval venous obstruction, cardiac preload reserve and exercise limitation. *Journal of Cardiovascular Translational Research*, 13(4), 531–539.

Pellikka, P. A., Nagueh, S. F., Elhendy, A. A., Kuehl, C. A. and Sawada, S. G. (2007). American Society of Echocardiography recommendations for performance, interpretation, and application of stress echocardiography. *Journal of the American Society of Echocardiography*, 20, 1021–1041.

Pieske, B., Tschope, C., de Boer, R. A., Fraser, A. G., Anker, S. D., Donal, E., Edelmann, F., Fu, M., Guazzi, M., Lam, C. S. P., Lancellotti, P., Melenovsky, V., Morris, D. A., Nagel, E., Pieske-Kraigher, E., Ponikowski, P., Solomon, S. D., Vasan, R. S., Rutten, F. H., Voors, A. A., Ruschitzka, F., Paulus, W. J., Seferovic, P. and Filippatos, G. (2020). How to diagnose heart failure with preserved ejection fraction: The HFA-PEFF diagnostic algorithm: A consensus recommendation from the Heart Failure Association (HFA) of the European Society of Cardiology (ESC). *European Journal of Heart Failure*, 22, 391–412.

Poole, D. C., Richardson, R. S., Haykowsky, M. J., Hirai, D. M. and Musch, T. I. (2018). Exercise limitations in heart failure with reduced and preserved ejection fraction. *Journal of Applied Physiology (1985)*, 124, 208–224.

Savarese, G. and Lund, L. H. (2017). Global public health burden of heart failure. *Cardiac Failure Review*, 3, 7–11.

Schaun, G. Z. (2017). The maximal oxygen uptake verification phase: A light at the end of the tunnel? *Sports Medicine Open*, 3, 44.

Smirmaul, B. P., Bertucci, D. R. and Teixeira, I. P. (2013). Is the $\dot{V}O_2max$ that we measure really maximal? *Frontiers in Physiology*, 4, 203.

Stöhr, E. J. (2019). Bionic women and men: Heart failure and an artificial heart pump. *Research Features*. https://cdn2.researchfeatures.com/wp-content/uploads/2018/2010/Eric-Stohr.pdf

Stöhr, E. J. and McDonnell, B. J. (2020). The unique physiology of left ventricular assist device patients: Keep your finger on the pulse! *Experimental Physiology*, 105, 747–748.

Stöhr, E. J. and Samuel, T. J. (2020). Echocardiographic assessment of myocardial deformation during exercise. *InTechOpen*.

Truby, L. K. and Rogers, J. G. (2020). Advanced heart failure: Epidemiology, diagnosis, and therapeutic approaches. *Journal of the American College of Cardiology Heart Failure*, 8, 523–536.

Upadhya, B. and Kitzman, D. W. (2020). Heart failure with preserved ejection fraction: New approaches to diagnosis and management. *Clinical Cardiology*, 43, 145–155.

Wasserman, K. (1990). Measures of functional capacity in patients with heart failure. *Circulation*, 81, II1–II4.

Wasserman, K., Zhang, Y. Y., Gitt, A., Belardinelli, R., Koike, A., Lubarsky, L. and Agostoni, P. G. (1997). Lung function and exercise gas exchange in chronic heart failure. *Circulation*, 96, 2221–2227.

Winter, E. M. (2007). *Sport and Exercise Physiology Testing Guidelines: The British Association of Sport and Exercise Sciences Guide*. London: Routledge.

Index

Note: Page numbers in *italics* refer to figures; those in **bold** refer to tables.

abnormal respiratory function **73–74**
absolute contraindications, CPET testing and 63
accelerometers 92
acquired heart diseases 223; exercise testing in 224
active physiological movement 150
activity counts, free living and 143
activity reporting and monitoring 17
aerobic exercise tests: in children 280; for obesity 217–219; in older adults 288; submaximal 217–218, **218**
allometric cascade 56
anaerobic performance testing in children 280–281
angiotensin-converting enzyme (ACE) inhibitors 35–36
ankle brachial pressure index (ABPI) 267, 268–269; defined 267, 268; interpretation of **269**; measuring 268–269
anthropometric data, interpretation of 84
anthropometry, defined 79
apical four-chamber view (A4CH) 188, 189, 190–191, *191*, *192*
arm span, measuring 81
arterial disease *see* peripheral arterial disease (PAD)
arterialised venous blood sampling 129
arterial stiffness of conduit arteries 159–160
arterial structure, vascular function and 159
arteries: conduit 155–160; resistance 155, 160–162
assent, physiological testing and children providing 14–15

asthma **73**, 74
Astrand Rhyming cycle test 217–218, **218**
atherosclerosis 155
autonomic neuropathy 232

BACPR Reference Tables Booklet 111
balance tests in older adults **289**
Bergström needle 205
beta-blockers 36
biological hazards **21**
blood flow *156*, 156–157
blood sampling 126–130; arterialised venous 129; capillary 129; and handling 126–129; overview of 126; pre-sampling standardisation 126–128; safety issues 130; treatment of blood following 129–130; venous 128–129
BMI *see* body mass index (BMI)
body composition: anthropometry and 278, **279**; measurement techniques 215; positioning, DXA 173–174, *174*, *175*, 176
body fat composition analysis 216
body mass, measuring 81
body mass index (BMI) 215–216
bone density assessment, DXA interpretation of **172**, 172–173, *173*, 175
bone mineral density (BMD) 167; *see also* dual energy X-ray absorptiometry (DXA)
breath-by-breath method 100–101
British Association of Sport and Exercise Sciences (BASES) 1; Code of Conduct 19–20, 24; introduction to 1–2; laboratory accreditation 66; professional competency and 5; on safeguarding and welfare importance 26–29
Bruce Protocol 225, **226**

calibration of laboratory/field equipment 66–67

cancer; *see also* exercise testing, breast/prostate cancer: overview 258; treatments 258–259

capillary blood sampling 129

cardiac structure and function assessment 182–195; apical four-chamber view 188, 189, 190–191, *191, 192*; left parasternal long axis view 187–188, *188, 189, 190*; overview of 182; resting transthoracic echocardiogram 184, 185, 186–187, *187*; stress transthoracic echocardiogram 194; subcostal four-chamber view 191, *192*; suprasternal window 191, *192*, 192–193, **193**; 12-lead electrocardiogram 182, *183*, 184, **185**, *186*

cardiopulmonary exercise test (CPET) 224–226, **225**, **226**, 250–255; absolute contraindications **252**; in heart failure 307, 311–312; incremental exercise phase 254; infection control 251; interpretation 254–255, *256*; in-test measurements **253**; modality and equipment set-up 251; in obstructive *vs.* restrictive disorders 250; overview of 250; for peripheral arterial disease 272; pre-test procedures 251, **253**; quality control 251, **252**; recovery phase 254; relative contraindications **252**; reporting, results 255; response patterns 255; resting phase 251, **253**, 254; risk assessment 251; unloaded phase 254

cardiorespiratory-metabolic estimates of exercise intensity, FBAs and 132–133, **133**

cardiovascular disease (CVD) 222–227; acquired diseases as 223; congenital diseases as 222–223; diseases covered by term 222; exercise testing in 223–227, **225, 226**; future directions for 227; inherited diseases as 223; mortality rate 222; overview of 222

carotid artery reactivity (CAR) 156, 158

carotid-femoral pulse wave velocity (cfPWV) 160

chemical hazards **21**

children: exercise testing in (*see* exercise testing in children); perceived exertion in 115, *116*

Children's Effort Rating Table (CERT) 115

chronic kidney disease (CKD) 241–248; disability 247; function limitations 246–247; introduction to 241; neuromuscular function 246; peak exercise capacity 242, 246; physical function assessment in **241**, 241–242, **243–245**; stage, classification of **241**

chronic obstructive pulmonary disease (COPD) **73**, 74

client engagement, data intelligence and 46–47

coefficient of variation (CV) 49

comorbidities, obesity related 216

complications, obesity related 216

conduit arteries: arterial stiffness of 159–160; carotid artery reactivity and 158; defined 155; flow-mediated dilation and 157–158; ultrasonography of 155–157; vascular function of 157–159

confidentiality, physiological testing and 15–16

congenital diseases 222–223; defined 222; exercise testing in 224

consent, physiological testing and 14–15

consumer devices, energy expenditure 93

control samples, quality of 67, **68**

control tests, laboratory and field equipment 67

coronary artery disease (CAD) 222

CPET *see* cardiopulmonary exercise test (CPET)

cross calibration 177

Cytochromes P450 (CYPs) 34, **35**

data access/usage, physiological testing and 15–16

data collection 44, **45**

data fatigue 46

data intelligence 43–47; client engagement and 46–47; data collection and 44, **45**; data fatigue and 46; defined 43; feedback and 45–46; health questions and 44; overview of 43; pitfalls 46; visualisation and 44, 45

data interpretation and visualisation 44, 45

data management and analysis **45**

desirable skills and knowledge 6

diabetes 231–238; categories of 231, 232; contraindications 232–233; diagnosis criteria **231**; exercise participant preparation 233, *234*; exercise test use for 232–238; introduction to 231–232; screening 232–233; symptoms of untreated 231; type 1, exercises 233–236; type 2, exercises 236

diabetic kidney disease (nephropathy) 233

Dialysis Outcomes and Practice Patterns Study (DOPPS) 247

Diet-Induced Thermogenesis (DIT) 91

disability, chronic kidney disease and 247

doubly labelled water (DLW) 92

Douglas bag technique, respiratory gas analysis using 97–99, **99**

dual energy X-ray absorptiometry (DXA) 167–178; body composition positioning for 173–174, *174*, *175*, 176; bone density, interpretation of **172**, 172–173, *173*, 175; calibration 171–172; communication, professional practice and 177–178; cross calibration 177; defined 167; indications/ contraindications for 168–170, **169**; interpretation and reporting 175–176; longitudinal 176–177; overview of 167; precision study samples 176–177; pre-scan standardisation 170, **171**; radiation dose 168; technology 167–168; training requirements 178

duty of care, health and safety in 19–24; hazards, identification of 20; overview of 19; professional obligations 19–20; risk assessment 20–24

DXA *see* dual energy X-ray absorptiometry (DXA)

ECG *see* 12-lead electrocardiogram (ECG)

ECHO *see* resting transthoracic echocardiogram (ECHO)

elastic similarity, scaling and 55

elimination of medications 34, 35

energy expenditure (EE) 91–94; application considerations for 94; components of 91; device-based measures of 92–93; expression of, data *93*, 93–94; Physical Activity Energy Expenditure 91–93

enterohepatic circulation 33, *34*

E-P scale, perceived exertion and 115, *116*

equipment calibration and maintenance *see* laboratory and field equipment

ergometry in children 278, 279–280

ergonomic hazards **21**

essential skills and knowledge 6

ethical issues: activity reporting and monitoring 17; confidentiality 15–16; consent/assent 14–15; data access/ usage 15–16; information to participants 14–15; minimising risks 13; participant withdrawal 16; power relationships 14; recruitment process 13–14; related to physiological testing 12–18; risks *vs.* benefits 12–13

ethical principles applied to physiological testing 10–12

evidence-based practice 8

excretion of medications 34, 35

exercise echocardiography 309

exercise immunology 197–203; assessing illness and infection 198–199; considerations before testing 197–198; introduction to 197; mucosal immune function, assessing 200–201; symptom data, collecting 198–199, **199**; systemic immune function, assessing 201–203, *202*

exercise-induced bronchospasm (EIB) 74

exercise intensity, RPE and measures of 111–112, **112**

exercise intensity domains: lactate threshold 103–105, **105**; maximal steady state/critical power 106–108, *107*; overview of 102

exercise-related cardiovascular events, risk modulators of 61

exercise testing, breast/prostate cancer 258–263; cancer overview 258; cancer treatments 258–259; during/after breast cancer treatment 260, **261 262**; during/ after prostate cancer treatment 260, **261–262**, 262–263; overview of 259; pre-treatment physiological/functional testing 260; safety considerations 259

exercise testing, cardiac disorders 223–227; cardiopulmonary 224–226, **226**; in congenital, inherited and acquired heart disease 224; contraindications to 224, **225**; functional capacity assessment 226; heart rate (HR) measurement and 227; incremental shuttle walk test 226–227; overview of 223–224

exercise testing, chronic kidney disease 241–248; function limitations 246–247; gait speed tests 246–247; neuromuscular function 246; physiological impairment peak exercise capacity 242, 246; sit-to-stand performance tests 247; walking ability tests 246–247

exercise testing, chronic lung disease *see* cardiopulmonary exercise test (CPET)

exercise testing, diabetes 232–238; interpretation of, outcomes 238; participant preparation 233, *234*; post-test recommendations 237–238; pre-test recommendations 237; protocol and supervision 236–238; during test recommendations 237; type 1 diabetes 233–236; type 2 diabetes 236

exercise testing, obesity 215–221; aerobic 217–219; fitness and functional assessment 217; flexibility 219; functional testing 219; maximal 219; physical function assessment considerations 219–220; pre-physical fitness/function assessment considerations 217; strength and muscular endurance 219; submaximal 217–218, **218**

exercise testing in children 277–281; aerobic performance 280; anaerobic performance testing 280–281; body composition, anthropometry and 278, **279**; ergometry and 278, 279–280; fitness/performance field testing 281; isokinetic strength testing 281; maturation assessment 277–278; overview of 277

exercise testing in females 291–295; considerations for 294; framework for *292*; interpreting 294; menstrual cycle and 291, 292–293; monitoring 293–294; overview of 291; performance tests for 294–295; screening 293

exercise testing in older adults 284–289; aerobic capacity 288; arm curl test 287; balance and mobility 288–289, **289**; chair sit-to-stand performance 287–288; end-of-test criteria 285; functional fitness assessment 285, **286**; grip strength 287; maximal/submaximal cardiopulmonary 284; mode of 284–285; muscular strength/endurance 287–288; overview of 284; six-minute walk test 288; speed/grade increases 285

exercise testing in pregnancy 297–303; clinical considerations 303; fetal monitoring and 301, 302; maternal monitoring and 301, **301**; maximal 300; modality of 299–300; post-test considerations 302; pre-test considerations 297–299, **298**; reporting and results of 302; submaximal 300–301

FBAs *see* field-based assessments (FBAs)

feedback, data intelligence and 45–46

field-based assessments (FBAs) 132–138; cardiorespiratory-metabolic estimates of exercise intensity and 132–133, **133**; changes in exercise capacity based on 137–138; objectives of 132; overview of 132; physical activity guidance using 137; risk stratification 134, 137; testing protocol methods 134, **135–136**

fitness to practice, professional competency and 6

flow cytometry, immune cell types and 202–203

flow-mediated dilation (FMD) 156, 157–158

fractional exhaled nitric oxide (FeNO) 76

free-living physical activity and sedentary behaviours, measurement of 143–146; monitoring technologies for 145; monitor selection/data collection for 143–144; overview of 143; physical activity patterns, data processing and 144–145, *146*

Functional Movement Screen (FMS) 87–88

functional screening 86–89; defined 86; landing error scoring system 88–89; overview of 86; reasons to employ 87; tools 87–88

gas exchange threshold (GET) 103–105

gastric emptying 33

gastric motility 33

gestational diabetes 232

girth measurements 82–83, **83**

Global Lung Function Initiative (GLI) 255

global positioning system (GPS) recorders 271

graded exercise testing (GXT) 111–112; *see also* rating of perceived exertion (RPE)

haemodilution, blood sampling and 127

hazards: identification of 20; types of **21**

Health and Safety at Work Act (1974) 19

Health and Safety Executive (HSE) 21

health and safety practice in duty of care 19–24; hazards, identification of 20; overview of 19; professional obligations 19–20; risk assessment 20–24

health questions, data intelligence and 44

heart failure 307–314; categories of 307–308; clinical thresholds 307–309; CPET and 307, 311–312; data

interpretation 313; definition of 307; exercise testing, value of 309, *310*, 311; exercise echocardiography 312; future directions for 313–314; introduction to 307; monitoring vital non-primary parameters 312; New York Heart Association classification of **308**; standardising exercise protocols 311–312
heart rate reserve (HRR) method 133
human research ethics, core principles of 11
Human Tissue Authority 11
hygiene, infection control and 22

illness and infection, assessing 198–199; symptom data collection 198–199, **199**
immune cell functional responses 203
immune cell numbers 201
immunology *see* exercise immunology incidents 24
incremental protocol exercise testing method 134
incremental shuttle walk test (ISWT) 226–227, 246
information to physiological testing participants 14–15
Informed Consent Form (ICF) 13
inherited heart diseases 223; exercise testing in 224
insurance, risk assessment and 24
interclass correlation coefficient (ICC) 50
interdisciplinary teams: professional competency and 7–8; in sport and exercise sciences 7
International Safeguards **27–28**, 29
intima-media thickness (IMT) 159
Ionising Radiation for Medical Exposure Regulations (IRMER) 168
Ionising Radiation Regulations 2017 (IRR17) 168
isokinetic strength testing 281
isokinetic testing 121–122; described 121; protocol for 122
isometric testing 122–123; described 121; protocol for 123
isotonic (isoinertial) testing 123–124; described 121; 1-RM formulas for **123**; protocol for 124

Jackson Common Cold Questionnaire 198, **199**
joint integrity tests 150
joint tests 150

laboratory and field equipment 66–71; calibration of 66–67; control samples,

quality of 67, **68**; control tests 67; documentation and user training 69; frequency of calibration 67, 68–69, *70*; introduction to 66; maintenance tasks, type and frequency of 69; preventative maintenance 69
lactate threshold (LT) 103–105, *104*, **105**
Landing Error Scoring System (LESS) 87, 88–89
left parasternal long axis view (PLAX) 187–188, *188*, *189*, *190*
license to practice, professional competency and 6
lung and respiratory muscle function 72–78; abnormal **73–74**; fractional exhaled nitric oxide 76; mouth pressure 76–77; overview of 72, 74; results feedback of assessments 77–78; single breath gas transfer 75–76; spirometry 74–75; static lung volumes, measurement of 75
lung disease exercise testing *see* cardiopulmonary exercise test (CPET)

magnitude interpretation of reliability estimate 50–51
maintenance tasks, type and frequency of 69
maturation assessment in children 277–278
maximal exercise tests, obesity and 219
maximum strength, defined 121
measurement pre-requisites, anthropometry 79–80
mechanical hazards **21**
medications: common **32**; defined 30; half-life of 31, **32**; types of 30
medications, exercise response influence of 30–37; angiotensin-converting enzyme inhibitors 35–36; application examples of 35–37; beta-blockers 36; elimination and 34, 35; enterohepatic circulation and 33, *34*; first-pass (pre-systematic) metabolism and 34, **35**; gastric emptying 33; gastric motility 33; introduction to 30; ionisation 33; pharmacodynamics 31–32, **32**, *32*; pharmacokinetics 31–32, **32**, *32*; prescription 30–31; splanchnic blood flow and 33; thyroxine 36–37
menstrual cycle, exercise testing and 291, 292–293
Metabolic Equivalents (METs) 143
metabolic threshold testing 102–109; exercise intensity domains overview 102; heavy-severe, maximal steady state/critical power 106–108, *107*; moderate/heavy, lactate threshold 103–105,

104, **105**; overview of 102; prognostic prescriptive value of 108–109

micro-biopsy technique 205, 207; *see also* skeletal muscle biopsy

mouth pressure, respiratory muscle function and 76–77

Movement Quality Tests (MQTs) 86

mucosal immune function, assessing 200–201; saliva sample collection 200–201

multidisciplinary teams: professional competency and 7–8; in sport and exercise sciences 7

muscle biopsy *see* skeletal muscle biopsy

muscle tissue treatment post-biopsy collection 208–209

musculoskeletal assessment 148–152; approaches 148–149; core, tests 150; described 148; influences on test outcomes of 149–150; special, tests 150, **151**, 152

near-infrared light spectroscopy (NIRS) 272

non-isometric growth 55–56

obesity: aerobic exercise tests for 217–219; body fat composition analysis 216; body mass index and 215–216; defined 215; exercise testing in 215–221; fitness and functional assessment for 217; flexibility testing 219; functional testing 219; maximal exercise tests 219; measurement and classification of 215; physical function assessment considerations 219–220; pre-physical fitness/function assessment considerations 217; related complications/comorbidities 216; strength and muscular endurance testing 219; submaximal exercise tests 217–218, **218**; waist circumference and 216

obesity systems map 215

older adult; *see also* exercise testing in older adults: defined 284

optimal cutting temperature compound, embedding tissue sample 209

over the counter (OTC) medication 30

paraffin wax, embedding tissue samples 209

Participant Information and Consent Form (PICF) 15

Participant Information Sheet (PIS) 13

participant withdrawal 16

passive physiological movement 150

perceived exertion in children 115, *116*

perceptually regulated exercise testing (PRET) 113

percutaneous needle biopsy technique 205; *see also* skeletal muscle biopsy

peripheral arterial disease (PAD) 267–273; ankle brachial pressure index 267, 268–269, **269**; classifications for **268**; CPET testing for 272; described 267; diagnosis of 267, 268; exercise testing for 269–271; GPS recorders 271; muscle oxygenation, peripheral blood flow and 272–273; overview of 267; six-minute walk test 271; treadmill walking protocols for, patients 269–270

peripheral blood flow/vascular function assessment 155–162; *see also individual classified arteries*; conduit arteries 155–160; flow-mediated dilation and 157–158; overview of 155; resistance arteries 160–162

personal indemnity, risk assessment and 24

pharmacodynamics 31–32, **32**, *32*

pharmacokinetics 31–32, **32**, *32*

Physical Activity Energy Expenditure (PAEE) 91; assessing 91–93

Physical Activity Level (PAL) *93*, 93–94

Physical Activity Readiness Questionnaire (PAR-Q) 217

physical function assessments 242

physical musculoskeletal examination 150

physical performance/functional fitness tests 86

physiological exercise testing 10–18; activity reporting and monitoring of 17; confidentiality and 15–16; consent/assent and 14–15; data access/usage and 15–16; ethical issues related to 12–18; ethical principles applied to 10–12; information to participants and 14–15; minimising risks of 13; overview of 10; participant withdrawal and 16; power relationships and 14; privacy and 15–16; recruitment process 13–14; risks *vs.* benefits of 12–13; safeguarding in 26–29

plethysmography 160–161

power relationships, participant recruitment and 14

practice-based evidence 8

pregnancy 296–303; *see also* exercise testing in pregnancy; exercise testing in 297–303; overview of 296, *297*; screening 296, 297

prescription only medicines (POM) 30
PRET *see* perceptually regulated exercise testing (PRET)
pre-test preparation/evaluation 61–64; absolute contraindications 63; to establish cardiorespiratory fitness 63–64; overview of 61–62; relative contraindications 63; screening process 62
professional competency 5–8; introduction to 5; maintaining/extending 6–7; multi- and interdisciplinary teams and 7–8
pulse wave velocity (PWV) 159–160

Quantitative Movement Tests (QMTs) 86

radiation dose, dual energy X-ray absorptiometry and 168
rating of perceived exertion (RPE) 111–117; in children 115, *116*; effective use of 115–117; factors influencing 113–114; measures of exercise intensity and 111–112, **112**; modes of using 111; overview of 111; to predict/assess VO_2max 112–113; PRET as method of determining 113; scale use for 115; and strength/power testing and training 114–115
ratio standards 53–54
reflective practice 7
relative contraindications, CPET testing and 63
relative energy deficiency in sports (RED-S) 167
reliability: applications **51**, *51*, 51–52; defined 48; designs 48; interclass correlation coefficient and 50; magnitude interpretation of 50–51; mean change and 49; and measurement error 48–52; overview of 48; standard error of measurement and 49; statistics from, analyses 49–50
resistance arteries: blood flow 160–161; defined 155; vascular function and structure *161*, 161–162
respiratory gas analysis 97–101; breath-by-breath method 100–101; Douglas bag technique 97–99, **99**; overview of 97
Resting Metabolic Rate (RMR) 91, 143
resting transthoracic echocardiogram (ECHO) 182, 184, 185, 186–187, *187*
risk assessment: accidents and 24; emergency procedures and 24; field-based 134, 137; findings, recording 22; in health and safety practice 20–24; hygiene

and 22; incidents and 24; insurance/personal indemnity and 24; resources for 22; standard operating procedures and 24; steps to 20, 21–22, **23**
risk evaluation 21–22, **23**
RPE *see* rating of perceived exertion (RPE)

safeguarding in physiological testing 26–29; for children in sport **27–28**; introduction to 26, 29; responsibilities 29
safety: blood sampling and 130; in breast/prostate cancer exercise testing 259; in duty of care 19–24 (*see also* duty of care, health and safety in); of skeletal muscle biopsy 209
scaling 53–57; allometric cascade 56; allometry 54–55; elastic similarity 55; introduction to 53; non-isometric growth 55–56; ratio standards 53–54; recommendations for 56–57; surface law 55; uses of 53
screening process 293; objective assessment 62; pre-test preparation/evaluation 62; subjective assessment 62
segmometer 80
Short Physical Performance Battery (SPPB) 246
Siconolfi step test 217
single breath gas transfer 75–76
sit-to-stand performance tests (STS) 247
six-minute walk test (6MWT) 271, 288
skeletal muscle biopsy 205–209; background 205, *206*, 207; common sites for 207; introduction to 205–207; procedure 207–208; risks/safety aspects of 209; tissue treatment post-collection 208–209
skinfold calipers 80
skinfolds, measuring 81, **82**
special musculoskeletal tests 150, **151**, 152
speckle tracking echocardiography (STE) 187–188
spirometry 74–75
splanchnic blood flow 33
standard error of measurement (SEM) 49
standard operating procedures 24
static lung volumes, measurement of 75
statistics from reliability analyses 49–50
strength/power testing and training, RPE and 114–115
strength testing 121–124; isokinetic 121–122; isometric 122–123; isotonic (isoinertial) **123**, 123–124; overview of 121
stress ECHO 182, 194

stress transthoracic echocardiogram (stress ECHO) 182, 194
stretch stature, measuring 80
subcostal four-chamber view (S4CH) 191, *192*
submaximal aerobic graded exercise tests 217–218, **218**
submaximal incremental protocol exercise testing method 134
suprasternal window 191, *192*, 192–193, **193**
surface anthropometry 79–84; data, interpretation of 84; defined 79; equipment 80; girths 82–83, **83**; measurement error 83, 84; measurement pre-requisites 79–80; overview of 79; procedures 80–81; skinfolds 81, **82**
surface law 55
systemic immune function, assessing 201–203, *202*; flow cytometry 202–203; immune cell functional responses 203; immune cell numbers 201

Technical Error of Measurement (TEM) 83, 84
test-retest designs 48
thyroxine 36–37
timed endurance task exercise testing method 134
transcutaneous oxygen pressure ($TcpO_2$) 273
12-lead electrocardiogram (ECG) 182, *183*, 184, **185**, *186*

type 1 diabetes 231, 232; exercises 233–236
type 2 diabetes 232; exercises 236
typical error of measurement (TEM) 46, 49

ultrasonography: of conduit arteries 155–157; to examine blood flow *156*, 156–157; to examine intima-media thickness 159; for vascular function examination 157

vascular function: arterial structure and 159; carotid artery reactivity and 158; of conduit arteries 157–159; flow-mediated dilation and 157–158
venous blood sampling 128–129
venous occlusion plethysmography 160–161; and pharmacology 161–162
VO_2max: aerobic performance in children 280; Astrand Rhyming cycle test for 217–218, **218**; cardiopulmonary exercise test 254–255; FBAs to estimate 132–133; heart failure and 313; for older adults 285; protocols to estimate 134, **135–136**; for risk stratification 134; RPE to predict/assess 112–113

Wisconsin Upper Respiratory Symptom Survey (WURSS) 198, 199
World Health Organisation (WHO): BMI obesity classes 216; obesity definition 215; physical health assessment 241, 242